Computer-Aided Design of User Interfaces VI

T0137906

Computer-Aided Design of User Interfaces VI

Víctor López-Jaquero · Francisco Montero
José Pascual Molina · Jean Vanderdonckt
Editors

Computer-Aided Design of User Interfaces VI

Proceedings of the Seventh International
Conference on Computer-Aided Design
of User Interfaces (CADUI 2008)

 Springer

Editors
Víctor López-Jaquero
Escuela Superior de Ingeniería Informática
University of Castilla-La Mancha
Albacete, Spain

José Pascual Molina
Escuela Superior de Ingeniería Informática
University of Castilla-La Mancha
Albacete, Spain

Francisco Montero
Escuela Superior de Ingeniería Informática
University of Castilla-La Mancha
Albacete, Spain

Jean Vanderdonckt
Université catholique de Louvain
Louvain-la-Neuve
Belgium

ISBN: 978-1-84996-826-3   e-ISBN: 978-1-84882-206-1
DOI 10.1007/978-1-84882-206-1

British Library Cataloguing in Publication Data
A catalogue record for this book is available from the British Library

Printed on acid-free paper

Springer Science + Business Media
springer.com

Contents

Sponsors

Oficial CADUI Web site

Computer-Aided Design of User Interfaces
http://www.isys.ucl.ac.be/bchi/cadui
http://cadui2008.albacete.org

Scientific Sponsors

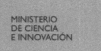

Corporate Sponsors

Programme Committe Members

General co-chairs

Víctor López-Jaquero, University of Castilla La Mancha, Spain
José Pascual Molina, University of Castilla La Mancha, Spain
Francisco Montero, University of Castilla La Mancha, Spain

PC members

Julio Abascal, Univ. of País Vasco, Spain
Lawrence Bergman, IBM T.J. Watson Research Center, USA
Niels Ole Bernsen, University of Southern Denmark, Denmark
Birgit Bomsdorf, Univ. Hagen, Germany
Marcos Borges, Univ. Federal do Rio de Janeiro, Brasil
Gaelle Calvary, Univ. Joseph Fourier, France
Pedro Campos, Univ. of Madeira, Portugal
Karin Coninx, Univ. of Hasselt, Belgium
Larry Constantine, Univ. of Madeira, Portugal
Angélica de Antonio Jiménez, Univ. Politécnica de Madrid, Spain
Olga De Troyer, Vrije Univ. Brussel, Belgium
João Falcão e Cunha, FEUP, Porto, Portugal
Clive Fencott, University of Teesside, UK
Peter Forbrig, University of Rostock, Germany
Elizabeth Furtado, Univ. Fortaleza, Brazil
Toni Granollers, Univ. of Lérida, Spain
Geert-Jan Houben, Vrije Univ. Brussel, Belgium
Javier Jaén, Univ. Politécnica de Valencia, Spain
Anthony Jameson, DFKI, Germany
Joaquim Jorge, IST, Lisbon, Portugal
Christophe Kolski, Univ. de Valenciennes, France
Quentin Limbourg, SMALS-MVM, Belgium
Kris Luyten, Univ. of Hasselt, Belgium

José Antonio Macías, Univ. Autónoma de Madrid, Spain
Mark Maybury, The Mitre Corp., USA
Pedro J. Molina, Capgemini, Spain
Kizito Ssamula Mukasa, Fraunhofer IESE, Germany
Jeff Nichols, IBM Almaden Research Center, USA
Erik Nilsson, SINTEF, Norway
Nuno Nunes, Univ. of Madeira, Portugal
Philippe Palanque, IRIT, Université Paul Sabatier - Toulouse III, France
Fabio Paternò, ISTI-CNR, Italy
Óscar Pastor, Univ. Politécnica de Valencia, Spain
Beryl Plimmer, Univ. Of Auckland, New Zealand
Angel Puerta, RedWhale Corp., USA
David Ragget, W3C, UK
Arcadio Reyes Lecuona, Univ. of Málaga, Spain
Gustavo Rossi, Univ. De La Plata, Argentina
Dominique Scapin, INRIA, France
Robbie Schaefer, Universitaet Paderborn, Germany
Montserrat Sendín, Univ. of Lérida, Spain
Orit Shaer, Tufts University, USA
Daniel Schwabe, Pontifícia Universidade Católica do Rio de Janeiro, Brazil
Constantine Stephanidis, ICS-Forth, Greece
Hallvard Traetteberg, Norwegian Univ. of Science and Techn., Norway
Jean Vanderdonckt, Université Catholique de Louvain, Belgium
Marco Winkler, IRIT, Université Paul Sabatier - Toulouse III, France

Steering committee

Gaelle Calvary, Univ. Joseph Fourier, France
Christophe Kolski, Univ. de Valenciennes, France
Fabio Paternò, ISTI-CNR, Italy
Angel Paternò, RedWhale Corp., USA
Jean Vanderdockt, Université Catholique de Louvain, Belgium

Organizing committee

José Eduardo Córcoles, University of Castilla-La Mancha, Spain
José A. Gallud, University of Castilla La Mancha, Spain
Arturo S. García, University of Castilla La Mancha, Spain
Jose Manuel Gascueña, University of Castilla La Mancha, Spain
Pascual González, University of Castilla La Mancha, Spain
María Teresa López, University of Castilla La Mancha, Spain
María Dolores Lozano, University of Castilla La Mancha, Spain
Diego Martínez, University of Castilla-La Mancha, Spain
Elena Navarro, University of Castilla-La Mancha, Spain
Víctor M. R. Penichet, University of Castilla La Mancha, Spain
Manuel Tobarra, University of Castilla-La Mancha, Spain

Chapter 1
The Challenges of User-Centred Design

William Hudson

Abstract A number of perceptual and psychological issues conspire to make the successful design of interactive systems – and user interfaces in particular – much more difficult than it would seem at first sight. This paper describes the author's keynote address to the CADUI conference and investigates these issues, touching on attentional, change and mud splash blindnesses. It also explores the diffculties technologists can have in understanding user's needs, as demonstrated by a recent study in empathizing and systemising skills within the IT sector.

1.1 People Are Not Perfect

While human beings are amazing creatures, we have our limitations. In the field of design, one glaring limitation is our willingness to overlook them. We design and develop systems that assume the visual acuity of an eagle; memory of an elephant; navigation skills of a bat; stamina of a camel; and the dexterity of a monkey (see Fig. 1.1) [1].

There are several reasons for this. The first is that, by default, designers and developers focus very intently on the problem at hand *in the abstract*. Issues that stem from human limitations or needs (such as leaving the office to eat or sleep) are peripheral to the solution being designed. However, to make matters worse, there are several human limitations relevant to interactive systems that are not very well known within the field of Human–Computer Interaction (HCI). All these stem from failings of visual perception and so are called 'blindnesses': attentional blindness, change blindness, and mud splash blindness.

Attentional blindness is well known within the field of visual perception [2]. It is best illustrated through demonstration, but even a description of the problem is fairly impressive. Perhaps the best-known example is a short video clip of two teams of students wearing either black or white T-shirts (depending on the team). The audience is told simply to count the number of times the teams pass a ball between them as

W. Hudson
Syntagm Ltd, Oxford, UK
e-mail: william.hudson@syntagm.co.uk

V. López-Jaquero et al. (eds.), *Computer-Aided Design of User Interfaces VI*,
DOI: 10.1007/978-1-84882-206-1_1, © Springer-Verlag London Limited 2009

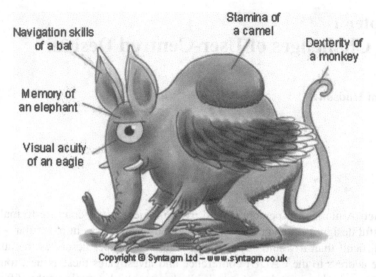

Navigation skills
of a bat

Stamina of
a camel

Dexterity of
a monkey

Memory of
an elephant

Visual acuity
of an eagle

Copyright © Syntagm Ltd – www.syntagm.co.uk

Fig. 1.1 The perfect user

they move about in a fairly distracting manner. About half way through the clip, someone dressed in a gorilla suit walks into the scene, beats their chest and then walks off. They are on screen altogether for about 5 s. At the end of the clip the audience is asked if they observed anything unusual. Only about half of the audience will have noticed the gorilla. The other half of the audience was so intent on performing the task in hand that they were oblivious to this unexpected event.

Another surprising aspect of visual attention is our inability to see changes on a screen when a brief blanking field is present – the kind that separates virtually all web pages as the browser loads new content. The phenomenon is called change blindness [3]. Its effect is a little harder to predict than inattention blindness as some participants will notice the change straight away but others may give up after a minute or two.

The third perceptual issue is related to change blindness. Rather than a blanking field between screens, its contents are changed at the same time as simulated mud splashes – hence its name, mud-splash blindness. Participants find it almost impossible to say what has changed.

All three of these issues have important implications for design. Users who might be very distracted by their tasks risk not noticing important information (a gorilla!) on their screens. Changes to web pages may not be seen on reload because of change blindness. And finally, animations or popup boxes, similar to mud splashes in their effect, may mask other changes that occurred at the same time.

1.2 Designers Are Not Perfect

Twenty years on from Don Norman's *The Psychology of Everyday Things* [4] designers are still creating even simple technology with unhelpful user interfaces. The two examples shown here from a recent hotel stay made it difficult to know

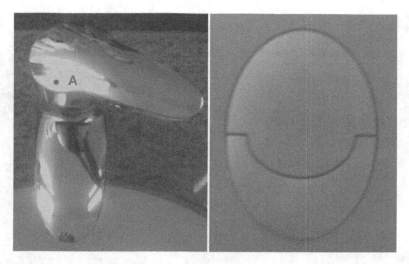

Fig. 1.2   Designs are not perfect

what temperature the water would be (contrary to what might be expected from the left-hand image in Fig. 1.2, where the dot marked 'A' is red, this is the cold setting). In the same hotel room, it is hard to understand why a toilet would have two different flush controls when it is impossible to guess what they do.

The difficulty in these and many screen-based examples of poor design is that we still do not teach (or understand) visual language. We would understand it better if we worked more directly with the users of our creations, but that is still relatively rare. So, for every well-designed web site, desktop application or phone, there are hundreds that could be more self-explanatory and easier to use.

For example, an early version of the Microsoft web site page for Intranet Explorer version 8 should have been fairly straightforward (see Fig. 1.3). But the visual language used suggests that selecting an operating system (A) will show appropriate system requirements (B). On the contrary, the two parts of the page are unrelated. Once the operating system is selected and the Go button pressed, the page is abandoned and replaced with a new one to perform a download.

1.3   User-Centred Design (UCD) ≠ Usability ≠ Cool

Design examples of this kind are plentiful, but there is an even deeper problem. The pressures to engage and excite customers have created a fog of confusion around the concepts of user-centred design (UCD), usability, and 'coolness'.

These three ideas are related but, as Fig. 1.4 shows, not equivalent. User interfaces can be *usable* without being *useful* (as represented by the UCD circle) and they can be *cool* without being either. And regrettably, for customers and users, the current trend is towards coolness without substance. Microsoft Windows Vista,

Fig. 1.3 The new Microsoft web site page for Intranet Explorer version 8

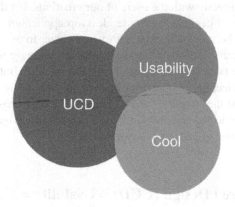

Fig. 1.4 The concepts of user-centred design (UCD), usability, and 'coolness'

Office 2007 and Apple's iPhone are all examples of user interfaces that have been designed to be appealing, but in many cases are actually more difficult to use than their predecessors. (The iPhone requires that users have appropriate-sized fingers, for example. It does not recognize a stylus.)

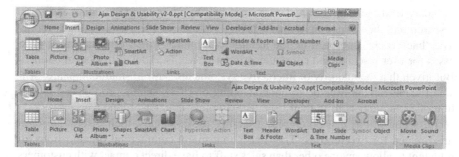

Fig. 1.5 Two views of the same toolbar from Microsoft PowerPoint 2007

Consider Fig. 1.5. This shows two views of the same toolbar from Microsoft PowerPoint 2007. The only difference is the window size. In smaller windows, the toolbar is compressed to fit. Cool, but very difficult for technical support departments who are trying to assist colleagues without seeing their screen. And, unlike all previous versions of Microsoft Office applications, the 'ribbon' as this interface is called, completely replaces the menus.

An additional challenge has been introduced for Windows Vista. The title bars are translucent, which, although attractive to some, makes it difficult to see where the title bar ends and the next window begins. Since users must drag the title bar to move windows on the screen, they sometimes end up clicking in the wrong window. It is hard to imagine what user need has been addressed by these and many other changes on the path to coolness. Yet, at the same time, truly helpful features are overlooked. As a case in point (and through no fault of Microsoft), it is not possible to buy a flight and a hotel package from a travel web site if you would like a hotel that is not near an airport. So, booking a flight and overnight stay in Heidelberg (Germany) is impossible in a single transaction since there is no airport in Heidelberg. It is left to the customer to find an appropriate airport, means of transport, and hotel.

1.3.1   Why Is There Not More UCD?

Apart from the drive for coolness, what is holding UCD back? One of the most common reasons was expressed perfectly by Jack Warner of the Hollywood studio bearing his name:

I don't want it good, I want it Tuesday.

UCD and usability are thought of as either optional (when thought of at all) or as enhancements that can be added later. A further complication with usability is that it is actually very limited in its scope. If a travel web site does not offer the means of booking a hotel away from an airport, then that missing functionality will not be usability-tested by definition. It is a very brave usability specialist that tells their customer or employer that they have built the wrong system.

Many of these shortcomings stem from an unwillingness to conduct early user research and the continuing trend of hiding systems builders away in back rooms. The 'back room' approach is fine in large companies with well-established processes for user-research and communicating user needs in detail to system builders. But given that the majority of interactive systems are built in small companies with small teams having little or no understanding of UCD, such a pronounced separation of technologists from their users is extremely counter-productive.

In organizations that do employ usability professionals, their efforts are often misdirected for two reasons. The first is that many commercial organizations are reluctant to allow anyone other than sales staff to have direct contact with customers. The second is that where bespoke usability facilities exist (such as an expensive lab with video cameras and observation rooms), there is enormous pressure to make good use of them, at the expense of the design process itself. In this latter case, success is often measured as a fully booked usability lab, even if the work that is booked – user research, for example – should be conducted in the field [5].

1.3.2 Empathetic Design

Before we look at solutions to some of these challenges, there is one further problem area to explore. Like the visual perception issues discussed earlier, it is inherent in the human condition: the people who are best at creating technology are often the worst at the understanding how and why other people find it difficult to use. The evidence for this comes from a different branch of psychology, investigating the causes of autism and Asperger's syndrome (AS). Simon Baron-Cohen and his colleagues at the Autism Research Centre have developed a model they use to explain the significant differences in behaviour between men and women, called empathizing–systemizing theory [6, 7]. A related theory, known as the 'extreme male brain' [8] characterizes the more extreme differences between the normal population and suffers of autism and AS.

Empathizers are interested in people and social interaction while systemizers are more focused on the physical world and causality. On average, men score higher than women on systemizing while women score higher than men on empathizing. Not surprisingly, a large study of empathizing and systemizing within the IT field (441 participants) showed systemizing scores for men and women that were both substantially higher than the average population [9]. However, men whose job roles were predominantly technical had significantly lower empathizing skills, as illustrated in Fig. 1.6. (The few women who stated that their job roles were primarily technical also showed this effect, but it was less significant.)

Ideally, we would have equivalent technology for interactive systems that would allow designers and developers to empathize with users. They would do this by showing how a web page looked to a 60-year-old (that is the purpose of the yellowed goggles and helmet visor in Fig. 1.7) or simulate how difficult it is to select a menu when you have trouble moving the mouse in a straight line.

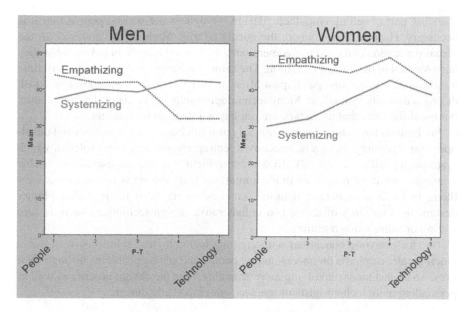

Fig. 1.6   Men whose job roles were predominantly technical had lower empathizing skills

Fig. 1.7   Examples of empathy-assistive technology (images courtesy of the University of Lough-borough, except bottom-right: Meyer-Hentschel [10])

A big part of selling empathetic design, though, is persuading people that it is necessary. Happily, this is where the gorilla returns. Many of the audience in the visual perception demonstrations mentioned earlier are truly stunned by what they have learned of the human condition. The same revelations occur almost every time a developer watches one participant after another fail at the same point in a task during a usability evaluation. Many technologists may not be naturally empathetic, but the difficulties that users face are not beyond their understanding.

So, humans have shortcomings not only as users but also as designers and developers (and possibly managers, executives, entrepreneurs, and other roles in which systemizing skills are valued). To overcome them – to design useful and usable systems – we must recognize those limitations and take steps to compensate for them. In UCD in particular, it further emphasizes the need for multidisciplinary design, field research of users, and collaborative design techniques such as card sorting or affinity diagramming.

But for everyone concerned with creating technological solutions, it means a much greater emphasis on understanding people and seeing problems through their eyes. To do that means involving more empathizers in the design process as well as persuading more technologists of the need for empathetic design.

References

1. Hudson, W. (2002). Simulating the Less-Than-Perfect User. SIGCHI Bulletin, 34 (March–April 2002).
2. Simons, D. and Chabris, C. (1999). Gorillas in our midst: sustained in attentional blindness for dynamic events. Perception, 28, 1059–1074.
3. Hudson, W. (2002). Designing for the Grand Illusion. SIGCHI Bulletin, 33 (November–December 2001).
4. Norman, D. A. (2002). The Design of Everyday Things. (Basic Books).
5. Hudson, W. (2004). My Place or Yours: Use and Abuse of Research Facilities. In Interactions, 11(3).
6. Baron-Cohen, S. (2003). The Essential Difference: Men, Women and the Extreme Male Brain Allen Lane (Penguin Press).
7. Baron-Cohen, S., Richler, J., Bisarya, D., Gurunathan, N. and Wheelright, S. (2003). The systemizing quotient: an investigation of adults with Asperger syndrome or high-functioning autism, and normal sex differences. Phil. Trans. R. Soc. Lond. B, 358(1430), 361–374.
8. Baron-Cohen, S. (2002). The extreme male brain theory of autism. Trends Cogn. Sci., 6(6), 248–254.
9. Hudson, W. (2009). Reduced Empathizing Skills Increase Challenges for User-Centered Design. In Proceedings of CHI 2009.
10. Meyer-Hentschel. URL http://www.mhmc.de/HTML/age_explorer.html.

Chapter 2
Model-Driven Engineering of Workflow User Interfaces

Josefina Guerrero García, Christophe Lemaigre, Jean Vanderdonckt
and Juan Manuel González Calleros

Abstract A model-driven engineering method is presented that provides designers
with methodological guidance on how to systematically derive user interfaces of
workflow information systems from a series of models. For this purpose, a workflow
is recursively decomposed into processes that are in turn decomposed into tasks.
Each task gives rise to a task model whose structure, ordering, and connection with
the domain model allows a semi-automated generation of corresponding user interfaces by model-to-model transformation. Reshuffling tasks within a same process
or reordering processes within a same workflow is straightforwardly propagated as
a natural consequence of the mapping model used in the model-driven engineering.
The various models involved in the method can be edited in a graphical editor based
on Petri nets and simulated interactively. This editor also contains a set of workflow user interface patterns that are ready to use. The output file generated by the
editor can then be exploited by a workflow execution engine to produce a running
workflow system.

2.1 Introduction

The introduction of Workflow Management Systems (WfMS) in organizations has
emerged as a major advantage to plan, control, and organize business process. The
WfMS in a modern organization should be highly adaptable to the frequent
changes. The adaptability of the WfMS includes changes on User Interfaces (UIs)
that are used to control business process. To increase adaptability of contemporary
WfMS, a mechanism for managing changes within the organizational structure and
changes in business rules needs to be reinforced [1, 2]. Even that several approaches
have addressed workflow modeling problems, including: graphical notations [3, 4],

J.G. García (✉), C. Lemaigre, J. Vanderdonckt and J.M.G. Calleros
Université Catholique de Louvain, Louvain School of Management (LSM),
Place des Doyens 1, 1348, Louvain-la-Neuve, Belgium
e-mail: josefina.guerrero@uclouvain.be

V. López-Jaquero et al. (eds.), *Computer-Aided Design of User Interfaces VI*,
DOI: 10.1007/978-1-84882-206-1_2, © Springer-Verlag London Limited 2009

description languages [3–5], supporting tools [1, 4, 6, 7], workflow patterns [8], and UIs derivation from workflow specifications [9, 10]; integrate all the domains have been poorly explored. Some issues encountered while deriving UI from a workflow specification are the following:

- *User interface hand coded design.* UI derivation from a workflow specification has been used on commercial tools [9], even though the UI is still manually designed and correlated to workflow components. In some cases, several UIs can be predefined for basic UI action types, for instance, Open a File.
- *Lack of integration models of the organization and UI generation.* There are some efforts [4] trying to model the organization and workflow. This second category refers to a totally different problem and is not intended to generate information systems (IS) but to model workflow.
- *Lack of adaptation to organizational changes.* Workflow tools allow managers to design their organization "how it is" and simulate changes on the workflow models to compare whether there are improvements in time, cost, etc. The problems arise when the changes are applied to the organization. Especially when IS are affected. The correct propagation of changes is very difficult to assure, what is more, this work must be hand coded.

These shortcomings stem from the need for a logical definition of workflow models to derive UIs that further allows a computational handling of them as opposed to a physical handling hard coded in particular software. The remainder of this chapter is structured as follows. Section 2.2 explains the conceptual model. Section 2.3 illustrates the different steps that followed in order to derive UIs. Section 2.4 introduces a case study using a tool support. Section 2.5 provides a brief discussion and a comparison with the related work. Section 2.6 gives a final conclusion.

2.2 Conceptual Model of a Workflow Information System

FlowiXML is a methodology [11] for developing the various user interfaces (UIs) of a workflow information system (WIS), which are advocated to automate processes, following a model-driven engineering based on requirements and processes of the organization. The methodology applies to (1) integrate human and machines based activities, in particular those involving interaction with IT applications and tools; (2) identify how tasks are structured, who perform them, what their relative order is, how they are offered or assigned, and how tasks are being tracked. Figure 2.1 represents the UML class diagram of this meta-model without any attributes or methods, more details about the attributes and methods of these classes could be found in [11]. The meta-model involves the following models:

- *Workflow model.* It describes how the work in organization flows by defining models of process (what to do?), tasks (how to do it?), and the organizational structure (where and who will perform it?). A workflow model has at least one process and each process has at least two tasks. The heuristics to identify a

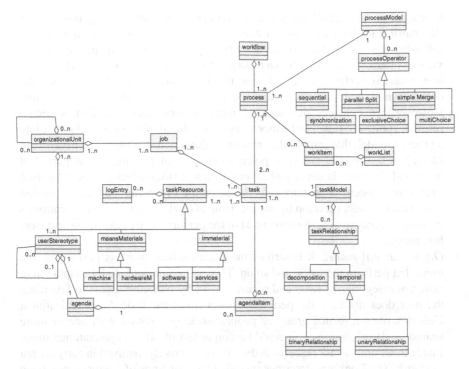

Fig. 2.1 Partial view of meta-model

workflow model are: it is associated to the operational and/or administrative objectives of organization, is performed within the same organization and it is associated to the automation of a business process.

- *Process model.* The definition of a process indicates the ordering of tasks in time, space, and resources. Our model is an adaptation of the Petri net notation proposed in [2, 12] and is compatible with the workflow resource patterns proposed in [8]. The concept of *work List* is introduced, which stocks the processes of the whole organization. Managers are benefited as they can identify resources performing tasks, status of the workflow, bottlenecks in the processes and the identification of the organizational unit where the task is performed. The heuristics to identify a process model are same group of resources, continuous period of time, specific ordering of tasks, the work is developed within groups, among groups, or by a group as a whole, is not further divided into sub-processes and it could be primary (production), secondary (support), or tertiary (managerial).
- *Task model.* Task models are used to collect the requirements of a workflow system. Task models are mechanisms to represent user's tasks along with their logical and temporal ordering. An adapted version of ConcurTaskTree (CTT) [13] is used in this work. A task is an activity that has to be performed by users (human, systems, humans interacting with systems, or a combination of them)

to reach a given goal related to the business processes. Introducing task models description to the workflow models corresponds, but is not limited, to the following reasons: (1) Task models describe, opposed to process models, end users' view of interactive tasks while interacting with the system. This allows describing how a task is performed. (2) It is true that in a process model we can add the detail desired, with process hierarchies, to represent a detailed task description. However, we consider that specific temporal operators, iteration, suspend/resume, applied to task, can be more naturally defined in a task model rather into a process model, that implies the creation of dummy transitions. The heuristic to identify a task model are same place, same type of resource, same period of time, and the work is developed by one resource (individual), it could be user, interactive, system or abstract task. Based on the organizational model, we can add a machine task (develop by any mechanical or electrical device that transmits or modifies energy to perform or assist in the performance of tasks. For instance: fax, robot).

- *Organizational model.* It describes the places where work is performed, the users that perform the work, and so on. This part contributes to UI adaptation to different categories of users and security of IS by blocking access to UIs when the user does not have the permission to perform the task. An organizational Unit describes a formal group of people working together with one or more shared goals or objectives. It could be composed of other organizational units. Inside these units a task resource is directly or indirectly involved in carrying out the work. The LogEntry describes specific characteristics of the resources. Each resource may have a log Entry associated with them. A Job represents the total collection of tasks, duties, and responsibilities assigned to one or more positions which require work of the same nature and level, for instance, a surgeon. At this level an Agenda is defined showing assigned tasks to the user. It allows the description of the different status of a task (for instance: not started, in progress), the date when the task begins, the deadline, the date when the task could be assigned or delegated, and the date when the task is completed.

- *Mapping model.* In a model-based approach [14] all the components are models. Even transformation among models and relationships are described in terms of a meta-model. The mapping model defines the relationships between the models. This mapping model allows the specification of the link of elements from heterogeneous models and viewpoints. Several relationships can be defined to explicit the relationships between models. We extended the existing mapping model of UsiXML (www.usixml.org(as depicted in Fig. 2.2. The extended model contains mappings describing task execution (rules to specify: complex and dynamic users' interaction within the organization), such as: *Is Grafted On* mapping, this relationships is useful when a task (Tj) has been executed, and a task complementary (Ti) is defined to realize the first task where Ti is completely autonomous to Tj. When work is executed tasks are *defined by* a userStereotype. Then, they can be *allocated to task Resource*s, following the set of predefined workflow resource patterns, proposed in [8]. These patterns represent the different ways in which tasks are advertised and ultimately bound to specific resources for execution.

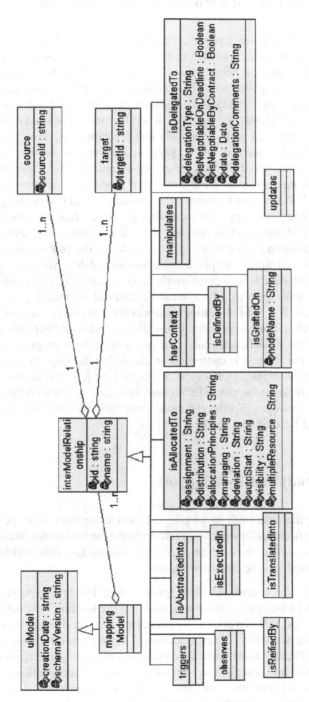

Fig. 2.2 Mapping model

2.3   A Method to Design Workflow User Interfaces

A User Interface Description Language (UIDL) consists of a high-level computer language for describing characteristics of interest of a UI with respect to the rest of an interactive application; it helps define UIs linguistically with a general trend to do so in an XML-complaint way. In a previous work [15] a number of XML-compliant languages for defining user interfaces were identified and analyzed. We select for our work UsiXML as a UIDL for several reasons. The most relevant is its flexibility to be expanded with the models that we proposed. Also, more than a language, UsiXML is a methodology to generate UIs on a model-based approach. The conceptual framework of UsiXML relies on the Cameleon Reference Framework [16]. Reusing this mechanism the UI of a workflow model, that includes task models, can be generated. Model-based approach is intended to assist in designing UIs with a more formal computer supported methodology rather than the more common information paper design, such as storyboarding. It attempts to explicitly represent knowledge that is often hidden in the application code. The problem of generating user interfaces from a workflow specification has several dimensions to be tackled. It is necessary to have UIs to support user's tasks specified in task models, user's communication with agendas which must be updated accordingly as tasks are assigned or ended, and tasks allocation with workflow resource patterns. Also we need a framework not just to generate those UIs automatically but also to specify workflows and task models, integrating the concepts that we propose in previous section. Hence, our method is composed on the following steps to achieve these goals: (1) define the organizational units, (2) define the jobs and user stereotypes, (3) define the workflow, which includes process model, (4) define workflow patterns, (5) define the task models, (6) mapping model from task models to UIs, (7) generate UIs: agendas, UI for each task model.

2.4   Case Study and Tool Support

The purpose of the case study is to give a concrete application of the concepts through the specification of a workflow representing a medical center. We developed a tool (Fig. 2.3) to support the description of workflow models. This workflow editor allows the graphical specification of workflow.

- *Step 1: where? Organizational units' specification.* The first step, which is not mandatory to be the first, consists in specifying the location in which the work must be done. Organizational units' attributes are then specified in the editor and graphically the workflow designer identifies the different components of the organization. Organizational units are represented by rectangles (big rectangles in Fig. 2.3), which will contain a set of ordered tasks and the available resources. It is the way to locate those elements inside the organization. The following organizational units are the structural decomposition of the hospital: (i) reception:

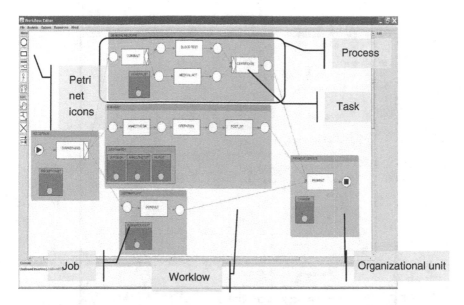

Fig. 2.3 Workflow editor

patients coming to this unit will be dispatched through the medical units of the
hospital; (ii) general medicine: diagnostic and simple medical acts are realized in
this unit; (iii) surgery: patients will be operated in this unit; (iv) dermatology: unit
involved in every dermatological resource and the performance of the related
medical acts; (v) payment service.

- *Step 2: who? Specification of jobs and user stereotypes.* This step consists in the
  description of all the actors involved in the workflow. For this purpose we define
  different levels of users, who are the resources that will be in charge of performing
  the organization work. Jobs are ways to structure the crew of people inside the
  organization (Fig. 2.4). It involves the complete collection of knowledge and
  practices needed by a definite human resource to perform a task. Jobs specified
  in the definition of the case study are the following: Receptionist, Generalist,
  Surgeon, Anesthetist, Nurse, Dermatologist, and Cashier. Once jobs are defined
  it is possible to incorporate user stereotypes, people able to carry out tasks of a
  particular job. The workers editor (Fig. 2.5) is used for this purpose. Workers are
  defined in terms of attributes (name, experience, hierarchy level) and the list of
  jobs they can perform. For instance, we define a user stereotype called Robert
  Wink, having 4 years experience in the third hierarchy level. He is able to carry
  out tasks as a generalist and surgeon. Also, it is necessary to assign them a place
  into the organizational scheme. A user stereotype may be assigned to several
  organizational units. The graphical representation used for the workflow editor
  is based on a first resource container inside the organizational unit. It allows the
  workflow designer to group resources. Job boxes are put inside of the main
  resource box. Each job box is instantiated by user stereotypes able to perform

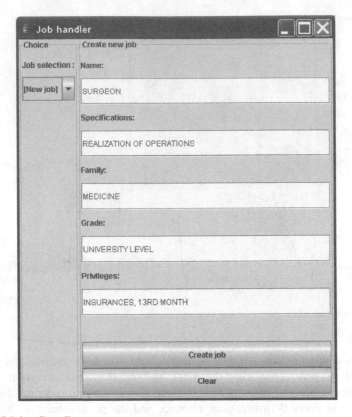

Fig. 2.4 Job handler editor

the job of the box. This leads to the kind of representation given in Fig. 2.3 (small rectangles). The organizational unit contains a resource box made of three job boxes. Every job box instantiates user stereotypes of a certain job (there are two surgeons, one anesthetist and one in the given example). This lets managers know which resources are available for execute a task in an organizational unit.

- *Step 3: what? Workflow specification.* The workflow specification, depicted in the process model, takes place inside of the organizational unit framework. Concretely, the workflow represents the business process and determines the right resource for the right task at the right time. This part of the graphical notation (Fig. 2.3) of the workflow is based on Petri nets [12].
- *Step 4: whom? Defining workflow resource patterns.* It is important to specify who will be in charge of what. For that purpose, we use workflow resource patterns [8] to assign or offer tasks. As, we have already defined jobs and user stereotypes, now we add rules defining the way work will be undertaken. The resource pattern editor (Fig. 2.6) allows the workflow designer to specify resource patterns. At first a list of jobs required to carry out task is specified in the editor. The workflow designer selects one ore more jobs allowing a user stereotype to realize the task. For the moment, 43 workflow resource patterns [8] have been incorporated so that

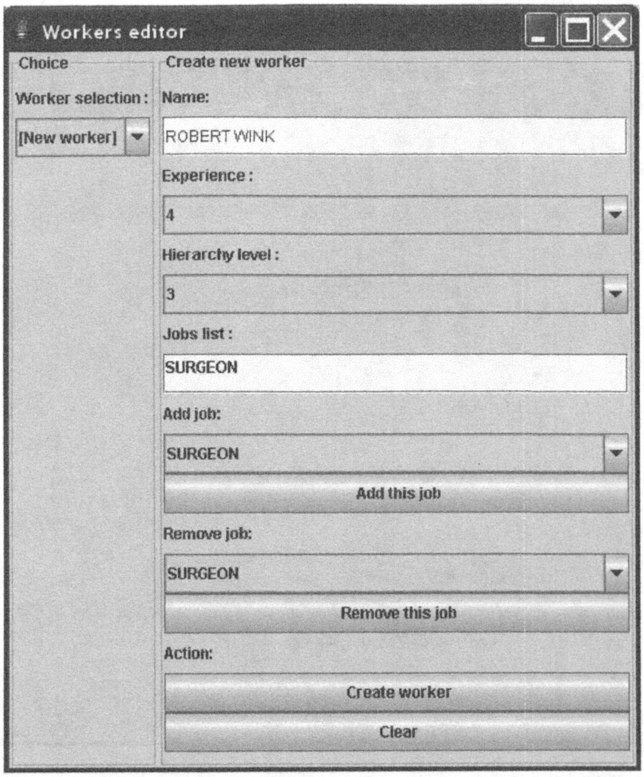

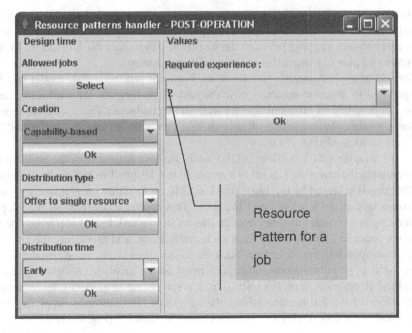

Fig. 2.5 Workers editor

Fig. 2.6 Resource patterns editor

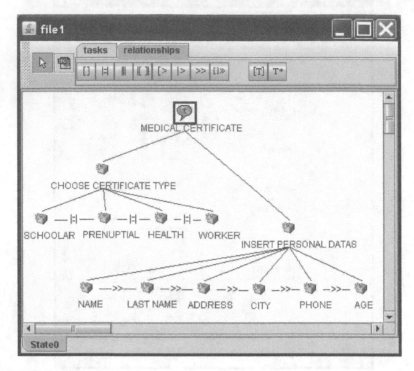

Fig. 2.7 Task model editor

the designer may apply them directly using a predefined UI. Each UI pattern is
expressed in UsiXML and is stored in a pattern repository. For the moment, there
is a one-to-one mapping between the workflow pattern and the UI pattern. In the
future, we plan to expand this mapping with parameters.

- *Step 5: how? Task models specification.* For each process a task model can be
  specified to describe in detail how the task is performed. By exploiting task
  model descriptions different scenarios could be conducted. Each scenario represents a particular sequence of actions that can successfully be performed to
  reach a task goal (Fig. 2.7).
- *Step 6: Mapping the workflow to UI.* Finally we have to deal with the problem of
  generating the complete UIs set to support all the designed workflow in run-time.
  This step is achieved by relying on the UsiXML method that progressively moves
  from a task model to a final user interface. This approach consists of three steps:
  deriving one or many abstract user interfaces from a task model, deriving one or
  many concrete user interfaces from each abstract one, and producing the code of
  the corresponding final user interfaces. To ensure these steps, transformations are
  encoded as graph transformations performed on the involved models expressed
  in their graph equivalent. For each step, a graph grammar gathers relevant graph
  transformations for accomplishing the sub-steps. For instance, applying this
  method to the task model we obtain its correspondent UI (Fig. 2.8).

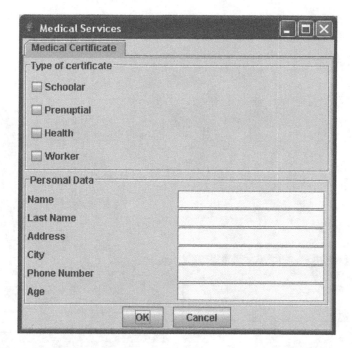

Fig. 2.8 User interface (UI) derived from task model

2.4.1   The Simulator Tool

After we develop all the UIs for each task, we have control of how the work is flowing inside the organization, for this purpose we have a workflow editor. Following the Petri net representation, resource choice is made when a token is in place preceding a transition. It is managed following resource patterns defined with the editor. When a task is started the associated token goes from a place to the associated transition. In this way, work in progress is represented in the workflow simulation diagram. Each user that participated in the workflow should have an *agenda* to view and manage the tasks that are assigned or offered to him. Each agenda can be visualized as a queue of tasks assigned to a resource. Through agendas we can support the work among resources or groups (Fig. 2.9). As we said, one important aspect to consider is any change in the workflow and to have the possibility to manage it.

2.5   Discussion and Related Work

While reviewing the literature one can easily see the extensive research of the organization, their process, adaptability, etc. In the same venue, WfMS research includes graphical notations [3, 4], description languages [3–5], supporting tools [1, 4, 6, 7],

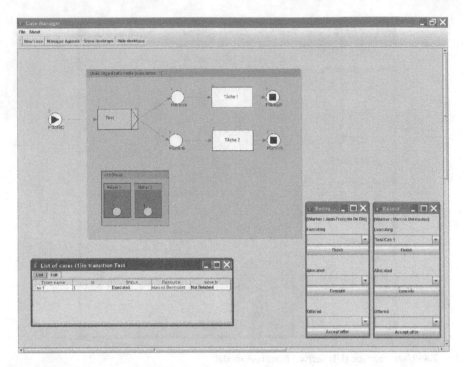

Fig. 2.9 Workflow manager tool

and workflow patterns [8], each tackling specific and independent issues of modern organizations. In this chapter we introduced a model that includes all these aspects, which are relevant and have an impact one to each other when changes are applied. We use a model-driven engineering approach for the user interface design, as it aids in creating interactive software that considers multiple factors, such as users, tasks, and so on. Still there are missing points regarding our model. First, we consider that it is fundamental to address Mandviwalla & Olfman [17] criteria for support group interactions, such as the following ones: (a) support multiple group tasks, (b) support multiple work methods, (c) support the development of the group, d) provide inter-changeable interaction methods, (e) sustain multiple behavioral characteristics, (f) accommodate permeable group boundaries, (g) adjustability to the group context. In [18] there are usability guidelines that can be considered, for a future work, as a principle that has to be taken into account for building UIs respecting cognitive and sensory-motor capabilities of users. By linking user interfaces of a WfMS we expect to solve the problem of synchronizing the communication between UIs (agendas and task UIs) and the workflow view. One option can be client–server architecture. So far we can just simulate agendas interaction. The solution should provide communication channels from the workflow manager application (server) to every userStereotype agenda (clients). In the domain of model-driven engineering, Stavness [1] presents a progression model in order to support workflow execution, but not a complete decomposition of processes along with jobs and organizational units is included.

The same observation holds for [6, 10]. In particular, in [10], a task model is indeed used, but only its hierarchical decomposition is used. Therefore, our method and our supporting tool differ from the state-of-the-art in that it is based on several models (not just data or tasks), some coming from theory of organizations. The graphical notation is based on Petri nets as in [2, 3]. In [19] a method called AMOMCASYS is presented, this method is also based on Petri nets, it is aimed at modeling and simulating complex administrative systems.

2.6   Conclusion

This chapter defined a method for designing UI of WISs where UI are directly derived from a model of the workflow, which is decomposed into processes to end up with tasks. Based on workflow patterns, it is possible to model an entire workflow with high-level mechanisms and automatically generate the workflow specifications and their corresponding UIs. All models are uniformly expressed in the same XML-based specification language so that mappings between models are preserved at design-time and can be exploited at run-time in needed. Then, the different *steps* of the approach have been properly defined based on the underlying models and a *tool* has been developed to support the method enactment. The major benefit of the above method is that all the design knowledge required to progressively move from a workflow specification to its corresponding UIs is expressed in the model and the mapping rules. The method preserves continuity (all subsequent models are derived from previous ones) and traceability of its enactment (it is possible to trace how a particular workflow is decomposed into processes and tasks, with their corresponding user interfaces). In this way, it is possible to change any level (workflow, process, task, and UI) and to propagate the changes throughout the other levels by navigating through the mappings established at design time. In order to partially support this method, a software tool has been developed in Java 1.5 that supports the graphical editing of the concepts introduced in an integrated way. It then enables designers to pick any of the predefined 43 workflow resource patterns that are later attached to a corresponding UI pattern in UsiXML. This method has been so far validated on four real-world case studies (e.g., a hospital dept., a triathlon organization, a cycling event, and personalized order of compression stockings over Internet). More information, including a video demo of the software can be found at: http://www.usixml. org/index.php?mod=pages&id=40.

References

1. Stavness, N., Schneider, K.A.: Supporting Flexible Business Processes with a Progression Model. In: Proc. of the 1st Int. Workshop on Making model-based user interface design practical: usable and open methods and tools MBUI'2004 (Funchal, January 13, 2004) CEUR Workshop Proceedings, Vol. 103. Accessible at http://sunsite.informatik.rwth-aachen.de/Publications/ CEUR-WS//Vol-103/stavness-et-al.pdf.

2. van der Aalst, W.M.P., van Hee, K.: Workflow Management: Models, Methods, and Systems. The MIT Press, Cambridge (2002).
3. van der Aalst, W.M.P., ter Hofstede, A.H.M.: YAWL: Yet Another Workflow Language. Information Systems 30, 4 (2005) 245–275.
4. van Hee, K., Oanea, O., Post, R., Somers, van der Werf, J.M.: Yasper: a tool for workflow modeling and analysis. In: Proc. of 6th Int. Conf. on Application of Concurrency to System Design (2006) 279–282.
5. Dumas, M., ter Hofstede, A.: UML Activity Diagrams as a Workflow Specification Language. In: Proc. of 4th Int. Conf. on the Unified Modeling Language, Concepts, and Tools UML'2001 (Toronto, October 1–5, 2001). Lecture Notes in Computer Science, Vol. 2185. Springer, Berlin (2001) pp. 76–90.
6. Lee, H. B., Kim, J. W., Park, S. J.: KWM: Knowledge-based Workflow Model for Agile Organization. Journal of Intelligent Information Systems 13 (1999) 261–278.
7. van der Aalst, W.M.P., Kumar, A.: XML Based Schema Definition for Support of Inter-organizational Workflow. In: Proc. of 21st Int. Conf. on Application and Theory of Petri Nets ICATPN'2000. LNCS, Vol. 1825. Springer, Berlin (2000) 475–484.
8. Russell, N., van der Aalst, W.M.P., ter Hofstede, A.H.M., Edmond, D.: Workflow Resource Patterns: Identification, Representation, and Too Support. In: Proc. of 17th Conf. on Advanced Information Systems Engineering CAiSE'2005 (Porto, June 13–17, 2005). Lecture Notes in Computer Science, Vol. 3520. Springer, Berlin (2005) 216–232.
9. Kristiansen, R., Trætteberg, H.: Model-Based User Interface Design in the Context of Workflow Models. In: Proc. of 6th Int. Workshop on Task Models and Diagrams for User Interface Design TAMODIA'2007 (Toulouse, November 7–9, 2007). Lecture Notes in Computer Science, Vol. 4849. Springer, Berlin (2007) pp. 227–239.
10. Stolze, M., Riand, Ph., Wallace, M., Heath, T.: Agile Development of Workflow Applications with Interpreted Task Models. In: Proc. of 6th Int. Workshop on Task Models and Diagrams for User Interface Design TAMODIA'2007 (Toulouse, November 7–9, 2007). Lecture Notes in Computer Science, Vol. 4849. Springer, Berlin (2007) 2–14.
11. Guerrero, J., Vanderdonckt, J., Gonzalez, J.M.: FlowiXML: A Step Towards Designing Workflow Management Systems. Journal of Web Engineering 4, 2 (2008) 163–182.
12. van der Aalst, W.M.P.: The application of Petri Nets to Workflow Management. Journal of Circuits, Systems, and Computers 8, 1 (1998) 21–66.
13. Paternò, F. Model-based design and evaluation of interactive applications. Springer (1999).
14. Puerta, A.R.: A Model-Based Interface Development Environment. IEEE Software 14, 4 (1997) 41–47.
15. Souchon, N., Vanderdonckt, J.: A review of XML-compliant user interface description languages. In: Proc. of DSV-IS'2003. Springer, Berlin (2003) 377–391.
16. Calvary, G., Coutaz, J., Thevenin, D., Limbourg, Q., Bouillon, L., Vanderdonckt, J.: A Unifying Reference Framework for Multi-Target User Interfaces. Interacting with Computers 15, 3 (2003) 289–308.
17. Mandviwalla, M., Olfman, L.: What do groups need? A proposed set of generic groupware requirements. ACM Transactions on Computer-Human Interaction 1, 3 (1994) 245–268.
18. Palanque, P., Farenc, Ch., Bastide, R.: Embedding Ergonomic Rules as Generic Requirements in a Formal Development Process of Interactive Software. In: Proc. of IFIP TC 13 Int. Conf. on Human-Computer Interaction Interact'99 (Edinburgh, September 1–4, 1999). IOS Press, Amsterdam (1999) 408–416.
19. Adam, E., Kolski, C., Mandiau, R., Vergison, E.: A software engineering workbench for modeling groupware activities. In: C. Stephanidis (Ed.), Universal Access in HCI: inclusive design in the information society. Lawrence Erlbaum Associates, Mahwah, NJ (2003) pp. 1499–1503.

Chapter 3
User Interface Development Life Cycle for Business-Driven Enterprise Applications

Kenia Sousa, Hildeberto Mendonça and Jean Vanderdonckt

Abstract This work presents how business process models are described in terms of task models to solve traceability issues for large systems. The proposed approach presents a method with activities specifically selected for the scenario of developing user interfaces (UIs) for enterprise applications founded on extensive business processes. Furthermore, some of these activities are detailed to make the work on UIs aligned with business processes. With the use of the tool proposed in this research, it is then possible to identify the UI components that are impacted whenever changes are made on business processes.

3.1 Introduction

The use of Information Technology (IT) has evolved over time from its traditional use as an administrative support toward a more strategic role to enforce business processes (BP). In addition, there is a growing interest on the alignment of IT with organizational objectives from different perspectives, such as from business executives, IT managers, and academics.

It is observed in the IT domain that most researches are focused on specifying the association between models from business and IT to support propagating changes [1, 18]. Another observation is that many of these researches use software engineering models to address alignment issues. However, such strategies lack the consideration of a major aspect of information systems: their user interfaces (UI). The impact of focusing on functional aspects is that many changes on business processes that affect UIs are not carefully treated, thus leaving the decision of how changes impact UIs to be done in an ad hoc manner. This effect is even more negative when we address large systems in which changes in business process rules are common

K. Sousa (✉), H. Mendonça and J. Vanderdonckt
Université catholique de Louvain, Louvain School of Management (LSM),
Place des Doyens 1, 1348, Louvain-la-Neuve, Belgium
e-mail: kenia.sousa@student.uclouvain.be

and may have impact on even hundreds of UIs, thus leading to the need to define strategies to maintain the traceability between business process and UIs whenever changes are requested.

Certain changes on business processes that have a direct impact on UIs may be related to different reasons, and therefore can be classified to aid in organizing their impact on UIs: (1) components, new data that need to be informed may result in new elements on UIs; (2) navigation, updating organizational goals that influence responsibilities of professionals may result in new navigation between screens; (3) internal structure, change in the way of working and approaching users may result in new sequence of fields; (4) external structure, new activities that professionals must execute may result in new UIs.

Such details about ordering of components, of screens, positioning of components on screens, and navigation aspects are only expressed in UI models, and are not present, for instance, in use case, class, and activity diagrams of UML. However, there are few works in the literature that study the alignment of business process and UI models, such as [13] and [14]. Aiming at supporting the development of UIs and their alignment with business processes, the overall research goal is to correlate business and UI by (1) defining the association of business process with UI models, and (2) presenting a prototype of a tool for model transformation that addresses both semiautomatic generation of UIs and traceability. This proposal is mainly aimed toward organizations that are driven by their business processes, and therefore want their systems to address such processes in a way that as the processes are created, maintained, and evolved, so are its supporting systems.

3.2 Related Work

There are recent works on the domain of model-driven architecture that discuss about traceability in model-driven development and its importance for analyzing alignment to requirements, impact, and propagation of changes, etc. However, the most common use of traceability in model transformations is between data models and class diagrams, such as in [17], which discovers useful trace information from model relations. In the work of Rummler et al. [9] on the traceability in model-driven development of business applications, they link artifacts from the development process that range from software requirements, test cases, design objects, and code fragments. It does not mention any artifact for UI and the artifacts are not necessarily models but sometimes text documents, for instance. On the other hand, it focuses on how software development techniques aid in traceability; in their case, they use aspect orientation.

Moving toward valuing integration with UI, it has been agreed by academics and practitioners that the potential of IT in enterprise applications depends on how it is used, which is directly influenced by the UI [16]. Therefore, there is a growing interest on UI in the business domain, as it is possible to verify in some works done in IBM research centers, such as [14], in which the focus is on designing low-fidelity prototypes based on business process models. Another example is a recent work of Stolze et al. [12], in which they call attention to the fact that only relying on work-flow models may be problematic to represent aspects of the user interaction because it is difficult to consider specific user requirements in such models.

Aligned with the idea that information from business processes is not enough for UI design, the work of Pontico et al. [8] advocates for a hybrid approach for modeling combining task models and process models. Similarly, Kristiansen and Traetteberg [4] propose a solution to use both workflow and task models to design role-centered UIs. It associates tasks in the BPMN model with the highest level of task models. However, there is a limitation in this approach because even though the company in their case study decomposed their business process models in tasks, not all business process models have only one level of decomposition. It is possible to have processes composed of at least three different levels: subprocesses, activities, and tasks. When modeling task models, they adopt a hierarchical sequence-oriented style, but fixed sequence is not as broad as the variety of possibilities provided by different operators that enable a richer user interaction. Besides these two diver-gences, this approach is similar to ours since it adopts a process that starts with business processes (in their case, more specifically a workflow model, responsible to manage business processes) and results into a final UI (FUI) using several models (task, domain, dialogue, a similar abstract UI, and a similar concrete UI).

Sukaviriya et al. [15] use data group concepts to link design elements to business process models, which is different from our approach. A data group is a subset of data elements that appear together on a UI. In our case, we use task models as the link between business process and UIs, without neglecting data elements, which are related with tasks. Since tasks are related to UIs, there is, thus, an implicit relationship between data elements and UIs. Therefore, besides associating business with data, we also add the concern on behavior, provided by task models.

3.3   Business Process and User Interface Model Alignment

With a detailed analysis of the specification on business process modeling notation, it was detected that some business process elements can be transformed into elements in a task model. For more details on the description of business process elements, refer to the specification [7].

The relationships between tasks in a task model are different from the ones used in business processes; therefore, there is a need to correlate them. Table 3.1 specifies the association of the relationships in business processes and in task models, with the rationale behind the decisions explained as follows. (1) Sequence flow and enabling operator represent the order in which activities are performed. (2) In cases when an activity passes information for the execution of the next activity, a data object can be associated to a sequence flow. (3) Considering two activities A1 and A2, the use of a rule intermediate event before A2 can trigger a named rule that momentarily pauses the execution of A1 while A2 is executed, and a link intermediate

Table 3.1 Association of business and task elements

No.	Business process	Task model
1	Sequence flow	Enabling
2	Sequence flow + data object	Enabling + information passing
3	Rule intermediate event + link intermediate event	Suspend/resume
4	Exclusive decision	Deterministic choice
5	Inclusive decision + exclusive merge	Nondeterministic choice
6	Cancel intermediate event	Disabling
7	Ad hoc marker in subprocess	Independence
8	Parallel gateway	Concurrency
9	Parallel gateway + data object	Concurrency + info passing

Table 3.2 Association of activity attributes and task properties

No.	Activity attribute	Task property
1	Conditional flow	Optional
2	Standard loop	Iteration
3	Multi-instance loop + MI condition	Finite iteration

event after A2 is finished connects to an intermediate event in A1, going to the moment where A1 was paused. The use of these triggers is in accordance with the suspend/resume operator that affects the flow of activities by momentarily interrupting one activity as another one is executed. (4) Both the exclusive decision and the deterministic choice represent a point in the process where the first alternative that is chosen determines the flow that will be taken. (5) Many combinations of the alternatives can be selected with inclusive decision, but it is also necessary to use the exclusive merge to express that only one of the activities is expected to be fully accomplished and its result to be passed through the flow, as a manner to be aligned with nondeterministic choice. (6) When two activities are competing and one is being performed, it may be interrupted by the second one, but the interrupted one is canceled by triggering the cancel event as soon as the second one starts, similar to disabling. (7) Ad hoc marker in a subprocess composed of activities that can be performed in any order using the attributes of an embedded subprocess addresses the same function as an independence operator. (8) In cases when two or more activities may be executed in parallel, the parallel gateway and concurrency serve the same purpose. (9) When activities are performed in parallel, similar to the previous situation except that data are synchronized, data objects and information passing are added.

Table 3.2 associates activity attributes from business processes with task properties from task models. (1) The conditional flow can have expressions that determine whether the task in this flow will be used, which can express that a task is optional, depending on a certain condition. (2) Standard loop determines that an activity is performed repeated times, similarly to the iteration. (3) Multiinstance loop has a numeric expression (its attribute MI Condition) that is evaluated once before the activity is performed and the result of this evaluation specifies the number of times that the activity will be repeated. This is in alignment with finite iteration, which expresses that a task can be iterated n times.

Table 3.3 Association of process activities and task types

No.	Process task type	Task type
1	User	Interaction
2	Service	Application
3	Manual	Single user
4	None	Abstract
5	User + attribute performers	Multiple users

Table 3.3 associates types of process activities and of tasks. Task types provide detailed information that helps in designing UIs. In business processes, tasks are the most atomic activities and in accordance to task models, they also have types. (1) User and interaction types represent tasks performed by a human with the assistance of a system. (2) Service and application represent an automated task performed by the system. (3) Manual and single user are related to tasks that are performed by a human without any aid from a system. (4) Abstract is used to group tasks; it has no specific meaning, which can mean that the type *none* is suitable for this case. (5) User type can be also appropriate to represent multiple users when the attribute *performers* is informed to specify if it is performed by a group or an organization.

This association of the main elements of business process with task models brings a contribution for UI development of information systems that are based on business process. This proposed approach closes the gap in UID life cycle, which most commonly started with task models, leaving aside business processes.

It is crucial to make it clear that the transformation of business process models into task models represents a first version of task models that need refinement. Such refinement can be done by human factors experts and UI designers, who update tasks and their relationships when new aspects may need to be created to address the richness and particularities of user interaction. The task model refinement can certainly be done with the participation of business analysts to allow consistency and alignment of task models with the business processes.

3.4   Case Study

Our experience [11] comes from analyzing an organization decomposed in bank and insurance subdivisions. The bank has a business department composed of a large group composed of around 50 business analysts, who are devoted to working on analyzing and evolving the business processes that drive the functioning of the bank and insurance. The insurance subdivision designs and develops systems that support the business processes.

In their methodology, they specify business processes with flows of subprocesses and activities until reaching an atomic level in which tasks are associated to business rules and data. However, some organizations do not detail their business processes to such a level; instead, they maintain business process models in a high level description and detail them when necessary for system development using software engineering artifacts (e.g., use cases), as proposed in [3].

Since we can come across organizations that follow these divergent methodologies, it is aimed that our approach addresses both realities. Therefore, our proposal is also applicable in the prior example of high-level business process description. In such cases, task models are also created from business processes; the main difference is that the refinement is more fine-tuned. This scenario is not addressed in this research work, which focuses on the context of the studied organization that has a great set of business process models that are specified into details.

We conducted interviews with three business analysts, two system analysts and developers, and two UI designers. During the meetings, we worked with examples of business processes and screens for insurance contracts. The main issues we detected and addressed in this organization were related to lack of correlation between business process and UI design, difficulties in doing impact analysis after changes, and difficulties to understand, to find, and to keep updated information spread in many different artifacts. In general, their business process models are composed of 60 elements that are handled for each process, which includes subprocesses, activities, and tasks, not even mentioning their business rules, which would increase this number by nearly 100 more elements to be considered. In the next section, we, then, present how these issues are addressed through method specification and tool support.

3.5 Method and Tool Support

Using the associations between models to transform a source model into a target one provides a traceability chain among the models. This chain supports identifying the impact of model changes on the system UI. Therefore, a tool called Usi4Biz (User Interface for Business) is being developed to manage these models using XML, enabling communication with other tools, such as modeling business processes in commercial tools that provide XML schemas that can be exported.

Once the models are imported into Usi4Biz (or even created within it), it is time for associating the models. Using the strategy proposed here to transform business process models into task models, their association is automatically created as the transformation is executed. This argument also applies for AUIs created from task models and domain models, and for CUI created from AUIs, since our proposal is founded on the Cameleon Reference Framework [2], which is composed of four development steps: create conceptual models (e.g., task model, data model, user model), create AUI, create CUI, and create FUI, and supported by UsiXML [5]. However, there is also the scenario in which transformations between models are not performed; rather, models are created, thus making it necessary to make manual mappings between them.

Therefore, in the organizational context under study, we propose the following method as depicted in Fig. 3.1 by applying the method engineering strategy presented in [10], which considers their needs and goals, thus making it more suitable for their reality and more feasible to be applied in the industry: (1) Business analysts design business process models in a business modeling tool, (2) Business analysts export

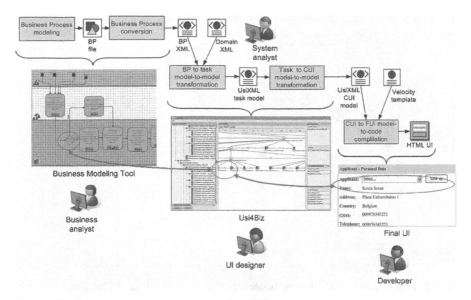

Fig. 3.1 Outline of the method with roles, artifacts, and tools

the XML from the BP tool and import it into Usi4Biz, (3) System analysts create the domain model (goal: design UIs focused on the application domain), (4) Business analysts request to generate task model based on the BP XML, (5) UI designers and human factors experts refine the generated task models by updating tasks and relationships (goal: design UIs considering users' mental models to perform their tasks), (6) UI designers list screen components based on task models (screen group, screen, screen fragment, and screen element), (7) UI designers create CUI models from task models (goal: design focused on the look-and-feel of the system), (8) Programmers develop FUIs from CUI models.

The complete description of this method, i.e., model-to-code compilation, is out of the scope of this paper and has already been addressed in several related papers, for instance, TERESA [6], supporting automated generation of UIs. Also, subject to further explanation in a future work is considering that CUI models in UsiXML have many details about the presentation but not for design creativity in a Web environment, for instance. To provide this, we consider the use of templates, with which the CUI is merged to produce a version closer to user's needs. To manage templates, we consider the Apache Velocity [19], an open source template engine widely applied in Web projects, without being restricted for them. However, the contribution here is that the task model is obtained from the business process model and that the UI resulting from task models is rigorously structured in terms of UI components and the support for traceability.

Usi4Biz supports Identifying the impact of changes; whenever the business processes are updated, this tool can provide information of which other models are impacted, which is a parallel research work that is focused on traceability. However,

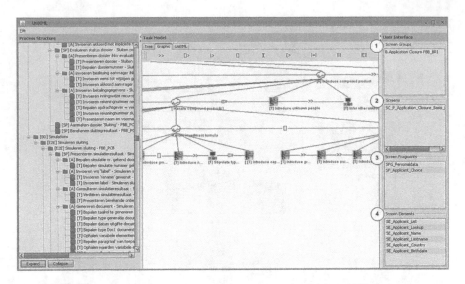

Fig. 3.2 Prototype of Usi4Biz showing business process, task model, and UI components

in this paper we want to emphasize on the support for UI design, by demonstrating how the hierarchical structure of task models can aid in organizing UIs and its components, which are numbered in Fig. 3.2: (1) screen group, a group of closely related screens; (2) screen, a state of the user interface when executing a task or part of a task; (3) screen fragment, a container of related elements; and (4) screen element, the most atomic component.

Figure 3.2 depicts the prototype of Usi4Biz, through which we aim at demonstrating the structure of the tool, not the contents of the models. On the left of the tool there is the business process extracted from the business process XML of a commercial tool, shown in a tree structure. On the middle, there is the task model generated from this business process. On the right, there are the UI components, which are applicable to generate both AUI and CUI models since the main difference between them is that CUIs are more detailed than AUIs with style guide specifications. This tool is being implemented in Java 6 using JAXP and JAXB libraries to process XML code.

The definition of organizational standards for UI organization is of primordial interest for this organization; therefore, the use of the hierarchical structure of task models can enrich their UI standards by considering both structure and user interaction. One example that well illustrates the effective use of task models as a bridge between business process and UI design is the following: a joint work between different departments has reached the resolution of defining that a screen is composed of screen title, screen fragments, and an action button. Considering that they directly associate screens to subprocesses, this leaves no flexibility for UI designers. The result is that they have screens that resemble long forms, with a long scroll bar. In cases like that, the task model can be analyzed by UI designers to help group tasks that are most similar and group them in separate screens.

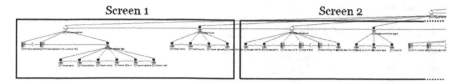

Fig. 3.3 UI design decision to organize screens depending on complexity of activities

Providing an overview of the complexity of their business processes, it is possible to understand the impact of fixing the association of screens to subprocesses. One of the subprocesses under analysis in this case study contains 17 activities, in which each activity is composed of a varied number of tasks, ranging from 5 to 30 tasks, and each task runs business rules that also vary in quantity from only 1 to as much as 99.

Figure 3.3 depicts the situation in which the UI designer analyzes the complexity of the tasks and decides to organize them in two screens, which are interlinked. For space reasons, this figure depicts a decision toward grouping tasks on screens, not the contents of the tasks. The process of making the decision of how to group tasks in screens is very complex and requires experts to consider various aspects, such as correlation between tasks, correlation of data manipulated by different tasks, smooth navigation from a certain domain to another, among others. Figure 3.4 depicts a CUI designed for the task model according to organizational standards. To illustrate a problematic situation in this CUI, knowing that tasks run business rules, consider that as users fill out fields, certain rules are executed in parallel. One possibility is that the return of a rule that requires correcting values may appear on the side of a specific field that is positioned outside the user sight since the scroll is down on the screen and the return is on the top of the screen. When users finish filling out the fields and press the confirm button on the bottom of the page, they receive a second warning, which could be avoided if the screen was not so long, which imposes restrictive range of vision and extra navigation (i.e., scrolling). On the other hand, Fig. 3.5 reproduces the CUI for the second screen of the task model, which is a second version that is much more compact and enables a better user experience.

This strategy has been analyzed by top managers from the business department, who have given positive feedback considering cost analysis, feasibility of tool support, and acceptance of change for the examples in which it was applied. The next steps are to select a pilot project and test the tool in future case studies.

3.6 Conclusion

This work presented a model-driven UI development life cycle aimed for enterprise applications in organizations with extensive business processes. The experience in a large bank/insurance company enabled us to propose a solution for aligning business processes and UIs of their supporting systems, a major issue in this company as well as in many others in the competitive business word. This reality encourages us to

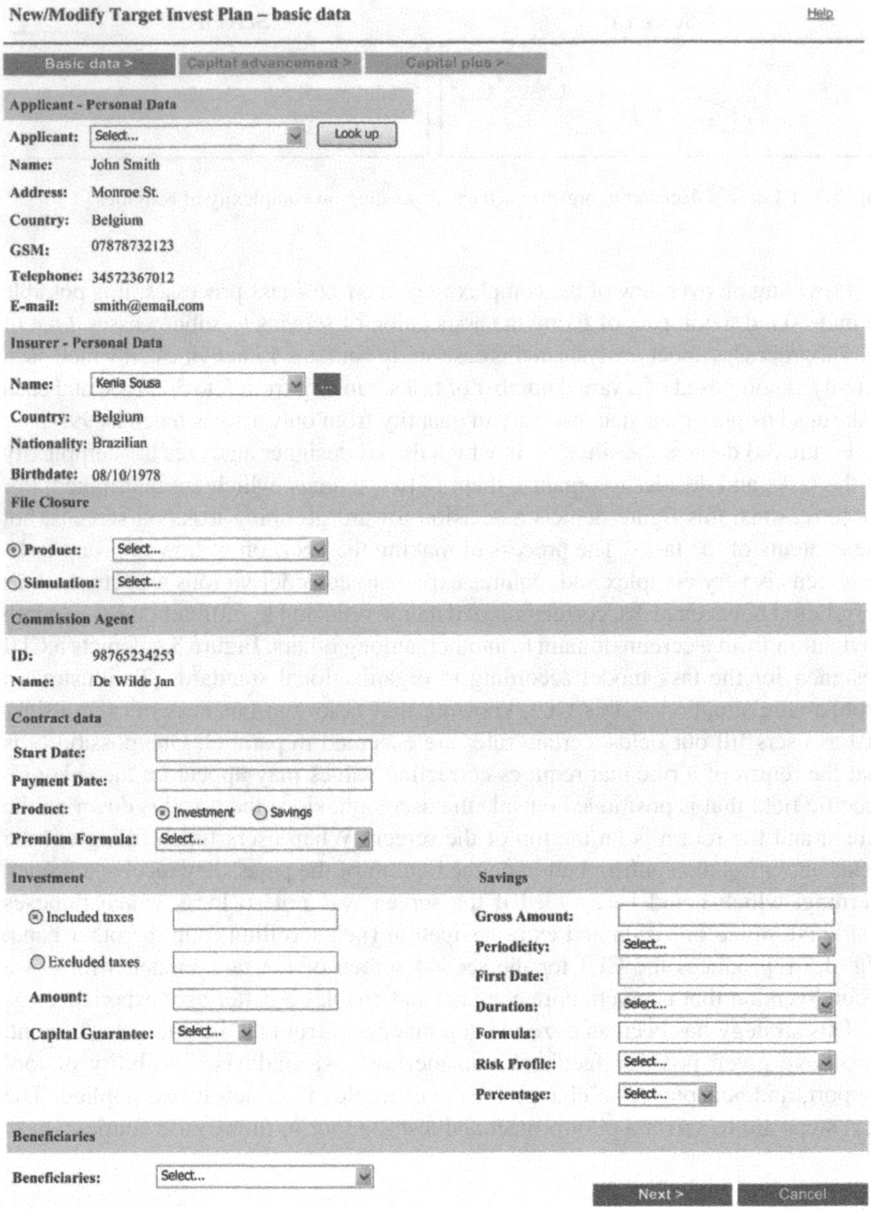

New/Modify Target Invest Plan – basic data   Help

| Basic data > | Capital advancement > | Capital plus > |

Applicant - Personal Data

Applicant: Select... ▾   [Look up]
Name: John Smith
Address: Monroe St.
Country: Belgium
GSM: 07878732123
Telephone: 34572367012
E-mail: smith@email.com

Insurer - Personal Data

Name: Kenia Sousa ▾ [...]
Country: Belgium
Nationality: Brazilian
Birthdate: 08/10/1978

File Closure

◉ Product: Select... ▾
○ Simulation: Select... ▾

Commission Agent

ID: 98765234253
Name: De Wilde Jan

Contract data

Start Date: [   ]
Payment Date: [   ]
Product: ◉ Investment ○ Savings
Premium Formula: Select... ▾

Investment

◉ Included taxes [   ]
○ Excluded taxes [   ]
Amount: [   ]
Capital Guarantee: Select... ▾

Savings

Gross Amount: [   ]
Periodicity: Select... ▾
First Date: [   ]
Duration: Select... ▾
Formula: [   ]
Risk Profile: Select... ▾
Percentage: Select... ▾

Beneficiaries

Beneficiaries: Select... ▾

[Next >]   [Cancel]

Fig. 3.4 UI designed for one subprocess

validate this approach in other organizations with different business profiles aiming at analyzing their interest on the strategy and their openness to change.

The proposed solution is composed of a method supported by Usi4Biz, a tool that maps models starting with the business process model, going to the task models until

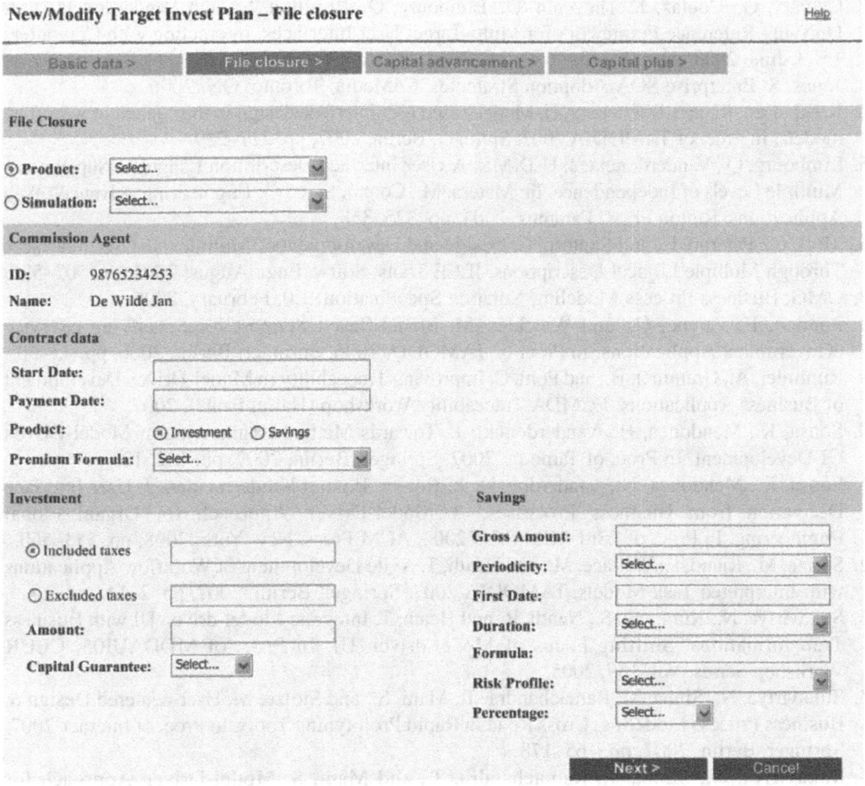

New/Modify Target Invest Plan – File closure   Help

Basic data > | File closure > | Capital advancement > | Capital plus >

File Closure

◉ **Product:** Select...
○ **Simulation:** Select...

Commission Agent

ID: 98765234253
Name: De Wilde Jan

Contract data

Start Date:
Payment Date:
Product: ◉ Investment ○ Savings
Premium Formula: Select...

Investment | **Savings**

◉ Included taxes | **Gross Amount:**
 | **Periodicity:** Select...
○ Excluded taxes | **First Date:**
Amount: | **Duration:** Select...
 | **Formula:**
Capital Guarantee: Select... | **Risk Profile:** Select...
 | **Percentage:** Select...

Next > | Cancel

Fig. 3.5 UI designed for a subset of activities in the subprocess

reaching UI components. Such mapping is possible through semiautomatic transformation or manual mappings, thus letting designers free to decide whether the context is more appropriate for transformations or not. For future work, we intend to provide the transformations from business process model into task models through Web services to enable interoperability by allowing many tools to access them.

Acknowledgments Our special thanks to the company for allowing us to share information of our joint project. We gratefully acknowledge the support of the program Alban, the European Union Program of High Level Scholarships for Latin America, under scholarship number E06D103843BR.

References

1. Aversano, L., Bodhuin, T., and Tortorella, M. Assessment and impact analysis for aligning business processes and software systems. In Proc. of ACM Symposium on Applied Computing SAC'2005. ACM Press, New York, 2005, pp. 1338–1343.

2. Calvary, G., Coutaz, J., Thevenin, D., Limbourg, Q., Bouillon, L., and Vanderdonckt, J. A Unifying Reference Framework for Multi-Target User Interfaces. Interacting with Computers 15, 3, June 2003, pp. 289–308.
3. Jones, S. Enterprise SOA Adoption Strategies. C4Media, Toronto, ON, 2006.
4. Kristiansen, R., and Traetteberg, H. Model-based user interface design in the context of workflow models. In Proc. of TAMODIA'2007. Springer, Berlin, 2007, pp. 227–239.
5. Limbourg, Q., Vanderdonckt, J. UsiXML: A User Interface Description Language Sup-Porting Multiple Levels of Independence. In: Matera, M., Comai, S. (eds.): Engineering Advanced Web Applications. Rinton Press, Paramus, 2004, pp. 325–338.
6. Mori, G., Paterno, F., and Santoro, C. Design and Development of Multidevice User Interfaces Through Multiple Logical Descriptions. IEEE Trans. Softw. Eng., August 2004, pp. 507–520.
7. OMG, Business Process Modeling Notation Specification, 1.0, February, 2006.
8. Pontico, F., Farenc, C., and Winckler, M. Model-Based Support for Specifying eService eGovernment Applications. In Proc. of TAMODIA'2006. Springer, Berlin, 2006, pp. 43–50.
9. Rummler, A., Grammel, B., and Pohl, C. Improving Traceability in Model-Driven Development of Business Applications. ECMDA Traceability Workshop (Haifa, Israel), 2007.
10. Sousa, K., Mendonça, H., Vanderdonckt, J., Towards Method Engineering of Model-Driven UI Development. In Proc. of Tamodia'2007. Springer, Berlin, 2007, pp. 112–125.
11. Sousa, K., Mendonça, H., Vanderdonckt, J., Rogier, E., and Vandermeulen, J. User Interface Derivation from Business Processes: A Model-Driven Approach for Organizational Engineering. In Proc. of 23rd ACM SAC'2008, ACM Press, New York, 2008, pp. 553–560.
12. Stolze, M., Riand, P., Wallace, M., and Heath, T. Agile Development of Workflow Applications with Interpreted Task Models. TAMODIA 2007, Springer, Berlin, 2007, pp. 2–14.
13. Sukaviriya, N., Kumaran, S., Nandi, P., and Heath, T. Integrate Model-driven UI with Business Transformations: Shifting Focus of Model-driven UI. In Proc. of MDDAUI05, CEUR Workshop Series, Vol. 159, 2005.
14. Sukaviriya, N., Sinha, V., Ramachandra, T., Mani, S., and Stolze, M. User-centered Design & Business Process Modeling: Cross Road in Rapid Prototyping Tools. In Proc. of Interact'2007. Springer, Berlin, 2007, pp. 165–178.
15. Sukaviriya, N., Sinha, V., Ramachandra, T., and Mani, S. Model-Driven Approach for Managing Human Interface Design Life Cycle. In Proc. of MoDELS 2007. Springer, Berlin, pp. 226–240.
16. Sujitparapitaya, S., Janz, B.D., Wetherbe, J.C., and Sammet, D. Ascension Health Systems: Enterprise user Interface Approach to Organizational Data Management. In Proc. of 34th Hawaii International Conference on System Science, 2001.
17. Vanhooff, B., Van Baelen, S., Joosen, W., and Berbers, Y. Traceability as Input for Model Transformations. ECMDA Traceability Workshop (Haifa, Israel), 2007.
18. Vasconcelos, A., Caetano, A., Neves, J., Sinogas, P., Mendes, R., and Tribolet, J. A Framework for Modeling Strategy, Business Processes and Information Systems. In Proc. of IEEE EDOC'2008. IEEE Computer Society Press, Los Alamitos, CA, 2008.
19. The Apache Velocity Project. Available at http://velocity.apache.org. Accessed on Jan 1, 2008.

Chapter 4
Using Profiles to Support Model Transformations in the Model-Driven Development of User Interfaces

Nathalie Aquino, Jean Vanderdonckt, Francisco Valverde and Oscar Pastor

Abstract The model-driven User Interface (UI) development life cycle usually evolves from high-level models, which represent abstract UI concepts, to concrete models, which are more related to the UI implementation details, until the final UI is generated. This process is based on a set of model-to-model and model-to-code transformations. Several industrial tools have applied this approach in order to generate the UI. However, these model transformations are mainly fixed and are not always the best solution for a specific UI. In this work, the notion of Transformation Profile is introduced to better specify the model-to-model transformations. A Transformation Profile is made up of a set of predefined Model Mappings and a Transformation Template. The mappings connect initial and target UI models in a flexible way, whereas the Transformation Template gathers high-level parameters to apply to the transformation. As a consequence, a Transformation Profile enables designers to define parameterized transformations that could be reused for another UI development project.

4.1 Introduction

The Cameleon Reference Framework [1] defines a model-driven engineering (MDE)-compliant [13] development life cycle for multi-target User Interfaces (UIs) and structures it into four levels of abstraction: *Task and Concepts*, to describe tasks and domain-oriented concepts; *Abstract User Interface* (AUI), to express a UI in terms of Abstract Interaction Objects (AIOs) in a way that is independent of the interactors available in the target computing platform; *Concrete User Interface* (CUI), to concretize the AIOs of an AUI into Concrete Interaction Objects (CIOs) which are independent of a specific toolkit; and *Final User Interface* (FUI), the UI code in any programming or mark-up language.

N. Aquino (✉), J. Vanderdonckt, F. Valverde and O. Pastor
Centro de Investigación en Métodos de Producción de Software, Universidad
Politécnica de Valencia, Camino de Vera s/n, 46022 Valencia, Spain
e-mail: naquino@pros.upv.es

V. López-Jaquero et al. (eds.), *Computer-Aided Design of User Interfaces VI*,
DOI: 10.1007/978-1-84882-206-1_4, © Springer-Verlag London Limited 2009

This chapter focuses on the transformation from an AUI model to a CUI model. On the one hand, there are approaches where transformation rules are implicit in the transformation tools, resulting in a lack of flexibility to customize transformations [4, 12]. On the other hand, typically there are similarities and differences among UI development projects. Therefore, it is not a reasonable approach to define the transformation rules for the AUI to CUI model transformation each time for each project, nor is it reasonable to use the same transformation rules for every UI development project.

The main purpose of this work is to optimize AUI to CUI model transformations. To achieve this goal, Transformation Profiles are introduced as a mechanism to externalize and customize the AUI to CUI model transformations and to reuse knowledge between different UI development projects. A Transformation Profile is composed of a set of Model Mappings and a Transformation Template. The Model Mappings specify how to concretize an AIO into a CIO. Therefore, the connections between the AUI model and the CUI model are externalized from the tools that perform the transformations and can be customized according to computing platforms and users. The Transformation Template parameterizes the transformation with high-level parameters that can be applied in two dimensions: UI fragments or UI patterns.

The rest of the chapter is organized as follows: Section 4.2 presents Transformation Profiles, Model Mappings, and Transformation Templates. Section 4.3 presents a case study with a practical application of the Transformation Profile in the generation process of UIs in OO-Method, a software development method. In the case study, the OO-Method Presentation Model (PM) plays the role of the AUI model, and the UsiXML CUI model plays the role of the CUI model. In Sect. 4.4, the AUI to CUI model transformations of others MDE-compliant UI development methods are analyzed. Finally, Sect. 4.5 presents some conclusion.

4.2   Introducing the Transformation Profile Approach

In a model-driven architecture (MDA)-compliant [9] UI development process, an AUI model is transformed to one or more CUI models. This transformation is based on mappings from elements of the AUI model to elements of the CUI model. The mapping problem has been defined as the difficulty of linking abstract and concrete elements in a UI model. This problem has been identified by Puerta and Eisenstein [12] as a non-trivial one. One of the main issues raised by the mapping problem is that, most of the time, the models and their mappings are hardcoded in their supporting tools. As a consequence, they have limited flexibility for modifications and customizations [4].

In order to solve these problems, this work introduces the Transformation Profile concept. The Transformation Profile is intended to externalize the knowledge of how to transform the AUI model to the CUI model. Figure 4.1 illustrates the use of a Transformation Profile. A Transformation engine takes as input an AUI model and a Transformation Profile. The Transformation Profile provides the rules that

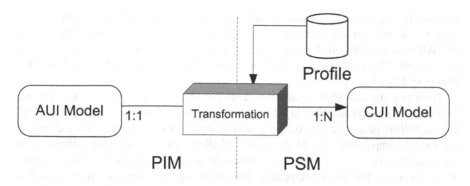

Fig. 4.1 AUI model to CUI model transformation using a Transformation Profile

specify how to transform the AUI to the CUI model. To organize the transformation knowledge, the Transformation Profile is structured in a set of Model Mappings and a Transformation Template. In other words, one Transformation Profile is the sum of one set of Model Mappings and one Transformation Template.

The Transformation Profile approach provides flexibility for the modification and customization of transformation rules, as well as interesting reusability potential. Model Mappings and Transformation Templates are introduced in Sects. 4.2.1 and 4.2.2.

4.2.1   Model Mappings

A mapping model is a well-known issue in the MDA of UIs. Puerta and Eisenstein [12] presented a general framework to solve the mapping problem in model-based UI development systems. Following the same line, Montero et al. [7] introduced a formal definition of potential mappings among UsiXML models with its corresponding syntax. UsiXML is an XML-compliant UI Description Language that allows designers to apply a multi-directional development of UIs at multiple levels of independence (http://www.usixml.org). In the UsiXML Mapping Model, the *isReifiedBy* relationship indicates that a CIO is the reification of an AIO through a transformation (see ref. [7] for more details). This relationship has been used in this work to define the Model Mappings.

Our Mapping Model is composed of relationships of reification type between an AUI model and a CUI model. Each mapping is specified by one Source, zero or more Conditions, one Target, and a Priority. The Source is an AIO of the AUI model, and the Target is a CIO of the CUI model. A graphical CUI model can represent a UI in terms of CIOs that can be containers (such as *window*, *horizontalBox*) or individual components (such as *outputText*, *inputText*) [15]. The containers can contain other containers or individual components defining a tree-like structure. Therefore, the Target could be a CIO which is the root of a CIO tree. If Conditions are specified, each of them must be satisfied in order to the Source be reified in the Target. A Condition is a Boolean expression that can be specified over elements of the AUI model. Finally, the Priority allows specifying the prevalence of some mappings over others. The Conditions and Priority constitute extensions over the UsiXML Mapping Model.

To clarify the idea of the mappings, a simple textual example is given: let *input* be an AIO that represents the input argument of a method of the domain model, let *horizontalBox* be a concrete container, and let *outputText* and *inputText* be concrete individual components. The Mapping Model allows us to specify the reification of the *input* into an *horizontalBox* that contains an *outputText* at the left and an *inputText* at the right. The Model Mappings allow the designer to specify widget selection and layout. In addition, different Model Mappings can be defined to address different UI platforms and end-user preferences.

4.2.2   Transformation Templates

In order to give more flexibility to the transformation from the AUI model to the CUI model, a Transformation Template is used in conjunction with the set of Model Mappings. A Transformation Template is composed of parameters that specify how the CUI model and subsequent final UI are going to be structured and/or stylized.

A model is composed of elements that have attributes with their corresponding data types and values. Well-defined meta-models specify default values for the attributes of their elements. The Transformation Template parameterizes the model transformation with parameters that overwrite default values of attributes of CIOs of a CUI model, for example, style parameters like colours or font types.

High-level parameters, which are not directly related to a single attribute of an element, can also be specified in a Transformation Template. These parameters can be related to a group of attributes of one or more elements, or to the elements themselves and relations among them. Several customizations can be achieved with high-level parameters gathered in the Transformation Template. There can be parameters for specifying the widgets to be used, the layout options, the dialog style (e.g. by *wizard* or by *tabbed dialog box*), the location of objects (e.g. position of a *toolbar*), or the alignment of elements (e.g. alignment of *labels* with respect to their associated input elements). Furthermore, high-level parameters can overwrite some of the mappings of the previously defined Model Mapping.

Each parameter is described by its name, set of possible values, default value, and the elements where it is applied. The scopes of application of the parameters can be specified in two dimensions: UI *fragments* or UI *patterns*.

Regarding the *UI fragment* dimension, the following scopes of application specify that the parameter is applied to:

- *Intra-application*: all fragments of the application UI.
- *Inter-container*: all UI containers of a particular type (e.g. *windows*, *dialog boxes*, *tabbed dialog boxes*, *toolbars*) within the application.

- *Intra-container*: all UI containers of a particular type with all their contained UI fragments (e.g. *images*, *icons*, *widgets*) within the application.
- *Inter-individual component*: all UI individual components of a particular type (e.g. all *buttons*).

Some of the above categories can be combined to obtain more refined applications. For instance, by combining the inter-individual component and inter-container scopes, the parameter will be applied only to a particular type of UI individual component within a particular type of UI container (e.g. *buttons* of a *dialog box*).

For the *UI pattern* dimension, the following scopes of application specify that the parameter is applied to:

- *Inter-pattern*: all UI patterns.
- *Intra-pattern*: a UI pattern of a specific type.
- *Inter-sub-pattern*: all UI sub-patterns of a specific UI pattern.
- *Intra-sub-pattern*: a specific UI sub-pattern of a particular UI pattern.

Once developed, a Transformation Template can be applied to a range of interactive applications, for instance, in order to ensure compliance with corporate style guides or to make a family of applications consistent in their look and feel. Besides, some of the parameters could be implemented in a user preference's configuration file in the final software product, so as to enable the final users to adapt some aspects of the UI to their personal preferences (colours, font types, position of windows, etc.) by means of a suitable editor. The adherence to style guides and the adaptability affect the usability of a software product [3]. The use of high-level parameters and the combinations of their scopes of application give a lot of flexibility and power to the notion of Transformation Profile.

4.3 Applying Transformations Profiles in the Generation Process of UIs in OO-Method: A Case Study

OO-Method [10] is a software development method that is an MDA-compliant. It uses models in order to specify the structural and functional aspects of information systems. It also uses a PM [6] that is based on interface patterns in order to specify the UI in an abstract way. OO-Method is supported by OlivaNova – The Programming Machine (a commercial product of CARE Technologies – http://www.care-t.com/) that edits the various models involved and automatically applies subsequent transformations until the final code of a fully functional application (not limited to database or UI) is generated.

The first level of the OO-Method PM is made up of Interaction Units (IUs) that represent the main interactive operations to be performed. One of the IUs is the *Service IU* which is used for specifying the presentation of a service that modifies an object, their attributes, and relationships. The next level of decomposition of the PM consists of restricting and specifying the behaviour of each IU using elementary patterns. In a *Service IU*, the following elementary patterns, among others, could be defined:

- *Argument Grouping*: It enables the arrangement of input arguments of a service in groups and subgroups, and establishes the order in which groups and input arguments are shown to the user. An *Argument Grouping* element of type group corresponds to a group of input arguments, whereas an *Argument Grouping* element of type argument corresponds to one input argument.
- *Defined Selection*: It enables the definition of a set of valid values and can be associated to an input argument.
- *Introduction*: It allows the specification of edit masks, valid value ranges, and help and validation messages, and can be associated to an input argument.

The application selected to illustrate the Transformation Profile approach is a photography agency management system. Consider a *Service IU*, of the OO-Method PM, to register photographers. In the registration process, the photographers must supply personal data: name, DNI, age, gender, and contact data: telephone and e-mail. The *Service IU* is structured with two *Argument Grouping* elements of type group (Personal Data and Contact Data), which contains *Argument Grouping* elements of type argument which are related to the input arguments of the service (name, DNI, telephone, etc.). A *Defined Selection* pattern is used to specify a set of valid values for gender: male and female, and an *Introduction* pattern is used to define a valid value range for age (between 0 and 120). Figure 4.2 reproduces the described *Service UI* as generated by OlivaNova for a desktop platform.

Note that the OO-Method PM corresponds to an abstract representation of a UI without any details of the visual appearance. The OlivaNova transformation engine generates the source code of the UIs from this model by applying transformation rules that are implicit in the tool. Therefore, if the final UI does not satisfy the end-user's requirements, manual modifications must be applied.

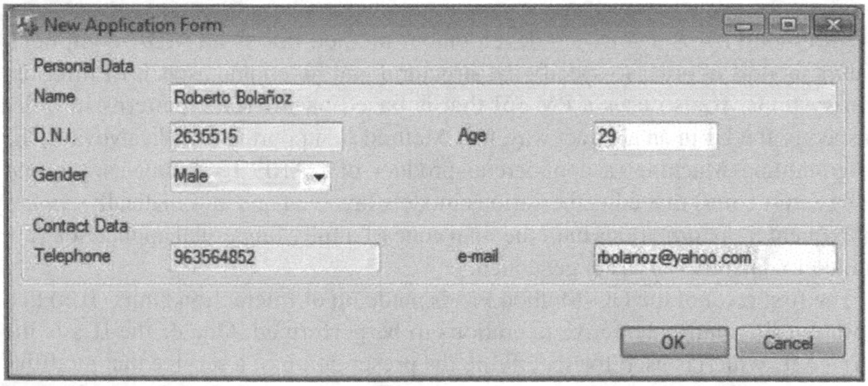

Fig. 4.2 UI generated by OlivaNova for the photographer registration example

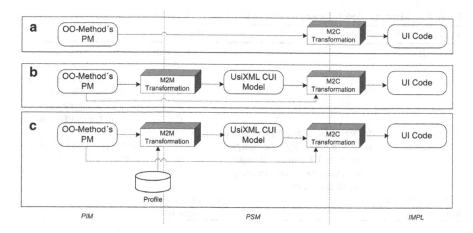

Fig. 4.3 OO-Method UI generation process: (**a**) in its current state, (**b**) as proposed in [11], and (**c**) using a Transformation Profile

Pederiva et al. [11] introduced a Beautification Process for OO-Method in order to address the shortcomings related to the generation of the UIs and manual modifications. The first step of the process proposes to derive a CUI model from the OO-Method PM. In the mentioned work, the UsiXML CUI model was selected for this purpose.

A UsiXML CUI model consists of an abstraction of a final UI independently of the particular widgets used in a specific computing platform, thus resulting in a characterization of a UI in terms of CIOs. In this work, only graphical CIOs such as *separator* (a decorator), *inputText* (a graphical individual component), or *window* (a graphical container) are considered. Further details about the CIOs provided by UsiXML can be found online at http://www.usixml.org/documentation/usixml1.8.0/UsiXML.xsd.html.The Transformation Profile approach could be introduced into the OO-Method UI generation process to add flexibility to the PM to UsiXML CUI model transformation. Figure 4.3 illustrates the proposed evolution for the OO-Method UI generation process.

Table 4.1 represents a subset of the Mapping Model that externalizes the mappings used by the OlivaNova compiler in the generation of the UI shown in Fig. 4.2. The Source column represents an interface pattern from the OO-Method PM, the Conditions column lists the conditions that must be satisfied for the mapping to be applied, and the Target column shows the UsiXML CUI model transformation result. Table 4.1 presents the mappings in ascendant order of priority, so that, for example, an *ArgumentGrouping* of type argument, related to an input argument of type integer or string, which has a *Defined Selection* associated, will be mapped to a *comboBox*.

The default mappings provided by OlivaNova are enough from a functional point of view but do not always meet the customer's requirements. To solve this problem, an alternate Transformation Profile could be applied. Table 4.2 represents

Table 4.1 Mapping Model (subset) for PM to UsiXML CUI model transformation

Source	Conditions	Target
Service IU		*window* that contains a *borderBox* which encloses a *topBox* and a *bottomBox*. The *topBox* contains a vertical-oriented *box*. The *bottomBox* contains a right-aligned *flowBox* with OK and Cancel *buttons*
Argument Grouping	*Argument Grouping* type is group	*groupBox*
	Argument Grouping type is argument and *Argument Grouping* is related to a string or integer input argument	Horizontal-oriented box that contains an outputText and an inputText
Defined Selection		*comboBox*
Introduction		*inputText*

Table 4.2 Alternate Mapping Model (subset) for PM to UsiXML CUI model transformation

Source	Conditions	Target	Mapping Number
Service IU	*Service IU* does not have *Argument Grouping* elements of type group	*window* that contains a *borderBox* which encloses a *topBox* and a *bottomBox*. The *topBox* contains a *groupBox*. The *bottomBox* contains a right-aligned *flowBox* with OK and Cancel *buttons*	1
Argument Grouping	*Argument Grouping* type is group and the *Argument Grouping* is the last group of a *Service IU*	*window* that contains a *borderBox* which encloses a *topBox* and a *bottomBox*. The *topBox* contains a *groupBox*. The *bottomBox* contains a right-aligned *flowBox* with OK and Cancel *buttons*	2
	Argument Grouping type is group and the *Argument Grouping* is not the last group of a *Service IU*	*window* that contains a *borderBox* which encloses a *topBox* and a *bottomBox*. The *topBox* contains a *groupBox*. The *bottomBox* contains a right-aligned *flowBox* with Next and Cancel *buttons*	3
	Argument Grouping type is argument and *Argument Grouping* is related to a string or integer input argument	horizontal-oriented *box* that contains an *outputText* and an *inputText*	4
Defined Selection		*radioButton*	5
Introduction	*Introduction* type is integer and *Introduction* specifies a valid value range	*Spin*	6

a subset of an alternate Mapping Model that allows *Service IUs* with more than one *Argument Grouping* element of type group to be displayed like a wizard. This option can be useful when several input arguments must be entered and the user need only focuses on one arguments group. Furthermore, the *Defined Selection* pattern is mapped to a *radioButton*, and the *Introduction* pattern of type integer that specifies a valid values range is mapped to a *spin*. Table 4.2 presents the mappings in ascendant order of priority.

In order to provide a better customized UI, the alternate Transformation Profile includes a Transformation Template, which is represented in Table 4.3. The Transformation Template defines font properties (*textFont* and *isItalic*) and a vertical alignment of the labels for all the UI fragments of the application. The *labelAlignment* is a high-level parameter that overwrites the mapping number 4 of Table 4.2. Furthermore, visual and font properties are specified for all the containers of type *window* and all the individual components of type *button*.

The Transformation Profile, which is composed of the Mapping Model and the Transformation Template presented in Tables 4.2 and 4.3, could be an input for the Model Compiler so as to generate a UsiXML CUI model from which the final UI could be generated according to the required changes. This approach enables the designer to choose the most suitable Transformation Profile for a concrete UI development. Figure 4.4 represents the UI which could be obtained if the new Transformation Profile is applied.

Table 4.3 Transformation Template (subset) for PM to UsiXML CUI model transformation

Parameter name	Parameter value	Scope of application (UI fragment)	Container to apply	Individual component to apply
textFont	Times new roman	Intra-application	All	All
isItalic	Yes	Intra-application	All	All
labelAlignment	Vertical	Intra-application	All	All
bgColor	C2EADD	Inter-container	All *windows*	None
isBold	Yes	Inter-individual-component	None	All *buttons*
textFont	Arial	Inter-individual-component	None	All *buttons*

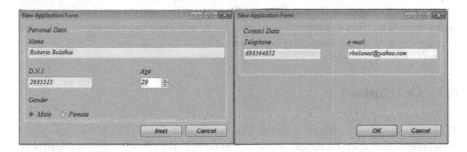

Fig. 4.4 Expected UI applying the alternate Transformation Profile

4.4 Related Work

The approach described in this chapter is original since it combines a set of Model Mappings and a Transformation Template in a single Transformation Profile to support transformations that are tailored to each application.

Some software tools support a transformation-based approach for generating a UI (e.g. Teallach [2], TERESA [8]), but the transformations are not made explicit and, therefore, cannot be edited or parameterized. In particular, MOBI-D [12] and Mastermind [14] cannot be considered as genuine transformation approaches since only the models are explicit: the transformations are not explicit and there is no true transformation engine. Mastermind is based on a rule-based approach while MOBI-D directly generates code from the models. TransformiXML [5] does support explicit transformations since it interprets mappings written in UsiXML and converts them into graph transformations. Although these transformations are explicit, and therefore can be edited, they cannot be conditioned, prioritized, nor parameterized, which limits their flexibility. In TransformiXML, the designers themselves must enter new transformation options, which is a complex process reserved to specialists, as opposed to parameterizing existing transformations thanks to their parameters. This tailoring process is much more affordable to designers.

There are also other software tools that support a template-based approach, but they are restricted to only modifying the values of some widget properties. For instance, Genova (http://www.esito.no/) gathers predefined values of UI properties, like colour, font, and style, in a template that is then applied to a UI. Our approach generalizes the notion of template to high-level parameters and also handles the notion of UI pattern, which, as far as we know, does not exist in similar works.

When comparing the Transformation Template with Cascading Style Sheets (CSS) [16], we can say that while CSS is a mechanism for adding style to Web documents, the Transformation Template is thought to be used in an MDE-compliant UI development life cycle in order to specify not only the style but also the structure of UIs for different computing platforms (e.g. desktop, web, mobile). Furthermore, parameters of the Transformation Template can be associated to UI patterns besides UI containers or individual components.

To the best of our knowledge, no existing work today provides both a transformation-based approach (e.g. based on Model Mappings) and a template-based approach (e.g. based on Transformation Templates) in a single and unified way of developing UIs. This combination enables us to combine the powerfulness of the first approach with the flexibility of the second.

4.5 Conclusion

To summarize, the contribution of this chapter is twofold: (1) From the *conceptual* viewpoint, it has introduced the notion of Transformation Profile, which consists of a Transformation Template and a set of Model Mappings to be applied during the model-to-model transformation steps in MDE of UIs. The Transformation Profile externalizes the transformation rules and makes them editable, customizable, and reusable. The Model Mappings can be conditioned and prioritized. With regard to the Transformation Template, the different application dimensions (UI fragments and patterns) allow designers to apply the parameters in the same way as the *selector* does in CSS. Since the Transformation Profile is independent of the underlying models, nothing prevents its reuse in any other work in MDE of UIs. In principle, the Transformation Profile notion could be used in any model-to-model transformation or model-to-code compilation. (2) From the *methodological* viewpoint, this approach has been incorporated in OO-Method, which is an MDE method for automatically generating an entire interactive system (and not just the UI).

Nowadays, the hardest challenge consists of identifying the parts of the tools to be expanded when new parameters need to be incorporated. A new abstraction could be included in the model editor, but this would affect the high-level modelling activity and may introduce unnecessary levels of detail at this step. A new parameter could be inserted in the various transformation steps, but this would largely affect the transformation engine implementation. Therefore, we think that the easiest solution is to introduce a Profile *during* the transformations themselves. Of course, this still affects the model-to-code compiler, but only in a way that augments its capabilities in an incremental way.

Therefore, the most important shortcoming of this approach relies in its implementation cost. Even though this cost is relatively high, this approach allows designers to apply the Transformation Profile to tailor the MDE process to end-users needs. End users love to specify their own needs and really appreciate seeing them incorporated in the MDE process, as opposed to a traditional MDE process where all the transformations are predefined and lead to a predetermined UI.

Acknowledgements This work has been developed with the support of MEC and MITyC under the projects SESAMO (TIN2007-62894) and PISA (FIT-340000-2007-110).

References

1. Calvary, G., Coutaz, J., Thevenin, D., Limbourg, Q., Bouillon, L., and Vanderdonckt, J. A Unifying reference framework for multi-target user interfaces. Interact. Comput. 15, 3 (2003) 289–308
2. Griffiths, T., et al. Teallach: a Model-based user interface development environment for object databases. Interact. Comput. 14, 1 (2001) 31–68
3. ISO/IEC 9126-1 (2001) Software engineering – Product quality – Part 1: Quality model
4. Limbourg, Q., Vanderdonckt, J. Addressing the mapping problem in user interface design with UsiXML. In: Proc. of 3rd Int. Workshop TAMODIA 2004 (Prague, November 15–16, 2004). ACM Press, New York (2004), pp. 155–163
5. Limbourg, Q., Vanderdonckt, J., Michotte, B., Bouillon, L., López-Jaquero, V. UsiXML: a language supporting multi-path development of user interfaces. In: Proc. of 9th IFIP EHCI-DSVIS'2004 (Hamburg, July 11–13, 2004). LNCS, Vol. 3425, Springer, Berlin (2005)
6. Molina, P.J., Meliá, S., Pastor, O. JUST-UI: a user interface specification model. In: Proc. of 4th Int. Conf. on Computer-Aided Design of User Interfaces CADUI2002 (Valenciennes, May 2002). Kluwer, Dordrecht (2002), pp. 63–74

7. Montero, F., López-Jaquero, V., Vanderdonckt, J., González, P., Lozano, M., Limbourg, Q. Solving the mapping problem in user interface design by seamless integration in IdealXML. In: Proc. of 12th Int. Workshop on Design, Specification and Verification of Interactive Systems DSV-IS2005 (Newcastle upon Tyne, 13–15 July 2005), Harrison, M. (ed.). LNCS, Vol. 3941. Springer, Berlin (2005), pp. 161–172
8. Mori, G., Paternó, F., Santoro, C. Design and development of multi-device user interfaces through multiple logical descriptions. IEEE Trans. Softw. Eng. 30, 8 (2004) 507–520
9. Object Management Group, MDA Guide Version 1.0.1 (2003). http://www.omg.org/docs/omg/03-06-01.pdf. Accessed 25 January 2008
10. Pastor, O., Molina, J. C. Model-Driven Architecture in Practice. A Software Production Environment Based on Conceptual Modeling. Springer, New York (2007)
11. Pederiva, I., Vanderdonckt, J., España, S., Panach, I., Pastor, O. The beautification process in model-driven engineering of user interfaces. In: Proc. of 11th Int. Conf. INTERACT'2007. LNCS, Vol. 4662. Springer, Berlin (2005), pp. 409–422
12. Puerta, A. R., Eisenstein, J. Towards a general computational framework for model-based interface development systems. Knowledge-Based Systems 12 (1999) 433–442
13. Schmidt, D.C. Model-driven engineering. IEEE Comput. 39, 2 (2006) 41–47
14. Szekely, P., Sukaviriya, N., Castells, P., Muthukumarasamy, J., Salcher, E. Declarative interface models for user interface construction tools: the MASTERMIND approach. In: Proc. of 6th IFIP Int. Conf. on Engineering of Human–Computer Interaction EHCI'95 (Yellowstone, August 1995). Chapman & Hall, London (1996), pp. 120–150
15. Vanderdonckt, J. A MDA-compliant environment for developing user interfaces of information systems. In: Proc. of 17th Conf. on Advanced Information Systems Engineering CAiSE'05 (Porto, 13–17 June 2005). LNCS, Vol. 3520. Springer, Berlin (2005), pp. 16–31
16. World Wide Web Consortium (2007) Cascading Style Sheets Level 2 Revision 1 (CSS 2.1) Specification. http://www.w3.org/TR/CSS21/. Accessed 28 April 2008

Chapter 5
Translating Museum Visual Contents into Descriptions for Blind Users: A Multidisciplinary Approach

Barbara Leporini and Ivan Norscia

Abstract Accessibility and usability guidelines are available to design web sites accessible to blind users. However, the actual usability of accessible web pages varies depending on the type of information the user is dealing with. Museum web sites, including specimens and hall descriptions, need specific requirements to allow vision-impaired users, who navigate using a screen reader, to access pieces of information that are mainly based on visual perception. Here we address a methodology to be applied for the proper creation and elaboration of alternative image descriptions in museum web pages. Such methodology has been applied to a gallery of the Museum of Natural History and Territory (University of Pisa). Such indications allow the user: (1) to address indexed contents and to link to information in more details, (2) to calibrate image descriptions (with a command providing alternative explanations for specimens), and (3) to access extra information for the blind (via hidden labels). A multidisciplinary approach is necessary to obtain effective and comprehensive descriptions. In this perspective, a cooperative environment is eventually proposed for team work facilitation.

5.1 Introduction

Most museums make part of their content available in their websites, for self-advertisement and to light up the interest of potential visitors. An online preliminary visit can help planning the real visit and/or provide in-depth and complementary information to be used for educational purposes.

While the preliminary visit can improve the quality of the visit for "regular" users, it can represent the key of a successful visit for special users, such as blind people. In fact, through an online previsit, blind users have the possibility (a) to

B. Leporini (✉) and I. Norscia
ISTI – CNR, Pisa, Italy
e-mail: barbara.leporini@isti.cnr.it

prepare a "mental plan" of the spatial display of museum specimens, exhibitions, and halls and (b) to start dealing the museum contents, in order to avoid information overload during the real visit. The informational gap experienced by blind users (visual display and content location) cannot be properly filled by museum operators, who are constrained by the short time of an average visit. Since time constrains clash with multifaceted information, the visit may eventually result in a simple specimen list or in a sloppy presentation of the overall content.

In order to be really fruitful and effective for disabled users, the virtual visit must be not only well organized and appealing but also accessible. Although a plethora of guidelines, criteria, and suggestions has been proposed to gain or increase web accessibility and usability [2, 3, 6–9], a recent international survey of 125 museum web sites showed that only a minority of them fulfilled the basic accessibility requirements [5]. Consistently, user trials revealed that a Non negligible part of visually and cognitively impaired users was not able to recuperate pieces of information or accomplish simple tasks on most of the web sites included in the survey [5].

Museum web sites need additional accessibility requirements to allow vision-impaired users, who navigate using a screen reader, to access contents that are largely based on visual perception. A crucial aspect for the suitability of museum web sites is image description since pictures, figures, and illustrations are an important means for understanding properties and value of scientific specimens, pieces of art, or collections. Of course, comprehensive and effective descriptions (including visual cues, notions, and cultural meaning) can be provided by a combination of experts in different fields (e.g. biology, history, web designer, photography, and accessibility).

In this chapter, we address the issue of image description in museum web sites by presenting the case of the Museum of Natural History and Territory of the University of Pisa. Here, we propose a multidisciplinary approach in order to overcome the problem of content accessibility prevented by the imprecise, or even missing, translation of the image content into screen reader language (descriptive text). The chapter is organized as follows: introduction (current section), theoretical problem (Sect. 5.2), methodology (Sect. 5.3), case study (Sect. 5.4), and possible solution via cooperative approach (Sect. 5.5).

5.2   The Problem

Accessibility and usability guidelines should allow the creation of web sites suitable for disabled users. However, most guidelines have been created considering accessibility as invariant with respect to content type. Instead, actual usability and accessibility of web pages varies depending on the type of information the user is dealing with. As a consequence, the guidelines are often loose and their successful application is too much dependent on personal interpretation.

For example, the checkpoint 13.1 "Clearly identify the target of each link" reported in the WCAG 1.0 guidelines for accessibility [8] states that "Link text should indicate the nature of the link target," providing indications like "more information about sea lions" or "text-only version of this page" rather than "click here" or "more information." Nevertheless, a study conducted on 100 web sites reported that link description is one of the accessibility problems still encountered during web navigation [4].

A further controversial issue is represented by the application of alternative descriptions to nontext elements, as indicated by the checkpoint 1.1 "Provide a text equivalent for every nontext element (e.g. via 'alt,' 'longdesc,' or in element content)" [8]. On the basis of this checkpoint, web designers should apply different levels of description, short, more extensive, or alternative. However, the application is controversial since the type of description cannot be univocally predicted basing on the typology of nontext elements, as in the case of images.

For example, no long description needs to be associated to images if they refer to products sold via e-commerce: in this case, the blind customers are more interested in identifying the item they are willing to buy than in getting an in-depth description of the visual features of the product. In this case, short and clear labels are welcome. On the contrary, the visual features of a scientific specimen or a piece of art are necessary to understand their intrinsic value and properties, thus a detailed and more comprehensive image description is in order here.

Although possible solutions have been proposed to help web designers to create alternative descriptions [1], assigning a proper description remains a difficult task, since web designers must determine, as a first step, the underlying role of an image. In a museum web site, at least three situations are likely to occur. An image can represent a link (e.g. to the home page) and the relative alternative description falls more into checkpoint 13.1 than into checkpoint 1.1 [8]. In this case, it is more appropriate to label the image function (e.g. "home page") than providing a description of the image itself, which can reported (once for all) in the home page. An image can also be purely ornamental (e.g. pictures of museum building): in this case, a short description is probably enough. Finally, pictures or illustrations can be related to museum specimens and, consequently, the description must be extended since such elements are necessary to understand web page content.

Alternative descriptions can be classically assigned via "alt" attribute (short text), "longdesc" attribute (longer descriptions), or an external link addressing an entire explanatory page. Here we provide a new option to insert longer descriptions without the use of an external link or the "longdesc" attribute. Since description typology varies according to the type of specimen or piece of art described, a multidisciplinary approach must be considered in order to make such new option effective.

5.3   The Methodology

In order to make the online visit both accessible and usable, it is important that image location be well organized. Often many images and videos, with relative information, are clumped in a single page because they are related to a specific exhibition or hall. Even if such organization can make sense for "regular" users, who are able to detect both the image set and the whole visual layout all at once, vision-impaired users can be disoriented because they process the contents in a sequential way, via screen reader [9]. Scrolling down all the images is not only time consuming but also confusing and unpractical during information search. Instead, a list of short descriptions of visual items could allow vision-impaired users to pick up specific items only on request.

In this view, web pages, each one referring to a hall/gallery, can be organized according to two levels: (1) a summary listing the items exhibited and their location in the hall (index page) and (2) a descriptive page for each items (item detail page), which can be entered on request by linking on each piece listed in the index page.

- *Index page* – here the following information is reported:
    - *"Welcome description"* – a summary of the main content of the hall/exhibition.
    - *"Memo description"* – a reminder for blind users on how to use the page.
    - *"Spatial description"* – a map to help orientation in the hall.
    - *"Inventory description"* – list of the items with a link to a new window (item detail page, *see below*).
- *Item detail page* – here all information about a piece of art or specimen is reported, well separated from any other confounding element. Vision-impaired users have the possibility to concentrate on a single item and, if not totally blind, they can use specific software to magnify and navigate the page. The page is organized as following:
    - *Magnified image* – a picture with a short description suitable for exploration by low-vision users.
    - *Notional caption* – in-depth description for all users. This part provides information on origin, nature, meaning, and cultural relevance of the item.
    - *Visual caption* – description of visual cues important for a complete understanding of the presented items. Such information can be read via screen reader only. Colors, shapes, spatial dislocation (if the item is composed by different elements), and other features appearing in the image (e.g. if an animal is hairy or not) need to be included in this description. It should be noticed that this part does not carry any background information on the item itself. As a matter of fact it has nothing to do with the notional caption (necessary to all users). The visual caption only provides visual cues that a blind user would not get otherwise.

The possibility of inserting the different types of descriptions must be considered by web designers since the beginning, in order to integrate all the pieces of information in a clear and well-structured way. However, notional and visual descriptions must be scrupulously prepared by experts in the field, and not by web designers, because details are important for the analysis of scientific specimens (e.g. animal or plant reconstructions) or pieces of art (e.g. a marble statue). Moreover, since a museum can include different disciplinary fields (e.g. paleontology, zoology, and botany), several experts can be required to provide appropriate descriptions and information to all the items shown in the museum web site.

In this perspective, the team work for web site realization is needed and it should involve the following people:

1. Web site designer, for the creation and the technical development of the web site.
2. One or more experts in the field, for providing item descriptions.
3. A coordinator, who should gather and integrate the information prepared by the experts.
4. A sample of final users with special needs, to test the web site via assistive technology tools (e.g. screen reader and magnifier).

5.4   The Case Study

When we focus on the web page describing a specific exhibition/hall, the questions to address are:

- How to structure the index page containing the information on the exhibition/hall and the list of specimens that can be "explored" during the visit?
- How to organize the item detail page assigned to each specimen image?
- How to create and insert the additional description to be used by vision-impaired users?

In order to address such questions, we referred to the web site of the *Museo di Storia Naturale e del Territorio, Università di Pisa* and, specifically, to the page describing the gallery of human evolution and early hominids (*home > esposizioni > zoologia > ominidi*). Such gallery includes only four different dioramas (partially three-dimensional models), thus representing an ideal model to implement, for the first time, a new methodology.

Following the methodology proposed in Sect. 5.3, we structured the index page as follows:

- A "welcome description," a short opening part reporting main subject (a sort of an expanded title); in our case: *"The gallery of human history presents human evolution from early hominids to Homo sapiens."*
- A "memo description," for users navigating through screen reader; this part reminds the users that they can click on each item link (reported below in the page) to open a new window containing an in-depth explanation and a specific hidden description for the blind.
- A "spatial description" reporting hall shape (square), size (20 m × 20 m) and the location of the four dioramas (in this case, one per each side); this part is important for orientation and can be analyzed before the visit. In bigger exhibitions, this part can take the form of a map, with its own detail page associated.
- An "inventory description," reporting a list of diorama titles: (1) the study of an anthropologist of nineteenth century, (2) Laetoli footprints and *Australopithecus afarensis* in the African savannah, (3) *Homo neanderthalensis* in an everyday life scene, and (4) drawings by early *Homo sapiens* from the Chauvet cage. Each title is associated with a small image, which can be clicked on to get into a new window page dedicated to the diorama (*see* Fig. 5.1).

Ricostruzione di uno studio dell'antropologo
degli inizi del 1900

Diorama di *Australopithecus afarensis*.

Diorama dell'uomo di Neanderthal

Riproduzione di incisioni rupestri.

Fig. 5.1 List of items in the index page

Subsequently, we organized the item detail page by including: (1) the diorama picture (magnified image), (2) an explanation for all users (notional caption), and (3) a hidden description for vision-impaired users (visual caption). We inserted the alternative description for blind users via hidden labels. Normally, when the description is not short, the attribute "longdesc" or a descriptive link ("[D]" type) is used. However, when the description is rather complex and multifaceted, the navigation procedure can become confusing and misleading. Consequently, we decided to insert an alternative description that can be read only by the screen reader (thus hidden to "regular" users), so that the vision-impaired users can find all the information in the same page. Figure 5.2 (below) shows an example of item detail page for the exhibition considered here.

The detail page associated to diorama 1 (Fig. 5.2) can be opened by clicking on the correspondent diorama small image contained in the index page. Such small image is associated to the link text "study of an anthropologist: picture – link to a new window." The part "link to a new window" is inserted only if JavaScript is active, otherwise the detail page will open in the main browser window.

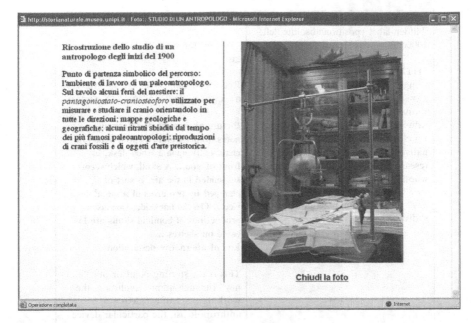

Fig. 5.2   An example of an item detail page

Figure 5.3 shows the HTML code used for the visual caption (*left*) and the infor-mation sequence read by the screen reader (*right*). It should be noticed that the screen reader detects, as first, the presence of the image with the alternative short label, then the hidden description and, eventually, the general explanation appearing on the left side of the window. Such sequence, different from the order that can be detected by the visual layout, is caused by the HTML code flow and by the CSS properties used for page editing. We decided to give priority to the hidden description because the picture itself could contain elements that are important to understand the explanation. In this specific case, it is crucial to know that a clamping metal device is located on the table, in order to understand the general explanation.

5.5   Preliminary User-Based Evaluation

We conducted a preliminary test in order to evaluate if the application of our criteria was successful in allowing blind users to collect information that they could not obtain otherwise. The test involved 16 blind users with similar computer skills (they were all participating in the same computer training class, at the intermediate level). They were asked to perform a virtual visit to the gallery of human evolution and early hominids: half of them were asked to navigate an accessible site without our additional criteria, whereas the other half used the site including our criteria.

| ```
//CSS fragment
.hidden-label {position:absolute; left:-
1000em; z-index:-1;}
...
//HTML fragment<div id="rightfoto">
<img          src="../images/photo.jpg"
alt="the study of an anthropologist" />
</div> <!-- fine foto-->
<div id="leftfot o">
<p class="hidden-label">Picture alter-
native description: notes, papers, and
research books lie chaotically upon a
wood desk...</p>
<p>This is starting point of our "jour-
ney" through human evolution...</p>
</div>
``` | Photo:: The study of an anthropologist<br><br>*Graphic:* **the study of an anthropolo-gist**<br><br>Reconstruction of the typical study of an anthropologist of the XIX century.<br><br>**Picture alternative description: notes, papers, and research books lie chaotically upon a wood desk, in front of you... A skull, which seems suspended in the air, is sort of clamped by two arms of a metal de-vice... On the backside, various re-productions of hominid skulls are lo-cated on shelves...**<br>**End of alternative description**<br><br>This is the starting point or our "jour-ney" through human evolution: the working place of a paleo-anthropologist. the particular device upon the table is used in physical anth-ropology for craniometric measure-ments...<br><br>*Link* shut the window |

Fig. 5.3 HTML and CSS code (on the *left*, **a**); page portion read by the screen reader (on the *right*, **b**)

After a fixed navigation time (15 min), they were asked to answer five questions included in a multiple choice questionnaire. The questions were relative to basic information that could be obtained by both pictures (with the short alternative description always included) and text. A score of 5 points was assigned for each exact answer. On average, the users navigating the implemented site could obtain a higher score (mean ± standard error: 20.63 ± 5.63) than the users using the site without additional criteria (mean ± standard error: 6.88 ± 4.58). Even if quantitative and more in-depth analyses are in progress, this preliminary result suggests that our additional criteria are effective in expanding the background information that a blind user can obtain during the virtual visit of a museum gallery.

5.6 Multidisciplinary Approach in a Cooperative Environment

An integrated cooperative environment on the web is important to enhance and improve the team work required to plan, organize, develop, and successfully implement museum web pages (a working page is shown in Fig. 5.4).
```

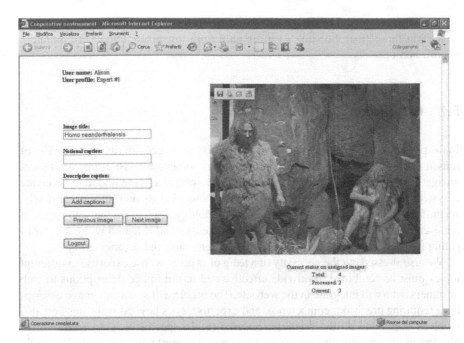

Fig. 5.4 A working page in a cooperative environment

Such environment needs to have the following features:

- *Web-based system.* The environment must be created via Web technology and accessible from everywhere. In this way, web site creation is relieved by the necessity of having all team members in geographical proximity. An immediate consequence would be a wider array of options for team members selection. In our case study, the experts in different fields could cooperate from there "home base": Department of Anthropology, CNR, Museum of Calci, etc.
- *User profile differentiation.* The environment needs to include different access profiles, following an identification/authentication process, in order to separate system subsets, differing according to the role of each team member. In this case study, a web designer, a museum expert, a photographer, an anthropologist, and a CNR researcher entered the system via different access profiles.
- *Content-based database.* The environment is based on a database gathering all the pieces of information provided by the team members. In our case, for example, the museum expert provided information on the exhibit (spatial organization and dioramas), the anthropologist entered biological information on the early hominids recreated in the hall, and the CNR researcher managed to ensure that accessibility criteria were followed.
- *Collaborative and cooperative interaction.* The environment should allow team members to communicate and exchange information with each other, in order to allow proper integration, combination, and connection of all contents.

Collaboration and cooperation are crucial in order for the content (1) to remain consistent throughout the site, (2) to be uniformly organized, and (3) to maintain overall homogeneity.

5.7 Conclusions

In the present work, we addressed the important issue of accessibility and usability of museum web sites that should allow online visits suitable for vision-impaired users navigating through screen reader. In particular, we provided a methodology to create a system of additional and alternative descriptions able to present, appropriately, scientific specimens and art pieces. Such methodology, applied on the web pages of a museum, has been studied to provide complements of information without complicating the web page framework, thus avoiding confusion and disorientation.

We also stressed out the necessity of a team of experts, whose expertise in different topics must be combined to provide effective and useful image descriptions to web designers, who will integrate in the web site. The problem of scientific image description, requiring precision, competence, and expertise, goes beyond web sites and also involves books and all the scientific material (tools, specimens, etc.) addressed to blind users. The cooperative environment proposed to create museum web sites could be easily recycled for any type of elaboration involving scientific subjects.

Acknowledgments The authors wish to thank Walter Landini and Elisabetta Palagi (director and curator of the vertebrate section, respectively) of the Museum of Natural History and Territory (University of Pisa): without them this work would not have been possible.

References

1. Ahn, L., Ginosar, S., Kedia, M., Liu, R., Blum, M. (2006). Improving accessibility of the Web with a computer game. In the Proceedings of the SIGCHI Conference on Human Factors in Computing Systems. Montréal Québec, Canada, April 22–27, 2006, pp. 79–82
2. Leporini, B., Paternò, F. (2004). Increasing usability when interacting through screen readers. International Journal Universal Access in the Information Society, 3 (1), 57–70.
3. Leporini, B., Paternò, F. (2008). Applying Web usability criteria for vision-impaired users: does it really improve task performance? International Journal of Human–Computer Interaction, 24 (1), 17–47
4. Petrie, H., Hamilton, F., King, N. (2004). Tension, what tension?: Website accessibility and visual design. In the Proceedings of the 2004 International Cross-disciplinary Workshop on Web Accessibility (W4A), ACM International Conference Proceeding Series, Vol. 63, pp. 13–18
5. Petrie, H., King, N., Weisen, M. (2005). The accessibility of museum Web sites: results from an English investigation and international comparisons. In: J. Trant and D. Bearman (eds.). Museums and the Web 2005: Proceedings, Toronto: Archives & Museum Informatics, published on March 31, 2005 at http://www.archimuse.com/mw2005/papers/petrie/petrie.htm
6. Stephanidis, C., Akoumianakis, D., Sfyrakis, M., Paramythis, A. (1998). Universal accessibility in HCI: process-oriented design guidelines and tool requirements. In: C. Stephanidis and

A. Waern (eds.). Proceedings of the 4th ERCIM Workshop on "User Interfaces for All," Stockholm, Sweden, October 19–21

7. Theofanos, M.F., Redish, J. (2003). Bridging the gap: between accessibility and usability. ACM Interactions Magazine, New York: ACM Press, November–December 2003 issue, pp. 36–51

8. Web Content Accessibility Guidelines 1.0 URL: http://www.w3.org/TR/WAI-WEBCONTENT

9. Web Content Accessibility Guidelines 2.0 Draft December 2007–January 2008 URL http://www.w3.org/WAI/GL/WCAG20/WD-WCAG20-20071218/

Chapter 6
A Location-Aware Guide Based on Active RFIDs in Multi-Device Environments

Giuseppe Ghiani, Fabio Paternò, Carmen Santoro and Lucio Davide Spano

Abstract In this chapter, we propose a multi-device, location-aware museum guide. It is a mobile guide able to opportunistically exploit large screens when they are nearby the user. Various types of games, which can exploit multi-device environments, are included in addition to the museum and artwork descriptions. The mobile guide is equipped with an RFID reader, which provides information useful to automatically detect nearby artworks. We also present example applications of this solution and then briefly discuss the results of first empirical tests performed to evaluate the usefulness and the usability of the enhanced mobile guide.

6.1 Introduction

Recent technological advances (including increasing availability of various types of interactive devices, sensors, and communication technology) enable novel interactive software environments to support users in several contexts for different objectives. In the edutainment area, museums are an interesting domain because of the large amount of digital information and the increasingly prevalent technological resources adopted in such environments. Thus, they are a particularly suitable context in which to experiment with new interaction techniques for guiding mobile users and improving their experience. However, at the same time, such a wealth of both information and devices might become a potential source of disorientation for users, if not adequately supported.

Traditionally, the support for museum visits is limited to audio guides and interactive kiosks, which are limited in different ways from various viewpoints. It is important to exploit new technologies to identify new solutions able to enhance the user experience. Games for mobile guides can provide an interesting and amusing way to promote user interaction and learning. In this regard, the use of different types of devices within the museum (e.g. mobile devices and large screens) can be

G. Ghiani, F. Paternò, C. Santoro and L.D. Spano
ISTI-CNR, Via G.Moruzzi, 1, 56124 Pisa, Italy
e-mail: Giuseppe.Ghiani@isti.cnr.it

seen as a means to enrich user experience by enabling further functionality, such as displaying the visitors' position and supporting games on the large screen while the user visits the museum using the mobile guide.

For lack of space we cannot discuss the many proposals put forward in the area of mobile guides. One important example was the GUIDE project [1] which developed an intelligent and context-aware tourist guide: each point of interest is associated with a geographic area, each one supported by a Wireless LAN, and when the user enters these areas, the corresponding information is automatically provided as text descriptions, images, and audio comments. Among other examples of mobile guides that exploit various kinds of information to adapt the services they provide, we mention Hippie [2] which provides the visitors of an art exhibition with comments on the artworks in sight, adapting the information to user's location, interests, and knowledge that is derived from the interaction. However, solutions based on automatic generation of comments on the closest artwork may sometimes be judged annoying by the user. CRUMPET [3] personalizes its services, both on PDAs and mobile phones, not only according to the position of the user and her interests but also according to previous interaction with the system. Lol@ [4] is a tourist guide for the city of Vienna, using GPS as localization techniques and a GIS support for generating the maps. It adapts the information to the device, but not to the user's characteristics. However, differently from our approach, no multi-device support has been deployed in such guides.

We found interesting the idea of developing games to enhance interactivity in museums, which has been extensively explored mainly through more conventional media such as paper-based treasure hunts. However, little research has been reported in the role of digital adaptive games inside galleries, even if similar research in other contexts has been carried out [5]. Furthermore, an increasing interest has been attracted by the use of RFID technology in order to supplement physical artwork with associated digital information. Mantyiarvi et al. [6] have proposed the scan and tilt interaction paradigm. Physical selection is obtained by scanning RFID tags associated with the artworks and single-handed tilt gestures are used to control and navigate the user interface and multimedia information. By pointing at the artwork of interest and controlling audio information with small single-handed gestures, the visual channel is not too overloaded, resulting in a less intrusive interaction technique. We performed a first empirical evaluation on this prototype. The test showed an overall good acceptance among users but, at the same time, highlighted some limitations. For example, the passive RFID tags used in this prototype forced the users to stand in very close proximity to the artworks, which is not very natural in museum environments.

Here we present a new environment (UbiCicero) aiming to support multi-device interaction and games to improve museum visitor learning integrated with a location-aware support exploiting RFID technology. The goal is to improve the experience of museum visitors facilitating the access to the information available and increasing the interactivity of the environment.

In this chapter, we first discuss related work, including our previous experiences with mobile guides, then we present our novel approach for mobile guides exploiting in an integrated manner RFID technology, games, and large shared screens and report on some first evaluations. Finally, we provide some concluding remarks and indications for future work.

6.2   The Visit

Our interactive environment for museum visitors has been implemented for two museums: The Marble Museum (Carrara) and the Museum of Natural History (Calci). Our mobile guide provides visitors with a rich variety of multimedia (graphical, video, audio, etc.) information regarding the available artworks and related items. In addition to information regarding artworks, sections, and the museum, the application is able to support some services such as showing the itinerary to get to a specific artwork from the current location. Most information is provided mainly vocally in order to allow visitors to freely look around; however, the visual interface can show related videos, maps at different levels (museum, sections, and rooms), and specific pieces of information.

One feature in the guide is the use of active RFID tags for automatically detecting nearby artworks. Figure 6.1 shows the museum guide implemented on the PDA device equipped with the compact flash (CF) RFID reader, which is a small add-on that can be plugged into a standard PDA interface. RFID-based solutions are composed of two main parts: the set of tags, or radio transponders and the tag reader, or transceiver. Tags basically have a static identification (ID) number, but can also store different type of information such as sensed data (e.g. environmental temperature). The reader scans for available tags and, depending on their features, may interrogate them for additional information stored on their embedded memory. To make our mobile guide as small and as light as possible, we opted for a totally handheld-based solution consisting of CF RFID reader with small-sized antenna. The PDA does not need any additional expansion or adapter because the reader plugs directly into the CF slot. In general, RFID technology can be applied by using *passive* or *active* tags:

1. *Passive* RFID tags do not have any internal battery and exploit the energy electromagnetically inducted by a neighbouring antenna. Thus, passive tags can respond with their IDs when and only when a reader within a few centimetres' range interrogates them.
2. *Active* RFID tags are equipped with an internal power source and are able to transmit by themselves at any time. There are two different types of active tags, depending on the way they work: beacon and respond.
   (a) *Beacon* tags have a radio transmitter and they continuously send their data at certain intervals of time. The reader tunes into the proper radio frequency and listens to the tag information and the detection is not affected by the number of users, since the readers do not send any request to the tags. Also, beacon technology uses read-only tags

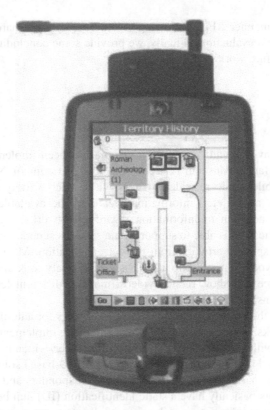

Fig. 6.1 The museum mobile guide

(b) *Respond* tags (which, differently from the previous ones, are read and write tags) wait for a reader request before responding. Because of the need for both transmitter and receiver modules, respond tags involve more complex architectures, larger dimensions, and higher costs than beacon tags. However, while the battery life of beacon tags (2–4 years) depends on how frequently they transmit, the battery life of respond tags depends on how often they are interrogated (in any case more than 6 years).

An undeniable benefit of active tag technology is the wide read range (up to 100 m). Museum artworks are equipped with physical tags and each tag has a unique ID number. Note that a single tag can be associated with more than one neighbouring artwork, when they are very close. This is due to the difficulty of distinguishing two or more tags that are too close to each other. Indeed, if two tags were placed in a very small area, the reader would see both of them with the same received signal strength indication (RSSI). The use of RFID technology for localization and the problems related to tag density are also discussed in Bellotti et al. [7]. When the user enters a new room, the guide activates the museum map highlighting the new room and corresponding vocal comments.

Continuous monitoring of the tags' signal allows the guide to calculate artworks closest to the user among those inside the current room. When a new tag is detected, that is a new area is being visited, an audio clip is played to alert the user and a vocal message indicating the number of neighbouring artworks is generated. Tag detection enables the computation of user's position; however, the proximity of an artwork does not imply that the user is interested on that artwork (s/he could be even looking to another one). For this reason, and depending on user preferences, the guide may ask confirmation before describing any artwork or even describe them automatically. A more affordable support would detect user's orientation through an electronic compass (see Sect. 6) besides user location to determine which item s/he is actually watching at.

We chose the active beacon tags for our RFID-based solution because it is more scalable with respect to the number of users. Actually, the RFID reader just tunes into the proper radio frequency and "listens" to the tag(s) information, reporting the list of visible tags together with their RSSIs. However, when tags are sending their IDs, overlap may occur and data may be lost. For this reason, the detection of all the visible tags may take a few seconds (depending on the number of tags in range).

Localization at the application layer is performed by estimating the nearest tag and obtaining the associated artwork(s). Access to the RFID hardware is achieved via the libraries provided by the hardware supplier (http://www.identecsolutions. com/) whose functions allow the application to configure and interrogate the RFID reader. For each query (queries are performed with the frequency of 2 per second) from the localization support, the RFID reader provides the list of visible tags. Each list element contains data related to a visible tag, such as ID and RSSI. The application localization support keeps a list of all the tags that have been detected at least once. In the application, each tag is associated with its last reported RSSI and the time elapsed since its last detection. Only tags that have been detected recently are considered in the computation. The best tag is always the one with the highest RSSI. However, a "new tag event" is generated only if the new tag is the best candidate for N consecutive queries. The value of N is specified in the application settings to achieve a trade-off between reliability and speed of the localization: the higher it is, the more reliable the localization will be, but also the more time it will take to update the identification of the closest artworks. The value of N must be carefully chosen, especially when tag density is high (i.e. artworks are very close), in order to avoid erroneous detections. To facilitate localization, an RSSI threshold is used to adjust the reader sensitivity. In our case, we are able to detect tags up to 5 m, also because of the limitations of the small antenna. Lower sensitivity makes the reader report only the nearest tags and simplifies the application layer computation. Nevertheless, when many artworks are too close to each other, they may be detected as a single tag. Indeed, if two tags were placed in a very small area, the reader would see both of them with the same RSSI. The guide automatically detects this movement through the RFIDs and highlights nearby artworks with squared frames around the corresponding icons. Then, when the user accesses the description of the artworks, the

colour of the associated icons changes again to signal the fact that the related
artworks have been visited.

6.3   Software Architecture

The main elements of the software architecture are the modules in the PDA, in the
stationary device, and the communication protocol of the environment. The PDA
module is composed of five layers, each one provides the others with services.
From the bottom they are:

1. *Museum DB*, which provides information about the artworks;
2. *Core and Communication*, which provides the basic mechanisms including network services for sending/receiving messages;
3. *Localization*, which provides support for localizing the nearby artworks and the
   user location exploiting various technologies (such as RFID and IrDA), when
   available;
4. *Visit*, supporting interactive access to museum info; and
5. *Games*, supporting the interactive games.

In particular, the database provides information about museum artworks to the
upper layers.

The core implements data structures useful for the upper layers, for example
support for configuration and help and the XML parsers. It also provides functionality used to update the information regarding the state of the players, to connect to
shared stationary displays and to exchange information among palmtops and therefore implements algorithms for managing sockets, messages, and group organization. When the user explicitly starts the interface splitting, the mobile application
sends a connection request message to the stationary device. If the connection is
successful, a pre-computed desktop version of the application is activated, a series
of messages encoding the state data is sent by the mobile version to the stationary
one to replicate the state. State synchronization must be maintained when the interface is split between the mobile and the situated display. Thus, the mobile has to
send update messages anytime its state changes.

The localization layer contains the concurrency manager of IrDA and RFID
signals (infrared signals are used to detect when the user enters a room). Such layer
is exploited by the visit and game layers. The visit layer supports the presentation
of the current room map and a set of interactive elements. Each artwork is associated with an icon identifying its type (sculpture, painting, picture, …) and positioned in the map according to its physical location. By selecting such icon, users
can receive detailed information on the corresponding artwork. In addition, this part of
the application allows users to receive help, access videos, change audio parameters,
and obtain other info.

The games layer extends the museum visit application and supports games displaying and solving. Game contents are defined using an XML format to allow easy
modifications and additions.

6.4   Visit and Games in Multi-Device Environments

While some preliminary ideas regarding the use of games in mobile guides were introduced by Dini et al. [8] but without using any localization support, here we present a comprehensive solution, tested into two museums, with a wider set of games. Such games have been integrated with an RFID-based localization support. In particular, in our new environment in order to increase the learning experience, six types of individual games are considered:

1. In the associations game, users must associate images with words, for example the author of an artwork or the material of an artwork.
2. In the details game, an enlargement of a small detail of an image is shown. The player has to guess which of the artwork images the detail belongs to.
3. The chronology game requires the user to arrange the images of the artworks shown chronologically according to the creation date.
4. In the hidden word game, the users have to guess a word: the number of characters composing the word is shown as help.
5. In the memory game, the user has to look at an image (which then disappears) and s/he has to answer to a question associated with the previously shown image.
6. The quiz is a single-choice question.

The artworks that have an associated game show an additional star icon, through which it is possible to access the game. If the game is solved correctly, the icon becomes a green check, otherwise it turns to a red cross (Fig. 6.2).

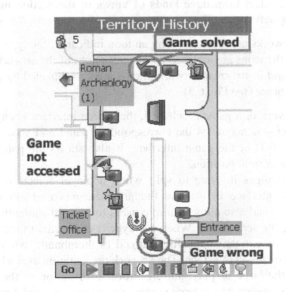

Fig. 6.2 Representation of the game state

The main feature of our solution is to support visit and game applications exploiting both mobile and stationary devices equipped with large screens. The typical scenario is users freely moving and interacting through the mobile device, who can also exploit a larger, shared screen of a stationary device (which can be considered a situated display) when it is nearby. Shared screens connected to stationary systems can increase social interaction and improve user experience, otherwise limited to individual interaction with a mobile device. They also stimulate social interaction and communication with other visitors, though they may not know each other. A larger shared screen extends the functionality of a mobile application enabling the possibility to present individual games differently, share social game representations, show the positions of the other players in the group, and also perform a virtual pre-visit of the entire museum. Each large shared display can be in different states:

1. *Standalone:* the screen has its own input devices (keyboard and mouse) and it may be used for a virtual visit of the museum. It can be exploited by visitors who do not have the PDA guide.
2. *Split:* one visitor has taken control of the display. The PDA displays name and group of the controller.
3. *Search:* the display shows the current position of the other players, according to the RFID localization.
4. *Game:* the display shows one individual game.

Since a shared display has to go through several states, the structure of its layout and some parts of the interface remain unchanged in order to avoid disorientating users. This permanent part of the user interface provides information such as the current section map and its position in the museum, an explanation of the icons used to represent the artworks and the state of the final enigma game. In standalone mode, users can select from three kinds of views of the section map, using the toolbar on its top-left corner. These views are:

1. *Icons*: the artworks are represented by an icon indicating the type.
2. *Thumbnails*: the icons are replaced by a small photo of the artwork.
3. *Thumbnails and icons*: small artwork photos are accompanied by icons on their bottom-left corner (*see* Fig. 6.3).

When an artwork or a game is selected, the screen interface changes its layout adapting the focus: it magnifies the correspondent panel and shows the artwork details (*see* Fig. 6.4) or the game interface. It also shows the path to reach the artwork from the current position.

The screen changes its state to split when a player selects the connection through the PDA interface. In this case, the large screen is used both to show additional information and also allow multiple users to focus the attention on a given game exploiting the screen size. When a player is connected to the large screen, its section map view is automatically changed to thumbnails, while the artwork types are shown on the PDA screen. The artwork presentation uses a higher resolution image on the large display, adding more information to the description. The game representation on the large screen is used to share and discuss it among

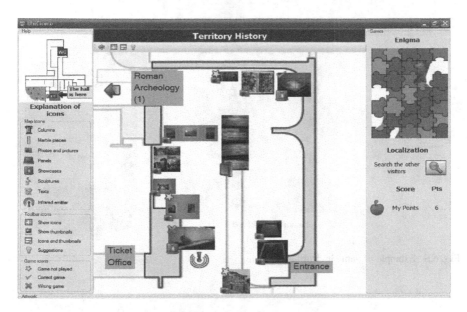

Fig. 6.3 Museum room in large screen using thumbnails plus icons

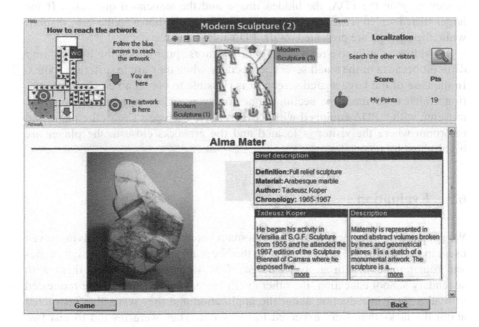

Fig. 6.4 Artwork presentation on large screen

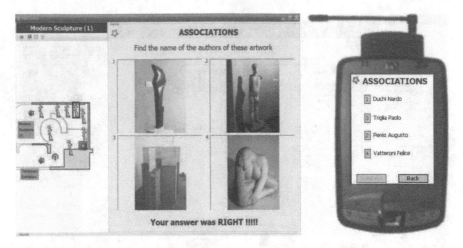

Fig. 6.5 Example of game in distributed mode

multiple users. In the split representation, the possible game answer choices are shown only on the PDA interface, while game information and higher resolution images are shown on the larger screen (*see* Fig. 6.5).

The visualization of the enigma game differs depending on the availability of the large screen: if only the PDA is used, it is composed of two presentations visualized sequentially on the PDA, the hidden image and the associated questions. If the larger shared screen is available, then the hidden image is shown on the large display, while the answers are presented on the PDA user interface.

Providing an effective representation of visitors' position on the PDA is very difficult because of the small screen, especially when they are in different rooms. In the case of the large shared screen, it is possible to obtain a better representation which is divided into sections, one for each visitor currently visiting the museum with a PDA equipped with RFID reader. Each part shows the name and the room where the visitor is located and the artworks close to the player are highlighted by rectangles.

6.5 Evaluation

We performed a first evaluation of our nomadic application guide involving seven users in the Marble Museum and five in the Natural History Museum (eight males and four females), with an average age of 36.4 years old, three of them with secondary school education, the others with laurea degree. Users were requested to read a short introduction about the application and they were also instructed about the tasks they were expected to carry out. They were invited to test two versions of the mobile guide. One version was equipped with the multi-device support, the RFID module for detecting proximity of artworks within a museum room. The other version was a basic one without the multi-device support and no RFID support.

They were asked to visit some sections of the museum using the two versions. With the enhanced prototype, they were also requested to access and solve some games and to perform at least one splitting between PDA and a large screen available in a museum section. Half of the users started the visit by using the enhanced version and then continue with the basic one; for the others, the vice versa held. Afterwards, the users had to fill in a questionnaire.

Almost all people involved in the tests reported not to have good experience in using PDAs, a few of them had previous experience in using digital museum guides, even less reported to have used digital games in museum settings.

The possibility of the enhanced museum guide of detecting the current position of the user and therefore to present information dependent on such a position (by surrounding with a frame the icon representing the artwork(s) closest to the user) was judged useful by testers (in a 1–5 scale in which 1 is the worst case and 5 is the best one, $M = 3.58$; $SD = 1.16$), especially for orientation and for helping in identifying an artwork and associating an icon in the map to the related artwork in the museum. Delays in the localization support were noticed by some users, which brought about some hesitations during the visit. In addition, they judged useful ($M = 3.75$; $SD = 0.87$) the support given by the enhanced guide for presenting descriptive information about the artworks currently closer to the user. As for the multi-device support, users appreciated the guide/games support offered in the PDA version ($M = 3.73$) and in the desktop one ($M = 3.2$). Also the way in which the functionality was split between the PDA and the large screen was rated quite positively ($M = 3.1$). Regarding the splitting, some of them noted that it might be not so easy for the user to follow a description which is partially visualized on a PDA and partially on a large screen because of the division of attention.

People who preferred the visit with the basic prototype appreciated the possibility of having a quicker visit and the fact that the basic version supported a visit that allows more user's initiative with respect to the enhanced version. The UI for visualising the games associated to the various artworks in the museum was rated quite good ($M = 3.67$; $SD = 1.37$), although some users reported problems in selecting the icon representing the game associated to a specific artwork; regarding the content of the games, users judged them in a quite good way ($M = 3.58$; $SD = 1.24$), although they emphasized the opportunity of providing games that are easy for being solved by museum visitors. Games were judged amusing ($M = 3.67$; $SD = 1.15$) and useful in stimulating and improving learning ($M = 3.5$; $SD = 1.31$), one of the most favourite games was the quiz.

All in all, the application was acknowledged useful, interesting, and with good potentialities. Improvements were suggested in order to further improve the precision of user localization within the museum sections and its performance in the location support and to simplify as much as possible the interaction.

6.6   Conclusions and Future Work

In this chapter, we proposed a multi-device, location-aware guide supporting museum visits, including the possibility of enriching the museum visits through games. Its main contribution is in the ability to exploit multi-device environments, in which users can freely move about with their mobile guide but also exploit large screens connected to stationary PCs when they are nearby. Both the access to museum information and the associated games can benefit from the availability of multiple devices as well as additional services, such as the presentation on the large screen of the locations of other visitors, which are detected through RFID tags. We have also developed an authoring environment that allows developers to easily customize the guide for new museums.

We are investigating new ways to further enhance personalization of the guide user interface, in particular in group visits, and the possible automatic detection of user's orientation. Orientation, combined with localization, would better support the identification of the user's interests in the exhibition area.

Future work will be dedicated to carry out further empirical validation of our guide in order to better understand the advantages and possible improvements of the enhanced version with respect to the basic one.

References

1. Cheverst, K., N. Davies, K. Mitchel, and P. Smyth: Providing Tailored Context-Aware Information to City Visitors. In Adaptive Hypermedia and Adaptive Web-Based Systems (AH 2000), LNCS Vol. 1892. Springer, Berlin/Heidelberg/New York, 2000, pp. 73–85
2. Opperman R., M. Specht, and I. Jaceniak: Hippie: A Nomadic Information System. In Handheld and Ubiquitous Computing. Springer, Berlin, 1999, pp. 330–333.
3. Poslad, S., H. Laamanen, R. Malaka, A. Nick, P. Buckle, A. Zipf: CRUMPET: Creation of User-Friendly Mobile Services Personalised for Tourism. In Proceedings of the 3G Mobile Communication Technologies, London, UK, 2001, pp. 26–29.
4. Pospischil, G., M. Umlauft, and E. Michlmayr: Designing LoL@, A Mobile Tourist Guide for UMTS. Information Technology & Tourism 5(3), Cognizant Communication Corporation, 2003, pp. 151–164
5. Bell, M., M. Chalmers, L. Barkhuus, M. Hall, S. Sherwood, P. Tennent, B. Brown, D. Rowland, S. Benford, M. Capra, and A. Hampshire: Interweaving Mobile Games With Everyday Life. In CHI 2006 Proceedings Games and Performances, Montréal, Canada, 2006.
6. Mantyiarvi, J., F. Paternò, Z. Salvador, and C. Santoro: Scan and Tilt – Towards Natural Interaction for Mobile Museum Guides. In Proceedings Mobile HCI 2006, Espoo. ACM, New York, September 2006, pp.191–194.
7. Bellotti, F., R. Berta, A. De Gloria, and M. Margarone: Guiding Visually Impaired People in the Exhibition. Mobile Guide 2006, Turin, Italy, 2006 (http://mobileguide06.di.unito.it/pdf/Bellotti&al.pdf).
8. Dini R., F. Paternò, and C. Santoro: An Environment to Support Multi-User Interaction and Cooperation for Improving Museum Visits through Games. In Proceedings Mobile HCI'07, Singapore. ACM, New York, September 2007.

Chapter 7
Design of Adaptative Video Game Interfaces: A Practical Case of Use in Special Education

José Luis González Sánchez, Francisco L. Gutiérrez, Marcelino Cabrera and Natalia Padilla Zea

Abstract The use of new technological and learning methods that help to improve the learning process has produced the inclusion of the video games as active elements in the classrooms. Video Games are ideal learning tools since they provide training skills, promote independence, increase and improve students' concentration and attention. For special education students with learning difficulties, it is very important to adapt the game to each student's cognitive level and skills. The present work describes our experience in the design and the use of video game as new forms to create didactic learning tools to pupils with serious communication problems as autism, dysphasia, ictus, or cerebral palsy.

7.1   Introduction

Humans, through history, have had the ability to administrate their leisure time and have used this factor as cultural development. According to Huizinga [1], the game with the relationship and abilities that humans acquire with the playing process is one of the most important aspects in the human social-cultural evolution. Video Games are the twenty-first century games.

Video Games [2] enable knowledge to be developed through game contents and increase cognitive abilities through play, but a special child/player has his/her own characteristics that make him/her unique in the world. In these situation, it is a very important factor that didactical video games must adapt to the player, not only to the context, also to interaction techniques, user interface, and the didactical contents to develop the most efficacious didactical video game.

In this chapter, we will describe our proposal to design and develop "player-centred Video Games" and apply them to a practical context: special education. We will describe how to introduce he educational contents into a game structure and how

J.L.G. Sánchez (✉), F.L. Gutiérrez, M.J. Cabrera and N.P. Zea
Video Games and E-Learning Research Lab (LIVE) – GEDES, Software Engineering Department, University of Granada, C/Daniel Saucedo Aranda, s/n, E-18,007, Granada, Spain
e-mail: joseluis@ugr.es

V. López-Jaquero et al. (eds.), *Computer-Aided Design of User Interfaces VI*,   71
DOI: 10.1007/978-1-84882-206-1_7, © Springer-Verlag London Limited 2009

to readapt the video game interface to make these contents and game dynamics (user interface and user interaction) the most suitable as possible to users/players. The second section of this chapter presents various considerations and ideas about special education video games and how to develop personalized video games using our game architecture and design techniques. Section 3 presents an example of our ideas, a video games to learn the vowels. Finally, Sect. 4 outlines our conclusions and future lines of work.

7.2 Learning by Playing, Playing to Learn: The Design of Adaptative Video Games to the Player

Can we learn playing videogames? This is a question largely debated by specialists in psychology and pedagogy. A video game could be an unequal pedagogical tool in special education classroom. We should take into account a series of user's factors in order to get the most effective possible educational process when we are designing an educational video game: *Motivation*, *Attention*, *Concentration*, and *Emotion* [3–6]. But, in special education field, the game must be easy to personalize using the player's cognitive and physical characteristics because every child is unique in the classroom.

Our didactical video games proposal starts from this main idea: The principal child activity must be playing; the consequence of this action (playing) will be that the child learns the educative contents in an implicit way.

It is essential to design and develop a high-quality video game that the game process stimulates player's fun and entertainment. We denominate *Playability* the set of properties to describe the player's experience with a particular game system, that the principal goal is fun/entertainment to the player in a satisfactory and credible way, playing alone or with other players. Playability reflects the player's pleasure, experience, sensations, and feelings when he/she is playing the video game.

In the Design Process, the first step is creating a complete StoryLine. It must be attractive to the future players who play the game. A good story offers a "good connection" between game and player, and helps to catch the player's attention and consequently to create crucial motivation mechanisms that guarantee the interest of the child to play the game. The history should motivate, excite, and thrill the child/player.

The following step is the Gameplay Design. It includes all player experiences during the interaction (what the player can do and how to do) with game systems, for example, goals, rules, learning curve, etc. This term is used to describe the overall experience of playing the game excluding the aspects of graphics, sound, and the storyline. In Gameplay Design for the special education field, it is very important to offer a *feedback*, focused on the cognitive need, for each action. *Player's error* should be corrected without causing sadness or discouragement. It is recommendable to use a main character or *hero*, who acts as a mediator/guide in the learning process and game. This learning process should be in rise, based on *multi-levels* or missions, where the level of difficulty increases gradually. *Rewards* offer an extra motivation–satisfaction factor; they allow us to create mechanisms that influence the player to self-improvement and advance while playing.

In the educational contents design, it is crucial to identify the *player's profile*, his/her limitations, and cognitive capabilities in order to choose the best interaction and user interface mechanisms. We have to structure and adapt the *didactic unit* objectives to the player's characteristics and goals of the game. The *educational contents* should be introduced into the game structure in a hidden way.

Our main goal is to develop special education video games that adapt to the different player profiles. In order to do that, we proposes a software evolution framework, based in three-layer structure: the meta-game, the meta-phase, and the meta-level. With this meta-structure, we model the behaviour and the functionality of our game engine and video game mechanics: interaction, feedback, etc., independently from the player skills or concepts to be learned.

Meta-game layer offers the basic game architecture for training with a specific child. It has two dimensions: The *Accessibility dimension*, which describes the user interface and the interaction characteristics according to the player's skill profile and *Gameplay dimension*, which defines the principal characteristics of the game (goals, multi-levels or missions, rewards, etc.).

Meta-phase layer involves the educational contents. Finally, the *meta-level layer allows* defining educational exercises to train the concept defined in the specific phase. This game definition is saved in binary files to use them with the game engine to run a specific game. We can use the game reports to readapt the difficulty of levels dynamically, introducing adaptation/personalization rules (e.g., frequency of errors and hits) into the game engine. A graphical model of our adaptative/evolutive game architecture is represented in Fig. 7.1.

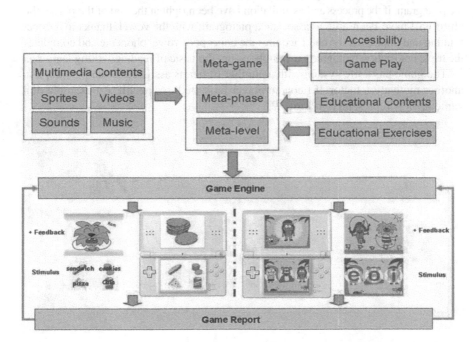

Fig. 7.1 Adaptative/evolutive video games architecture

7.3   A Practical Example: Leoncio and the Lost Vowels Island

As an example of video games using the ideas that we have presented in this chapter, we will introduce our prototype of didactical video game applied to special education: "Leoncio and the Lost Vowels Island" on Nintendo DS™ [2]. The main educational objective is to learn the vowels across the relationship between the stimuli that the game presents. With the correct stimulus we also introduce erroneous stimuli; in these cases, the player should discriminate to obtain the correct result. The game is based on learning method of reading/writing call "SuperLecto-Escritura" [7]. In every moment during the game exists parallelism between phoneme, text, and pictograms (vowel pronunciation, vowel writing, and vowel graphic representation). The development of the learning of vowels comes through an incremental way, using for it a multi-level system that is grouped in different phases. In each level, thanks to the audio device, the child can identify the phoneme of each pictogram touching on it with the stylus or using sweeping technique in each possible option, emphasizing the pictogram and the letter to be stimulated. When the child responds correctly (he/she correlates pictogram with pictogram, later pictogram with vowel, and finally with audio), the game shows an appropriate feedback and emphasizes the pictogram and audio with the vowel. If the child fails, the game emphasizes the right answer and encourages the child to re-select a new answer. If the process of selection is right, in the following level of the vowel-phase, the pictogram will decrease its clarity, appearing the letter, which is "hidden" behind the pictogram. At the end, the child correlates only the vowel with the pictogram. If the process and assimilation have been right at the end of the phase, the child will have been able to associate a pictogram with the vowel, thanks to a direct training and implicitly, the child acquires the concept of vowel phoneme and completes the triple association pictogram-vowel-phoneme, the basic of reading/writing learning.

The game has a life system with a number of hearts assigned to the players, it is another motivation factor. If Leoncio/player fails, he loses health. An example of a game level is represented in Fig. 7.2.

Fig. 7.2   Example level in "Leoncio and the Lost Vowels Island"

When you work with video games in special education, they have a crucial factor. Children must have to adapt to the game, and this process makes the learning process more complex. Our video game include an adaptative process because the game could personalize to the players/children cognitive/physics requirements, for example, the interaction methods, playability, or contents presentation using accessibility mechanisms to rapidly adapt the game to several cognitive user profiles.

7.4   Conclusions and Future Works

In this chapter, we have presented our proposal of player-centred video games for special education, following the idea "Learning by playing, playing to learn." The learning process must be implicit in the video game dynamics.

We are designing a visual platform to create evolving video games following a development process in which aspects as user interface, educational contents, multimedia, and interaction methods are described in separated and incremental steps. To improve the playability and the game efficacy, we use entertainment devices as Nintendo DS. Finally, we have presented one of our prototypes: "Leoncio and the Lost Vowels Island."

In next months, we will begin an experiment with a group of children to check the efficacy of our method in "special schools" and elementary schools. We will keep on working in the software evolution framework development and video game theoretic model that allow us working with adaptation/personalization techniques. Also, we are working in defined playability attributes and properties/qualities and use them in the video game software development to obtain more fun and playable video games to play alone or in company.

Acknowledgments   This study and work is financed by the Spanish International Commission for Science and Technology (CICYT) and DESACO project (TIN2008-06596-C02-2) and the F.P.U. Programme of the Ministry of Education and Science, Spain.

References

1. Huizinga, J.: Homo Ludens (Ed.) Alianza Editorial, SA Madrid, Spain (2002). ISBN: 9788420635392
2. González Sánchez, J. L.; Cabrera, M.; Gutiérrez, F. L. Diseño de Videojuegos aplicados a la Educación Especial. VIII Congreso Internacional de Interacción Persona-Ordenador. INTERACCION-2007. pp. 35–45 (2007).
3. Malone, T.W., Lepper, M.R. Intrinsic Motivation and Instructional Effectiveness in Computer-based Education. In R.F. Snow& M.J. Farr (Eds.) Aptitude, Learning and Instruction. Volume 2: Conative and affective process analyses. pp. 243–286. Lawrence Erlbaum, Hillsdale, NJ (1987).
4. Keller, J.M., Kopp, T.W. An Application of the ARCS Model of Motivational Design. In C.M. Regeluth (Ed.) Instructional Theories in Action: Lessons Illustrating Selected Theories and Models. pp. 289–320. Lawrence Erlbaum, New York (1987).

5. Csíkszentmihályi, M. Flow: The Psychology of Optimal Experience. Harper and Row, New York (1990)
6. Norman, D. A., Emotional Design: Why We Love (or Hate) Everyday Things. Basic Books, New York (2004)
7. García, C. V; Luciano, M. C., SuperLecto-Escritura. Programa para el aprendizaje de la Lectura y Escritura. Ediciones Némesis, S. L. ISBN: 84-922930-8-X

Chapter 8
A Preliminary Study of Two-Handed Manipulation for Spatial Input Tasks in a 3D Modeling Application

Antonio Capobianco, Manuel Veit and Dominique Bechmann

Abstract We developed a free form deformation application for an immersive environment in which users can interact freely using data gloves. To ensure better comfort and performances, we added the possibility of bimanual interaction in our environment. To investigate the actual gain obtained by this interaction technique, we designed an experimental protocol based on spatial input tasks. In our experiment, we asked our subjects to use only the dominant hand to achieve the different tasks or, on the contrary, to use both hands. Comparison of users' performances – time and precision – shows that, without proper training, executing a task using two hands can be more time consuming than using one hand. In fact, the degree of symmetry of the tasks performed with each hand seems to have a significant impact on whether users take advantage of bimanual possibilities. Our results also show that bimanual interaction can introduce proprioceptive cues that can be of help to achieve more precision in the placement or selection only when proper visual information are missing.

8.1 Introduction

Virtual reality and 3D interaction are often presented as a major step toward real direct and intuitive manipulation. Indeed, immersive virtual environments (IVEs) allow users to interact with virtual objects using everyday actions and commands. For example, users can manipulate – grab, move, rotate, etc. – an object using their bare hands, as they would with a real object. It is also possible to experiment 3D scenes exploration with total immersion in a virtual world. This has proved to be useful to enhance users understanding of the environment explored. For example, a large-scale multimodal virtual system for archaeological purposes has proved to be efficient during

A. Capobianco (✉), M. Viet and D. Bechmann
LSIIT UMR 7005 CNRS, Pole API Bd Sebastien Brant,
BP 10413, 67412, Illkirch Cedex, France
e-mail: capobianco@lsiit.u-strasbg.fr

V. López-Jaquero et al. (eds.), *Computer-Aided Design of User Interfaces VI*,
DOI: 10.1007/978-1-84882-206-1_8, © Springer-Verlag London Limited 2009

an exhibition for the public whose aim was to teach the process of constructing columns as part of the structure of an ancient Greek temple [1].

However, the evolution of virtual environments seem disappointing, with few actual applications. The main application field seems to be information visualization and virtual scene exploration. But except for a few examples, and despite all the efforts provided, interaction with the environment in this kind of applications generally remains poor, and frequently needs specific interaction metaphors for each task (sometimes integrating the use of physical devices, "props," to complete the task). It seems that major manipulation and perception problems remain, despite an early identification of these difficulties in precocious studies on virtual reality [2, 3]. At present time, these specific issues still need to be resolved before drawing a real profit from IVE potentialities. For example, no effective solutions have been provided for effective spatial selection and input in IVE graphical applications: techniques are usually poor and lack of precision and efficiency. Exploiting bimanual interaction and proprioception have been suggested and are promising solutions to some of the known fundamental issues [4–8].

We developed a free form deformation application called *Odd Mesh Maker* (OMM) that allows a user to perform simple 3D modeling tasks in IVE using data gloves. Our objective with this application is to provide a set of intuitive and efficient interaction techniques to realize simple modeling tasks. Relying on previous studies, showing the potential manual and cognitive benefits obtained from bimanual interaction [9], we developed several bimanual interaction techniques for deformation tasks. In this chapter, we propose a preliminary survey investigating the benefits of some basic bimanual interaction techniques in IVEs for 3D input. Our study aims at investigating whether bimanual interaction can be used as a significant improvement toward effective and convenient spatial input in IVE, and how they influence the users' performance and comfort.

8.2 Bimanual Interaction

The justification of research interest in bimanual interactions seems obvious. We spontaneously use bimanual interactions to ensure efficiency, precision, and comfort in the realization of everyday tasks. Thereby, bimanual interactions techniques are becoming more and more present in 2D applications, and have been exploited to lead to intuitive interactions modalities in IVE (e.g., two-handed ray-based interactions [8], over the shoulder deletion and two hands flying [10], and two-handed selection techniques for volumetric data [11]).

The Kinematic Chain Theory [12] provides a theoretical framework to describe bimanual techniques. *Guiard* propose that two-hand interaction can be symmetrical or asymmetrical. In symmetrical tasks, the two hands perform the same action. In asymmetrical tasks, each hand performs a different action. In that case, the non-dominant hand usually sets the frame of reference for the action of the dominant hand. Our interaction modality, manipulating objects using non-dominant hand while deforming with dominant hand, is based on these principles: the user can use the non-dominant hand as a reference frame to correct dominant hand gesture [13] and make precise manipulations on an object.

As well, using bare hands to achieve a task can bring gains in motor efficiency and lower cognitive load. In bimanual interaction, motor efficiency is mainly due to parallelism, that is, the simultaneous execution of the two tasks assigned to each hand. According to *Buxton and Myers*, there is a correlation between degree of parallelism and performances [14]: the results of their study show that it is possible to improve users performance by splitting the sub-tasks of compound continuous tasks between the two hands. This procedure leads to improvement of performances for both novices and experts users. Their study also shows that when two hands are used sequentially, each one making separate tasks, it can avoid time-consuming task switching, thus reducing task completion times. However, these encouraging results must be taken with proper care considering the fact that the expected benefits may depend on the interaction device or input modalities, on the subtasks involved in the task, and on the environment [6]. For example, a study realized on a docking task necessitating manipulation and navigation in an IVE showed no significant gain from bimanual interaction [15], whereas an experiment conducted to evaluate the effectiveness of bimanual interaction techniques in the VLEGO environment showed that two-handed cooperative manipulation led to shorter completion times and lower error rates [16].

In addition, bimanual interaction introduces proprioception in the environment. Proprioception is the sense of the relative position of neighboring parts of the body. Using a persons' sense of position and orientation of his body and limbs can be exploited as an additional sensory-motor channel that provides useful information to the user [10].

8.3 OMM: A 3D Modeling Application

8.3.1 Manipulation Paradigm

Direct deformation applications in IVEs (i.e., manipulating 3D forms freely in a 3D environment, allowing designers to grab and deform free formed surfaces at any point of the surface) were considered as an important breakthrough toward more efficient and intuitive design interfaces [17].

As a matter of fact, in these environments, users can experience an unmediated direct manipulation situation [18]. Assuming that the actions are performed directly on the objects by the user with his/her bare hands, the environments do not necessitate acting through artifacts such as display control points, widgets, icons. In that extent, it shortens the distance (between one's thoughts and the physical requirements of the system under use) and increases the engagement (the feeling that one is directly manipulating the objects of interest) [19].

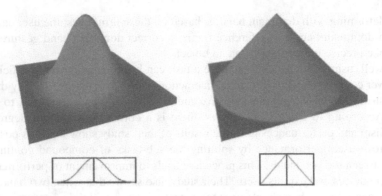

Fig. 8.1 Deformation tasks can be performed using both hands, in asymmetric situation. The use of both hands is expected to increase users control over the deformation and gesture range

8.3.2 The OMM Application

Our protocol implementation is based on *OMM*, a deformation application based on the *Twister* deformation model [20], in which users can freely perform deformation on 3D objects using their hands.

To control the application, users are provided with a menu allowing them to load or save an object, modify the current application mode (moving, scaling, or warping), and modify the objects parameters and the deformation parameters. Moving, scaling, and warping an object can be performed using unimanual gestures. The application can be used indifferently with one or both hands. The two hands can be used simultaneously (Fig. 8.1) or alternatively to manipulate or warp an object. Every deformation is defined by a deformation volume and a deformation function. Deformation volume defines the part of the object that will be warped. If the deformation volume intersects the object, every vertices laying inside the volume will be moved by the deformation. In OMM, the deformation volume is spherical and can vary in radius. The deformation function is a function f: R -> R, f(x) = y, with y in [0, 1], which defines how vertices laying inside the deformation volume will be affected by the deformation. When $f = 0$, it means not affected by the deformation, and when $f = 1$, it means fully affected by the deformation (*see* Fig. 8.2). This parameters can be modified using the menu.

The user uses a data glove to interact with the environment, position the starting point of the deformation gesture, and control the deformation shape (*see* Figs. 8.3–8.5). Our objective with this application is to develop an environment that proposes 3D modeling tools that will not require ad hoc devices to interact. In that purpose, we developed a wide range of tools that allows a user to rotate, translate, replace, and add objects with the sole use of the data gloves as an interaction device. Since these tools still need to be evaluated, we will not present them further here.

Fig. 8.2 Deformation examples with same deformation volume but different deformation functions

Fig. 8.3 An influence sphere is attached to the users' dominant hand. The deformation area is defined by the intersection of the selection sphere and the surface

8.4   Design Study

This study aims at investigating whether using bimanual interaction can improve performance in spatial input tasks, and how proprioception can be exploited to enhance users control over the task. In this section, we present our experimental setup and the hypothesis we investigated.

Fig. 8.4 By grasping the surface, the user validates the warped area

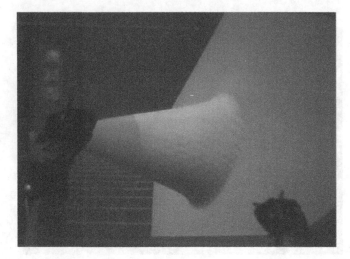

Fig. 8.5 The deformation is defined by both the position and the orientation of the hand at any moment during the deformation gesture

8.4.1 Subjects

We selected eight subjects with no prior experience with IVE. They were divided into two groups: group 1 achieved the two tasks using only the dominant hand, and group 2 had to use both hands. All subjects were right-handed and had normal or corrected to normal vision. We first presented the FFD application and hardware device to the subjects. We then allowed them to use it freely for a few minutes period. During this training session, they were allowed to use both unimanual or bimanual interaction to perform a deformation.

8.4.2   Apparatus

Experiments were conducted on a Barco Consul, a semi-immersive virtual reality environment using stereoscopic display – resolution 1,400 × 1,050, refreshed at 100 Hz – and CrystalEyes CE-2 glasses. Images were generated using two HP Workstation XW8000 – one for each screen – fit out with a 3 GHz Quad Xeon and a NVIDIA Quadro FX 3000. Head and hands tracking is ensured by the ART tracking system and magnetic trackers. Users used 5DT data gloves to interact with the virtual reality environment. Each result is converted to centimeters because of tracking system's precision.

8.4.3   Tasks

Subjects were asked to achieve two different tasks; each task was repeated 16 times.

In the first task, the designation task, the subject had to interact with a cube placed at a random position in the workspace. One at a time, each of the four corners belonging to the face in front of the user was highlighted by a red coloring. The user was required to grab – or designate – highlighted corner as precisely as possible and make a deformation to validate designation. During this session, the dominant hand of the user was surrounded with a colored sphere representing the deformation area. This sphere was here to help the user perceive the volume of the cube that would be influenced by the deformation. The user perfectly grabbed the corner when the center of the sphere attached to the user's hand perfectly matched with it. In the first condition, the user could only use the dominant hand to grasp the corner, while in the second condition, the user could manipulate (move and orientate) the object with the nondominant hand whereas the dominant hand would grab the highlighted corner. We hypothesized that the use of nondominant hand would bring higher comfort and efficiency in this designation task, leading to shorter completion times and higher accuracy. The accuracy was measured using the Euclidean distance between corner and center position.

In the second task, the docking task, two spheres were presented in the user's workspace. A red sphere represented a fix target, and a white sphere was to be manipulated by the user. The two spheres were randomly positioned. The user had to grasp the white sphere and put it in the target. To make a perfect match, the two centers had to coincide. In the first condition, the user had to grasp and put the sphere using the dominant hand; in the second condition, the user had to grasp the target sphere using the nondominant hand before grasping the white sphere using the dominant hand. The precision is measured by the Euclidean distance between the two spheres' centers. For this task, we did not expect shorter completion times, assuming that the subjects had to realize two separate tasks: grab the target and then grab and drop the movable sphere. However, we hypothesized higher accuracy for the bimanual condition, assuming that the second hand would allow the subject to exploit that proprioception has an additional information to perform the task (Fig. 8.6).

8.5   Results

Regarding task completion times in the designation task, while we expected group 2 to be faster than group 1, results show the opposite. For the first task, subjects of group 1 took an average time of 11.39 s to designate a vertex, whereas group 2 took an average of 14.05 s. This result is statistically significant ($p = 0.02$). For the second task, group 2 took an average of 15.02 s (this result was not statistically significant). These time values include the preliminary evaluation of the situation by the user, the realization of the task, and the validation of the action.

We expected bimanual interaction to prove faster than unimanual interaction for task 1, taking into account that it seems to be a more natural way of interacting with objects. As a matter of fact, holding an object with one hand while performing an operation on the object with another is a day-to-day activity. However, our results, with completion times increased by 2.66 s for group 2 in comparison of group 1, show that it may not be so intuitive to realize such a manipulation in IVE. Previous studies showed that the degree of parallelization is dependent on the conceptual integration of both subtasks into a single one [7]. This result tends to show that the positioning – using the nondominant hand – and the designation task – using the dominant hand – were not conceptually integrated as a unique task, which, we hypothesized, would have led to shorter realization times.

Concerning task 2, we hypothesized shorter completion times for the unimanual situation. This expectation mainly comes from the necessity of performing one supplementary action in the bimanual situation (grabbing the target), and assuming that this action could not be integrated to the main task at hand (positioning the sphere):

Fig. 8.6 The *designation task* with the user's sphere in blue (*left*) and the *docking task* (*right*)

the subjects first had to grab the target before turning their attention to the movable sphere. However, results show that the bimanual condition leads to shorter completion times for the overall measures, with completion times increased by 1.48 s for group 1 in comparison of group 2. Regarding placement times (the time to displace the sphere, after grabbing the two objects), group 2 is faster than group 1 with a mean difference of 3.54 s ($t = 7.40$ s vs $t = 10.94$ s; this result is statistically significant, with $p = 0.006$). This important difference can explain why group 2 was faster than group 1: the time spent for grabbing the target was regained during the docking phase, where the bimanual modality proved to be more efficient. It is surprising that such a gain was not observed during task 1. We think that this may be because in that case the two subtasks performed by each hand can easily be integrated in a unique conceptual objective – making the two spheres closer, while in task 1, each subtask had its own semantic objective: orientate and designate.

From the second result, we can assume that bimanual interaction can lead to shorter completion times for fully integrated task. However, the first result tends to show that bimanual interaction, although intuitive with real objects, is not fully exploited in IVEs. It may be because users need a learning period to integrate both subtasks into one conceptual task (which makes a deformation on a precise vertex), since the proper use of bimanual techniques for a combined operation may be more difficult to learn, as suggested by Gribnau [21]. In our experiment, the learning period consisted of manipulating a plan and a cube using one or two hands. Although this learning period was not limited, almost every subject took only about 5 min to try different modalities. It probably would have needed a longer learning period for users to fully exploit the whole potential of bimanual interaction.

These results are consistent with previous works that led to some doubts about whether bimanual interaction can lead to real improvements in the effectiveness of user interaction in IVEs [22]. Whereas our result shows significant improvements in the second task, the comparison with the results of task 1 suggests that it strongly depends on the structure of the task. Thus, considering that bimanual interaction is compelled to save time because each hand works in parallel may not always be an effective way to think about two-handed interface design. Bimanual interaction should be analyzed further to know how we should structure two-handed manipulations proposed to the final users.

Regarding precision, our results shows no difference between group 1 and group 2 for task 1. The two groups have the same average performance of 0.07 m. Performances for task 2 (Table 8.1) show that all distances of group 2 are smaller

Table 8.1 Docking task precisions measures: Euclidean distance, distance along each axis, and time needed to place the sphere on the target

	Group 1	Group 2	t-test
Distance$_{tot}$	0.058	0.012	$p = 0.024$
Distance$_x$	0.016	0.0036	$p = 0.14$
Distance$_y$	0.025	0.0067	$p = 0.04$
Distance$_z$	0.040	0.0061	$p = 0.03$

than those of group 1 and are statistically significant (except for x distance). These two results seem contradictory: for the two tasks, group 1 and 2 differ only in the use of bimanual interaction, but results indicate a positive influence of the bimanual modality in terms of precision only for task 2. We explain this result by whether or not the visual cues provided by the environment are sufficient to perform the task. In fact, subjects experienced difficulties for task 2 linked to the data glove sensitivity for postural detection between open hand and close hand. These difficulties lead to some involuntary drifts of the displaced sphere. It seems that in that case, the non-dominant hand presence as a reference was used to improve gesture control, whereas in task 1, only visual information (sphere of influence) was exploited. In task 2, it seems that the subjects actually used proprioceptive information, prob-ably because of the interferences' nature, which were linked to the proprioceptive information about the hand position during the target release stage.

Moreover, the gain in precision is more important regarding depth axis. It seems that the subjects' tendency was to place objects at height of sight, leading to occlu-sion phenomenon that canceled visual information about depth information. In this case, absence of visual cues is overcome using information from proprioception cues: the relative positions of each hand.

8.6   Conclusions and Perspectives

Our results show that bimanual interaction lead to better efficiency and comfort without the need for prior training only under a certain set of conditions. Concerning completion times, it seems that symmetrical tasks are performed quicker. Asymmetrical tasks, on the other hand, did not allow our subjects to take advantage of the bimanual interaction condition. We think that maybe with further practice, subjects would have obtained better performances.

We also found that bimanual interaction introduces proprioception that can be exploited when proper visual cues are missing. For task 1, the groups did not show any differences concerning precision. We think that this is because of the influence sphere we added in *OMM*. We think that the subjects, in that case, only relied on visual information to perform the task at hand. Yet, proprioception cues seem to have been used when visual information was inappropriate (problems to control the release of the sphere in task 2) or missing (depth information in task 2). In a future study, we would like to further investigate those results. We will analyze the impact of proper training to exploit bimanual interaction for asymmetrical tasks. We would also like to further evaluate the importance of proprioceptive cues to replace missing visual information. For example, we could intentionally create a lack of visual information, by avoiding the sphere around the subjects' hand in a designation task. We could also create a new task with an environment visually overloaded and see if bimanual interaction helps.

We would also like to investigate the impact of bimanual interaction on the possibility to ensure greater control and precision during the deformation gesture.

In a desktop modeling application, users generally refer to several visual cues to control the task at hand. In an IVE, adding the same visual clues could lead to a visual overload that would hinder the activity of the user. We think that it is possible to exploit proprioception to replace certain visual information, thus allowing the user to actually realize the deformation planed without relying only on the visual capabilities of the environment.

References

1. Christou, C., Angus, C., Loscos, C., Dettori, A., Roussou, M.: A versatile large-scale multi-modal VR system for cultural heritage visualization. In: M. Slater, Y. Kitamura, A. Tal, A. Amditis, Y. Chrysanthou (eds.) VRST. ACM, New York, pp. 133–140 (2006). URL http://dblp.uni-trier.de/db/conf/vrst/vrst2006.html#ChristouALDR06
2. Grossman, T., Balakrishnan, R.: Pointing at trivariate targets in 3D environments. In: CHI'04: Proceedings of the SIGCHI conference on Human factors in computing systems. ACM, New York, pp. 447–454 (2004). DOI http://doi.acm.org/10.1145/985692.985749
3. Wanger, L.C., Ferwerda, J.A., Greenberg, D.P.: Perceiving spatial relationships in computer-generated images. IEEE Comput. Graph. Appl. 12(3), 44–51; 54–58 (1992). DOI http://dx.doi.org/10.1109/38.135913
4. Boeck, J.D., Weyer, T.D., Raymaekers, C., Coninx, K.: Using the non-dominant hand for selection in 3D. In: 3DUI'06: Proceedings of the 3D User Interfaces, IEEE Computer Society, pp. 53–58, (2006)
5. Hinckley, K., Pausch, R., Goble, J.C., Kassell, N.F.: A survey of design issues in spatial input. In: UIST'94: Proceedings of the ACM symposium on User interface software and technology. ACM, pp. 213–222 (1994)
6. Kunert, A., Kulik, A., Huckauf, A., Fröhlich, B.: A comparison of tracking- and controller-based input for complex bimanual interaction in virtual environment. IPT/EGVE 2007: Eurographics Symposium on Virtual Environments, Weimar, Germany (2007)
7. Owen, R., Kurtenbach, G., Fitzmaurice, G., Baudel, T., Buxton, B.: When it gets more difficult, use both hands: exploring bimanual curve manipulation. In: GI'05: Proceedings of Graphics Interface. Canadian Human-Computer Communications Society, Ontario, pp. 17–24 (2005)
8. Wyss, H.P., Blach, R., Bues, M.: iSith – intersection-based spatial interaction for two hands. In: 3DUI'06: Proceedings of the 3D User Interfaces. IEEE Computer Society, Washington, pp. 59–61 (2006)
9. Leganchuk, A., Zhai, S., Buxton, W.: Manual and cognitive benefits of two-handed input: An experimental study. ACM Trans. Hum. Comput. Interact.5(4), pp. 326–359 (1998)
10. Mine, M.R., Brooks F.P., Sequin, C.H.: Moving objects in space: exploiting proprioception in virtual environment interaction. In: SIGGRAPH'97: Proceedings of Computer graphics and interactive techniques conference. ACM Press/Addison-Wesley, New York, pp. 19–26 (1997)
11. Ulinski, A., Zanbaka, C., Wartell, Z., Goolkasian, P., Hodges., L.F.: Two handed selection techniques for volumetric data. In: IEEE Symposium on 3D User Interfaces 2007. Charlotte, North Carolina, March 10–11. pp. 107–114 (2007)
12. Guiard, Y.: Asymmetric division of labor in human skilled bimanual action: the kinematic chain as a model. J. Mot. Behav. 9(18), 486–517 (1987)
13. Bagesteiro, L.B., Sarlegna, F.R., Sainburg, R.L.: Differential influence of vision and proprioception on control of movement distance. Exp. Brain Res. 171, 358–370 (2006)
14. Buxton, W., Myers, B.: A study in two-handed input. In: CHI'86: Proceedings of the SIGCHI conference on Human factors in computing systems. ACM, New York, pp. 321–326 (1986). DOI http://doi.acm.org/10.1145/22627.22390

15. Huckauf, A., Speed, A., Kunert, A., Hochstrate, J., Fr¨ohlich, B.: Evaluation of 12-dof input devices for navigation and manipulation in virtual environments. In: INTERACT. Springer, Berlin, pp. 601–614 (2005)
16. Kiyokawa, K., Takemura, H., Katayama, Y., Iwasa, H., Yokoya, N.: Vlego: A simple two-handed modeling environment based on toy block (1997). URL citeseer.ist.psu.edu/kiyoka-wa97vlego.html
17. Yamashita, J., Fukui, Y.: A direct deformation method. In: M. Slater, Y. Kitamura, A. Tal, A. Amditis, Y. Chrysanthou (eds.) Virtual Reality Annual International Symposium, 1993 IEEE, pp. 499–504 (1993)
18. Shneiderman, B.: Direct manipulation. Designing the User Interface. Addison-Wesley, Reading, MA (1992)
19. Hutchins, E.L., Hollan, J.D., Norman, D.A.: Direct manipulation interfaces. *Hum. Comput. Interact.* 1(4), 311–338 (1985)
20. Llamas, I., Kim, B., Gargus, J., Rossignac, J., Shaw, C.: Twister: A space-warp operator for the two-handed editing of 3D shapes (2003). URL citeseer.ist.psu.edu/llamas03twister.html
21. Gribnau, M.: Two-handed interaction in computer supported 3D conceptual modeling, Doctoral thesis, Delft University of Technology (1999)
22. Hinckley, K., Pausch, R., Proffitt, D., Kassell, N.F.: Two-handed virtual manipulation. *ACM Trans. Comput. Hum. Interact.* 5(3), 260–302 (1998)

Chapter 9
Design of a Model of Human Interaction in Virtual Environments

Javier Carlos Jerónimo, Angélica de Antonio, Gonzalo Méndez and Jaime Ramírez

Abstract In this chapter, we present a generic model for human interaction in virtual environments and the design of a software component that has been built according to this model for its use in the MAEVIF platform for intelligent virtual environments for education and training. We present the motivations and the main objectives and we detail the key design decisions and the way in which they have been realized in an object-oriented approach based on design patterns. Improved adaptability and extensibility are the main properties of the resulting interaction module.

9.1 Introduction

The real world is complex and the approaches to its 3D graphical representation are more and more detailed and accurate, but visual representation is only one part of the problem. Additionally, we need to provide the user with an interaction model which is, just like the graphical representation, as realistic as possible. This interaction model should go beyond basic actions like *move* or *touch*, dealing with the complex interactions that could take place in the real world, those in which a person moves and manipulates objects in a concrete order to achieve a certain goal.

The main objective of our work is the design of a software model of complex human interaction in virtual environments. Some requirements were considered essential for our design:

1. *Scalability*: The model must be applicable and easy to use for simple as well as for complex interactions.
2. *Extensibility*: The model must allow its easy expanding and making changes in some parts of the design while not affecting the others. This is one of the most

J.C. Jerónimo (✉), A. de Antonio, G. Méndez and J. Ramírez
Universidad Politécnica de Madrid, Campus de Montegancedo s/n, 28660,
Boadilla del Monte, Spain
e-mail: jcjeronimo@alumnos.upm.es

V. López-Jaquero et al. (eds.), *Computer-Aided Design of User Interfaces VI*,
DOI: 10.1007/978-1-84882-206-1_9, © Springer-Verlag London Limited 2009

important things we had in mind when creating the model because it will be probably expanded several times along its lifetime (to include new kinds of interactions or devices).

3. *Ease of integration*: Although the design is focused in a concrete platform that has fostered its design and implementation, it must be abstract enough to be easily integrated into other platforms. The overall goal is to design a generic model for human interaction in virtual environments, and the particular one, to implement and integrate it as a part of the MAEVIF platform.

MAEVIF is a platform for the development of education and training systems based on virtual environments [1, 2]. It is divided into two parts: (1) *Agent-based intelligent tutoring subsystem (ABITS):* this is the central part of the platform. It is composed of a group of software agents that collaborate for teaching and training. Each agent is focused in a particular topic of the teaching process: tutoring actions, student tracking, learning objectives... (2) *Graphics and interaction subsystem (GIS):* this is the program that runs in the users' terminals. Its purpose is to bring the user a 3D representation of the virtual world and to provide them with the possibility to interact with the environment using the devices available to them.

The agents in ABITS must share and analyze information about the actions that the students perform in the virtual environment. These actions must be assessed and evaluated to determine if the learning objectives are being achieved or not. This knowledge about the actions performed by the students is abstract in the sense that generally it does not matter how the user has effectively executed them (for instance, it may be important to know that the student opened the door, but not if he pressed the handle with his hand or if he pushed the door with his shoulder). Consequently, there is a need for an abstraction process that transforms the interactions that the user performs in the virtual world into the final actions that are important to the teaching process.

There could also be restrictions associated to the way actions can be performed. For instance, there could be actions that require a group of simple interactions to be conducted in a concrete order. Following the previous example, opening the door using the handle is composed of two elemental interactions: *put the hand on the handle* and *press down the handle*. Consequently, actions will be made up of groups of simple interactions with ordering constraints.

Additionally, nowadays there are a great variety of interaction devices that can be used in VR environments, ranging from simple ones such as keyboards, joysticks, and mouses to immersive VR devices such as data-gloves, haptic devices, tracking systems, and caves. The interaction model must not depend on the devices available in a particular execution environment, that is, it should support any kind of peripheral connected to the client's computer to allow the user to perform actions in the virtual world. Using the previous example of "*user A opens door X,*" the movement of his hand can be detected by a tracking system, and then he can press the handle by clicking a button or by doing a gesture with his real hand (which can be detected and interpreted by a data-glove or by a system of digital video cameras). Therefore, the interaction model should offer another abstraction from the concrete devices being used to the interaction events that are meaningful for the system.

9.2   Related Work

Trying to separate interaction devices control from VR applications is a problem that has been addressed in quite a lot of publications, such as in ref. [3]. However, as in the cited work, it is usual that ad hoc solutions are designed, so that the same problem has to be solved now and again every time a new system is built.

There are several systems that have addressed the same problem described in this chapter. One of the most popular is the VR Juggler suite [4], and more specifically one of its modules called Gadgeteer [5]. This module acts as a hardware device management system. It contains a dynamically extensible Input Manager that treats devices in terms of abstract concepts such as *positional*, *digital*, or *gesture*. Although designed to be modifiable, it is thought to be used together with the rest of the VR Juggler suite, which makes it unsuitable in cases where other VR platforms are preferred.

Other solutions include MR Toolkit [6] and VRPN [7]. Both are designed to support the transmission of peripheral data via packets on a network. This way, input devices can be moved to different machines or replaced with different devices (even at runtime) without requiring any changes to the source code of the applications that use them. CIDA [8] is a plug-in based input devices management platform that aims to abstract the type of the device used. According to the authors, the plug-in mechanism allows an easier addition of new devices.

Other applications such as the ones described in [9, 10] also provide a library or a framework to develop device-independent VEs. As in the case of VR Juggler, it appears that the whole bundle is needed in order to support different kinds of devices, while in the current work, given its layered structure, the devices level can be used separate from the rest.

There is another kind of tools that mainly consist of libraries that are best suited to interact with specific framework, as in the case of CAVELib and CAVE or EQUIP and MASSIVE-3 [11]. Although they may support a wide variety of devices, the fact that they are mainly crafted to work with a specific platform makes them less suitable for extensive use.

Finally, some approaches make use of unusual interaction devices such as the ones described in [12], where eye gaze is used as the main interaction technique. Although using an appropriate abstraction should be easily done, it is still necessary to experiment how this kind of interaction can be integrated.

9.3   General Design of the Interaction Module

9.3.1   Abstraction Layer

Following the requirements and considerations presented in Sect. 9.2, our interaction model design provides an abstraction layer made up of three different levels: (1) abstract actions that the ABITS can understand (we will call these *operators*).

Some example operators are *give something to someone, take something somewhere, activate some object, establish a relationship between two objects....* (2) Basic interactions (we will call these *behaviors*). Example behaviors are *touch, grab, release, push...* Behaviors can be grouped to define operators. (3) Interaction devices that can be used to perform the basic interactions. We will call *device* to any process that can collect input from the user. It can be implemented with a physical peripheral or some other software elements like a menu, a voice recognition system, a pseudo-device like a remote administration console, or a collision detector active in the 3D graphics engine. In short, it can be anything that launches events that can be considered as user input.

The separation between the three levels provides an extraordinary flexibility to the system, allowing the developer to reuse existing behaviors and/or operators and making easier the design of new ones. The model also allows us to associate any existing or future device to any behavior. This is fundamental because of the great amount of different peripherals that could be alternatively used in the system. Furthermore, we could use various devices at the same time to generate the same behavior, which could be useful under some circumstances. This design brings us the possibility to expand any of the levels without making changes to the others.

9.3.2   World Objects Representation

Every object in the virtual world is known as an *entity*. This concept also includes the parts of an object or avatar representing the user: body, arms, head, etc.

An *entity* is any virtual object that has the following characteristics:

1. A 3D representation. Commonly known as a *model* in 3D terms.
2. A collection of attributes: 3D coordinates and orientation, name, parent, and children *entities*...
3. Behaviors that indicate what can be done with the object, and what the object can do with its environment (other *entities*).

This representation of objects comes from the design of the MAEVIF GIS, and has been adopted because of its power and ability to be easily used and expanded. An *entity* as it is defined in the GIS can be expanded with additional attributes and methods by the modules connected to the GIS (our interaction module is a module of the GIS). Only a few entities will be managed by the interaction module, namely those representing the parts of the user body that he/she can use to interact with the world: fingers and hands, for instance. The connection of operators, via behaviors, to these avatar entities will make it possible for the user to interact with other entities of the virtual world.

We have defined three main software object classes representing the actions executed by the user, in three levels of abstraction: *Operator*, *Behavior*, and *Device*. The additional *Entity* class, besides the properties related to interaction, has information about the behaviors that the entity can launch. Two manager classes will store and keep under control the instances of the relevant classes: *OperatorsManager* and *DevicesManager*.

9.3.3   Adaptability and Extensibility Mechanisms

In order to enforce the adaptability of the interaction module, we need to be able to create different types of instances of these classes (the ones which are relevant for a given virtual environment and hardware setting) and to establish relationships between them with a minimum coupling. We also want to maximize the extensibility of the module, minimizing the effort required to add new behaviors or devices that were not considered in the initial design.

For instance, we want behaviors to maintain relationships with all the devices that can be used to launch it. A specific behavior such as *push* could be launched using used, keyboard, data-glove, etc. We would need to define different subclasses of the *Device* class for different types of devices, but we do not want the behavior to know any details about the creation of device instances nor even be aware of the device types.

The solution adopted is the definition of abstract factories that create the necessary objects based on external definition files provided to them. For example, if we need to create a device object, we only need to read the definition of that device and send it to the proper abstract factory, which in turn will make use of the concrete factory available for the device's subclass. In this way, the only class that will have knowledge about the relevant classes and their relationships is the *configuration manager* (Fig. 9.1).

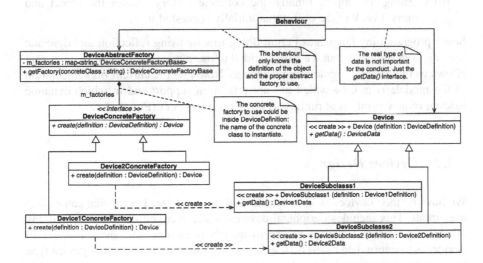

Fig. 9.1 Use of abstract factories to create the devices associated to one behavior

The *configuration manager* is an essential part of the interaction model. It deals with a lot of configuration settings, most of them detailing the relevant entities and devices in a given virtual environment and hardware setting. But it also allows for an easy extension of the interaction module with new *behaviors* and *device types*. The latter extensions will require, in addition to new configuration settings, the definition of new subclasses as an extension of the base classes in the framework, and the definition of new concrete factories, but without any modification of the existing code except for the *configuration manager*.

The initialization method responsible for the creation of all the required objects is as follows:

1. *Registration of subclasses*: the *configuration manager* registers all the subclasses he/she knows in the proper abstract factories, establishing the relationship with their corresponding concrete factories. New subclasses added in the future will require the modification of this registration process.
2. *Definitions of objects*: the *configuration manager* creates a definition object for each subclass of the system from the configuration settings it loads.
3. *Creation of an object*:
    (a) Asking for a definition: when one object (e.g. the behavior push) needs to create and establish a relationship with an instance of another class (e.g. a certain mouse device), it asks the configuration manager for the corresponding definition.
    (b) Calling the abstract factory: the object sends the definition to the proper abstract factory.
    (c) Delegating to concrete factory: the abstract factory locates the concrete factory corresponding to the class, as it was previously registered, and sends the definition to it.
    (d) Creating the object: Finally, the concrete factory creates the object and returns it back to the object that initially requested it.

Some programming languages permit doing this by using reflection and dynamic loading of new classes, but we have decided to use a more general mechanism that allows us to use any programming language. Note that the current implementation of the module is in C++ which has not reflection support and in which dynamic loading of new symbols at runtime is platform dependent (Fig. 9.2).

9.3.4 Devices Design

We have defined devices as an abstraction of any software library that can collect user input. This includes peripheral devices, voice recognition libraries, and any other software that we want to use to launch behaviors. The main purpose of devices is to return data based on user input. In order to consider a new device type by the interaction module, the abstract method *getData()* must be implemented in

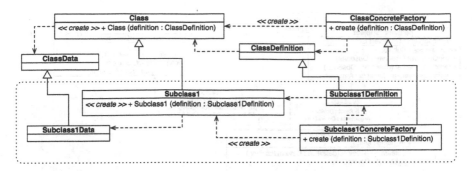

Fig. 9.2 Example of a class in the design with its own concrete factory, definition, and data. Using this structure in the class and registering it in the proper abstract factory (in the *configuration manager* initialization) will make its creation accessible from any other class of the design

the new device subclass. The separation between behaviors and devices also requires that all devices return the same class of data. This is achieved by another abstraction: *DeviceData*.

We have defined two steps for the process of obtaining data from the device:

1. *Poll*: device objects are periodically polled to update its internal state with new data available in the underlying software. The *devices manager* calls the *getData()* method of each device, which is implemented in the concrete subclass.
2. *Notify*: devices notify associated behaviors only when new data is available.

The first step is executed several times per second (every frame in most of the cases). Most of the device drivers use polling to obtain new data from the peripheral. When the underlying device software library provides notification mechanisms, polling can be ignored. It is possible that in most polls, no updated data is available. This is why we have decided to introduce the second step: to prevent the system from overloading behaviors with messages containing redundant data. The second step ensures that only messages containing new data are sent from devices to behaviors.

To achieve this goal, a device makes two uses of the observer pattern: first, as an observer in polls; and second, if there is new data available in any poll, as a subject to notify the registered behaviors (Fig. 9.3).

9.3.5 Behaviors Design

A behavior is any basic interaction that the user is allowed to perform in the virtual environment. A group of behaviors, in a concrete order, can launch an operator and so let the simulation system know what the user is doing in the virtual environment.

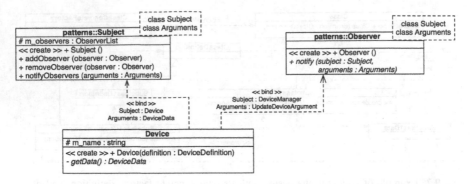

Fig. 9.3 Use of the observer design pattern by the *device* class. There is also an example of a special device that notifies about collisions between entities detected in the 3D engine

As explained in earlier sections, a behavior can have a group of devices associated to it. This provides us the possibility to launch it in various different ways. The problem here is that some devices will return a vector of real numbers, others a pair of entities (for instance, a pseudo-device that detects collisions in the 3D engine), or even a sentence uttered by the user and recognized by a voice software library.

When a device notifies a behavior that it has new data and sends the data, the processing of the data to determine if the launching requirements for the behavior are met would require the behavior to have knowledge of the type of data and the way to process it, adding a dependency of the behavior on the device. Another option would be having the device itself make that decision, and not simply returning the data, but then we would have the same problem reversed: a dependency of the device on the behavior; if we created a new behavior, we should modify the existing device to introduce the knowledge related to the new behavior and its activation.

To avoid any dependency, we have introduced an external *evaluator* class. There will be an evaluator specialized in each behavior–device association. For example, let's suppose we have a *touch* behavior and a *device* for joysticks that returns a float. When the user moves the joystick axis, the position is represented in the interval [−1.0…1.0] and when the user pushes a joystick button, the data shows if it is pressed or not (−1.0 not pressed, 1.0 pressed). Let's suppose that we already have an *evaluator* that processes this kind of data and determines whether or not the behavior must be launched. Now we introduce a voice recognition library as a device, returning strings like *touch object*. It is obvious that the existing *evaluator* does not work with the new kind of data, but the only thing we must do is to create a new *evaluator* for each behavior we want to be activated by the new device.

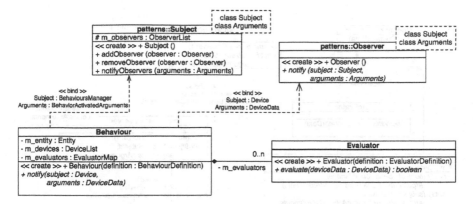

Fig. 9.4 Behavior class with its two uses of the observer design pattern: it receives events from the devices associated and it sends events to the behavior manager

With this design, we keep devices and behaviors clearly separated, allowing new additions to the system with the minimum changes to existing classes (Fig. 9.4).

9.3.6   Operators Design

An *operator* represents an abstract interaction of the user with the virtual environment, such as *take something* or *give something to someone*. These operators are independent from initiator and targets, as the action is always the same but with different arguments. Therefore, there is only one instance of each operator class. Furthermore, an operator can be made of several behaviors executed in a concrete order. Thus, we have introduced a concept similar to the *evaluator* that here is called *detector*. A *detector* is an external class that the operator uses to know when it has been activated. The detector will process behaviors executed by the user and it will launch the operator when the requirements are meet.

We have designed *detector* as an abstract class to avoid restricting its internal design. Different types of detectors can be implemented if the existing ones are too not enough for new operators to be created. For a *detector* to do its job, it is required to detect the creation of new behaviors. Moreover, whenever a behavior is executed by the user, all the detectors depending on it must know about this event. These two situations have been solved with two applications of the observer pattern (*see* Fig. 9.5): first, when a behavior's concrete factory creates a new object, it notifies the behaviors manager so that it can notify this event to all the detectors; second, after a behavior has been created and the detectors are notified, if the behavior is

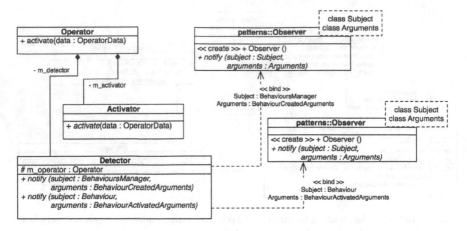

Fig. 9.5 Operator design with its detector and activator

relevant to the operator's requirements, it will be observed so that when it is launched by the user, the detector is notified of this event.

Our detector class implements a finite state automaton that tracks the behaviors launched by the user and determines when the requirements of the operator are met. Figure 9.6 shows an example: the *take something* operator's detector has been implemented as a finite state automaton with three states. The requirement to pass from the initial state to the intermediate one is the *touch object* behavior. Then, the transition from this intermediate state to the final one is allowed by the *take* behavior (with the meaning of *close hand*). In the final state, we can be sure that the user wants to launch the operator *take something* as he/she has touched an object and has closed hand (in this order).

This design is very simple and allows us to completely define the specific automata in the configuration file. For more complex operators, if automata are not powerful enough, it will be possible and easy to define a new kind of detector (for instance, based on a Petri net) directly usable by the system.

We have created an automata template library in such a way that it is easy for the user to completely define a new automaton just by using configuration settings (the system will create dynamically the automata at runtime). The assignment of a detector object to a particular operator is done at runtime.

The activation of the operator by the detector when the activation requirements are met is realized by a message from the detector to the operator containing all the arguments related to the abstract action that the operator represents. For example, in the *take something* operator, this message must contain the actor and the object.

In the MAEVIF platform, the process of activating an operator implies the creation of a JSON message which is sent to the ABITS, but we anticipate that in other uses of this interaction module, the consequence might be different. This led us to design the operator in such a way that it uses an external class to do the real activation of the operator. In our case, this activation object will be a network client that will marshal the operator's activation arguments in a JSON string that will be sent across the network to the agents platform. Figure 9.7 summarizes the data flow involved in the process of collecting user input data and analyzing it.

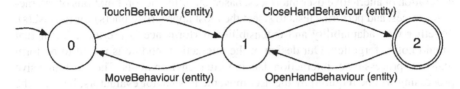

Fig. 9.6 Operator's detector designed as a finite state automaton

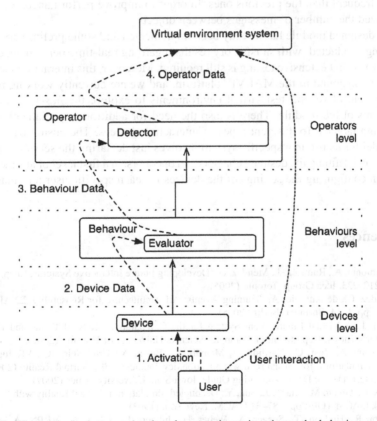

Fig. 9.7 When a device has new data based on user input, it activates the behaviors associated and they process the data using the corresponding evaluator object. If the device data meets the requirements for activating the user behavior, the data flow will reach the top level of operators in which there will be more processing to determine whether or not an operator must be activated

9.4 Conclusions

Our main goal when designing our interaction model was to create a powerful but at the same time simple design, and an easily extensible module. This chapter presents the resulting design detailing the rationale for the most important design decisions. The flexibility of the designed interaction module allows for an easy generation of alternative user interfaces, based on different combinations of interaction devices, and performs tests to select the most appropriate one(s) for the task(s). Together with adaptability and extensibility, performance is a critical factor that should not be forgotten. Our design of the interaction module is meant to perform real-time processing of interaction data in virtual environments. The most intensive processing will be required by the user movement behavior evaluators, because the user will probably update those peripherals every frame. Other behaviors will be associated to asynchronous events too, but those events (*take*, *push*, *touch*) will be less frequent than the previous ones. In order to improve performance, we have minimized the number of messages between objects.

The designed module has already been implemented and some preliminary tests are being conducted, with satisfactory results regarding real-time performance and memory use, but extensive testing is still required. Moreover, this interaction module has been integrated in the MAEVIF platform, and we are currently working in the development of several test virtual environments to explore the possibilities and constraints of the module. There is also the need for additional specializations of the design targeted to different types of interaction devices. The customization of the model for its use in a specific system involves just declaring the set of available devices, and defining the desired behaviors and operators, in a first level of abstraction, and then configuring the settings of the devices for each specific user terminal.

References

1. de Antonio, A., Ramírez, J., Méndez, G.: Developing Future Interactive Systems, Chap. VIII, pp. 212–233. Idea Group, Toronto (2005).
2. Méndez, G., de Antonio, A.: Training Agents: An Architecture for Reusability. LNAI, vol. 3661, pp. 1–14. Springer, Berlin (2005).
3. Chen, J.: A Virtual Environment System for the Comparative Study of Dome and HMD. Master's Thesis, Department of Computer Science, University of Houston (2002).
4. Bierbaum, A., Just, C., Hartling, P., Meinert, K., Baker, A., Cruz-Neira, C.: VR Juggler: A virtual platform for virtual reality application development. IEEE Virtual Reality (2001).
5. Gadgeteer: Device Driver Authoring Guide. Iowa State University, Ames (2007).
6. Shaw, C., Green, M., Liang, J., Sun, Y.: Decoupled Simulation in Virtual Reality with the MR Toolkit. ACM TOIS, pp. 287–317. ACM, New York (1993).
7. Taylor, R., Hudson, T., Seeger, A., Weber, H., Juliano, J., Helser, A.: VRPN: A Device Independent, Network-Transparent VR Peripheral System. VRST, pp. 55–61. ACM. New York (2001).
8. Kelner, J., Teichrieb, V., Farias, T., Rodrigues, C., Pessoa, S., Teixeira, J., Costa, N.: CIDA: An Interaction Devices Management platform. Proceedings SVR 2006, pp. 271–284 (2006).

9. Blach, R., Landauer, J., Rsch, A., Simon, A.: A Highly Flexible Virtual Reality System. Future Generation Computer Systems Special Issue on Virtual Environments (1998).
10. Kessler, G.D., Bowman, D.A., Hodges, L.F.: The Simple Virtual Environment Library: An Extensible Framework for Building VE Applications. Presence 9(2), 187–208 (2000)
11. Greenhalgh, C., Izadi, S., Rodden, T., Benford, S.: The EQUIP Platform: Bringing Together Physical and Virtual Worlds. Technical report, University of Nottingham, UK (2001).
12. Vinayagamoorthy, V., Garau, M., Steed, A., Slater, M.: An Eye Gaze Model for Dyadic Interaction in an Immersive Virtual Environment: Practice and experience. Computer Graphics 23(1), 1–11 (2004).

Chapter 10
A Space Model for 3D User Interface Development

José P. Molina, Pascual González, Jean Vanderdonckt,
Arturo S. García and Diego Martínez

Abstract Space deserves a special attention when designing 3D user interfaces. However, many proposed methods rely on simple sketches and/or maps. Besides, those methods usually leave aside the 2D interfaces that may be found in the 3D environment or that surround it. This chapter presents an attempt to formalize 2D and 3D spaces by the definition of a meta-model. This is one of three meta-models that have been defined in *three-dimensional user interface development* methodology, which is also described here along with some case studies, focusing the description on space.

10.1 Introduction

As a definition, a 3D user interface (3D UI) is one in which the language used by the user to introduce commands and information into the computer and/or the language used by the computer to present information to the user are based on the physical space and its three dimensions. That is, either the user employs 3D devices to interact with the system, or the system renders 3D images to the user, or both. Over the years, there has been a remarkable effort to understand these 3D UIs through the tasks, the interaction techniques that were proposed to support them and the systematic evaluation of such techniques. However, if there is anything that characterizes these interfaces, this is precisely the 3D space, so it is important to understand and model it.

In the case of 2D graphical user interfaces (2D GUIs), the methods proposed for their development frequently included some sort of 2D space modelling, for example with diagrams that specify the layout of the controls on a window or diagrams that specify navigation paths through windows. These specifications are then used by programmers to create the final interface, for example LUCID [1] and OVID [2],

J.P. Molina (✉), P. González, J.Vanderdonckt, A.S. García and D. Martínez
Laboratory of User Interaction and Software Engineering (LoUISE), Instituto
de Investigación en Informática de Albacete (I3A), Universidad de Castilla-La Mancha,
Campus universitario s/n, S-02071 Albacete, Spain
e-mail: jpmolina@dsi.uclm.es

V. López-Jaquero et al. (eds.), *Computer-Aided Design of User Interfaces VI*,   103
DOI: 10.1007/978-1-84882-206-1_10, © Springer-Verlag London Limited 2009

or compiled to generate it automatically, for example IDEAS [3]. In the case of 3D
UIs, proposed methods usually rely on sketches and maps to specify the position of
objects in 3D space, for example Fencott [4], SENDA [5] and IDEAS-3D [6], a sort
of similar specification that, this time, is delivered to content creators that shape this
space and its objects using 3D modelling tools.

However, previous methods usually forget that 3D environments do not exclude
2D GUIs [7], so it must be considered how to specify not only the two spaces but
also their relationships. Granollers et al. [8], for instance, introduced an augmented
dialogue model to match positions in the real world with the dialogues of a conventional interface, in the context of an Augmented Reality (AR) system. Furthermore,
real space is not only of interest in systems that augment real places with virtual
objects, but it is the space that devices and users belong to, so it should also be
considered in the development of any kind of interface.

In this context, this chapter examines the problem of understanding and modelling
space, or rather the spaces, and the relationships between them. To do so, this chapter
will first present an extension to the Reality–Virtuality continuum by Milgram and
Kishino [9], in order to cover three spaces, the real, the virtual and the so-called
digital one, which is also useful to understand the evolution of UIs from one to
three dimensions. Then, based on this new continuum, it will be presented the space
meta-model proposed in this work, again distinguishing between those three
spaces, but also describing their relationships.

This meta-model is actually one of the three that have been proposed for the
development of 3D UIs. With respect to the other two, there is one that tackles objects
and their classification, and the other one defines interaction elements and their
relationships. The latter is described in [10]. Together they provide the language
that supports a new methodology called *ThRee-Dimensional uSer interface Development*
(TRES-D), a structured approach that is oriented to task and interaction as well as to
objects and content, being space the third apex of this triangle. The process defined in
this methodology is also described in this chapter, as well as some case studies,
focusing on space and the proposed meta-model.

10.2   Extending the UI Continuum

On the basis of continuum by Milgram and Kishino, a new one is proposed with the aim
of offering a wider view of UIs, considering not only 3D UIs, but also 2D GUIs and
command-based interfaces, that is, 1D UIs. Figure 10.1 shows this new continuum.

In this proposal, the UIs are distributed along one axis according to their number
of dimensions, from one to three. This way, the continuum represents a wider one,
named *digital–virtual–real*, using "digital" to refer to the world of binary digits
used in computers as opposed to the world of real objects where humans live.
Besides, in the same way, the intermediate space between the real and the virtual is
called *Mixed Reality*; there is an intermediate space between the digital and the
virtual too, named *Mixed Virtuality*. 3D desktops fit in this new intermediate

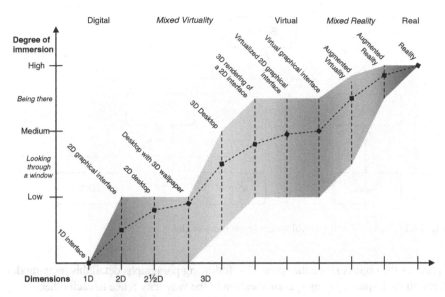

Fig. 10.1 Digital–virtual continuum for user interfaces

space, such as Win3D [11] or 3DNA [12], where the wallpaper is replaced by a 3D world, and so do Cube [13], SphereXP [14], Looking Glass [15] and Compiz Fusion [16], where windows are rendered as textures on flat surfaces that can be moved further or closer, and even be rotated. Transforming widgets into true 3D objects takes the UI one step further, resulting in a virtualized user interface (VUI) [7].

Furthermore, this new digital–virtual–real continuum adds a second axis that is related to the degree of immersion that, compared to reality, is experienced by the user when interacting with the space provided by the interface. This vertical axis follows this scale: *zero, low, medium, high*. Thus, when an interface is classified between the first two values, it means that users do not feel immersed in the space, or that feeling is very poor. In these interfaces, some depth cues may be given, such as shadows or overlays in 2D desktop interfaces, but that does not make the user feel in the space. Between low and medium, the user looks at the space through a window, possibly interacting with objects within using the "TV model," using the same term as by van Dam [17]. Between medium and high, the user does feel immersed in the 3D space. Current limits of Virtual Reality (VR) technology prevent it from offering the highest degree of immersion, which belongs to reality.

10.3   A Space Meta-Model

This meta-model is inspired in the digital–virtual–real continuum introduced in Sect. 10.2, making a distinction between these three spaces, as the diagram shown in Fig. 10.2 illustrates. That diagram also shows an aggregation relationship between objects and

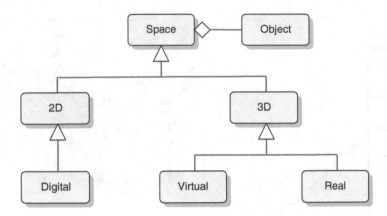

Fig. 10.2 Digital, virtual and real spaces in the meta-model

space, as the objects shape the space. The following paragraphs detail this meta-model through each space, paying special attention to the way they relate to each other.

10.3.1 The Digital 2D Space

As stated in Sect. 10.1, the idea of modelling space is not associated to the design of 3D UIs alone, and these interfaces do not exclude 2D interaction. Examples of modelling 2D space in conventional interfaces are the dialogue interaction and the component specification diagrams introduced by the IDEAS methodology in its dialogue model, graphically defining the navigation paths and the layout of window elements.

In general, the layout of controls in a window can be formalized defining a set of spatial relationships. Trevisan et al. [18] explain how to generalize Allen's 13 temporal relationships to 2D space, building a matrix (*Allen's 2D matrix*) that formalizes the possible space relationships between two controls in a 2D GUI. This formalization can also be useful in this part of the meta-model that is being proposed, as 2D controls can also be found in 3D UIs. Indeed, there is one 2D control that deserves special attention, the viewport, which represents the link between the digital and the virtual space, as it will be explained next.

10.3.2 The Virtual 3D Space

When working on IDEAS-3D, a previous attempt to 3D UIs development by extending IDEAS methods, first thoughts led to relate *viewpoints* and *places* in virtual worlds to dialogues in 2D GUIs. In fact, a window represents a *view* of the application dialogue. And, in the same way, the user of a 2D interface navigates through windows, the user of a virtual world can also jump from one viewpoint to another, from place to place.

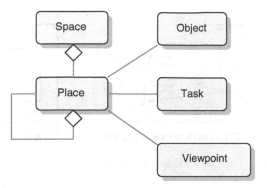

Fig. 10.3 The concept of place is common to all spaces

This follows the idea proposed in the RealPlaces design guide [19], so that the virtual space is structured in places in a hierarchical way, then associating an appropriate viewpoint to each place. In the IDEAS-3D methodology, that hierarchy of places mirrors the one of tasks, and so it is also a mechanism to relate space with the rest of models.

However, in both RealPlaces and IDEAS-3D, the world in mind was a horizontal, flat one, where the user navigates following the terrain, only taking off of it to jump from one place to another. However, such a conception of 3D space is limited for the general development of 3D UIs, such as the virtual interfaces found in many virtual worlds. Thus, places of interest are not always open spaces related to particular tasks; in some virtual worlds, the avatar can fly or orbit and, in general, there is not a single world but a set of interconnected worlds. At the same time, the identification of distinct regions in space can also be useful for other purposes, such as to specify the boundaries of the virtual world that limits the avatar movement, the maximum distance illuminated by the rays of a light source or reached by the waves of a sound source, or the view frustum associated to a viewpoint.

Then, even though the concept of place is included in this model, it gives way to a free structuring that can serve to different purposes needed in 3D UIs. As shown in Fig. 10.3, this concept of place is also common to the three spaces, although it is in the virtual one, here described, and in the real one, described later, where it has more relevance. That figure also shows the relationship that a place can have with objects, tasks and viewpoints. A place can also relate with other places, for instance building a hierarchy as in RealPlaces, and so making that hierarchy extensible to objects, tasks and viewpoints that relate to those places.

That freedom when structuring 3D space does not mean that this space cannot be formalized. In fact, the previous proposal from Trevisan et al. could be brought to this space too, generalizing Allen's relationships to 3D space by building a new matrix, which should now formalize the spatial relationships between two objects in a virtual world (and then named *Allen's 3D matrix*).

Furthermore, it could be said that this part of the model does not only cover the space in virtual worlds, featuring their three dimensions, but also the space of windows and widgets, as the latter could be described as a subspace of the former (Fig. 10.4).

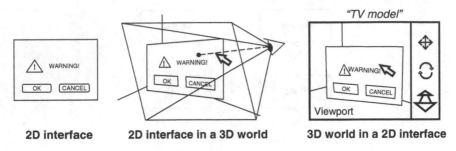

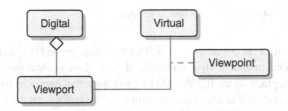

Fig. 10.4 A 2D interface in a 3D world and vice versa

Fig. 10.5 A viewport serve as a link between digital and virtual spaces

However, integrating both spaces is not usually a straightforward task. On the one hand, in contrast to the components of a window, the objects found in virtual worlds are not measured in screen units – pixels, but in physical units such as metres. One solution to this is to render 2D GUIs on the screen of a virtual computer in the 3D space, a solution proposed in [20] and realized in [7].

On the other hand, 3D environments are also integrated in 2D interfaces, in this case by means of an element named *viewport* (*see* Fig. 10.5), cited in Sect. 10.3.1, a 2D component that is used to project the virtual world onto a plane using a viewpoint as the centre of projection. The viewport is, this way, the retina of the eye of the user's avatar and, as such, is part of that avatar, as the rest of its virtual representation. As a 2D component, the viewport is integrated in a 2D GUI, being usually surrounded by other 2D controls in desktop applications, which represents the "TV model" cited before (*see* Fig. 10.4). In other cases, particularly in immersive applications, this component fully covers the screen, and those 2D controls are then rendered within the viewport as a *Head Up Display*. Besides, a 2D interface can have several viewports showing different views on the same virtual world, even in different screen displays, as it will be seen in the next section.

10.3.3 The Real 3D Space

In an AR application, space may be a building, for example a museum, or a place outdoors, for example an archaeological site. In the case of VR or Augmented Virtuality, it is easier to find smaller places, such as the one that fills a CAVE-like installation or even a simple desktop. As in virtual worlds, the concept of *place* is also necessary, describing the spaces that physical structures shape, for example the halls of a museum, or the spaces defined by the application, for example the space that surrounds a showcase in one of those halls.

Similarly, the concept of *viewpoint* is also important here. However, unlike the virtual worlds, where the user's avatar can lie exactly on the point of view just by clicking on a button, in the AR paradigm, it is the users who move, by their own means, to such position, or turn their own head to look in that direction, so the result is rather an approximation to the fixed positions and/or orientations. Despite differences such as this, the model of the real space is, so far, very similar to the model of the virtual world.

Indeed, the physical devices are the link between the real world and the digital or virtual one, and at this point, the model relies on previous ideas already presented in [21], particularly on the environment model that was developed for the UsiXML language [22]. That previous model describes the hardware platforms that the users interact with in their physical environment, with special attention to the surfaces associated with such platforms, such as the screen of a monitor or a projection system, considered as *interaction surfaces*. The latter term was introduced in [23], and defined as any physical surface that can be observed (e.g. by looking at the screen) or that can be acted on (e.g. by using the mouse pointer), which allows interaction with the system, either visible or embedded (Figs. 10.6 and 10.7).

However, there is no doubt that the concept of interaction surface was introduced with the 2D GUIs in mind, which are presented in flat panel displays. Instead, there is a need to extend it beyond 2D and introduce the concept of *interaction volume*, more suitable for 3D UIs where interaction is not constrained to the plane but takes place in the 3D of real space. Thus, an interaction volume can be defined by the scope of a tracking system, but also a computer monitor can create a volume of interaction in front of it when presenting 3D stereo images, overlapping the virtual with the real dimensions (Figs. 10.6 and 10.7). In fact, the representation of synthetic 3D images in a viewport on the screen of a monitor also creates a volume of interaction

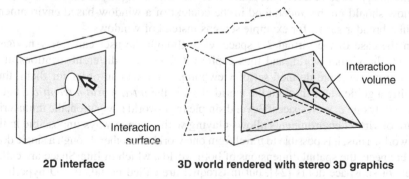

2D interface   **3D world rendered with stereo 3D graphics**

Fig. 10.6 Interaction surface and volume associated to a presentation device

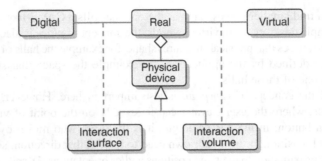

Fig. 10.7 Interaction surfaces and volume link real space to digital and virtual ones

behind that screen, although it cannot be reached by extending the hand. Moreover, these images are calculated on the basis of a point of view that has its correspondence with a point in the real world, so that the users will see the 3D effect if their position matches that point.

10.3.4 Intra-, Inter- and Trans-Spatial Transitions

The digital and virtual spaces are potentially infinite, only limited by technology, and the limits of the real space are beyond our world. However, digital and virtual content are usually bounded, as well as objects in the real world involved in the interaction. Nevertheless, the user's view of the previous spaces and their contents is often partial, incomplete. Some of the reasons for this are physical, related to human perception or presentation devices. Other reasons come from interface design, related to the tasks to be supported and the users' abilities to perform them. In any case, users must navigate to get a complete view, changing their viewpoint.

In the case of digital 2D space, proposed methods include specific diagrams to model these transitions, such as the Dialogue Interaction diagram in the IDEAS methodology, cited before. This is the *inter-window navigation*, but the concept of window should not be understood in the context of a window-based environment, but in a broader sense, for example screens instead of windows.

In the case of the virtual 3D space, even though the user can freely navigate through the virtual world, and thus explore it from very different locations, it is common to set a pre-defined set of viewpoints, and also an order for them, thus creating a guided tour through the world. This is the *intra-world navigation*, but is not the only one in such spaces. Beyond simple intra-world navigation, the immaterial nature of virtual environments allows playing with space in ways impossible in the real world. Thus, it is possible to travel from one world to another through a single door that connects the spatial dimensions of both worlds, which in InterSpace are called super- or subspace doors [24], but in Croquet are called portals or 3D hyperlinks [25]. Pre-defined viewpoints may well serve as entry points to the target world.

This is the *inter-world navigation*. The last type of navigation that is included in this meta-model is named *trans-spatial navigation*. It models transitions that occur in a space that is tied to another. This is what happens when the current viewpoint in a virtual world changes according to the movement of the user in the real world, thanks to the use of certain tracking devices. Another example, this time from an AR application, is the augmented dialogue that is described in [8], which binds the presentation of certain 2D GUIs to the arrival of a visitor at different points in the archaeological site.

10.4   The TRES-D Methodology

The process model of the TRES-D methodology is supported on the concepts and the terms provided by the space meta-model presented in Sect. 10.3, and the other two cited in Sect. 10.1, that is, the object and the interaction meta-models. This methodology derives from a careful study of previous approaches and one first attempt, named IDEAS-3D. It gives shape to a framework where different practices and tools for the general development of 3D UIs are gathered. The whole process is characterized by two main phases. The aim of the first one – the *previous study* – is to propose a solution to a given problem and, only if it is accepted, then the second phase follows – the *detailed study* – to complete the proposed design, and to implement and deploy it (Fig. 10.8).

In each stage, it is possible to prepare in advance some work of subsequent stages, so that the developer can foresee the problems that may need to be faced. In fact, the stage of solution proposal is meant to tackle in advance part of the work that would belong to the phase of detailed study. An agreement with the client mediates between both phases, as it is the client who has to approve the proposed solution. Once at the second phase, the design is addressed at two different levels, one detached from the implementation details – design I, and another one tightly related to that implementation – design II. A decision on which software and hardware will support the solution divides both design levels. In any case, both design I and II, and later the implementation stage, are divided in two parallel

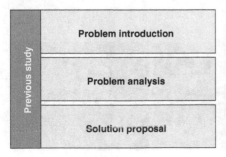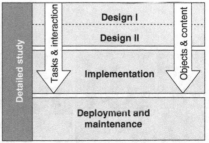

Fig. 10.8 TRES-D process model

activity chains. One of them is oriented to the interaction and the other one to the objects, following the proposed meta-models, translating the weight towards one or the other depending on each particular development, but in any case crossing both lines at several points of the development, specially due to their relationship with the third model, the space model. The last stage, deployment and maintenance, cannot be forgotten in the development of this kind of interfaces, which is quite often characterized by their non-conventional hardware.

10.5 Case Studies

Molina et al. [26] used three different projects to illustrate the structured development of 3D UIs that the TRES-D methodology proposes. This time, these projects are used to illustrate the meta-model presented in this chapter. One of these projects had the objective of creating a videogame for PC desktop that allowed the user to get into the game using 3D stereographics and a dataglove, and so the interest was to find a low-cost solution. The second of these projects pursued the virtualization of a block-based construction game in an immersive VR system, looking this time for the highest degree of naturalness. Finally, the third one was aimed at reproducing the UI shown in "Minority Report," the movie, using all available means for this purpose. Figure 10.9 shows all of them.

Starting with the videogame, it added stereo 3D graphics to the popular Tetris game, and so it was named TTristereo. It involved three spaces, the digital, the virtual and the real one. On the one hand, game menus were designed in 2D space, using a diagram to specify inter-window navigation. On the other hand, the urn and the blocks of the game were modelled in the virtual 3D space, and later shown from a fixed point of view on a viewport in the application window. Next to the viewport, a 2D panel displayed information related to the game in that window. A widescreen TV served as an interaction surface when displaying menus of the game, and as an interaction volume when showing the urn and the blocks with stereo 3D graphics. Another volume of interaction was associated with the optical system that tracked the P5 glove. Both volumes must correctly overlap in real space to allow the player to grasp, rotate and drop the blocks in the virtual space.

Fig. 10.9 TTristereo (*left*), VRPrismaker (*centre*) and "Minority Report" interface (*right*)

In the case of the block-based construction game, its VR counterpart was named VRPrismaker, exhibiting a complete 3D interface. The playground, table, shelves, game box, blocks and the user's avatar were modelled in the virtual 3D space. In order to immerse users in the virtual world, they put on a stereo-capable head-mounted display and a couple of datagloves (the PinchGlove system). Attached to these devices, a set of sensors tracked user's head and hands, within the interaction volume associated to an electromagnetic system. Such movements were mapped to the user's avatar, resulting in a trans-spatial navigation. Because of that mapping, the range of the tracking system in real space had to be taken into account when modelling objects in the virtual space, so to allow the user to play with the blocks without leaving this volume.

Finally, in the case of the "Minority Report"-like interface, this represents a 3D UI that does not render 3D images, they are 2D ones; it is the actions that are performed in 3D space. Then, elements in the 2D image were designed with a component specification diagram, and the presentation device played the role of an interaction surface. To track and recognize user's hand gestures, an electromagnetic tracking system was used too, with its associated interaction volume. In this case, it was necessary to adjust the position of this volume in from of the interaction surface, so that the user could correctly point to the images displayed.

10.6   Conclusions

This work represents an attempt to formalize 2D and 3D spaces in the context of 3D UI development by introducing a meta-model. A key feature is the distinction between digital, virtual and real space, based on a new continuum introduced here as an extension to Milgram and Kishino's Reality–Virtuality. This meta-model also contributes to define a language for a proposed methodology, named TRES-D, which has been described too, along with some case studies. However, TRES-D does not achieve the automation that was aimed when the first proposal, IDEAS-3D, was presented. Further work on the proposed meta-models must be done in order to address that goal, for instance merging them with UsiXML models so to benefit from its established model-based process.

Acknowledgements This work has been partially supported by the Ministerio de Educación y Ciencia of Spain (CICYT TIN2004-08000-C03-01) and by the Junta de Comunidades de Castilla-La Mancha (PAI06-0093).

References

1. Cognetics Corp. The LUCID Framework. URL: http://www.cognetics.com/lucid
2. Bardon D, Berry D, Bjerke C, et al. (2001) Crafting the Compelling User Experience Using a Methodical Software-Engineering Approach to Model Users and Design. Tutor. URL: http://www-3.ibm.com/ibm/easy/eou_ext.nsf/publish/1650

3. Lozano M (2001) A Methodological Approach for the Specification and Development of Object Oriented User Interfaces. Doctoral Thesis. Univ Politéc de Valencia, Valencia, Spain
4. Fencott C (1999) Towards a Design Methodology for Virtual Environments. UCDIVE Workshop, York, UK
5. Sánchez MI, de Antonio A, de Amescua A (2005) SENDA: A Whole Process to Develop Virtual Environments. In: Sánchez MI (ed) Developing Future Interactive Systems, Idea Group
6. Molina JP, González P, Lozano MD, et al. (2003) Bridging the gap: developing 2D and 3D user interfaces with the IDEAS methodology. In: Jorge J, et al. (eds) DSV-IS: Issues in Designing New-generation Interactive Systems, LNCS, Springer, Berlin, pp. 303–315
7. Molina JP, Vanderdonckt J, Montero F, et al. (2005) Towards Virtualization of User Interfaces based on UsiXML. 10th ACM Web3D Symposium, Bangor, UK, 169–179
8. Granollers T, Lorés J, Raimat G, et al. (2002) Vilars, un Nuevo Modelo de Diálogo Aplicando Realidad Aumentada. III Cong. Interacción, Leganés, Spain, 276–279
9. Milgram P, Kishino F (1994) A taxonomy of mixed-reality visual displays. IEICE Trans. Inf. Syst., Special Issue on Networked Reality, E77-D:12:1321–1329
10. Molina JP, García AS, Martínez D, et al. (2006) An Interaction Model for the TRES-D Framework. 13th IEEE MELECON, Benalmádena, Spain
11. ClockWise Technologies Ltd. Win3D. URL: http://www.clockwise3d.com
12. 3DNA Desktop. URL: http://www.3dna.net
13. Y. Fei. Cube Features. URL: http://www.infinite-3d.com/cube.html
14. The SphereXP. URL: http://www.spheresite.com
15. Sun Microsystems. Project Looking Glass. URL: http://www.sun.com/software/looking_glass
16. Compiz Fusion. URL: http://www.compiz-fusion.org
17. van Dam A (1997) Post-WIMP User Interfaces. Commun. ACM, 40:2:63–67
18. Trevisan DG, Vanderdonckt J, Macq B (2004) Conceptualising mixed spaces of interaction for designing continuous interaction. Virtual Real J., 8:2:83–95
19. IBM. RealPlaces Design Guide. URL: http://www-03.ibm.com/easy/page/580
20. Roberts D (2000) RealPlaces, 3D Interfaces for Office Applications. TFWWG Workshop, Biarritz, France
21. Molina JP, Vanderdonckt J, Gonzalez P, et al. (2006) Rapid Prototyping of Distributed User Interfaces. In: Computer-Aided Design of User Interfaces V, ISS, Springer, Berlin, pp. 151–166
22. UsiXML.org, User Interface eXtensible Markup Language. URL: http://www.usixml.org
23. Coutaz J, Lachenal Ch, Dupuy-Chessa S (2003) Ontology for Multi-surface Interaction. 9th IFIP INTERACT, Zurich, Switzerland, 447–454
24. Leftwich J (1993) InfoSpace: A Conceptual Method for Interacting with Information in a Three-Dimensional Virtual Environment. 3rd Int. Conf. on Cyberspace, Austin, USA
25. The Croquet Project. URL: http://croquetproject.org
26. Molina JP, García AS, Martínez D, et al. (2006) The Development of Glove-Based Interfaces with the TRES-D Methodology. 13th ACM VRST, Limassol, Cyprus, 216–219

Chapter 11
Evaluation and Optimization of Word Disambiguation for Text-Entry Methods

Hamed H. Sad and Franck Poirier

Abstract We study the key-characters assignment on ambiguous keyboards. We consider two cases: unconstrained and alphabetically constrained character arrangements on ambiguous keys. A genetic algorithm is used for searching the assignment that optimizes the text-entry performance. The results show that as the number of keys decreases, the gain in performance due to optimization increases. We also study the effect of the disambiguation word list layout on the text-entry usability. We demonstrate that adding words by completion to the word list always leads to better performance. The usability effect of changing the number of ambiguous keys, compared to changing the number of words displayed to the user, is investigated.

11.1 Introduction

One of the extensively used techniques for text entry on mobile devices is the word disambiguation. On keyboards based on this technique, each key is overloaded by more than one character. For typing a word, the user composes it by making a single tap on a single key for entering each character of the word. This means that there will be number of keystrokes equals to, or less than in some cases, the number of characters in the word. Since each key is assigned to more than one character, the resulting keystrokes usually refer to more than one word. This also means that another stage of disambiguating the resulting words is necessary. One of the simplest, and widely used, methods for disambiguation is to present all the words corresponding to the typed key sequence to the user in the order of their occurrence frequency and making the most frequent word ready for user confirmation. Word disambiguation text entry on mobile phones was first introduced by *Tegic Communications* (acquired by *Nuance*: http://www.nuance.com/), in the famous T9®, and proved to be theoretically more efficient than the dominant Multi-Tap entry method in [1].

H.H. Sad (✉) and F. Poirier
Université de Bretagne-Sud, VALORIA – Centre de Recherche, 56000 Vannes, France
e-mail: Sad@univ-ubs.fr

V. López-Jaquero et al. (eds.), *Computer-Aided Design of User Interfaces VI*,
DOI: 10.1007/978-1-84882-206-1_11, © Springer-Verlag London Limited 2009

There are, at least, two reasons for using such less direct entry, compared to normal desktop standard keyboards. The first is when there is no enough space for assigning a single character to each key. This is the case of mobile devices text-entry interfaces such as T9 on the standard telephone keypad. The second reason for using the word disambiguation entry is the reduction of motor movement, especially for users with some disability. Using less number of keys reduces the required movement for text entry, a significant example is the *UniGlyph* keyboard which use only three keys [2].

The performance of word disambiguation entry methods depends on the efficiency of its two stages: first, letter tapping followed by candidate words production, and second, word disambiguation. The effectiveness of the first stage is controlled by the keys design and the candidate word production algorithm. The keys size and placement affects user performance in tapping them and has been already extensively studied [3, 4]. In this work, we study the effect of candidate words production on the efficiency of the text-entry process. The second stage is the confirmation of the required word from the resulting word list which depends on the interface for presenting the words to the user and the selection mechanism of the desired word.

11.2 Candidate Words Production

There are many decisions concerning the design of word disambiguation entry methods. The resulting candidate words may be made to match only the typed key sequence as in the case of original T9®. Some methods add words with length greater than the key sequence under the condition that the beginning of those words match the typed key sequence so far [2]. Another design decision is the algorithm used in predicting the candidate words. The simplest and widely used method on mobile devices is using a simple ambiguous codes dictionary. When the user types a specific key sequence, he/she actually specifies a code that matches a group of words stored in code-words dictionary. The resulting words are presented to the user in their occurrence frequency order, that is the most frequent word appears as the first choice. The word-frequency based prediction is a special case of the prediction based on the n-gram [5]. In the n-gram, the prediction of the $n + 1$ word is based on information about the frequency of occurrence of a given word after the n words that precede it in the text corpus. The frequency prediction can be considered as n-gram prediction with $n = 1$. In other words, word-frequency based prediction is a non-contextual prediction scheme.

11.3 Word-Frequency Based Production

Word-frequency based production is widely used on mobile devices because it needs less storage space and simple word production algorithm. After typing a specific key sequence, word confirmation compromises word list search with or without scrolling, which is a time- and resource-consuming process. So, we identify three factors that affect user performance when using a frequency based production with word disambiguation text-entry technique: key-character assignment, size of the produced word list, and whether this list should contain words with length greater than the length of the typed key sequence (by word completion).

11.3.1 Key-Character Assignment

The number of words for each key sequence depends on the key-character assignment used and the total number of words in the dictionary. As the average number of words per ambiguous code increases, the time required for word confirmation increases. There have been many trials for optimizing ambiguous entry. Most of these trials are concerned with letter-based ambiguous entry, where the disambiguation is letters rather than word based [6, 7]. In another work, the average conditional probability was used to measure the efficiency of a given assignment but there was no given method to find a good assignment [8]. Alphabetically constrained key-character assignment was compared to an alphabetically unconstrained assignment in [9], but there were no clear description for the way of getting the desired assignment.

The problem of key-character assignment can be stated as: For a given list of word-frequency data (generated from a corpus), what is the assignment that gives the minimum average length for the resulting prediction lists for ambiguous codes? We present a genetic algorithm that can get the required assignment based on the key strokes per character (KSPC) to express the quality of a given key-character assignment [10]:

$$KSPC = \frac{\sum (K_w \times F_w)}{\sum (C_w \times F_w)}.$$

where K_w is the number of keystrokes required to type the word, F_w is the frequency of the word, C_w is the number of characters in the word, and the summation is over all the words in a specific corpus. K_w is equal to the number of characters of the word plus the index of the word in the disambiguation list. By this form, KSPC will be 1 if all the words in the corpus come in the first position in the disambiguation list (the ideal case) and will be more than 1 in typical cases. Larger KSPC means less-efficient disambiguation, and then the objective is finding the assignment with the minimum possible KSPC. A good point in the KSPC is that it weights each word by its frequency of occurrence when calculating the goodness of an assignment. This means that words with greater frequency will play the main role in the optimization and resulting assignment will give better performance for the frequent words.

11.3.1.1 Assignment Genetic Algorithm

The algorithm begins by collecting all given characters from a given corpus (in the form of word-frequency file), then it receives the following input information before searching the assignment:

- The required number of keys (less than the number of distinct characters in the corpus).
- The difference in number of character per key, given in percentage of the average number of characters per keys which is calculated by dividing the number of distinct characters by the number of keys and taking the ceiling number of the result. For example, if we have 39 characters, and 5 keys, the average number of character per key is 8. If the percentage is 20%, this means that the key may be assigned to 6–10 characters.
- Number of *individual* solutions (key-characters assignments) in a genetic algorithm *population*.
- Number of individual solution produced by *mutation* in each generation.
- Number of character interchange and character movement when doing a mutation on an individual solution (will be explained later).

All the above items are modifiable while the algorithm is running except the required number of keys.

The algorithm starts the search by generating a random population of number of individual solutions equal to twice the specified number of individuals in a generation. A random population individual is made by putting all the character in a single one-dimensional array in a random order. Then, a number of separators, equal to the number of required keys -1, are placed randomly in that array. Then the conditions of number of characters per keys is verified, if a valid solution has been produced, the algorithm continue, otherwise it repeats the process.

The fitness (KSPC) for each individual in the randomly generated population is calculated, then all the solutions are sorted and the first good half of the individuals is considered as the first generation. Each generation after the first one is produced by two processes: *Crossover* between the individual with the best *fitness*, and mutation on individuals chosen randomly from all the individuals of the current generation. The new individuals, resulted from the crossover and mutation, are ordered by their fitness, and the next generation individuals are selected by fitness priority.

Crossover is designed to satisfy the condition: The resulting individual inherits its main structure of his parents with some differences that maximize the probability that it will have better fitness. For satisfying the second part, a rough estimation is required for a bond of characters compared to another bond. For obtaining this estimation, we constructed a table of character frequencies for each possible character index in a word. For estimating a character bond, we add the character frequencies at each index for all the characters in the bond, the result is the bond frequency. The greater the bond frequency, the higher the cost for those characters when being in the same bond or key. Figure 11.1 illustrates the crossover process.

11.3.1.2   Application of the Assignment Algorithm

For testing our algorithm, we use a corpus of 100,000 French words. The corpus is made by loading the word-frequency list (http://www.lexique.org/listes-mots.php)

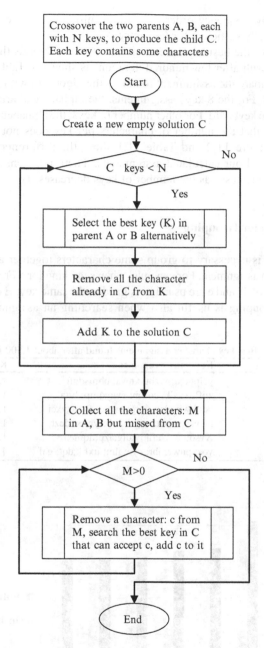

Fig. 11.1 Crossover operation

corpus of 129,000 French terms then clipping them with a list of 336,531 French words dictionary from the same site. The non-dictionary words in the word-frequency corpus are removed together with the repeated words. We then choose the first

100,000 entries by frequency order from the resulting list. We consider that this number is practically sufficient for text entry.

We searched for the best key-letter assignment for keyboards that have three to eight keys. The result after few hundred iterations is shown in Table 11.1. It is also interesting to compare the assignment found by the algorithm with the alphabetical based assignment. For the 8 keys assignments, the alphabetical arrangement is the standard telephone keyboard. For other number of keys, the alphabetical arrangement is constructed so that the number of characters per key does not differ so much between keys. Figure 11.2 and Table 11.1 show the differences in KSPC for the alphabetical and our calculated assignments. There is an enhancement in the performance that increases as the number of keys decreases.

11.3.1.3 Character Grouping

In some cases, it is necessary to group some characters together as one character when searching an assignment. For example, when searching for a French assignment, the letters like é, è, ê, ë, and e are usually assigned to the same key: E on the keyboard. The character grouping is useful also when searching an assignment for certain

Table 11.1 Best key-character assignments found after about 1,500 iterations

Keys number	Key-letter assignments	KSPC
3	yclpuejq; vrzbtkxnwa; ohmsdgfi	1.255
4	zjifluxwdk; coshn; evgyqmp; brta	1.070
5	bdukwl; qjat; yprg; hnme; fso; zvxci	1.020
6	takm; pqvwe; ujgsh; lib;fynox; dczr	1.019
7	Xvso;ublwh;fikjy;dtg;azp;nqme;rc	1.010
8	vos; pnwz; jhr; cye; ilm; uxbk;dqt; gaf	1.010

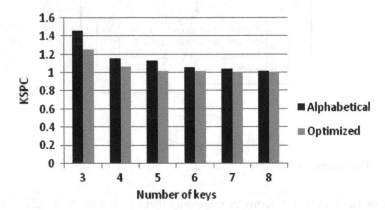

Fig. 11.2 The KSPC for both genetic algorithms optimized and alphabetical key-character assignments at different key numbers

keyboards like *UniGlyph* [2], where each group of letters is represented by a single glyph for reducing the number of keys. Using the character grouping feature with our algorithm, we get the assignment that is about 10% more efficient than the original *UniGlyph* assignment as shown in Table 11.2.

11.3.1.4 Best Alphabetical Keyboard

Although the key-characters assignment has less impact on the performance of an expert user, the alphabetical order is easy for new users. In searching for the best possible alphabetical assignment, we searched all possible arrangements for all the 26 characters with a specified minimum and maximum number of characters per key at the given keys number. For the 8 keys case, the best result is the arrangement: abc; def; ghij; klm; nop; qr; st; uvwxyz with a KSPC = 1.0148 compared with 1.012 for the optimized without the alphabetical condition one. For the fewest key arrangement (3 keys case), the best result was: abcdefgh; ijklmnopq; rstuvwxyz with a KSPC = 1.463 compared with 1.27 for the optimized without condition arrangement.

Figure 11.3 shows the number of words at each prediction index for the two arrangements for the 3 keys case. It is clear that the number of words that come as the first choices after typing a key sequence (prediction index = 0) is greater in the case of the optimized assignment.

Table 11.2 Original and optimized assignment for *UniGlyph*

Assignment	KSPC			
Original	/ \	( )	| -	1.423
Optimized	|)	/ \	(-	1.376

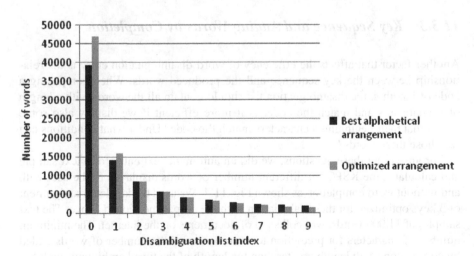

Fig. 11.3 Number of words at each word disambiguation index for the first ten indexes in case of three keys

Table 11.3 Displayed word list length and number of keys effects on the number of words entered without scrolling the list

Prediction list length	Number of words entered without scrolling		
	3 Keys	4 Keys	5 Keys
1	46,959	72,750	83,319
2	62,943	86,494	94,006
3	71,304	91,808	97,109
4	76,886	94,714	98,489
5	80,945	96,449	99,168

11.3.2 Size of the Word List Displayed to the User

The length of the word list produced for a given ambiguous code affects the usability of the word disambiguation text entry. More words lead to more searching time and more scrolling. Since the words are presented in their frequency order, not the familiar alphabetical order, the search process consumes a considerable amount of user resources. On most mobile phones, due to the small size of the screen, we have not enough space to display word lists. But this is possible in the case of PDAs, smart phones, or desktop. We calculated the number of words that can be entered without scrolling the list of displayed words for the optimized assignment arrangement of 3, 4, and 5 keys using a corpus of 100,000 words. Concerning the interface size, we noted that increasing the ambiguous keys number is more efficient than increasing the number of words displayed to the user. For example, using a 4 keys keyboard with disambiguation list length of 1 leads to 72,750 words, while using a 3 keys with disambiguation list length of 2 leads to 62,943 words, see Table 11.3.

11.3.3 Key Sequence and Adding Words by Completion

Another factor that affects the efficiency of word disambiguation entry is the relationship between the key sequence and the produced words. When composing a code of length n, the disambiguation list should contain all the words with a length of n characters and match the code. Is it more efficient if we display also some words that their beginning n characters match the code? Under what conditions can we chose these words?

For answering these questions, we did an automatic text entry for a text sample and calculated the KSPC for different number of words displayed to the user with and without word completion as shown Fig. 11.4. We used the key letter assignment of 3 keys optimized for these calculation with the corpus mentioned above. The text sample, of 11,000 words, was collected of documents on the internet. The minimum number of characters for prediction to occur is 3, and the number of words added by completion (with length greater than the length of the typed ambiguous code) to the disambiguation list is 5. We then calculated the total keystrokes required for

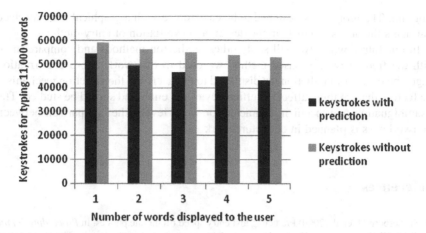

Fig. 11.4 The effect of number of words displayed to the user on the performance of word disambiguation entry

entering all the 11,000 words at different number of words displayed to the user. The result was that prediction always leads to better results, assuming that the user selects the desired words as soon as they appear in the prediction list.

11.4   Conclusion and Future Work

In this chapter, we studied the key-characters assignment in word disambiguation text entry. We used a genetic algorithm to search the assignment with the best possible KSPC. The results indicated that the number of keys decrease as the gain in performance between the two assignments, optimized and alphabetical, increases. Generally, for 5 or greater keys number, the increase is not sufficiently high. In other words, there is no motivation for changing the alphabetical assignments for more than 4 keys. Recently, small devices that need some form of text entry have appeared such as MP3 player and watch-size computing devices. On these devices, we need to optimize the entry with the fewest possible keys number.

We also searched the best possible alphabetical key arrangement for the cases of 3 keys and 8 (standard keypad) keys by trying all possible arrangement. The resulting assignments show that there is a remarkable gain in KSPC for the optimization under the alphabetical condition for the 3 keys but not for the 8 keys.

We used a text sample to test the effect of adding word by completion to the disambiguation list on the efficiency of text entry. The results indicated that the completion always leads to better performance. The study of word list size shows that adding a key leads to better performance than increasing the length of the word list displayed to the user by one word.

The key-character assignment algorithm and many other tools for evaluating text-entry methods, especially for mobile devices, are implemented as an application program. The program is designed to be easy to use with a graphical user interface that helps the non-specialists in the design and evaluation of entry methods.

In our future work, we will study other prediction methods and compare them with the frequency only based method we used in this work. Word confirmation stage, the design of prediction list displayed to the user, and the selection mechanism are factors that we think affect the efficiency of the entry and should be studied. The disambiguation may occur in characters or word levels; the comparison between the two levels is planned in our future work.

References

1. Silfverberg M, et al. (2000) Predicting text entry speed on mobile phones. In *Proceedings of the SIGCHI Conference on Human Factors in Computing Systems* (The Hague, The Netherlands, 2000). ACM, New York, NY, pp. 9–16, doi: http://doi.acm.org/10.1145/332040.332044
2. Poirier F and Belatar M (2006) Évaluation d'analogies scripturales pour la conception d'une méthode de saisie en mobilité – Uni-Glyph. Ergo-IA: 333–336
3. Zhai S, et al. (2002) Movement model, hits distribution and learning in virtual keyboarding. In *Proceedings of the SIGCHI Conference on Human Factors in Computing Systems: Changing Our World, Changing Ourselves* (Minneapolis, MN, April 20–25, 2002). ACM, New York, NY, pp. 17–24, doi: http://doi.acm.org/10.1145/503376.503381
4. James CL and Reischel KM (2001) Text input for mobile devices: comparing model prediction to actual performance. In *Proceedings of the SIGCHI Conference on Human Factors in Computing Systems* (Seattle, WA, 2001). ACM, New York, NY, pp. 365–371, doi: http://doi.acm.org/10.1145/365024.365300
5. Rosenfeld R (2000) Two decades of statistical language modeling: where do we go from here? *Proc. IEEE* 88: 1270–1278
6. Lesher GW, et al. (1998) Optimal character arrangements for ambiguous keyboards. IEEE Trans. Rehabil. Eng. (see also IEEE Trans. Neural Syst. Rehabil. Eng.) 6: 415–423
7. Nesbat S (2003) A system for fast, full-text entry for small electronic devices. In *Proceedings of the 5th international conference on Multimodal interfaces* (Vancouver, BC, 2003). ACM, New York, NY, pp. 4–11, doi: http://doi.acm.org/10.1145/958432.958437
8. Tanaka-Ishii K, et al. (2002) Entering text with a four-button device. In *Proceedings of the 19th International Conference on Computational Linguistics – Volume 1* (Taipei, Taiwan, 2002). Association for Computational Linguistics, Morristown, NJ, pp. 988–994
9. Gong J and Tarasewich P (2005) Alphabetically constrained keypad designs for text entry on mobile devices. In *Proceedings of the SIGCHI Conference on Human Factors in Computing Systems*. doi: http://doi.acm.org/10.1145/1054972.1055002
10. MacKenzie IS (2002) KSPC (Keystrokes per Character) as a Characteristic of Text Entry Techniques. In *Proceedings of the 4th International Symposium on Mobile Human–Computer Interaction* (Pisa, Italy, September 18–20, 2002). Springer, London, pp. 195–210

Chapter 12
Integrating Usability Methods into Model-Based Software Development

Stefan Propp, Gregor Buchholz and Peter Forbrig

Abstract Model-based software development is carried out as a well-defined process. Depending on the applied approach, different phases can be distinguished, for example, requirements specification, design, prototyping, implementation, and usability evaluation. During this iterative process, manifold artifacts are developed and modified, including models, source code, and usability evaluation data. CASE tools support the development stages well, but lack a seamless integration of usability evaluation methods. We aim at bridging the gap between development and usability, through enabling the cooperative use of artifacts with the particular tools. As a result of integration usability, experts save time to prepare an evaluation and evaluation results can be easily incorporated back into the development process. We show exemplary our work on enhancing the Eclipse framework to support usability evaluation for task model-based software development.

12.1 Introduction

Model-based software development describes a process which starts with abstract models and refines them iteratively. Models are transformed and adapted to more concrete models for different platforms and finally transformed into code which is deployed to the target platform. Traditional usability evaluation provides methods to evaluate a couple of different artifacts, but lacks a seamless integration into the development process and the applicability in early development stages. Therefore, we aim at bridging the gap between development and usability evaluation, through

S. Propp (✉), G. Buchholz and P. Forbrig
University of Rostock, Institute of Computer Science, Albert Einstein Street 21,
18059 Rostock, Germany
e-mail: stefan.propp@uni-rostock.de

V. López-Jaquero et al. (eds.), *Computer-Aided Design of User Interfaces VI*,
DOI: 10.1007/978-1-84882-206-1_12, © Springer-Verlag London Limited 2009

enabling the cooperative use of artifacts with developers and usability experts and pave the way towards a seamless integration of both processes.

Our work specifically focuses on the task model-based development of interactive systems [2]. Task models describe possible sequences of subtasks to accomplish a certain goal and temporal relations between the tasks [7]. The task model serves as a basis for the model-based development of a user interface. To evaluate the usability of the derived user interface, the underlying task model can be used to track the user interaction at a task-based level of abstraction. The particular advantage is a concise overview which hides the device-specific user interface events. Therefore, the analysis of a task trace is better readable and traces through an application deployed at different devices can be directly compared. Examples using this technique are RemUSINE [8] and ReModEl [1]. RemUSINE firstly captures the user interactions and subsequently maps the interactions to a trace of tasks, which were carried out. However, ReModEl deploys a task engine which natively recognizes the tasks at runtime and captures the task without mapping stage. For the subsequent analysis of task traces, Malý and Slavik suggested a visualization technique [5], further developed in [8, 9]. A task trace is depicted as time line to compare different users' behavior at a task-based level.

The previously stated approaches serve as individual methods and target deployed applications, but are not integrated into the development environment. This chapter discusses our approach of integration to provide usability testing at all stages of the development instantly on the artifacts currently under development. Within these evaluations, the focus lies on the efficiency of the system developed so far. The approach is discussed in Sect. 12.2. The integration into the development tools implemented as plug-ins for the Eclipse IDE is exemplified in Sect. 12.3.

12.2 Concept

12.2.1 Model-Based Usability Evaluation

It is a main principle of model-driven software development that both software engineers and user interface designers base their work on the same models. Progress in development is reflected in a sequence of transformations from the initial models (task model, user model, device model) as results of the requirements analysis to a finished software product. Those transformations cannot be done in a fully automated way but require humans using interactive tools. In the past, we have developed such tools providing support in the creation and transformation of models [2, 11]. Initially, a hierarchical task model describes the decomposition of the root task (also referred to as the user's goal) into subtasks that are to be carried out to reach the goal. Tasks can be optional and iterative and temporal relationships between different subtasks define the order in which the subtasks have to be executed. The user model describes the different roles a user can take on and by assigning roles

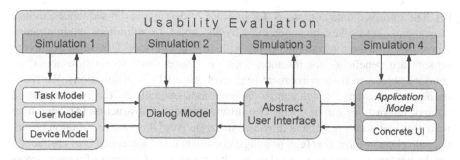

Fig. 12.1 Integration of usability evaluation into model-driven software development (MDSD)

to subtasks, cooperative behavior can be modeled where different users are involved in the work on a task (e.g. a customer and an employee of a travel agency take part in the task "book flight"). Device models specify the capabilities of different types of devices the software product is planned to be used at. It is also structured hierarchically. Hence, an include relationship can be modeled (e.g., if the subtask "seat reservation" is specified to be executable on a mobile, it can be performed on a PDA as well). On the basis of those models, the development of a user interface comprehends the creation of a device-independent abstract user interface (AUI), one or more device-specific concrete user interfaces (CUIs) specified by dialog graphs [2], and the final interfaces as device-specific rendering results. The integration of usability evaluation into this process of transformations is depicted in Fig. 12.1.

Each development stage is accompanied by usability evaluation tests (depicted as simulations 1–4 in Fig. 12.1): Task model simulations are used to reveal structural problems in the underlying model and can uncover lacking understanding of the task domain and indicate modeling mistakes. Evaluation techniques targeting the dialog model allow finding-deficient support of the user in providing access to the modeled tasks at the right time and the right place. Testing AUIs (first prototypical very simple UIs automatically generated from the dialog model) facilitates the pattern-based process of replacing very basic UI components with more specific ones, comparing the efficiency that is reached by executing tasks while using either one or another version of the interface. Finally, further evaluation methods based on UI-events, video recordings, and other techniques can be applied to ensure and optimize the final UI's usability.

The following sections will go into the details of model-related monitoring and other evaluation techniques in the successive development stages as outlined earlier.

12.2.2   Capturing of Interaction Traces

A common used technique of usability evaluation is to equip test users with devices and applications that have to be tested and observe the interaction with the device

[6]. The observed data comprises, for instance, video and audio sequences, mouse movements, keystrokes, or annotations by an expert. In ubiquitous environments, where users are moving and interacting with different devices' UIs, some additional sensors are beneficial, for instance, location sensors and information about the handled objects in the environment (e.g. exploiting RFID information). We focus on interaction events, which can be captured automatically by the system. Such a trace of interactions can be captured at different levels of abstraction [4]: beginning with physical events (e.g. hand moving a mouse), over UI events (e.g. button press), to goal-related information (e.g. printing a document). The lower levels of abstraction can be captured as system internal events, but cause a vast amount of data, whereas higher level events can be interpreted more directly, but normally need to be derived from the lower level events. We aim at reusing the models from software engineering to focus on the higher level events.

As described in Sect. 12.2.1, we use task models for the design of interactive systems. Therefore, our capturing mechanism of the usability evaluation expresses the interaction trace according to these models. Usability evaluation can be carried out at the four different stages of development (*see* Fig. 12.1).

1. In a very early stage of development, the task model is designed to reflect the tasks the users have to accomplish from the cognitive point of view. The task engine is capable of simulating the model and the interaction is captured to test whether all necessary tasks are covered appropriately structured.
2. To support different devices and user roles, customized dialogs are specified as dialog graphs [2] that are rendered as a prototypical UI, which simply contains buttons on different dialogs to execute tasks. While this UI is simulated, the execution of tasks is captured.
3. The generated UI can be refined according to the XUL specification with additional UI components (like input fields or menus) and JavaScript enhancements to provide a more realistic UI simulation. These more realistic UIs are simulated in the task framework and interactions are captured.
4. After having developed a final application, it can be transferred to a separate PC or PDA to evaluate the final application. The links to the task model are preserved to send the interaction events, for example, via http connection to the simulation environment. Each UI component that changes the status of a task is enhanced to send the corresponding event to the task framework to capture the interaction. The tool ReModEl [1] works in an analog way.

Our usability evaluation method aims at accompanying the whole development process while using the developed artifacts. To implement the concept, we enhanced the existing task engine to capture the interactions during a simulation of a task model or prototypical UI.

We are capturing information about the current time, the involved task model, the task, the new task status, and the event causing the progress within the task model. Furthermore, we include information about the user who is acting, the user role, the device, and optional context information like noise level or position of the tester when moving, depending on the sensors available in the environment.

An expert may annotate further information, like an unforeseeable influence disturbing the tester, or a user may annotate information, like a certain functionality which is currently needed but missing in the UI.

12.2.3   Data Processing

After having captured the interaction between user and system and having added some additional sensor data and annotations, the data is prepared according to the goal of the usability evaluation. To flexibly support a variety of individual goals, we utilize a pipeline for data processing. Subsequently, the different steps are described in their sequence of processing.

12.2.3.1   Merging Different Interaction Traces

Each interaction trace is captured as an individual trace according to a particular task model. Additional data like sensor data and annotations is added to the specific trace and task. If an evaluation incorporates different traces, they have to be merged, in order to visualize the cooperative work. We consider two cases:

- Different users can work cooperatively at the same task model. An example is a scenario within an accounting department, where one person enters the data and another person is required to double-check and approve the data. The individual interaction traces of both persons have to be joined.
- Different users can work concurrently at different task models with interdependencies between the models, for instance, if we consider a maintenance scenario with a maintenance person and a worker. The worker and the maintenance person both act according to their individual task model, while using the same machine. But if the worker is carrying out the "produce" task, the maintenance staff cannot carry out the "maintain" task with the same machine. To explain a delay within the "maintain" task, a joined view of both traces can be helpful.

We merge the different traces simply by time stamp.

12.2.3.2   Filtering

To support a broad variety of usability evaluations, the capturing mechanism collects a vast amount of data. To examine a specific evaluation goal, the currently irrelevant data has to be filtered out. We incorporate the following criteria:

- Task (task model, certain subtree of the task model, set of individual tasks, specific abstraction level within the task tree)
- User (specific user, all users related to a user role)

- Device (set of devices)
- Sensor (sensor value within a certain range)
- Time (date and time, duration of a task)
- Annotation (according to categories and values provided by the expert, according to the user)

Depending on the particular interest of the specific usability evaluation, suitable filter criteria can be combined.

12.2.3.3 Aggregation

To cope with the vast amount of captured data, we distinguish between two solutions: (1) removing the irrelevant data through filtering and (2) keeping all the data, but setting a focus on the data of interest through aggregation.

We apply a semantic lens for this aggregation. Analog to an optical lens, a semantic lens provides a high level of details within the area of interest, while lowering the level of details around. A lens is defined by a focus point, a lens size, and a lens function [3]. Applied at a task trace, the task instance of interest is focused, the lens size is the number of previous and successive tasks which are covered by the lens, and the lens function defines how the aggregation works. The lens function defines the level of aggregation for each position within the lens area. When considering a sequence of five-task instances, which are far away from the focus of the lens, they are out of the center of interest and therefore decreased in their level of detail. It is technically realized by replacing them by their parent task within the task model. The technique is further described in [9].

12.2.3.4 Normalization

To analyze the usability of a UI for a certain task, different users can be observed while working. If they differ in duration to accomplish the task, this might be an indicator for a usability issue, but in some cases, we faced the problem that the normal working speed was largely varying and there was no issue, for example, if one tester needs significantly more time for typing with the keyboard. We overcome this problem by normalization. When comparing different users' durations to accomplish a task sequence, their durations are scaled to eliminate the individual differences, if useful for the evaluation purpose.

Normalization proceeds as follows: the expert chooses a task and a certain user. The according time captured during observation is compared to the other users' and for each user a factor is derived. The factor is applied to all tasks of the respective user. As a result the duration of slower users is stretched and the duration of faster users is compressed. We suggest designing a short calibration task and appending it in front of the evaluation. As an alternative, all overall durations can be set to the same duration, to compare all users at 100% basis. Hence, normalization is applied to provide better comparability of users.

12.2.4   Visualization

After capturing and preparing the usability data, the visualization should help the usability expert to find usability issues and derive improvements for the UI. We provide a set of visualizations, which include:

- Log tables, to state the whole sequence of interaction events,
- Time lines, to compare different users working on the same task,
- Pie charts, to examine the tasks which caused the highest amount of time to be accomplished, and
- Gantt charts, to discover structural dependencies between concurrent tasks.

According to practical experiences, the set of visualizations will be extended.

Figure 12.2 depicts an example Gantt chart with a time line from left to right and the tasks on the left-hand side. Most tasks are fulfilled in a sequence, but also concurrent tasks can occur. The task "view calendar" is an example.

Each completed task is visualized with two bars: the first is the observed duration and the second the expected duration. The expected values provide a help to see at a glance where a usability issue might exist. The expected values can be provided manually or a trace of an expert is captured and compared.

12.2.5   Cooperative Work

Bringing together software developers and usability experts is not only a matter of working with the same concepts and more or less abstract models but has to be

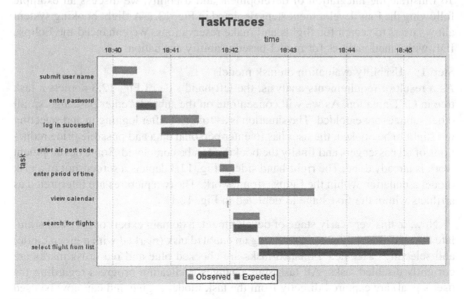

Fig. 12.2 Task trace visualization as Gantt chart

supported in the daily work. To overcome the drawbacks caused by media discontinuity in the process of having the usability test results interpreted by designers in order to deduce the necessary development steps in terms of improving the system's usability, developers and usability experts have to work on the same artifacts. Artifacts in the user interface-related steps of the software development can be dialog graphs, single dialog views, as well as UI components. Those artifacts are linked to or annotated with related usability test results visualizable in the project tree (*left part* of Fig. 12.4) to highlight elements requiring improvements or complete redesign. Thus, the utilization of test results becomes easier and progress in development stages gets more homogeneous. Moreover, operating in the same workspace helps developers and usability experts to establish a better understanding of each other's methods.

A version control system is used to maintain competing UI layouts and allows testing different interfaces for the same subtask(s) to find out which UI components and interface design support the users most efficiently and sufficiently. Different UI versions become measurable and comparable. By attaching recorded protocols (task traces) and analysis reports to each artifact's usability annotation, the process of an evolving interface becomes easily accessible and comprehensible, lowering the risk of making the same errors twice. We suggest maintaining and displaying the results of evaluations in a structured categorizable tree view to improve the communication between usability experts and UI developers [10].

12.3 Example

To illustrate the integration of development and usability, we discuss an example following the four development steps depicted in Fig. 12.1. A flight booking system allows users to search for flights and make reservations. We enhanced the Eclipse IDE with functionalities for model-based usability evaluation.

Step 1:   Usability evaluation on task models
As a result of requirements analysis, the left-hand side of Fig. 12.3 depicts a task tree in CTT notation. As we will concentrate on the subtask "enter passengers," all other subtrees are enfolded. The situation is as follows: After logging in and selecting the flight to be booked, the user has to enter personal data and possible price reductions of all passengers and finally the booking can be completed. Some development work is already done: The right-hand side of Fig. 12.3 depicts a screenshot of a task model simulation within the Eclipse framework. The two pictures are interpreted as artifacts within the first stage as depicted in Fig. 12.1.

Now, in this very early stage of development, a domain expert or user can simulate the task model by simply selecting an enabled task (marked with a green circle) and selecting "execute." Finished tasks are checked blue and red cross marks are currently disabled tasks. All task state changes (indicating progress regarding the user's goal) are captured directly from the task model engine and can now be used for further work. For instance, some users could complain about having to enter each discount (student, retired, etc.) separately and might want to have the discount input only after submitting the passengers' personal data.

Step 2:   Usability evaluation on dialog models
The next development step is to create a dialog model that is a dialog graph as depicted in Fig. 12.4a. An interface architect grouped actions together in dialogs. Before designing an interface, a usability evaluation is conducted to examine if and in which degree the arrangement meets the users' needs. Hence, an AUI is generated, where each view is used to create a dialog with buttons representing the tasks in the specific view. Users can simulate the execution of the tasks by simply clicking the buttons. One way to observe the users' behavior in real time is shown in Fig. 12.4b: A tree notation of the dialog graph displays the dialog structure and

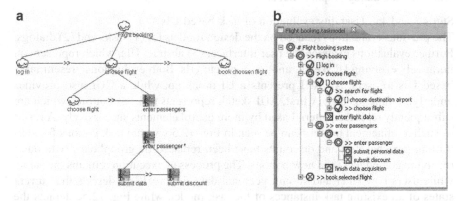

Fig. 12.3 (**a**) Task model (CTT notation) design time view and (**b**) task model runtime simulation

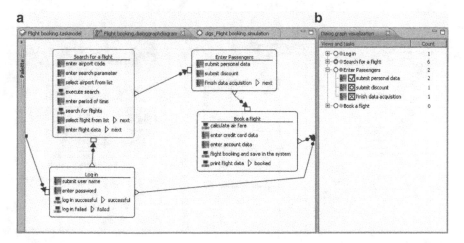

Fig. 12.4 (**a**) Dialog graph design time view and (**b**) dialog graph runtime simulation

tasks with the current states on it. The column on the right side shows for each element (can be view or task) the number of times an instance of the element has been activated. In this example, the dialog view "log in" has been shown one time and is not visible any more (indicated by the gray dot). The dialog "Search for a flight" has been used six times. The view "Enter passengers" is now active (green dot) for the second time and the tasks included have been executed in the first instance and now the user just submits the discount for the second passenger. "Book a flight" has not been active yet. There are a number of issues to analyze in this stage. Some examples given: Are tasks accessible when needed? How often are tasks executed at each dialog? Which ones can be considered as "main view(s)" according to the relevance for the users? Can subgoals be reached in a straightforward manner or do the users have to change the views very often? After answering these questions based on the result of usability evaluations, the UI architect can rearrange the dialog graph, if needed.

Steps 3 and 4:   Usability evaluation of task-based UIs
The previous evaluations focused on the design models for (1) tasks and (2) dialogs. Further evaluations examine the user interface: (3) abstract UIs, which represent an iteratively evolving UI sketch, and (4) concrete UIs. Both evaluations present task-based UIs to users. An AUI presents a UI mock-up, while a CUI also provides underlying functionality. A first, AUI sketch represents tasks as buttons, which are subsequently replaced pattern based by more useful elements successively. A result of such a refinement process can be seen in Fig. 12.5b, where task buttons for submitting personal data and discounts have been replaced by groupboxes with data-receiving components and new buttons. The process of execution remains the same, while users now enter and submit personal data. Figure 12.5a depicts the current states of all existing task instances of the task model, while Fig. 12.5c depicts the task trace visualization "time line," where already executed tasks are depicted with their duration. The underlying data is calculated from the task trace captured so far

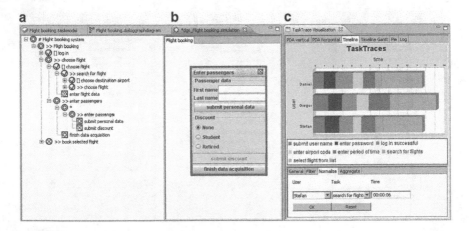

Fig. 12.5 (a) Task model runtime simulation, (b) concrete GUI runtime simulation, and (c) time line

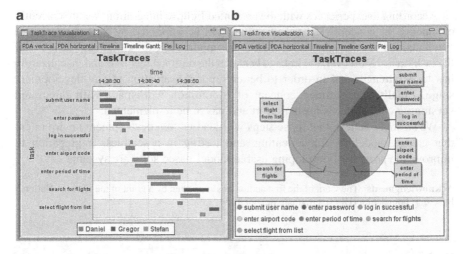

Fig. 12.6 Task trace visualization: (**a**) Gantt chart and (**b**) pie chart

and is updated in time. A filter has been applied to consider tasks represented by leaf nodes in the task tree only; hence, no higher level tasks are visible. During execution, it might be reasonable to aggregate the subtree "choose flight" to prevent the visualization from getting fragmented and unclear.

Figure 12.6 shows two other visualizations of task traces: a Gantt chart (Fig. 12.6a) and a pie chart (Fig. 12.6b). All visualization types are meant to support the usability expert in finding potential usability problems. In this example, the unusual long duration of "select flight from list" (Fig. 12.6b) is a strong indicator for a problem according to dialog "search for a flight" and should be examined further.

All these analysis and visualization techniques are implemented in the same environment as the development tools and can be applied in any stage. There is no need to export or import any kind of log files from elsewhere. Usability evaluations can be conducted right after a new development step has been taken and the results can flow directly into the further development process.

12.4   Conclusion and Future Work

In this chapter, we have shown how to integrate usability evaluation tools into model-based development software enabling the cooperative use of artifacts. Hence, usability experts save time to prepare an evaluation and results are easier to incorporate back into the development process. The example given demonstrated the tool support at different stages of development and provided a glance at the new opportunities of cooperative work on usability and development artifacts. Furthermore, software engineers, developers, interface designers, as well as usability experts may benefit from the insight into each other's work.

According to experiences with the presented Eclipse integration, we are currently enhancing the concept. The visualizations will be improved by further interactive elements and analytic algorithms to better support the exploration and analysis of the task traces. Moreover, the linkage between the outlined methods and visualization has to be strengthened in order to better support evaluation at any development stage. Finally, the outlined concept of a common workspace with integrated versioning control needs further effort and has to be implemented.

We strongly believe that those steps will lead us to a development environment that covers modeling, implementing, and testing in a seamless aggregation to improve the process of developing usable model-based software systems.

Acknowledgments The work of the first author was supported by a grant of the German National Research Foundation (DFG), Graduate School 1424.

References

1. Buchholz, G., Engel, J., Märtin, C., Propp, S.: Model-Based Usability Evaluation – Evaluation of Tool Support. HCII 2007, Beijing, China, pp. 1043–1052, 2007.
2. Forbrig, P., Dittmar, A., Reichart, D., Sinnig, D.: From Models to Interactive Systems – Tool Support and XIML. IUI/CADUI 2004, Funchal, Portugal, 2004.
3. Griethe, H., Fuchs, G., Schumann, H.: A Classification Scheme for Lens Techniques. WSCG'2005, Plzen, Czech Republic, 2005.
4. Hilbert, D, Redmiles, D.: Extracting Usability Information from User Interface Events. *ACM Computing Surveys*, vol. 32, no. 4, pp. 384–421, 2000.
5. Malý, I., Slavík, P.: Towards Visual Analysis of Usability Test Logs. Tamodia 2006, Hasselt, Belgium, pp. 25–32, 2006.
6. Nielsen, J.: Usability Engineering, Morgan Kaufmann, San Francisco, ISBN 0-12-518406-9, 1994.
7. Paternò, F.: Model-Based Design and Evaluation of Interactive Applications. Springer, Berlin, ISBN 1-85233-155-0, 1999.
8. Paternò, F., Russino, A., Santoro, C.: Remote Evaluation of Mobile Applications. TAMODIA 2007, Toulouse, France, pp. 155–169, 2007.
9. Propp, S., Buchholz, G.: Visualization of Task Traces. Interact 2007 Workshop on New Methods in User-Centered System Design, Rio de Janeiro, Brasil, 2007.
10. Pyla, P. S.; Howarth, J. R.; Catanzaro, C.; North, C.: Vizability: A Tool for Usability Engineering Process Improvement Through the Visualization of Usability Problem Data. Proceedings of the 44th Annual Southeast Regional Conference, ISBN 1-59593-315-8, pp. 620–625, 2006.
11. Wolff, A., Forbrig, P., Reichart, D.: Tool Support for Model-Based Generation of Advanced User Interfaces. MDDAUI 2005, Montego Bay, Jamaica, 2005.

Chapter 13
Supporting the Design of Mobile Artefacts for Paper-Based Activities

Marco de Sá, Luís Carriço, Luís Duarte and Tiago Reis

Abstract Current paper-based activities and practices are highly disseminated and intrinsic to our daily lives. Particular cases such as therapeutic and educational procedures, which rely strongly on paper-based artefacts (e.g. questionnaires, forms, manuals) assume special importance due to their critical content. However, their passiveness, limited interactivity, lack of adjustment, among other problems tend to obstruct personalization, hindering efficiency and preventing users from achieving desired goals. This chapter presents a framework that supports an easy and flexible design of tailored digital artefacts for mobile devices. The artefacts can be adjusted to the users' needs, providing support to various purposes by coping with and enhancing different procedures. The framework integrates a set of configurable domain-oriented guidelines that aid end-users through the creation of their personalized artefacts. It has been validated through two case studies by providing support to mobile learning and by offering means to achieve ubiquitous cognitive behavioural therapy.

13.1 Introduction

The recent advances in mobile devices and hand-held technology have extended their potentialities to multimedia and pervasive levels that were previously unavailable. Together with their usual characteristics (e.g. size, autonomy, portability, short usage learning periods, low-intrusiveness), these advances provide adequateness to a wide variety of ubiquitous activities that can benefit from computational support. Among other alternatives, this support can be easily offered by replacing traditionally

M. de Sá (✉), L. Carriço, L. Duarte and T. Reis
LaSIGE & Department of Informatics, Faculty of Sciences, University of Lisbon,
Lisbon, Portugal
e-mail: marcosa@di.fc.ul.pt

V. López-Jaquero et al. (eds.), *Computer-Aided Design of User Interfaces VI*,
DOI: 10.1007/978-1-84882-206-1_13, © Springer-Verlag London Limited 2009

used paper artefacts with a technological or digital medium [8], thus offering a large roll of potentialities unavailable on the original paper approaches.

In general, paper-based artefacts lack multiple communication modalities, hinder customization and configuration procedures and introduce the usual archiving and search difficulties. Moreover, given their passiveness, paper-based artefacts are unable to react to user interaction and cannot offer support to the on-going tasks through an interactive mode.

Mobile devices, hand-held in particular (e.g. PDAs or cellphones), can greatly enhance the underlying processes to paper-based activities without changing the common paper-based procedures. This is especially true since they can be easily carried along, still offering similar interaction possibilities to those of paper artefacts (e.g. touch screen, cursive writing) but providing the extra interactivity capabilities (e.g. storing, editing, audio and video feedback) that can enhance the process. Accordingly, their use on various domains and even critical scenarios is becoming more common [16]. More specifically, concepts such as m-health or m-learning are gaining momentum and offering ways to achieve specific tasks ubiquitously [2, 13].

However, existing applications that focus and support paper-based activities are generally predefined and focus particular domains. Most importantly, these are generally too generic, and fail to grasp important user details, or too specific to certain subjects offering low-flexibility levels. On the contrary, in many of these domains, there is the constant need to update, re-use and improve existing artefacts on a daily basis (e.g. forms, questionnaires). Contrastingly, power users (e.g. therapists, teachers, mediators) are rarely given the ability to quickly and easily modify and create digital items/artefacts according to specific requirements.

These problems, together with a couple of on-going projects, that focused psychotherapy [11] and education [12], were the base motivation for the design of a mobile-artefact design framework. It offers end-users the possibility of creating interactive artefacts and adjusting them according to the working domain or to their needs, including ubiquity and mobility requirements. The system offers means to exchange and transfer existing artefacts supporting cooperation and team work. Given the digital support, the framework also allows users to include behaviour in the resulting artefacts permitting the creation of proactive tools that facilitate users' tasks and daily activities, reacting to usage behaviour, time triggers and interaction patterns. Finally, the tool offers users embedded design guidelines that restrict component usage or provide suggestions for more suitable alternatives.

This chapter presents the mobile-artefact design tool and stresses the contribution that it has provided to the creation of effective tools that support multi-disciplinary activities. It focuses the features that support the design process, detailing the specification of the artefacts' behaviour capabilities and explaining how end-users are able to map their needs into psychotherapy and educational artefacts/tools. We start by addressing the current state-of-the-art within some of the aforementioned domains, stressing the features and problems that characterize most of the existing tools. Afterwards, the framework's architecture, components and features are described. The following sections present the case studies and the several steps that were taken to validate the framework and the resulting artefacts. Finally, some results are discussed and future work is drawn.

13.2   Related Work

The use of mobile devices to support paper-based activities is a growing field of research and practice. Existing examples range from simple annotation tools to more complex digital book readers, questionnaires or point-of-care services [6, 8, 12, 13].

In particular, hand-held applications directed to medical fields have been gaining some momentum in recent years. However, as in many other areas on the health care domain, they often focus on data gathering or visualization, analysis and especially organizational tasks [4]. Specific software, directed to the psychiatric and psychological use, allows patients to follow particular methods of therapy and even diagnosis [6]. Excluding patient solutions that, relying on expedite approaches of diagnosis, have revealed strong human rejection [1], studies have demonstrated the effectiveness of the computer role in the process of anxiety/depression therapy [7].

However, as in other domains, most of these systems provide either isolated therapist solutions or isolated patient solutions with no therapist control. Moreover, they only cover partial steps of the therapy process and do not allow the customization of the patients' tasks or artefacts. On the patients' side, some self-control or relaxation procedures are available on hand-held devices [2]. Still, they are generic and offer no adjustment options that suit patients' needs, problems or the therapy stage.

Within education, mobile devices are also generating some buzz and conquering the e-learning domain [10]. For instance, experiences in schools show that, when PDAs are used by children, besides lightening up their enthusiasm, they allow them to read e-books, communicate, play games and collaborate with each other in safety [9]. Their use in higher education has been tested as well. A group of computer science majors used PDAs as an adjunct to their student lives [3]. Results proved that most of the students frequently used their PDAs for lesson preparation, information sharing and even programming [3].

However, despite the abovementioned cases, their application on educational contexts is far from what it could be. Among others, the main reason for this low use, by teachers and students, is the limited number of relevant educational software for hand-held devices [13]. The existing software is mostly non-collaborative, which contrasts with researches that show that the learning process is more successful where there is strong collaboration [5]. Their use is generally limited to the assessment and evaluation of students. Nevertheless, results from previous studies [14] show that PDA-based artefacts used by students provide efficacy and efficiency levels that are identical or superior to paper-based ones. Moreover, advantages such as real-time scoring, for students, or less time spent on grading, for teachers, also promote the use of PDAs within schools and universities.

However, some relevant issues regarding the variety of items and artefact customization, the chosen subjects and courses or even the information exchange between users still retract from a more common use of such devices within or outside classes.

PDAs and hand-held devices in general are also being frequently used for the support of meetings and work flow processes. Here, given the nature of the various interactions and cooperating participants, the need to customize the used artefacts is even greater, requiring an adjustment to the domain as well as to the situation and various users [16]. Still, the construction of these tools must be standardized and supported by tools that provide sufficient flexibility in order to create powerful artefacts that cope with the demands of the various domains.

Overall, users within these domains (e.g. therapists–patients, teachers–students, mediator–participant), given their pervasive activities, share the need to carry artefacts with them, the need to extend their presence to ubiquitous locations and adjust their usage to specific requirements. Contrastingly, few of the existing applications offer ways for users to create their own artefacts [15]. Moreover, even those that do, do not provide visual design options and generally require programming skills, also failing to introduce behaviour within the artefacts, easily configuring them to react to usage behaviour or problems, extending the support ubiquitously. Furthermore, the possibility of integrating various modalities and media types together with reviewing and analysis capabilities is also rarely available, retracting from possible improvements both on the applications and on the processes.

13.3 Design Framework

In order to support paper-based activities, the design framework aims at offering means to construct interactive multimedia artefacts, capable of gathering and presenting data through various modalities. This support is particularly directed to end-users, providing a simple to use design and construction procedure that does not require previous design or programming knowledge. This process is facilitated through embedded design guidelines that aid users during design, improving the overall usability of the artefact or providing alternatives when needed.

The framework is composed by two main tools. The first one offers user the ability to create and configure their personalized interactive digital artefacts. It is available in a desktop/TabletPC version (Fig. 13.1 on the left) and in a light mobile counterpart that allows simple adjustments and updates to the used artefacts directly on the hand-held device (Fig. 13.1 on the right). The second tool is the runtime environment which is responsible for recreating and running the created artefacts. Furthermore, it contains the necessary mechanisms to store and log all the user data and interactions. The runtime environment also encompasses a playback mode that provides means to analyse and review all the user's interactions and created results. Artefact exchange between tools and devices is seamless and integrated into the

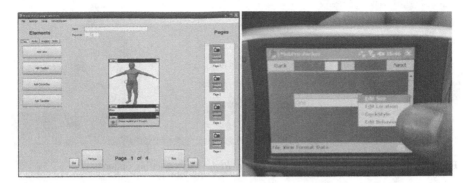

Fig. 13.1 The artefact design framework on its desktop version (left) and mobile one (right)

design tool. Artefacts, logs and results are stored in XML and can be exchanged through various means (e.g. e-mail, synchronization).

13.3.1 Artefact Design Tool

The artefact design tool (Fig. 13.1) is the framework's main component. It is composed by a wizard-based application that enables users to arrange artefacts, customizing them to their needs, usage situations, domain and devices (Fig. 13.2, right). It guides users on the design process by supporting the creation of each screen/page individually, not only organizing them sequentially but also allowing the configuration of different arrangements and sequences as needed, much alike pages within a book (right vertical bar – Fig. 13.1, left). Each screen/page is composed by a set of elements that can be added just by pressing a button. Currently, there are four main types of available elements (buttons on the left – Fig. 13.1, left) and each type can use different media formats and modalities (e.g. text, audio and video).

13.3.1.1 Output Elements

Output elements are mainly used for presentation purposes. They can be configured to display content to users on several ways using three media types: (1) *Text* – output elements are used to present textual content (e.g. book excerpts, questions) and can assume different configurations. For instance, labels can be used to show text with several characteristics (e.g. colours or font sizes). (2) *Audio and video* – output elements can be used with imported audio/video files, can be recorded directly on the designer through a microphone or webcam or, for audio only, can be synthetized from text (Fig. 13.2, left). (3) *Combined* – elements are composed by two or more output elements that present the same content. For instance, a text label can be used in concert with an audio file that contains the audio version of that same text.

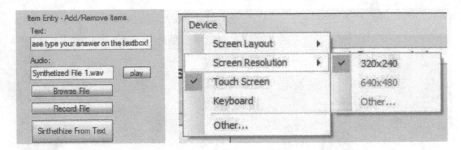

Fig. 13.2 *Left*: Audio label configuration screen. *Right*: Device setting options

13.3.1.2   Input Elements

Input elements are those that can be interacted with, providing users with the necessary mechanisms to create content and store it on the artefact. Here, elements can also assume various configurations and limitations or specific characteristics can be imposed. The same media types are available:

- *Text* – input elements allow users to type and store content on a textual format (e.g. text-boxes). These can be limited regarding size, font, characters, etc.
- *Audio and video* – input elements give users the ability to record sound or video clips directly into the artefact. The maximum length of the recording can also be configured during design.
- *Combined* – input elements can also be used. For instance, a specific element can be configured to request the user the same answer in two modalities that complement each other (e.g. text plus audio or video).

13.3.1.3   Mixed Elements

Mixed elements entangle output and input possibilities into one single element. They not only display content but also allow users to interact with, selecting or introducing data. The most common examples are track-bars or choice lists (e.g. radio button groups, combo-boxes), where each item of the list displays a particular type of media (e.g. text sentence, audio or video clips, image) and the user interacts with it by selecting the correct option(s).

13.3.1.4   Device and Domain-Oriented Elements

Device-specific elements, which depend on the used hardware, are also available. For instance, if the device has a touch screen, images or other elements can also be used as input elements. For example, an image divided into different areas can be used as a choice-list where the user selects, directly on the image, the correct choice. On the contrary, if using a normal cellphone, the element can be composed by the image and a corresponding drop-box with the available selections. Other examples provide navigation features over audio or video elements. The framework can also be easily extended with domain-oriented elements that include specific behaviours, limitations or icons that suit the demands of that particular domain (e.g. relaxation/emergency button, five column text entry element). Overall, elements can be used in concert with each other composing fairly elaborated screens and highly interactive artefacts (e.g. questionnaires, manuals, and games).

13.3.1.5 Actions and Triggers for Adaptation and Responsiveness

In order to create proactive digital documents/artefacts that offer hints and aids to users, manuals that omit or show new information according to the user's performance while completing it, the design framework also includes the customization of the artefacts' behaviour. Behaviour can be configured through the definition of rules. Rules are composed by time, interaction or content triggers and a consequent action. They can be attached to a specific element or to the entire artefact. On the former, depending on the interaction or usage within a specific element, a certain action can take place. On the latter, the interaction within various elements of the artefact (e.g. sequence of navigation or time to browse through various elements) defines the entire artefact's behaviour.

Time-based triggers can be configured to prompt warnings or change elements according to the time the user is taking to review/complete them. They can also be used to define alarms that alert users to use or complete an artefact at a given time.

Interaction triggers analyse the user's interaction with the device by counting clicks or detecting where on the screen the user has interacted. Content-based triggers activate actions depending on the content of the elements. For example, when the user chooses an option from a list or a value within a defined threshold, a certain action can be triggered (e.g. selecting 'YES' displays a warning).

In concert with the rules that are defined for each item or artefact, four different types of actions can be selected. The first one prompts a message that is composed by the user while the second jumps from the current screen or element to another within the artefact (e.g. first screen, end of the artefact, drawing, previous element). The two remaining actions hide or show elements (e.g. if a user checked a radio button a text-box is shown).

13.3.1.6 Design Guidelines and Suggestions

The usage of design guidelines and suggestions is paramount during the design process, especially taking into account that users creating their own artefacts may not have particular design or programming experience. Accordingly, the framework includes integrated design guidelines that assure acceptable usability levels while users are creating the artefacts' user interfaces. These guidelines automatically arrange screen elements according to specific values that can be configured and updated according to the targeted domain. Currently integrated guidelines allow the automatic docking and adjustment of elements to screen sizes and layouts. Moreover, the amount of elements per screen, as well as the amount of content per element (e.g. number of sentences within a label, size of an image, number of options within a list) can be limited according to various aspects (e.g. screen resolution, orientation). As a complement for these guidelines, when available, the system is also able to provide suggestions and alternative approaches to the current design. For instance, combo-boxes can be automatically replaced by radio buttons whenever options are longer than 25 characters or vice versa when the list contains more than 5 items.

13.3.2 Running Environment

The artefact running environment is the framework's second software component that is installed on a mobile device and is responsible for re-creating all the artefact/applications' descriptions, stored within XML files and built using the artefact editor. The environment is driven by a simple-to-use user interface which allows users to select which artefact to use as well as to review previously completed artefacts and results. The runtime environment application also includes a logging mechanism that, if switched on, gathers information about artefact usage for posterior analysis. Gathered data can be composed by the amount of clicks, location of the clicks, chosen values, typed characters, time to complete each question, time spent on an element or screen, etc. Currently, there are runtime environments for PocketPCs, PalmOS-based PDAs and desktop computers. This gathered data is used by the revision/log player feature that (r)enacts every event that was triggered, showing all the user's activities and interaction with the device and artefact (e.g. every typed character – one by one – or every selected choice). Events can be played at normal speed or browsed and searched as needed (Fig. 13.2, far right).

13.4 Case Studies and Usage Examples

Throughout the development stage, several domains were experimented and a wide set of artefacts was created using the framework (e.g. short interactive tutorials and organized diaries). However, to fully evaluate its potential, assess its usability and flexibility, the entire system was used on two real domains, psychotherapy and education, for real-life case studies.

13.4.1 Psychotherapy

Cognitive-Behavioural Therapy for the treatment of depression, anxiety or associated disorders relies heavily on the completion of paper questionnaires and thought registries throughout patients' daily lives. Accordingly, the introduction of a mobile-artefact developing framework was particularly suited to this scenario. Furthermore, the introduction of behaviour and pro-activeness without disregarding ubiquity was greatly needed in order to react to the patients' needs while away from therapy.

The design framework was used by psychotherapists and cognitive behavioural therapy researchers to create a wide set of existing therapeutic tools aiming to enhance the therapy process and to promote patient improvement [11]. Several specific originally paper-based artefacts (e.g. questionnaires, thought registering tables, pleasant activity records) were emulated and adjusted to patients. Therapists were requested to create similar digital versions with the available elements. For instance, thought registries were composed using text and audio output and input elements. The output elements requested the patient to register his or her thought while the input element allowed him or her to record it. Therapists created artefacts with both options, permitting users to select the most suited mode according to the location and time of completion. One therapist in particular included a quantifying element that allowed users to catalogue their thoughts and problems according to severity. All the therapists were given a short 30 min tutorial before using the framework.

Moreover, new approaches were also experimented and new artefacts were created. Some examples include anxiety assessment forms, pain measurement questionnaires, and relaxation tutorials. For instance, Fig. 13.3, on the middle, depicts an innovating pain therapy artefact that was arranged by a practising therapist. The artefact allows users to select the location of their pain through the image or the multiple-choice options. A similar artefact was created where users could point on an image their dislikes about their body and quantify them by using a track-bar.

Using the log player feature to review how patients completed their questionnaires and registered their thoughts, therapists were able to identify problematic thoughts where patients felt more uncomfortable (e.g. thoughts that took more time to register or were frequently revisited) and those that required further intervention during therapy sessions.

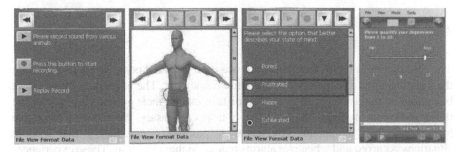

Fig. 13.3 Artefacts created with the design framework. *Far Right*: Log Player

13.4.2 Education

The framework was also used to create educational artefacts for students on a university setting, for a computer science course. Here, the main goal was to provide students with evaluation tests that could be answered on personal mobile devices (e.g. PPCs). Teachers also wanted to assess students' difficulties while using the tests and to understand if those problems pertained to the selected configuration of the artefacts or to the subject and content itself. The framework was provided to teachers in order to create the evaluation tests. Tests included several questions with different input and output elements (Fig. 13.3 on the left) and were distributed to a class of 30 students. This process was replicated at the university and at each student's home (e.g. tests sent to students through e-mail). All the results were gathered during the class or sent by mail and later reviewed by the teachers. The logging mechanisms allowed teachers to detect which questions took longer to respond, those that were revisited more frequently and those whose value was changed more than once. These three dimensions in concert allowed teachers to isolate questions that probably posed more difficulties to students. Moreover, it also provided detail on which input/output elements were more suited for a specific scenario [12].

Initial tests, composed by 20 screens/pages each, with two elements per page (e.g. one for output and one for input) took roughly 1 h to create. On the second iteration (the tests that were completed outside the class), teachers composed the artefacts with video and audio elements and took between 20 and 40 min. Students were given 1 h to complete each test. Log revision showed that most students completed the test in less that 30 min and revised their questions an average number of two to three times before locking their results.

On a qualitative analysis, students responded to questionnaires and results showed that they appreciated the fact of conveying within one device their annotations, exams and manuals provided by the teachers. Hints, the varied pictorial content and the visual appeal were also very well received. For teachers the major contributions were the ability to configure artefacts according to various dimensions and the ground breaking analysis that the log player features provided for class and homework, allowing them to replay all the students' interaction with the artefacts.

13.5 Results

The case studies in which the framework was used provided positive results regarding the functionalities and usability of the entire framework. The possibility of including behaviour on the artefacts allowed therapists to extend their presence outside of the therapy sessions, aiding patients whenever it was necessary. Patients also were able to complete their therapeutic artefacts more promptly, immediately after specific situations occurred and whenever alarms requested them to do so. These experiences solidified the initial beliefs that the framework could provide the needed features and flexibility to support a large roll of artefacts. When used in concert, the system's functionalities allowed users to adjust and tailor their artefacts taking into account the following dimensions: (1) Content – different types of media (e.g. images, text) were easily inserted, composing content or fetching information from several sources and compiling it into specific artefacts. These can contain various subjects (e.g. pain therapy, depression assessment, geometry, English). Together with the possibility of adjusting the content with different input types (e.g. touching the device's screen and pointing at a picture; selecting an option from a list of choices or writing free text), our system allowed users to create a varied set of artefacts for multiple purposes. (2) Location and time – using the same mechanisms mentioned above, users were able to compose artefacts according to the predicted location and time in which the tasks will be completed. For instance, if the user is not restrained by time, the artefact may be composed by open-ended questions (e.g. text-boxes). However, if the artefact must be completed while walking through a specific setting or similar context, lists, choice groups or audio input are better suited. (3) User requirements – different users (e.g. students/patients) have different requirements. Therefore, the system allows users (e.g. teachers or therapists) to personalize the used material (e.g. studying/therapeutic), including help and warnings, rewarding sentences, etc., according to the user and to his or her behaviour while completing the task. Furthermore, the inclusion of different media types and content also enhanced the usage process for users with different ages (e.g. pictorial content for younger ages and textual or both for older students). Using the log player functionality, therapists were able to identify problematic issues and concentrate their efforts on the most relevant problems. Teachers were also able to isolate questions that posed more problems to their students thus focusing specific subjects or customizing their tests accordingly. For students, advantages emerged from the possibility of using several artefacts on one device and even being able to carry on with their tasks (e.g. homework) wherever they were.

Regarding the design process, the outcome was extremely positive since users with no programming knowledge and no previous experience using the framework were able to design and materialize artefacts that suited their needs. Moreover, they were able, as initially aimed at, to enhance the processes and include features that were previously unavailable on the original artefacts.

Overall, the framework's adequateness to these two domains suggested that new boundaries can be found and other activities can be enhanced or supported by using mobile devices with proactive and customizable artefacts.

13.6   Conclusions and Future Work

Paper-based artefacts are used ubiquitously to support a wide set of activities on a daily basis. However, the used medium poses restrictions to the adjustment and tailoring of these artefacts hindering the underlying processes and obstructing cooperation, personalization and interaction with the artefacts.

In this chapter, we presented a design framework that supports the construction and utilization of multi-modal and multimedia artefacts by end-users. The framework provides a wizard-based user interface that aids users on the design, layout and user interface arrangements of highly flexible artefacts for mobile devices that can be carried along with users reacting and adjusting to their requirements as needed. The conducted experiments provided positive results, showing that users were able to create and customize their artefacts to their needs adjusting them to various dimensions. Globally, users that acted as designers or worked with the resulting artefacts were very pleased with the overall process.

As upcoming work, a group version of the framework is being developed. It will support cooperation from various users while composing artefacts that suit individuals or groups. Moreover, we aim at using the framework, individually or as a group version for prototyping purposes. Using the various elements that it integrates, together with the running (using actual devices), logging and revision capabilities, the framework can be used to create prototypes with various fidelities that automatically support active (e.g. usability questionnaires) and passive (e.g. log) evaluation procedures on real scenarios.

Acknowledgments This work was supported by LaSIGE and FCT, through project JoinTS, through the Multiannual Funding Programme and scholarship SFRH/BD/28165/2006.

References

1. K. Das. Computers in psychiatry: a review of past programs and an analysis of historical trends. Psychiatry Q, 73(4), 2002.
2. A. Przeworski and M. G. Newman. Palmtop computer-assisted group therapy for social phobia. J Clin Psychol, 60(2):179–188, 2004.
3. K. L. Alford and A. Ruocco. Integrating Personal Digital Assistants (PDAs) in a Computer Science Curriculum. IEEE Frontiers in Education, Reno, Nevada, October 10–13, 2001.
4. S. Garrard. Human–computer interactions: can computers improve the way doctors work. Schweiz Med Wochenschr, 130:1557–63, 2000.
5. K. M. Inkpen. Designing handheld technologies for kids. Personal Technol (3) 81–89, 1999.
6. J. G. Proudfoot. Computer-based treatment for anxiety and depression: is it feasible? Is it effective? Neurosci Biobehav Rev, 28:353–363, 2004.
7. J. H. Wright and A. WrightComputer-assisted psychotherapy. J Psychother Pract Res, 6:315–319, 1997.
8. S. Ljungblad, et al. Augmenting Paper-Based Work Practices. Ubicomp 2004.
9. R. L. Mandrik. Supporting Children's Collaboration Across Handheld Computers. In *CHI';01 Extended Abstracts on Human Factors in Computing Systems*, Seattle, WA, March 31–April 5, 2001, pp. 255–256.
10. D. Pownell and D. Bailey. The Next Small Thing – Handheld Computing for Educational Leaders. Learning and Leading with Technology, vol. 27, no. 8, International Society for Technology Education, 2000.
11. M. Sá, L. Carriço, and P. Antunes. Ubiquitous Psychotherapy. IEEE Pervasive Computing, Special Issue on Healthcare, vol. 6, no. 1, pp. 20–27, January–March, 2007.
12. M. Sá and L. Carriço. Detecting Learning Difficulties on Ubiquitous Scenarios, HCI International 2007, Beijing, China, July 22–27, 2007.

13. C. Savill-Smith and P. Kent. The Use of Palmtop Computers for Learning. Learning and Skills Development Agency, UK, 2003.
14. N. Segall, T. L. Doolen, and J. L. Porter. A usability comparison of PDA-based quizzes and paper-and-pencil quizzes. (English) Comput. Educ. 45, No. 4, 417–432 (2005).
15. M. Serrano, et al Multimodal Interaction on Mobile Phones: Development and Evaluation Using ACICARE. Mobile HCI'06, pp. 129–136, Helsinki, Finland, 2006.
16. G. Zurita, et al. Analyzing the Roles of PDA in Meeting Scenarios. CRIWG 2006, Spain.

Chapter 14
Integrating Dialog Modeling and Domain Modeling: The Case of Diamodl and the Eclipse Modeling Framework

Hallvard Trætteberg

Abstract For most applications, in particular data-intensive ones, dialog modeling makes little sense without a domain model. Since domain models usually are developed and used outside the dialog modeling activity, it is better to integrate dialog modeling languages with existing domain modeling languages and tools, than inventing your own. This chapter describes how the Diamodl language, editor, and runtime have been integrated with the Eclipse Modeling Framework.

14.1   Introduction

Domain modeling is one of the most fundamental software engineering activities. Besides being a tool for reaching a common understanding of the domain, a domain model may be utilized for engineering the actual system, both as a guidance for design and more directly as input to code and schema generators. There exist many languages that are well suited for this, and object-oriented class diagrams, as found in the Unified Modeling Language (UML), are very popular and well supported by modern tools.

A dialog model is an abstract description of the structure and behavior of a user interface, and in particular what information that each part mediates to the user as output and from the user as input. Hence, the domain model plays an important role in a dialog model, since the information that the user senses and manipulates by means of the user interface, should be part of it. This does not mean that the domain modeling activity must fully precede dialog modeling. For example, in a user-centered design process, prototypes are often used to elicit domain knowledge and requirements. If models are used for rapid prototyping, the domain model may result from or be refined by the dialog modeling process.

H. Trætteberg
Department of Computer and Information Sciences, Norwegian University of Science and Technology, Trondheim, Norway
e-mail: hal@idi.ntnu.no

V. López-Jaquero et al. (eds.), *Computer-Aided Design of User Interfaces VI*,
DOI: 10.1007/978-1-84882-206-1_14, © Springer-Verlag London Limited 2009

Since domain models are so important for dialog models, a dialog modeling language needs to include domain modeling concepts, like entity or class, attributes and associations, and operations. This does not mean you need to include a full domain modeling language in your dialog modeling language, but you must be able to reference, operate on, and utilize elements in existing models. At the language level, this means identifying every concept and construct where the domain model is relevant and where such references may be necessary. At the tool level, this means defining the role and scope of your own tools and existing ones, and their level of integration and interoperation. At the process level, this means identifying good practices for reaching specific goals.

This chapter details how the Eclipse Modeling Framework (EMF) [1] has been integrated into our Diamodl [2, 3] dialog modeling language, tool, and process. Section 14.2 gives an overview of related work. Section 14.3 briefly describes the Diamodl language and tool architecture, while Sect. 14.4 presents EMF. Section 14.5 explains how EMF concepts are integrated into the Diamodl language and how the EMF framework is utilized in the Diamodl tools. Section 14.6 outlines how the developer utilizes both EMF and Diamodl tools for developing and executing models, before we conclude in Sect. 14.7.[1]

14.2 Related Work

The topic of domain modeling has received some, but surprisingly little attention in the model-based user interface design (MB-UID) community in recent years. As the focus has shifted toward task-based design, domain modeling and data management get less focus than before. Paternò's work [4] lists domain models as one of several important abstractions, but it does not actually include a single domain model, although it does discuss UML, including class diagrams. Domain objects are mentioned as something operated upon by tasks, but little is said about how the structure of tasks relate to the structure of domain models, for example, specialization of task along inheritance relations and navigation along associations.

CTT, the most widely used task modeling notation, does not include objects in task diagrams itself, although it includes operators for data-based enablement. Several tools exist for working with CTT models, for example, CTTE [5] and Dialog-Graph-Editor [6], and although they both are able to generate running prototypes, they do not seem to be integrated with domain modeling languages or tools commonly used by industry.

Just-UI, with its heritage from a CASE method, acknowledges domain models by including a conceptual modeling stage using the object-oriented OO-Method, to obtain a conceptual schema of an Information System [7]. Code generation techniques

---

[1]More information is available at Diamodl's home page: http://www.idi.ntnu.no/~hal/research/diamodl.

are used for building a complete system, so it cannot be considered a rapid proto-typing tool.

Methods with roots from object-oriented design and software engineering are perhaps the most data-centric. OVID [8] is a method that combines object-oriented analysis and user interface design, to bridge the gap to software engineering. Hence, it has potential for integrating with domain modeling tools, but unfortunately, there is no tool support for OVID.

CanonSketch [9] is a tool for user-centered prototyping of user interfaces, where sketches of interfaces are evolved through canonical prototypes to executable HTML-based prototypes. In some ways, it is similar to the Diamodl approach presented in [3], in the focus on concrete representations and prototyping. However, their focus is on usability of developer-centric tools, while Diamodl is what they would call formalism-centric. CanonSketch is based on the Wisdom method [10] and hence supports UML, both for describing the logical structure of the user interface, the domain model and the link between them. However, CanonSketch does not seem to have support for combining the prototypes with rich example data, based on the domain model, for example, to aid user-centered evaluation.

UsiXML [11] is a family of XML-based languages, with a rich set of sublanguages and accompanying tools. UsiXML includes concepts (and tags) for task modeling, abstract and concrete user interface modeling, and domain modeling [12]. The domain model supports object-oriented modeling with classes, inheritance, attributes, associations, and methods. From the documentation on the Web site it is difficult, however, to understand how the domain model is handled by the existing editors, generators, and interpreters, for example, if code is implemented for representing the domain objects, like EMF does. The domain model has the concept of object and attribute, but there seems to be insufficient support for using rich example data in the generator and prototyping tools.

14.3   Diamodl and Domain Modeling

The Diamodl dialog modeling language is a hybrid language based on dataflow and state logic [2]. The dataflow part of the language includes concepts for storing, transforming, computing, and transmitting data, and is by nature data-intensive. Figure 14.1 shows a simple model fragment, with two variables (rectangles), a computation (triangle), and two gates (triangles) attached to an interactor (labeled rectangle). This particular fragment models how *a message* may be selected from the *set of messages* in *a mailbox*. A bit simplified, the logic is as follows: The value of the variable named "mailbox" flows into the computation named "messages." The computation is triggered whenever the input values change, and the resulting value[2] will

---

[2] The computation may also have side-effects, besides the resulting value.

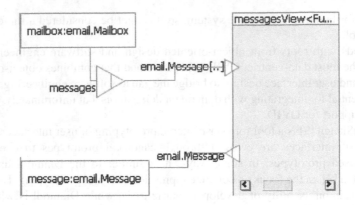

Fig. 14.1 Diamodl model fragment

flow into the gate pointing into the interactor. This gate is an *output-receive* gate, meaning that the interactor should make the value available for sensing by the end-user, typically by means of a graphical user interface component (widget). In the case of the fragment in Fig. 14.1, a listbox would be suitable, as it presents a set of values to the end-user and supports selection. If the interactor supports input of (new) values, as in this case, these values will flow out of the input-send gate, pointing out of the interactor. In the case of the fragment in Fig. 14.1, the selected item will flow out of the lower gate and into the variable named "message."

All these language elements are related to the domain model, for example, the variables and gates are typed with class names, the computation uses an association to compute-related values, and all of them (including the connections) operate on actual domain data.

While not shown in this model fragment, the Diamodl language supports states and transitions for controlling when various parts of the user interface are active. At first glance, these concepts are unrelated to the domain model. However, transitions are triggered by events and guarded by conditions, and they may refer to the domain data flowing into and out of variables and computations. In addition, transitions include actions that are executing when they are triggered, and states include actions that are executed upon entry and exit. These actions may operate on the domain data accessible in the context of the triggering model element.

Prototyping with Diamodl is supported by an editor and a runtime. The editor is based on GMF and includes actions for launching a runtime and executing the model. The behavior of the running prototype is animated in the editor to make it easier to understand the relationship between concrete and abstract structure and behavior. It is also possible to capture an event trace, to be able to inspect the execution in greater detail.

The Diamodl runtime is based on several open source libraries. The dataflow behavior is based on JFace Data Binding [13], data management on EMF [1], Statechart logic on the Apache SCXML engine [14], GUI execution on an XML format and renderer for SWT named XSWT [15], and finally, Javascript support is

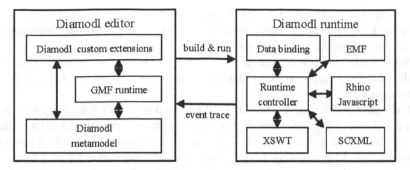

Fig. 14.2 Diamodl editor and runtime architecture

implemented by the Gnu Rhino engine [16]. All these libraries have been adapted and integrated to fit together both with Diamodl and with each other, as illustrated in Fig. 14.2.

14.4   Eclipse Modeling Framework (EMF) Concepts and Tools

EMF is a comprehensive Java-based framework and set of tools for modeling and managing domain data. Its core consists of a modeling language called Ecore and a compact runtime for managing models and instance data. Ecore supports a small subset of UML's class diagrams, similar to Object Management Group's MetaObject Facility [17], that is well suited for both in-memory manipulation and code generation. Since Ecore is its own meta-model, a fairly small set of concepts and a correspondingly small API may be used for understanding and managing Ecore objects.

An Ecore model describes a set of classes with attributes, references (associations in UML), and operations. In the typical case, a developer will generate a complete Java implementation of the model, and use the generated code in further development, for example, by filling in the body of operation stubs. Two standard languages, Java and OCL, are supported for specifying an operation's implementation, both of which rely on *annotations* on the operation that are recognized by the code generator, and appropriate code templates. Although a special, generated object factory is used to create the actual instances, the instances themselves will look and feel like ordinary Java objects and the application programmer will mostly use them as such.

EMF also supports a dynamic, reflective, meta-object-based API for managing instances, without any code generation. This API is typically used by generic tools that are independent of a specific Ecore model. In this case, the application typically loads one or more Ecore models and uses the contained meta-objects for creating instances and accessing attributes and references. Whether you use the generated or reflective API, a comprehensive set of features is provided by the framework core, including change notification and recording, automatic management of inverse references, and XML-serialization.

Several other Eclipse projects utilize and contribute EMF technology. The EMF Tools (EMFT) project contributes support for validation (e.g., using OCL), querying, and transactions.

EMF provides Eclipse-based views, editors, and wizards for working with both data and models. There are wizards that let you create an Ecore model from scratch, or built from Java code or an XML schema. The tree-based Ecore editor provides menu commands for creating model element according to context, a property sheet for editing details and drag'n drop for moving elements. There also exists a graphical Ecore editor contributed by the Graphical Modeling Framework (GMF) project. Although GMF is a generic framework for graphical editors for Ecore-based models, a graphical Ecore editor is provided as showcase of GMF's features.[3] A screenshot of both the tree-based and the graphical editor is shown in Fig. 14.3.

Given an Ecore model (file) it is possible to create and edit a data file containing instance data for the model. For instance, if the model contains the classes Library, Author, and Book, the data file may contain instances representing a specific Library containing a set of specific Books by specific Authors. The data editor is

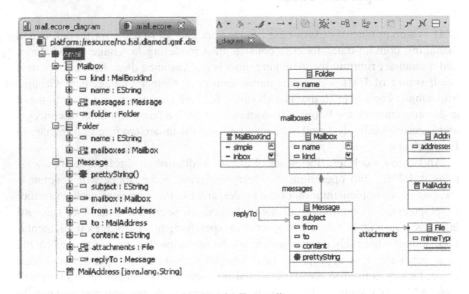

Fig. 14.3 Tree-based (*left*) and graphical (*right*) Ecore editors

---

[3] A newer and more feature-rich option is Ecore Tools (http://wiki.eclipse.org/index. php/Ecore_Tools).

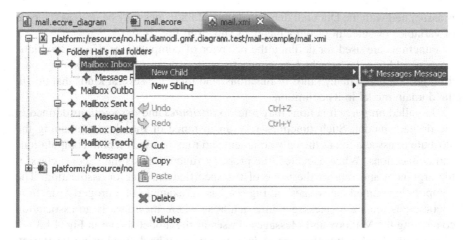

Fig. 14.4 Tree-based data editor

purely reflective, that is, it does not rely on generated code, only on the model. The editor makes sure only valid instance structures can be created, based on the rules defined in the model and implemented by custom validation code.

Figure 14.4 shows how the editor ensures that only a message may be created as a child of a Mailbox. Although the editor is simple and tree-based, it works well for creating example data for a domain.

EMF has extensive support for XML, in two ways. First, all instance graphs, including Ecore models, are serializable as XML. Second, any XML schema may be translated to an Ecore model. Later, when EMF serializes instance graphs for this model, it will make sure the XML is compliant with the original XML schema.

14.5   Utilizing EMF in the Diamodl Language and Runtime

Types and *functions* are the most important Diamodl modeling concepts where elements from the domain model need to be referenced. A type specifies a limited range of values that a variable may hold, that a function may take as argument or return, or that may flow along a connection. A type is a basic type like Integer, Boolean, or String, a user-defined class name or an array/list of one of the previous kinds. Diamodl does not support the definition of new classes; instead it relies on Java's classpath, for looking up Java classes, or Ecore models that are associated with the Diamodl model, for looking up Ecore classes. That is, to introduce domain-specific data in a Diamodl model, you must either add the necessary Java classes to your project or model the data using EMF's tools and associate the resulting Ecore model with your Diamodl model. As mentioned above, this may be done using the editors provided by the EMF and GMF projects. Once the Ecore model is associated with the Diamodl diagram, Ecore class names may be used as the type of variables by selecting from a menu, as shown in Fig. 14.5.

Functions are used for defining the behavior of computations. Unary functions may in addition be attached to connections, to transform values as they pass through. There are many kinds of functions, and there are several kinds that utilize the domain model in its definition.

So-called *property* functions may refer to *attributes* and *associations* defined in the domain model. Such functions take an instance of the class containing the attribute or association as the only argument and may be used on both computations and connections. When executed, the property function finds the (Ecore) class of the argument and returns the value of the specified attribute or association. The computation named "messages" in Fig. 14.1 is an example of a property function. It computes the set of messages in a mailbox, where messages is an association connecting the Mailbox and Messages classes in the model shown in Fig. 14.3.

A second kind of function, the *script* function, may be defined using Javascript, and the Javascript code may operate on the domain data accessible through the function's arguments. We use the Gnu Rhino engine, which is tightly integrated with Java. For example, it is possible to refer to any Java class and getters and setters are accessed using the Javascript property mechanism. To better support Ecore-based data, we have extended the Rhino engine to support Ecore instances. When a Javascript property of an Ecore instance (EObject) is read or set, we use EMF's dynamic meta-object-based API to access the corresponding attribute or association. This means that we may navigate through any instance graph with both ordinary Java objects and Ecore instances using Javascript's property access syntax.

As mentioned, Ecore supports specifying the implementation of operation using annotations. Unfortunately, since the support relies on code generation, it is less helpful in our prototyping tool. Therefore, we have added support for annotating the operation with Javascript. In Javascript, a method is a property with an anonymous function as its value. We have augmented the property lookup mechanism to look for our custom annotation. If the property currently has no value and the custom

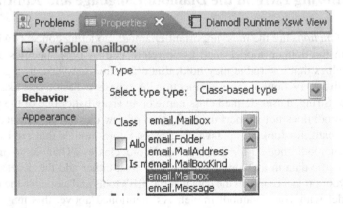

Fig. 14.5 Selecting an Ecore class as the type of a variable in the property sheet

annotation contains source code defining a function, an anonymous function object is created on-the-fly, installed as the property value (for later) and returned. For example, the prettyString operation defined by the Message class and shown in the class diagram in Fig. 14.3, is implemented by the following Javascript: $1.from + ":" + $1.subject; (The $1 symbol refers the implicit object argument, while $n for higher ns refers to the explicit arguments.) By supporting a scripting language like Javascript, more of the domain's meaning may be captured in the model and used it in our prototyping tool, without the need for code generation and a separate build operation.

Sometimes there is a need for referencing classes and other model elements in the domain model in Javascript code. This is necessary for testing whether some object is an instance of a specific Ecore class or for creating new instances of a specific Ecore class. To support this, all the Ecore packages associated with some Diamodl model are defined as global variables in Javascript's top-level scope. For example, in the model in Fig. 14.1, Javascript code will be able to refer to the Ecore package named "email" just by using its name. By using the getEClassifier()-method from the reflective Ecore-API it's then possible to locate a specific class by name, for example, email.getEClassifier("Message") will return the Message class. Since looking up contained objects by name is fairly common, we have introduced a shortcut that lets you read it as a property. For example, the expression email. Message will iterate across all objects contained by the email variable's value and return the one with a "name" attribute with the value "Message." This mechanism works for all Ecore instances, so any domain model using containment associations and "name"-attributes will support this shortcut.

The behavior of Diamodl is partly dataflow and partly Statecharts. The network of variables, computations, gates, and connections defines a graph through which data is propagated whenever some change occur. For example, when a variable changes, the value is propagated through the outgoing connections. Similarly, when one of the input values of a computation changes, a new output value is (re)computed and propagated through the network. In addition to reacting to changes of values, the Diamodl runtime also support reacting to changes of value properties, as this is necessary to ensure that dependent values are correctly updated. For example, a form field showing some property P of variable O must be updated both when O changes and when O's P property changes. In the Diamodl runtime, this is implemented by means of the JFace Data Binding framework and its "observable" values. Out of the box, this framework supports Java's standard way of listening to property changes. However, we have added support for Ecore's notification mechanism, to allow Ecore instances to also fully participate in dataflow. This makes it possible to have a variable typed with an Ecore class and ensure that property changes are reacted upon. For example, in the example in Fig. 14.1, this may be used to ensure that the listbox presenting the messages contained by the mailbox variable is correctly updated when a message is added or removed.

Conditions and actions are related to the Statechart "nature" of Diamodl. As mentioned above, they may both be attached to transitions and actions may also be attached to states. Conditions are evaluated in the context of some event, to guard the triggering of a transition after the appropriate event has been received. The event may include an event object which the condition may refer to. For example, if we want something special to happen when a message with a certain property is selected, the event will be that an object flows out of the appropriate gate, while the condition will check the property. Again, the domain model becomes central, and as for functions, Javascript support has been introduced as a generic solution. That is, conditions may be defined by means of Javascript expressions. Similarly, actions may be defined by Javascript statements that are executed in the context of the triggered model element, whether transition or state.

14.6 Using the EMF and Diamodl Tools Together

In this section, we will outline how the EMF and Diamodl tools are used together in practice.

It is often a matter of taste whether domain modeling is done before, during, or after dialog modeling. Fairly often, we model user interfaces for existing systems, and in such cases it is natural to develop the domain model first. EMF provides both tree-based and diagram-based editing of Ecore models, as shown in Fig. 14.3. In the initial development of the model, we prefer the diagram editor, but we find ourselves using the tree-based for details and annotations (used for scripting operations) as it is more responsive and has complete coverage of the Ecore language. Once a domain model is available, we can start referring to domain concepts in the Diamodl model, for example, define variables with type information and computations that access attributes and associations. If a concept name is used but missing, the Diamodl editor will insert problem markers. The editor includes actions for opening the domain model, so it is easy to add missing concepts to the domain model.

The editor has a palette of pre-defined model fragments to make modeling quicker, both abstract interactors and interactors containing references to a library of concrete user interface elements. To test a dialog, a runtime is launched, and all the concrete user interface elements are assembled into an XSWT file and rendered in a view in the Workbench, in a separate frame or inside the editor. Currently, layout information must be included by hand, by editing the XSWT file.

A qualitative evaluation of the user interface is possible without actual domain data, but little of the behavior may be tested without actual data to interact with and operate on. The Ecore editor includes an action for instantiating the model. EMF requires that a single object be the root of an instance tree, so an appropriate class must exist and be selected when creating the data file. A complete graph of Ecore instances may then be created using the reflective data editor, as shown in Fig. 14.4. Since the XML serialization format is based on the open XMI standard, it is straight-forward to export data from existing sources, using appropriate queries and transformations.

Once the example data are in place, they may be loaded by the runtime and utilized by the model elements. For example, each variable in the model has an

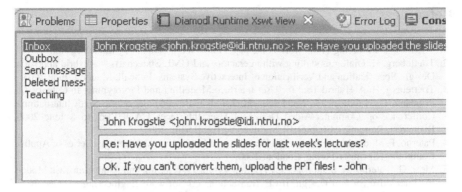

Fig. 14.6 The GUI prototype executing with example data from Ecore data file

enter action, that is executed when that part of the model is activated as a state. To initialize the variable with data from the data file, you will usually write a simple Javascript expression that navigates from the root instance to the desired data. A special action is provided for the common case where a variable is initialized to all the instances of a certain class.

The initialization of the variables will trigger the dataflow machinery and the user interface prototype will become alive, as the user interface elements are populated with data. The end-user may then start interacting with the prototype and cause values to flow according to the modeled behavior. Figure 14.6 shows an example prototype where the user first has selected a mailbox from a list and then selected one of this "mailbox" messages.

14.7   Conclusion and Further Work

The current version of the Diamodl editor and runtime, is the third in a series of implementations and the first that has fully been integrated with Eclipse and EMF. The EMF integration has and will allow us to utilize a plethora of modeling tools within the Eclipse ecosystem, since most of these also support EMF. Hopefully, this will make dialog modeling easier to combine with model-driven software engineering.

We are currently using Diamodl editor and runtime and the EMF tools in our master course TDT4250 on Model-driven development of information systems. In this course, we combine business process modeling with BPMN, domain modeling with EMF, and dialog modeling with Diamodl. Our experiences show that this combination works well from a modeling perspective. The next step is integrating Diamodl and EMF runtime systems with a BPEL engine, to enable Diamodl-based prototypes to participate in modern SOA-based process-oriented architectures. By building on Eclipse and EMF, we believe we have a good foundation for this work.

References

1. The Eclipse Modeling Framework home page: http://www.eclipse.org/modeling/emf/.
2. Trætteberg, H. Dialog modelling with interactors and UML Statecharts – a hybrid approach. Design, Specification and Verification of Interactive Systems. Funcall, Madeira, June 2003.
3. Trætteberg, H. A Hybrid Tool for User Interface Modelling and Prototyping. In Calvary, G., Pribeanu, C., Santucci, G., Vanderdonckt, J. (eds.), Proceedings of the Sixth International Conference on Computer-Aided Design of User Interfaces CADUI'06. (6–8 June 2006, Bucharest, Romania), Chapter 18, Springer-Verlag, Berlin, 2007.
4. Paternò, F. Model-based Design and Evaluation of Interactive Applications. Series of Applied Computing, Springer-Verlag, London, 2000.
5. Mori, G., Paternò, F., Santoro, C. CTTE: Support for Developing and Analyzing Task Models for Interactive System Design, IEEE Transactions on Software Engineering (August 2002, pp.797–813).
6. Reichart, D. Presented at the Tamodia 2007, Toulouse, France, demo session: http://liihs.irit.fr/tamodia2007/index.php?content=Demos.
7. Molina, P.J., Meliá, S., Pastor, O. JUST-UI: A User Interface Specification Model. Ch. Proceedings of the 4th International Conference on Computer-Aided Design of User Interfaces CADUI'2002, Kolski, J. & Vanderdonckt, J. (eds.), Valenciennes, France. Kluwer, Dordrecht, 2002.
8. Roberts, D., Berry, D., Isensee, S., and Mullaly, J. Designing for the User with OVID: Bridging User Interface Design and Software Engineering, MacMillan, Indianapolis, 1998.
9. Campos, P., Nunes, N. CanonSketch: A User-Centered Tool for Canonical Abstract Prototyping. Proceedings of the EHCI/DSV-IS'2004, International Conference on Engineering Human-Computer Interaction/International Workshop on Design, Specification and Verification of Interactive Systems, Hamburg, Germany, 2004.
10. Nunes, N. J., Cunha, J. F. WISDOM: Whitewater Interactive System Development with Object Models, in Mark van Harmelen (ed.), Object-oriented User Interface Design, Addison-Wesley, Object Technology Series, 2001.
11. Limbourg, Q., Vanderdonckt, J. UsiXML: A User Interface Description Language Supporting Multiple Levels of Independence, in Matera, M., Comai, S. (Eds.), Engineering Advanced Web Applications, Rinton Press, Paramus, 2004, pp. 325–338.
12. UsiXML language documentation: http://www.usixml.org/index.php?mod=pages&id=6, last visited at 1. February.
13. JFace Data Binding: http://wiki.eclipse.org/index.php/JFace_Data_Binding.
14. Apache SCXML engine: http://commons.apache.org/scxml/.
15. XSWT: http://sourceforge.net/projects/xswt (a bit outdated).
16. Gnu Rhino: http://www.mozilla.org/rhino/.
17. Object Management Group MetaObject Facility: http://www.omg.org/mof/.

Chapter 15
Inspector: Interactive UI Specification Tool

Thomas Memmel and Harald Reiterer

Abstract When the user interface should be specified, a picture is worth a thousand words, and the worst thing to do is write a natural language specification for it. Although this practice is still common, it is a challenging task to move from text-based requirements and problem-space concepts to a final UI design, and then back. Especially for user interface specification, actors must frequently switch between high-level descriptions and low-level detailed screens. In our research, we found out that advanced specifications should be made up of interconnected artefacts that have distinct levels of abstraction. With regards to the transparency and traceability of the rationale of the specification process, transitions and dependencies must be visual and traversable. For this purpose, a user interface specification method is introduced that interactively integrates interdisciplinary and informal modelling languages with different levels of fidelity of user interface prototyping. With an innovative experimental tool, we finally assemble models and design to an interactive user interface specifications.

15.1 Introduction

It is generally recognized by both software practitioners and Human–Computer Interaction (HCI) specialists that structured approaches are required to model, specify and build interactive systems with high usability [18]. This structure should be reflected in the Software Development Life Cycle (SDLC). Nevertheless, in many organizations, UI design is still an accidental or opportunistic by-product and HCI methods are not sufficiently embedded in the overall SDLC. If they are integrated, their contribution remains marginal, thus reducing the expected positive impact on

T. Memmel (✉) and H. Reiterer
Human-Computer Interaction Group, University of Konstanz, Universitätsstrasse,
10, 78457 Konstanz, Germany
e-mail: memmel@inf.uni-konstanz.de

V. López-Jaquero et al. (eds.), *Computer-Aided Design of User Interfaces VI*,
DOI: 10.1007/978-1-84882-206-1_15, © Springer-Verlag London Limited 2009

software quality. This reality can be explained by the fact that most Integrated Development Environments (IDEs) are inappropriate for supporting actors from different disciplines in designing interactive systems. Formal UI tools prevent many actors from taking part in collaborative design if they do not have adequate knowledge of specific terminologies. On the contrary, being too informal leads to misunderstandings and conflicts in communication with programmers. Moreover, on further examination, many tools turn out to be more focused on requirements management than on providing support in extracting requirements from user needs and translating them into good UI design. After all, despite – or perhaps precisely because of – the vast functionality of many tools, the outcome often is unsatisfactory in terms of UI design, usability and aesthetics. This is described as the *high threshold – low ceiling* phenomenon of UI tools [8]. In order to easily produce some results with reasonable efforts, an IDE should have a low threshold: the threshold with which one can obtain a reasonably good UI should be as low as possible. On the contrary, an IDE should have a high ceiling: the maximum overall performance of the IDE should be as high as possible. To these two dimensions, one usually adds a third one: *wide walls* (Fig. 15.1). An IDE should have walls that are as wide as possible, thus meaning that the range of possible UIs that can be obtained via the IDE should cover as much different UIs as possible.

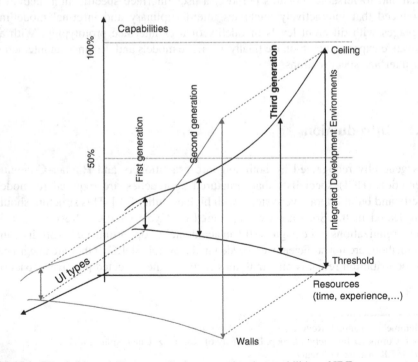

Fig. 15.1 Threshold vs. ceiling vs. walls for expressing the capabilities of IDEs

15.1.1   Actors in the UI Specification Process

Over the last 3 years, we observed UI development practice in the German automotive industry [14, 16]. As a consequence of the lack of appropriate tools, many actors tend to use tools they are familiar with and which can be categorized as being *low threshold – low ceiling – narrow walls* IDEs, which has been well observed by [8]. We distinguish between two different populations of tool-users, which can be assigned to two different areas of corporate UI development projects: (1) Client: Business personnel, marketers, domain experts or HCI experts use Office-like applications such as Word or Power Point [14] to document user needs and context of use in order to define the problem-space. They will translate the needs as analyzed, and their contextual conditions, into general usage requirements and evaluate their work at several quality gates. At this stage, responsibility is typically shared with, or completely passed on to, an IT supplier. (2) Supplier: Actors with a sophisticated IT background (e.g. programmers or designers) translate usage requirements into UI and system requirements, deliver prototypes and conclude the outcome in a UI specification. Working with UI builders, and using more formal, precise and standardized notations, they narrow the solution space towards the final UI.

15.1.2   Shortcomings of Current UI Specification Practice

smats. This makes it difficult to promote concepts and creative thinking down the supply chain without media disruptions and loss of precision [14]. The following negative factors therefore contribute to UI development failure:

1. The lack of a common course of action and the use of inappropriate, incompatible terminologies and modelling languages [24] that prevent even the minimum levels of transparency, traceability and requirements-visualization that would be adequate for the problem.
2. The difficulty in switching between abstract and detailed models due to a lack of interconnectivity (compare [9]).
3. The difficulty of travelling from problem space to solution space, a difficulty that turns the overall UI development into a black-box process.
4. The burial of mission-critical information in documents that are difficult to research and have very awkward traceability. Experts are overruled when the UI design rationale is not universally available in the corresponding prototypes.
5. The perpetuation of unrecognized cross-purposes in client and supplier communication, which can lead to a premature change or reversal of UI design decisions, the implications of which will not be realized until later stages.
6. The resulting misconceptions that lead to costly change requests and iterations, which torpedo budgets and time frames and endanger project goals.

Because of the immaturity of their UI development processes, industrial clients determined on a shift of responsibility. In our research for Dr. Ing. h. c. F. Porsche

AG and Daimler AG, we found the following sticking points that tend to change current UI specification practice: (1) Due to the strategic impact of many software products, clients want to increase their UI-related competency in order to reflect corporate values by high UI quality [16]. (2) Whereas conceptual modelling, prototyping or evaluation have always been undertaken by suppliers, the client himself now wants to work in the solution space and therefore needs to develop the UI specification in-house [14]. (3) The role of the supplier becomes limited to programming the final system. The client can identify a timetable advantage from this change, and an important gain in flexibility in choosing his suppliers. Having an in-house competency in UI-related topics, the client becomes more independent and can avoid costly and time-consuming iterations with external suppliers. (4) It is nearly impossible to specify a UI with Office-like applications. The existing actors, who are nevertheless accustomed to text-based artefacts, now require new approaches. The task of learning the required modelling languages and understanding how to apply these new tools must not be an unreasonably difficult one.

15.1.3 Tool Support that is Adequate for the Problem

This cultural change must be supported by an integrating UI tool that allows the translation of needs into requirements and subsequently into good UI design. In Table 15.1, we present a condensed overview of relevant UI tool requirements. In this chapter, we present both a set of models and a corresponding tool named INSPECTOR, still under development, which are designed to support interdisciplinary teams in gathering user needs, translating them into UI-related requirements, designing prototypes of different fidelity and linking the resulting artefacts to an *interactive UI specification*. The term *interactive* refers to the concept of making the process visually externalized to the greatest extent possible. This concerns both the artefacts and the medium of the UI specification itself. The latter should no longer be a text-based document, but a running simulation of how the UI should

Table 15.1 Requirements for UI tools for interactive UI specification; on the basis of [14, 20, 9]

Purpose/added value	Tool requirement
Traceability of design rationale; transparency of translation of models into UI design	Switching back and forth between different (levels of) models
Smooth transition from problem-space concepts to solution space	Smooth progression between abstract and detailed representations
HCI experts can build abstract and detailed prototypes rapidly	Designing different versions of a UI is easy and quick, as is making changes to it
Provide support for design assistance and creative thinking for everybody; all kinds of actors can proactively take part in the UI specification	Concentration on a specific subset of modelling artefacts, which can be a UML-like notation or one that best leverages collaboration
The early detection of usability issues prevents costly late-cycle changes	Allowing an up-front usability evaluation of look and feel; providing feedback easily

Table 15.2 Main differences between prototypes and interactive UI specifications

Interactive UI prototypes	Interactive UI specifications
Vehicle for requirements analysis	Vehicle for requirements specification
Exclusively models the UI layer; may be inconsistent with specification and graphical notations	Allows drill down from UI to models; relates UI to requirements and vice versa
Either low-fidelity or high-fidelity	Abstract first, specification design later
Supplements text-based specification	Widely substitutes text-based specification
Design rationale saved in other documents	Incorporates design knowledge and rationale

look *and* feel. Accordingly, we extend the meaning of UI prototypes to also include the provision of access to information items *below* the UI presentation layer.

Being interactively connected, all of the ingredients result in a compilation of information items that are necessary to specify the UI (Table 15.2). In Section 15.2, we link our research to related work. Section 15.3 presents the common denominator in modelling that we developed. We explain how our tool, called INSPECTOR, will utilize the resulting interconnected hierarchy of notations. We illustrate how abstract and detailed designs can be easily created and also exported in machine-readable XML formats such as XAML or UsiXML [12].

15.2   Related Work

Campos and Nunes presented the tools CanonSketch and TaskSketch [9]. CanonSketch was the first tool that used canonical abstract prototypes and a UML-like notation, supplemented by a functioning HTML UI design layer. TaskSketch is a modelling tool that focuses on linking and tracing use cases, by means of which it significantly facilitates development tasks with an essential use-case notation. Altogether, TaskSketch provides three synchronized views: the participatory view uses a post-it notation to support communication with end-user and clients, the task-case view is targeted towards designers and is a digital version of index cards (well-known artefacts of usage-centred or agile developers) and the UML activity diagram view is adequate for software engineers. As we will see in this chapter, we closely concur with the concepts of these tools, but our approach differs in some important areas. First, and in contrast to CanonSketch, we also support detailed UI prototyping because we found that the high-fidelity externalization of design vision is especially important in corporate UI design processes. Second, we provide more ways of modelling. INSPECTOR integrates earlier text-based artefacts, as well as task models and interaction diagrams. Some of them are also grounded in usage-centred design, but we focused on agile models as they proved to be helpful in bridging the gaps between the disciplines (see Sect. 15.3).

The tools DAMASK [13] and DENIM [19] used a Zoomable User Interface (ZUI) approach for switching between different levels of detail through a visual drill-down process. Based on our own experience with ZUIs, we followed a consistent implementation of this technique. Calvary et al. [7] presented the CAMELEON reference framework, which proposes four levels of abstraction for UI tools: tasks and concepts, abstract UI design, detailed UI design and the final UI. We will see that INSPECTOR supports this framework very well by the nature of the layers of abstraction used and the ZUI approach applied. However, as INSPECTOR is focused on UI specification rather than on actual UI development, it supports the final UI stage by means of UIs to other tools in the supply chain.

With respect to DAMASK and DENIM, INSPECTOR borrowed the idea of using animations to support transitions between contexts of use: when an actor needs to switch from one view to another, INSPECTOR applies a zoom-in, zoom-out technique so as to preserve continuity between the contexts of use, which has been largely demonstrated as a positive impact in SDLC [13].

15.3 A Common Denominator in UI-Related Modelling

An advanced IDE must be able to support all actors in actively participating in the UI specification process (Table 15.1). This requires it to deploy modelling techniques that can be used easily by everybody. We know that the Unified Modelling Language (UML) is a weak means of modelling the UIs of interactive systems [22]. As well as its shortcomings in describing user interactions with the UI, its notation also overwhelms most actors with too much (and mostly unnecessary) detail [2]. Designing UIs is an interdisciplinary assignment and many actors might be left behind due to any formality. For instance, UML is like Office-like artefacts in being inadequate for the specification of the look *and* feel of interactive UIs.

15.3.1 Bridging the Gaps with Agile Modelling

The identification of adequate means of modelling for UI specification is very much related to the ongoing discussion on bridging the gaps between HCI and SE. This discussion is also propelled by the very difference in the way experts from both fields prefer to express themselves in terms of formality and visual externalization. HCI and SE are recognized as professions made up of very distinct populations. In the context of corporate UI specification processes as outlined in Sect. 15.1, modelling the UI also requires the integration of the discipline of business-process modelling (BPM). The interaction layer – as interface between system and user – is the area where HCI, SE and BPM are required to collaborate in order to produce high-quality UIs. As actors in corporate UI specification processes come from all three disciplines, the question is which modelling notations are adequate to extend and align their vocabulary. As we found in our previous research, agile methods are close to HCI practice [15] and therefore represent a promising pathfinder for a course of action common to all three disciplines. Holt [11] presents a BPM approach that is based on UML class, activity, sequence and use-case notations. Ambler based its agile version of the Rational Unified Process (RUP) on a similar, but less formal,

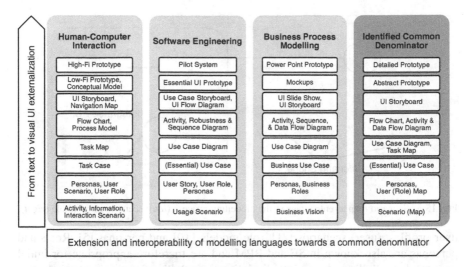

	Human-Computer Interaction	Software Engineering	Business Process Modelling	Identified Common Denominator
	High-Fi Prototype	Pilot System	Power Point Prototype	Detailed Prototype
	Low-Fi Prototype, Conceptual Model	Essential UI Prototype	Mockups	Abstract Prototype
	UI Storyboard, Navigation Map	Use Case Storyboard, UI Flow Diagram	UI Slide Show, UI Storyboard	UI Storyboard
	Flow Chart, Process Model	Activity, Robustness & Sequence Diagram	Activity, Sequence, & Data Flow Diagram	Flow Chart, Activity & Data Flow Diagram
	Task Map	Use Case Diagram	Use Case Diagram	Use Case Diagram, Task Map
	Task Case	(Essential) Use Case	Business Use Case	(Essential) Use Case
	Personas, User Scenario, User Role	User Story, User Role, Personas	Personas, Business Roles	Personas, User (Role) Map
	Activity, Information, Interaction Scenario	Usage Scenario	Business Vision	Scenario (Map)

From text to visual UI externalization

Extension and interoperability of modelling languages towards a common denominator

Fig. 15.2 Towards a common denominator in interdisciplinary UI-related modelling

BPM approach [1]. In general, agile approaches already exist in HCI [15], BPM [1] and SE [4] and we can define a common denominator for all three disciplines. We keep this denominator as small as possible. We filter out models that are too difficult to be understood by every actor. We do not consider models that are more commonly used to support actual implementation or that have been identified as mostly unnecessary by Agile Modelling [1, 2]. IT suppliers can deduce the structure of the UI much better from the resulting interactive specification than they can from Office-like documents.

We integrate different levels of modelling abstraction to visualize the flow from initial abstract artefacts to detailed prototypes of the interaction layer. On the vertical axis in Fig. 15.2, we distinguish the models according to their level of abstraction. Models at the bottom are more abstract (i.e. text-based, pictorial), whereas those at upper levels become more detailed with regard to the specification of the UI. On the horizontal axis, we identify appropriate models for UI specification. Accordingly, we differentiate between the grade of formality of the models and their purpose and expressivity. The models with a comparable right to exist are arranged at the same level. At each stage, we identify a common denominator for all three disciplines as a part of the thereby evolving interactive UI specification.

15.3.2 Text-Based Notations of Needs and Requirements: Personas and Scenarios

Text-based notations can be used at any stage to document early usability attributes (usability and user experience goals, constraints, etc.) with INSPECTOR's information bubbles (Fig. 15.3, left). For describing users and their needs, HCI recognizes

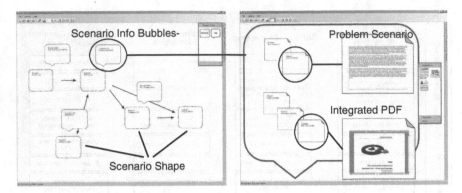

Fig. 15.3 Scenario map as entry stage to the modelling process (*left*); scenario info-bubble (*right*)

user profiles, (user) scenarios [21], role models [10] and personas [5]. Roles and personas are also known in SE and BPM and are therefore appropriate for initial user-needs modelling. As an interdisciplinary modelling language, research suggests scenarios [3] – known as user stories (light-weight scenarios) in agile development [4]. In SE, scenarios – as a sequence of events triggered by the user – are generally used for requirements gathering and for model checking.

Such a scenario is used to identify a thread of usage for the system to be constructed and to provide a description of how the system will be used. HCI applies scenarios to describe in detail the software context, users, user roles, activities (i.e. tasks), and interaction for a certain use case. BE uses scenario-like narrations to describe a business vision, that is, a guess about users (customers), their activities and interests. Starting up INSPECTOR, the user can create a scenario map that relates all scenarios that will be modelled (Fig. 15.3, left). The user can first describe a single scenario in a bubble shape (Fig. 15.3, right). For this purpose, INSPECTOR provides a build-in text editor with according templates and enables the direct integration of existing requirement documents into its repository. Later, the user will zoom-in and fill the scenario shape with graphical notations and UI design.

15.3.3 Graphical Notations: Requirements, Usage and Behaviour Modelling

Entering this stage, the user needs artefacts that support the important process of translating needs into requirements. Role maps [10] help to relate created Personas to each other (Fig. 15.4, left). Although different in name, task cases (HCI), essential-use cases (SE) and business-use cases (BPM) can be created in a classical use-case notation (Fig. 15.4, left). Moreover, use-case diagrams (SE, BE) overlap with use-case and task maps (HCI) [10]. The latter also help to separate more general cases from more specialized (essential) sub-cases. We considered different models for task and process modelling and, following Ambler [1, 2], we again selected related modelling languages.

Activity diagrams (Fig. 15.4, right) are typically used for business-process modelling, for modelling the logic captured by a single use-case or usage scenario, or for modelling the detailed logic of a business rule. They are the object-oriented equivalent of flow charts and data-flow diagrams. Data-flow diagrams model the flow of data through the interactive system. With a data-flow diagram, actors can visualize how the UI will operate depending on external entities. For the storyboard layer, we decided to keep the typical UI storyboards we know from HCI [5]. The storyboard serves as interface layer between needs and requirement models and the UI design (Fig. 15.5).

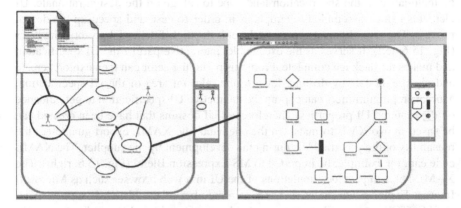

Fig. 15.4 Use-case diagram (*left*); activity diagram (*right*) with logic of single use case

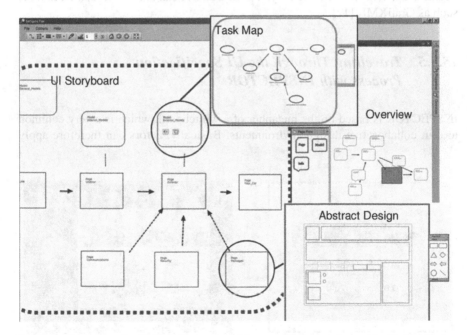

Fig. 15.5 UI storyboard with UI design and models; magnified areas show embedded artefacts

15.3.4   UI Prototyping and Simulation: Modelling Look and Feel

Prototypes are already established as a bridging technique for HCI and SE [22, 6].
HCI mainly recognizes them as an artefact for iterative UI design. Avoiding risk
when making decisions that are difficult to retract is a reason why prototyping is
also important for business people. Accordingly, we chose prototypes as a vehicle
for abstract UI modelling. They will help to design and evaluate the UI at early
stages and they support traceability from models to design. Alternate designs can
be maintained in the specification landscape to safeguard the design rationale. UI
elements can be assembled to templates in order to ease and speed up the design
process. The visually most expressive level is the high-fidelity UI prototyping layer
(Fig. 15.6, left). It serves as the executable, interactive part of the UI specification
and makes the package complete. From this point, the actor can then explore, create
and change models by drilling down to the relevant area of the UI specification.
Moreover, programmers can pop-up the interactive UI specification to get guidance
on the required UI properties. Therefore, all UI designs that have been created can
be saved in two XML formats. On the one hand, the XAML export guarantees the
reusability of the specified UIs during the development by the supplier. The XAML
code can, for example, be imported to MS Expression Blend (Fig. 15.6, right). The
XAML helps to provide simulations of the UI in a web browser such as Microsoft
Internet Explorer. On the other hand, as a member of the UsiXML supply chain,
INSPECTOR can contribute to the early phases of needs analysis and requirements
engineering. With its UI design layer, INSPECTOR can also be compared to tools
such as GrafiXML [12].

15.3.5   Travelling Through the UI Specification
Process with INSPECTOR

INSPECTOR is based on the metaphor of a whiteboard, which is a very common
tool in collaborative design environments. Basically, actors can therefore apply

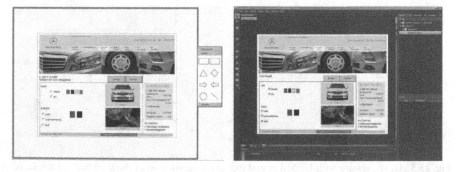

Fig. 15.6 INSPECTOR-made hi-fi UI design (*left*) in Microsoft Expression Blend (*right*)

the models and design capabilities of INSPECTOR in arbitrary order along the UI specification process. However, the scenario map is very well suited to work on early assignments of UI specification processes. Usability and user-experience goals, business and design vision as well as reusable requirements can be captured within the information bubbles at the scenario layer. At this initial stage, problem scenarios can be textually documented. They will be enriched by concrete artefacts at the UI storyboard layer, which functions as the mediator between interconnected models and design. It encapsulates the collection of linked and interrelated artefacts by means of panning and zooming as major interaction techniques [13, 19]. This provides actors with a feeling of diving into the information space of the UI speci-fication whiteboard. The appearance of INSPECTOR's UI is based on a linear scaling of objects (geometric zooming) and on displaying information in a way that is dependent on the scale of the objects (semantic zooming) [23].

Automatic zooming automatically organizes selected objects on the UI. Animated zooming supports the user in exploring the topology of an information space and in understanding data relationships. For switching between models and UI designs, the user can manually zoom-in and -out and pan the canvas. During user modelling, for example, a user shape can be linked to, and be part of, user roles, personas and use cases. Zooming-in on a user shape reveals more details about the underlying personas. The use-case shapes can be part of a superordinate task map and can be linked accordingly (Fig. 15.7). Moreover, zooming in a particular

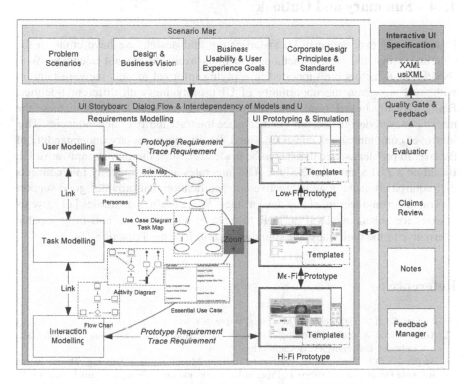

Fig. 15.7 Exemplified modelling and design throughput with INSPECTOR

case could link to an essential use-case description and reveal more detail on user and system responsibilities. At this stage, activity and data-flow diagrams help during interaction modelling. The user can link every model to UI designs of different fidelity and vice versa (Fig. 15.7). During modelling, or while traversing relationships by panning and zooming, hints about the current zoom factor and the current position in the information space can be given in order to avoid disorientation. A common way of supporting the user's cognitive (i.e. spatial) map of the information space is an overview window (Fig. 15.5). Navigating between artefacts can be an extensive task, however, if objects are widespread in terms of being some distance along the three dimensions of the ZUI canvas. For a much faster navigation, actors can switch between artefacts with a tree-view explorer that allows a jump zoom into areas far removed from the current user focus. In order to support the assessment of the UI specification quality, we are working on a feedback component for INSPECTOR. Annotations can be attached to any canvas object. They will be used to review requirements models, to integrate results of UI evaluation studies or to incorporate notes about trade-offs or design decisions. Annotations will be accessible through a management component, which allows a direct zoom-navigation to the artefacts concerned. Equally important for design rationale, the feedback will also be stored in the UI specifications such as XAML, UsiXML.

15.4   Summary and Outlook

Based on our experience in UI specification and design, we have come to the conclusion that the typical methods and tools available are not adequate. With INSPECTOR, actors are supported in applying informal models they are familiar with, and are given the opportunity of UI prototyping with different fidelities. Being logically linked, transitions from abstract to detailed artefacts increase the transparency of design decisions and enhance the traceability of dependencies. This improves communication, consistency and, finally, the necessary understanding of the overall problem space that has to be made accessible through an innovative UI. Based on a ZUI approach, INSPECTOR integrates and innovatively interconnects the required artefacts in an interactive UI specification that provides good support for roundtrip engineering at any design stage. Some evaluation studies [17] give us reasons for enhancing INSPECTOR to make it an innovative and fully capable alternative to the tool-landscape found in current industrial practice.

References

1. Ambler, Scott W. (2002): Agile Modeling, Wiley, NY
2. Ambler, Scott W. (2004): The Object Primer – Agile Model-Driven Development with UML 2, Cambridge University Press, Cambridge
3. Barbosa, S.D.J., Paula, M.G. (2003): Interaction Modelling as a Binding Thread in the Software Development Process,In Proc. of the workshop on bridging the gaps between software engineering and human-computer interaction, Oregon, USA

4. Beck, K. (1999), Extreme Programming Explained, Addison-Wesley, Reading
5. Beyer, H., Holtzblatt, K. (1998): Contextual Design: Defining Customer-Centered Systems, Morgan Kaufmann, San Francisco
6. Blomkvist, S. (2005): Towards a model for bridging agile development and user-centered design. In: Human-centered software engineering – integrating usability in the development process, Springer, Berlin, 219–244
7. Calvary, G., Coutaz, J., Thevenin, D., Limbourg, Q., Bouillon, L., Vanderdonckt, J. (2003): A Unifying Reference Framework for Multi-Target User Interfaces. Interacting with Computer 15(3): 289–308
8. Campos, P., Nunes, N. (2004): Canonsketch: a User-Centered Tool for Canonical Abstract Prototyping. In Proc. of 11th International Workshop on Design, Specification and Verification of Interactive Systems, Springer, Berlin, 146–163
9. Campos, P., Nunes, N. (2006): Principles and Practice of Work Style Modeling: Sketching Design Tools. In Proc. of Human-Work Interaction Design. Springer, Berlin
10. Constantine, L.L., Lockwood, L.A.D. (1999) Software for Use: A Practical Guide to Models and Methods of Usage-Centered Design, Addison-Wesley, Reading
11. Holt, J. (2005): A Pragmatic Guide To Business Process Modelling, British Computer Society, United Kingdom
12. Lepreux, S., Vanderdonckt, J., Michotte, B. (2006): Visual Design of User Interfaces by (De) composition, In. Proc. of DSV-IS'2006, Vol. 4323, Springer, Berlin, 157–170
13. Lin, J., Landay, James A. (2002): Damask: A Tool for Early-Stage Design and Prototyping of Multi-Device User Interfaces. In Proc. of the 8th International Conference on Distributed Multimedia Systems, San Francisco: 573–580
14. Memmel, Thomas; Bock, C.; Reiterer, Harald (2007): Model-driven prototyping for corporate software specification. Proceedings of the EHCI-HCSE-DSVIS'07 (IFIP International Federation for Information Processing 2008). In: J. Gulliksen et al., EIS 2007, LNCS 4940, 158–174
15. Memmel, T., Gundelsweiler, F., Reiterer, H. (2007): Agile Human-Centered Software Engineering, In Proc. of the 21st BCS-HCI, 167–175
16. Memmel, T., Reiterer, H., Ziegler, H., Oed, R. (2007): Visual Specification As Enhancement Of Client Authority In Designing Interactive Systems. Proc. of 5th WS of the German Chapter of the Usability Professionals Association, Weimer, Germany. In: Kerstin Roese, Henning Brau: Usability Professionals 2007, Frauenhofer IRB Verlag, Stuttgart, 99–104
17. Memmel, T.; Vanderdonckt, J.; Reiterer, H. (2008): Multi-fidelity User Interface Specifications. Proceedings of the 15th International Workshop on the Design, Verification and Specification of Interactive Systems (DSV-IS 2008), Jul 2008, 43-57
18. Metzker, E., Reiterer, H. (2002): Evidence-Based Usability Engineering. In Proc. of the CADUI 2002: 323–336
19. Newman, M.W., Jason, J.L., Hong, I., Landay, J.A. (2003), DENIM: An Informal Web Site Design Tool Inspired by Observations of Practice. HCI, 18(3): 259–324
20. Nunes, N. J., Campos, P. (2004): Towards Usable Analysis, Design and Modeling Tools. In Proc. of MBUI'2004, CEUR Workshop Proceedings, Vol. 103
21. Rosson, M.B., Carroll, J.M. (2002): Usability Engineering: scenario-based development of human computer interaction, Morgan Kaufmann, San Francisco
22. Sutcliffe, G. (2005): Convergence or competition between software engineering and human computer interaction, In: Human-centered software engineering – integrating usability in the development process, Springer, Berlin, 71–84
23. Ware, C. (2004): Information Visualization: Perception for Design, Morgan Kaufmann, San Francisco
24. Zave, P., Jackson, M. (1997): Four Dark Corners of Requirements Engineering. ACM Transactions on Software Engineering and Methodology 6, 1 (1997) 1–30

Chapter 16
Creating Multi-platform User Interfaces with RenderXML

Francisco M. Trindade and Marcelo S. Pimenta

Abstract As the technology evolves, the existence of different computational devices has made ad hoc software development no longer acceptable in the development of multi-platform software applications. This chapter describes RenderXML, a software tool developed to facilitate the creation of multi-platform applications. RenderXML acts as a renderer, mapping concrete user interfaces (UI) described in UsiXML to multiple platforms, and also as a connector, linking the rendered UI developed in one language to functional core code developed possibly in a different programming language.

16.1 Introduction

Computer software development has nowadays as an important requirement the possibility of execution in more than one platform, either through desktop computer, handhelds, or mobile phones. To address this demand, ad hoc software development is no longer acceptable in terms of the cost and time required for software construction and maintenance. In this way, many research projects were developed in order to allow the creation of software applications that can be executed in multiple contexts of use, with minimal alteration of its algorithms.

One of the proposed solutions is the development of user interfaces (UI) with plasticity, capable of adapting themselves to different use contexts. In order to obtain plasticity, High-level UI Descriptions (HLUID) are commonly used, enabling the definition of UIs in a platform independent form. Among the available

F.M. Trindade (✉) and M.S. Pimenta
Institute of Informatics, Federal University of Rio Grande do Sul, Av.
Bento Gonçalves, 9500, Bloco IV, Porto Alegre, RS, Brazil
e-mail: fmtrindade@inf.ufrgs.br

V. López-Jaquero et al. (eds.), *Computer-Aided Design of User Interfaces VI*,   177
DOI: 10.1007/978-1-84882-206-1_16, © Springer-Verlag London Limited 2009

HLUIDs, UsiXML [14] is based on the *Cameleon reference framework* [6], allowing the description of UIs for multiple use contexts.

This chapter describes RenderXML, a software tool developed to facilitate the creation of multi-platform applications. RenderXML acts as a renderer, mapping concrete UIs described in UsiXML to multiple platforms, and also as a connector, linking the rendered UI to functional core code developed possibly in multiple programming languages. Thus, RenderXML is intended to support not only the development of new (multi-platform) applications but also the migration of legacy applications to a multi-platform environment.

The main goal of this application is to help the UI developer, acting in the UI engineering process. Clearly, RenderXML has not the goal of helping designers in the UI design process. The main decisions of UI design process (definition of inter-active supported tasks, selection of interaction objects, definition of presentation and layout, etc.) are made in previous stages of UI design process, before the usage of RenderXML.

The chapter is structured as follows: first, we discuss the problem of developing multi-platform applications and some solution proposals, and then we present UsiXML and its role in the development of multi-platform applications. We describe some related work and the main concepts of RenderXML, discussing its features and benefits, and how to use it. An actual multi-platform application example illustrates the process of multi-platform UI rendering and multi-language functional core connection. Some concluding remarks and future work are presented in the final section.

16.2 Multi-platform Software Development

Recent years have seen the evolution of computational technology, which has allowed the development of many devices, providing users with access to process-ing power in different situations. This context has transformed the possibility of software execution in multiple platforms in an important requirement, proposing a new challenge for developers of interactive applications [20].

In fact, in this situation, the traditional ad hoc software development approach, with software (re)creation and maintenance for each platform is no longer accept-able because it is extremely costly and could result in users having many different versions of applications on different devices [4]. The growing proliferation of devices, each one with its unique requirements, demands a lot of technological knowledge of a developer in order to create applications for each device.

With this situation, research efforts are being made in order to develop tech-niques which permit the creation of applications that can be executed in multiple platforms, with minimal alteration of its algorithm. A straightforward solution is the usage of plastic UIs, capable of being executed in multiple contexts of use.

Specifically, in this chapter the term *multi-platform* corresponds to the definition of *context of usage* within the scope of plastic UIs, enclosing multiple devices, although some works also consider multiple modalities (e.g., graphical interface and voice interface) and multiple environmental attributes existent when the software is being executed (e.g., light conditions and user profile).

In order to develop plastic UIs, different techniques have been proposed. These propositions can be classified according to the World Wide Web (W3C) note on authoring technique for device independence [3], which identifies three classifications for authoring techniques: *single authoring, multiple authoring*, and *flexible authoring*. A brief description of each one of these categories is as follows [22]:

- Multiple authoring: The developer creates a specific version of the application for each device or device category. This situation, which includes (re)creation and maintenance for each platform, is extremely costly and has the drawbacks related previously in this chapter, but also provides the maximum control over the results.
- Single authoring: In this category, only one interface implementation is created, which is adapted to a specific device before being presented to the user. Single authoring techniques can be subdivided in techniques that use *platform independent vocabularies or toolkits*, like AUIML [4] or UIML [1], techniques that *extend established markup languages*, as RIML [8] or techniques which use *model-based UI development*, as XIML [21] or UsiXML [14].
- Flexible Authoring: Situation where the developer combines single authoring and multiple authoring techniques.

In this chapter, our solution approach is a model-based UI development single authoring technique, using a High-Level UI Description Language to allow the specification of multi-platform UIs.

A solution using HLUIDs was chosen because UI description languages have been widely used in multi-platform UI development, mainly because they abstract the UI description, providing a uniform way to develop multi-platform and even multimodal UIs. Besides that, the characteristic shared by many HLUIDs, which is to be a XML-based declarative language, makes these languages easy to be learned and understood, having potential to be adopted by a large developer community.

16.3 User Interface Extensible Markup Language: UsiXML

Different High-Level UI Description Languages have been proposed in order to design multi-platform UIs, like TERESA [20], UIML [1], XIML [21], and WSXML [11]. It is not the purpose of this chapter to investigate these languages, and a deeper analysis can be found in [14, 23].

Among the existent HLUIDs, we have chosen UsiXML because it is a language specially intended for context-sensitive UIs [14], having potential to become a W3C standard and being supported by an active and international research community.

Only the main concepts of UsiXML will be presented here. Further information can be found in related literature [14, 24].

In order to allow multiple platform UI development, UsiXML is based on the four abstraction levels of the *Cameleon reference framework* [6], which allows the description of a context-sensitive UI design cycle, as described by Fig. 16.1.

The four basic levels existent in this framework are as follows [14]:

- Final UI (FUI): UI running on a particular platform either by interpretation or by execution.
- Concrete UI (CUI): abstracts the FUI into a UI definition that is independent of any computing platform.
- Abstract UI (AUI): abstracts the CUI into a UI definition that is interaction modality independent (e.g., graphical/vocal interaction).
- Task and Concepts: higher level, where the user task is defined based on his viewpoint, along with the various objects that are manipulated by it.

16.4   Related Work

The creation of multi-platform UIs is also the goal of some related works in the literature, which can be classified in two categories: (a) tools working with UsiXML UI descriptions and (b) UI rendering tools, for UsiXML or other UI models.

Among the projects which use UsiXML, SketchiXML [9] can generate a UsiXML Concrete UI (CUI) and also a UIML UI specification, receiving as input hand sketched UI descriptions, having as main objective the creation of evolutionary UI prototypes. Working with another kind of input, GrafiXML [13] is a visual designer which allows the creation of UsiXML CUI specifications, based on the visual positioning of UI components by the developer.

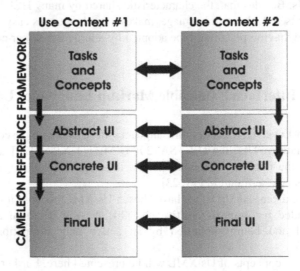

Fig. 16.1 The four basic levels of the Cameleon reference framework 14

In the category of UI rendering tools, QTKiXML [10] can map UsiXML description to the Tcl-Tk language. With the same objective, FlashiXML [5] can also map UsiXML descriptions, but to UIs described in vectorial mode, being interpreted by Flash or SVG plug-ins. InterpiXML [17] performs the mapping of UsiXML CUI descriptions using *Java Swing* UI components.

Using another UI models, Uiml.NET [15] and TIDE [2] map UIs specified in UIML [1] to the.Net and Java platform, respectively. TERESA (Transformation Environment for InteRactivE System representations) [16] uses the TERESAXML language to perform forward engineering design and development of multi-platform applications, supporting transformations from task models to desktop, phone UIs, and vocal interfaces.

Also in this category, the MONA project [22] has investigated multimodal interaction on mobile devices. One objective of the project was to devise a more "developer-friendly" single authoring method for cross-platform UIs.

16.5   RenderXML

In order to create multi-platform UIs based on the *Cameleon Reference Framework*, the life cycle shown in Fig. 16.2 must be followed. This life cycle is based on a generic task model, which envisions all the tasks to be performed by the interactive system, and is mapped to a final UI for a specific device through multiple reification steps.

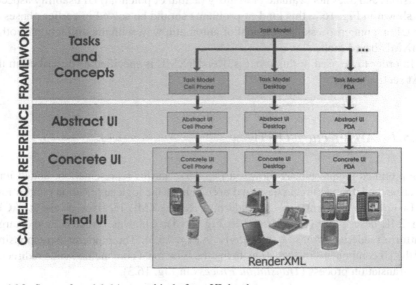

Fig. 16.2   Steps of model-driven multi-platform UI development

In practice, to obtain a final UI following the mapping steps presented in Fig. 16.2, a generic task model (Task Model) has to be created, which is transformed to a task model of a specific kind of device (Task Model Desktop). From the specific task model, the UI is further specified to an abstract UI (Abstract UI Desktop), which is dependent on the kind of interaction being used, and then to a concrete UI (Concrete UI Desktop), which depends on the target platform of the application. Finally, the concrete UI can be mapped to a final UI to be executed in a device (Desktop computer). All these steps can be performed supported by tools, which perform an automatic or semi-automatic mapping from one level to another.

RenderXML is a rendering tool projected to work in the last level of this transformation process (Concrete UI to Final UI), mapping concrete UIs described in UsiXML to final UIs for a specific device. In addition, RenderXML offers to the user another level of independence, allowing the connection of the rendered UI to functional cores developed in different programming languages.

With these features, RenderXML is a useful tool in the prototyping and development process of multi-platform applications. Since UsiXML allows the specification of all needed features of an UI, it can be used in the development of final UIs. In this particular situation, it is very important to have the possibility of developing UIs to multiple platforms using only one design language, setting the UI developer free from the need of mastering many different technologies. Using RenderXML the UI developer needs to know only UsiXML. In addition, the possibility of multi-language functional core connection allows applications developed in different programming languages to have their UI created with UsiXML.

It should be clarified here that RenderXML is a rendering tool, and not a UI design tool. In fact, RenderXML is not supposed to guide the designer's choice among design alternatives. Clearly, RenderXML does not check the designer's decisions and does not evaluate or identify (actual or potential) UI usability aspects. As shown in Fig. 16.2, this kind of problems should be solved in earlier phases of the UI mapping process, in a manual or automatic way, with the utilization of other UsiXML-based tools.

In order to be used in this process, RenderXML is specified as described in the next sections.

16.5.1   Architecture Overview

The proposed architecture is shown in Fig. 16.3. In this representation, dotted lines describe the UI rendering process, and normal lines the logic application connection.

In order to perform the UI rendering, RenderXML receives as input a CUI UsiXML description (*UsiXML UI* in Fig. 16.3), which is directed to the target platform renderer (*Platform 1 Renderer* in Fig. 16.3). The renderer is responsible for the UI components instantiation, being the functional core method calls redirected to a translation process (*Translation Process* in Fig. 16.3).

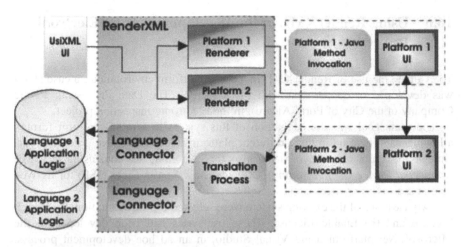

Fig. 16.3 RenderXML architecture

To connect the UI to its functional core, the translation process (*Translation Process* in Fig. 16.3) receives methods invocations and translates them to a language independent format. This description is forwarded to a plug-in for the target programming language (*Language 1 Connector* in Fig. 16.3), which calls the method in the functional core being executed.

The renderers (*Platform 1 and 2 Renderer* in Fig. 16.3) have the task of mapping the UI UsiXML CUI description to a final UI in a specific platform.

In order to accomplish this task, the rendering algorithm hierarchically covers the CUI description contained in the UsiXML file, instantiating at runtime the contained components with its specified characteristics.

During the rendering process, the UI content is obtained in the UI resource model, and the necessary functional core methods are obtained in the UI domain model.

To connect with the functional core, RenderXML has the definition of logic connectors (*Language 1 and 2 Connector* in Fig. 16.3). The connectors are responsible for receiving the description of the called method, translate it to the functional core's programming language, and invoke it.

In order to perform this task, the connector is subdivided in two different parts, the first one developed in Java, and the second developed in the target programming language. These two parts are connected by calls made through the *Java Native Interface* (JNI), which makes possible the connection between Java and other programming languages applications.

In this process, the method is described in a Java class, being this description passed through JNI. Reflection techniques are then used to realize the method call in the target programming language, based on its name and attributes.

16.6   Using RenderXML in the Development of an Electronic Inspection System

To evaluate the use of RenderXML in a multi-platform environment, a case study was developed in cooperation with PROCEMPA (The Data Processing Public Company of the City of Porto Alegre), in the Electronic Inspection project.

The main goal was the adaptation of this system to a multi-platform format, allowing its utilization in three different platforms, *Java Swing* for a desktop version of the application, *Java Swing* also for its mobile version, using the JME *Connected Device Configuration* (CDC), and *Java Server Faces* (JSF) for its Web version.

Two use cases of the existing system were selected for the adaptation: (a) Search License and (b) Enable License. These use cases had been developed in the Microsoft.Net platform using Visual Studio, in an ad hoc development process. Figure 16.4 shows the original UIs.

The adaptation begins with the specification of the original UIs in UsiXML. These descriptions contain not only the UI components, but also the UI behavior and content definition. In the "Search License" use case, the UI dynamic behavior contains the *getLicense* method invocation, which is responsible for searching a data repository and returning the license information based on the specified search parameters.

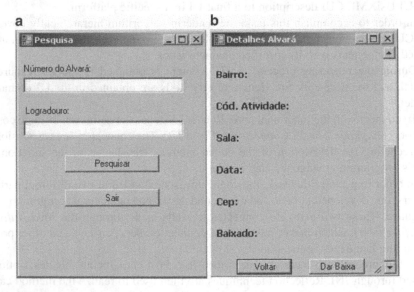

Fig. 16.4 Original UIs of (**a**) Search License (*Pesquisa*) and (**b**) Enable License (*Detalhes Alvará*)

Due to the programming language independence of RenderXML, the original functional core source code, developed in.Net could be used without any modification. To accomplish this, the method calls performed by the UI are forwarded to RenderXML, informing the name and parameters of the wanted method. This definition is translated by RenderXML to the target programming language, and the method is then executed. Figure 16.5 shows the code executed to perform the method call: the *getLicense* method, declared in the *LicenseFacade* class is prepared and called, using the RenderXML *logicConector* class, which is implemented based on the GoF *Command* design pattern [12].

With the original UIs specified in UsiXML, the application can be used in three different platforms. Due to RenderXML programming language independence, the original functional core source code did not have to be modified. The possible configurations are shown in Fig. 16.6, where platform 1 represents a mobile platform, based on the JME CDC configuration, platform 2 represents a desktop platform, based on JSE, and platform 3 is its web version, developed in JSF.

To change the UI platform, as in switching from A1 to A2 or A3 in Fig. 16.6, the user only has to adopt the RenderXML version corresponding to the desired platform: desktop, mobile, or web. To change the functional core's programming language, the only operation needed is a parameter change, specifying the logic connector to be used, as long as the two functional core versions implement the same interface.

```
logicConector.initializeMethod();
logicConector.prepareMethodClass
          ("LicenseFacade");
logicConector.prepareMethodName
          ("getLicense");
logicConector.
     prepareMethodStringReturnParameter
          (searchText,0);
logicConector.executeMethod();
```

Fig. 16.5 Method invocation source code

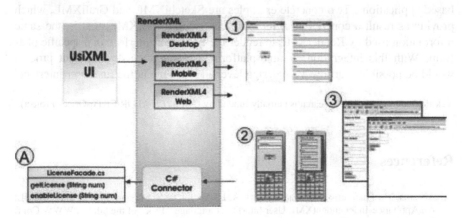

Fig. 16.6 Case study

16.7 Discussion, Conclusion, and Future Work

This chapter described a practical approach to the prototyping and development of
multi-platform applications, and described RenderXML, which acts as a UI renderer for multiple platforms. RenderXML stimulates the utilization of HLUIDs
(like UsiXML) in the development of multi-platform applications.

In addition to the contribution provided by RenderXML as a single application,
the tool is aimed to collaborate with other existing works based on UsiXML, helping in the multi-platform user interface development life cycle. Since it is the only
existing tool working between the concrete and final user interface levels in the
current UsiXML specification, this work actually fills an existing gap in the
UsiXML UI development process.

RenderXML is also innovative since it discusses the connection between the
rendered user interface and the application's functional core, allowing its utilization
with functional cores developed in possibly multiple programming languages, situation which has not been addressed by other works in this area.

Future work consists in the evolution of RenderXML, which can happen in three
different levels:

- Supported UsiXML concrete interaction objects.
- Supported platforms.
- Supported programming languages.

Examples of devices/platforms we intend to investigate are mobile phones, smart-
phones, PDAs, web-based interfaces, desktop interfaces, and even XO laptops from
the OLPC Project [18].

The final objective is to allow the creation of UsiXML-based UIs for a great
number of platforms and devices, and also expand the number of supported programming languages. In particular, our work aims to provide a tool which can be
used in actual UI developing in such diversity of contexts of usage.

Another possibility is the integration between RenderXML and other UsiXML-
based applications. Two concrete examples are SketchiXML and GrafiXML, which
provide as result a concrete user interface described in UsiXML, that is, the same
information used by RenderXML to render the final user interface in a specific platform. With this integration, a multi-platform user interface development process
would be possible, starting at the design level and arriving at the final user interface.

Acknowledgments This research is partially funded by CNPq (LIFAPOR/CNPq-Grices Project).

References

1. Abrams, M., Phanouriou, C., Batongbacal, A. L., Williams, S. M., and Shuster, J. E. "UIML:
   An Appliance-IndependentXML User Interface Language." Procs of the 8th Int. WWW Conf.
   Toronto, Canada. 11–16 May 1999. Elsevier Science Publishers, NY.

2. Ali, M.F., Pérez-Quiñones, M.A., Abrams, M., e Shell, E. Building Multi-Platform User Interfaces With UIML. In Proceedings of 2002 International Workshop of Computer-Aided Design of User Interfaces: CADUI'2002. Valenciennes, France.
3. Authoring Techniques for Device Independence. W3C Working Group Note 18 February 2004. http://www.w3.org/TR/2004/NOTE-di-atdi-20040218/
4. Azevedo, P., Merrick, R., Roberts, D. "OVID to AUIML - User Oriented Interface Modeling." http://math.uma.pt/tupis00/submissions/azevedoroberts/azevedoroberts.html
5. Berghe, Y. Etude et implémentation d'un générateur d'interfaces vectorielles à partir d'un language de description d'interfaces utilisateur, M.Sc. thesis, Université catholique de Louvain, Louvain-la-Neuve, Belgium, September 2004.
6. Calvary, G., Coutaz, J. Thevenin, D. Limbourg, Q., Bouillon, L. Vanderdonckt, J. A Unifying Reference Framework for Multi-Target User Interfaces, *Interacting with Computers*, Vol. 15, No. 3, June 2003, pp. 289–308.
7. Calvary, G., Coutaz, J., Thevenin, D., Limbourg, Q., Souchon, N., Bouillon, L., Florins, M., Vanderdonckt, J. Plasticity of User Interfaces: A Revised Reference Framework. In Proceedings of TAMODIA'2002 (Bucharest, July, 18–19, 2002), Academy of Economic Studies of Bucharest, INFOREC Printing House, Bucharest, pp. 127–134, 2002.
8. Consensus Project. http://www.consensus-online.org/
9. Coyette, A., Faulkner, S., Kolp, M., Limbourg, Q. SketchiXML: Towards a Multi-Agent Design Tool for Sketching User Interfaces Based on UsiXML. In Proc. of Tamodia'2004.
10. Denis, V. Un pas vers le poste de travail unique: QTKiXML, un interpréteur d'interface utilisateur à partir de sa description, M.Sc. thesis, Université catholique de Louvain, Louvain-la-Neuve, Belgium, September 2005.
11. Elting, Ch., Zwickel, J.and Malaka, R., Device-Dependent Modality Selection for User Interfaces – An Empirical Study, in Proceedings of 6th Int. Conf. on Intelligent User Interfaces IUI'2002 (January 13–16, 2002, San Francisco), ACM Press, New York.
12. Gamma,E., Helm, R., Johnson, R., and Vlissides, J. Design Patterns: Elements of Reusable Object-Oriented Software. Addison-Wesley, Reading, 1999.
13. Lepreux, S., Vanderdonckt, J., Michotte, B. Visual Design of User Interfaces by (De)composition, Em Proc. of 13th Int. Workshop on Design, Specification, and Verification of Interactive Systems DSV-IS'2006 (Dublin, 26–28 de Julho de 2006), G. Doherty and A. Blandford (eds.), LNCS, Vol. 4323, Springer-Verlag, Berlin, 2006, pp. 157–170.
14. Limbourg, Q., Vanderdonckt, J., Michotte, B., Bouillon, L., Florins, M. and Trevisan, D. UsiXML: A User Interface Description Language for Context-Sensitive User Interfaces. In Proc. of the AVI'2004 Workshop "Developing User Interfaces with XML: Advances on User Interface Description Languages" UIXML'04 (Gallipoli, May 25th 2004), pp. 55–62.
15. Luyten, K., Thys, K., Vermeulen, J., e Coninx, K. A Generic Approach for Multi-Device User Interface Rendering with UIML. In 6th International Conference on Computer-Aided Design of User Interfaces (CADUI'2006), Bucareste, Romênia.
16. Mori, G., Paternò, F., Santoro, C. Tool Support for Designing nomadic Applications. Em Proc. of 7th ACM Int.Conf. on IUI'03. ACM Press, New York, 2003, pp. 141–148.
17. Ocal, K. Etude et développement d'un interpréteur UsiXML en Java Swing, Haute Ecole Rennequin, Liège, 2004.
18. One Laptop Per Child (OLPC). http://www.laptop.org/index.en_US.html
19. Paterno, F. Model-Based Design and Evaluation of Interactive Applications, Springer-Verlag, Berlin, 2000.
20. Paternò, F., Santoro C. One model, many interfaces. In Proceedings of CADUI'02, pp 143–154. Kluwer, Dorchester, 2002.
21. Puerta, A. and Eisenstein, J. "XIML: A Common Representation for Interaction Data." Proceedings of IUI 2002, International Conference on Intelligent User Interfaces. San Francisco, California, USA. ACM Press.
22. Simon, R., Wegscheider, F., Tolar, K. Tool-supported single authoring for device independence and multimodality. Proceedings of the 7th international conference on Human computer

interaction with mobile devices ' services MobileHCI'05. Salzburg, Austria. Pages: 91 – 98
ISBN:1–59593–089–2
23. Souchon, N., Vanderdonckt, J., *A Review of XML-Compliant User Interface Description Languages*, Proc. of 10th Int. Conf. on Design, Specification, and Verification of Interactive Sys-tems DSV-IS'2003, LNCS, Vol. 2844, Springer-Verlag, Berlin, 2003, pp. 377–391.
24. Vanderdonckt, J., A MDA-Compliant Environment for Developing User Interfaces of Information Systems, Proc. of 17th Conf. on Advanced Information Systems Engineering CAiSE'05 (Porto, 13–17 June 2005), O. Pastor ' J. Falcão e Cunha (eds.), Lecture Notes in Computer Science, Vol. 3520, Springer-Verlag, Berlin, 2005, pp. 16–31.

Chapter 17
Analysis Models for User Interface Development in Collaborative Systems

Víctor M.R. Penichet, María D. Lozano, José A. Gallud and Ricardo Tesoriero

Abstract This chapter presents several models as a proposal to carry out the process of analysis for CSCW systems, a stage of the model process which is essential in this type of systems. The methodology presented to address the analysis stage provides the mechanisms to specify the organization of the participants of a system, the roles they play, the interaction of the users within the system and the interaction among participants through the system, that is, person–computer–person interaction.

17.1 Introduction

The analysis stage of any process model is a fundamental stage which provides the exhaustive study of certain characteristics from the problem domain. It is a matter of discovering *what*, just describing the system requirements without implementation details. Problem domain elements and their relationships are studied. The specification in the requirements gathering stage is achieved in a language which is 'closer to the person'. This information and some other newer will be specified closer to the developer in the analysis stage.

The chapter is organized as follows. Section 17.2 presents a review of some related works. The steps of the methodology regarding the analysis of CSCW systems are described in Sect. 17.3. Section 17.4 presents a simple case study to show how to model according to the proposed methodology. Sections 17.5 and 17.6 describe the analysis stage in detail as well as the diagrams we propose to model collaboration. Section 17.7 describes the importance of traceability between stages and also within the stage for modelling consistency reasons. Finally, Sect. 17.8 outlines some conclusions and final remarks.

V.M.R. Penichet (✉), M.D. Lozano, J.A. Gallud and R. Tesoriero
Computer Systems Department, University of Castilla-La Mancha, 02071, Albacete, Spain
e-mail: victor.penichet@uclm.es

V. López-Jaquero et al. (eds.), *Computer-Aided Design of User Interfaces VI*,
DOI: 10.1007/978-1-84882-206-1_17, © Springer-Verlag London Limited 2009

17.2   Related Works

The most commonly used language to model the real world is UML, now in its
version 2.0 [9]. The modelling of traditional systems has been carried out by means
of class diagrams, object diagrams and package diagrams to describe the static and
the structural part of the system. Activity diagrams are frequently used to model
behaviour issues in the system, that is, to describe the dynamic part. These charts
are part of the methodology in some well-known process models such as RUP [6].

However, these mechanisms to represent the real world do not provide a way to
specify person–computer–person interaction naturally. Typically, such kind of
interaction takes place in CSCW systems [4, 5, 7, 14], which are becoming more
and more common due to the growing necessities of users who need to interact with
others and the progress of the technologies and the network infrastructure.

Some other approaches such as AMENITIES or, more recently, CIAM address this
problem from a different point of view. AMENITIES (A MEthodology for aNalysis and
desIgn of cooperaTIve systEmS) [3] is a methodology that arose with the aim of
addressing the complexity of collaborative systems. It is focused on the concept of
group and tackles behavioural and structural issues. However, it does not take into
account the user interface ones. On the contrary, CIAM (Collaborative Interactive
Applications Methodology) [8] is a methodological framework based on a set of models
that allow engineers to guide the design and development process of user interfaces of
interactive groupware applications. CIAM is not a process model but a methodology.

The methodology for CSCW systems proposed in this chapter provides an analysis of the structure and the behaviour of the system focused on the user as a member
of a group and driven by the tasks they play. In the specification of the structure, the
actors of the system and how they participate, how they are organized and what roles
they play, in addition to the description of the objects of the system, are taken into
account. The study of the behaviour is carried out describing the functionality from
a CSCW point of view addressing their main features [15], as well as its space–
temporal features, which are especially important in these systems [7].

The description about what a system do may be represented with flowcharts, finite
state machines, workflow models, data flow diagrams or task modelling. Besides,
these models take into account collaborations in a CSCW system but they are
designed especially to model human–system interaction [10, 13, 16]. ConcurTaskTrees
or CTT [10] is one of the most widely used notations for task modelling. This notation has been adopted as part of the methodology we present. We also propose an
additional diagram that has been developed to ease the modelling of the collaboration
among the users involved in a CSCW system in a more natural way.

17.3   Steps in the Analysis Stage for Collaborative Systems

The steps defined to tackle the analysis stage in this process model are the following:
identification and description of roles, identification and description of tasks, analysis
of the system structure and analysis of the system behaviour.

The analysis of a collaborative system begins with the identification of roles and tasks from the information gathered in the requirements gathering stage. Once the initial roles and tasks are identified, they are described. At the same time, the task diagrams (TD), collaboration diagrams (CD) and organizational structure diagrams (OSD) are used to model the system from the analysis point of view. These diagrams will be described in the following sections.

On the one hand, the identification of the initial roles provides the analyst with an initial outline of the organizational structure of the actors of the system. This diagram as well as the UML class diagram models the structure of the system. Likewise, the identification of the first tasks eases an initial order, which provides an initial outline of the task diagrams and collaboration diagrams, which model the behaviour of the actors in the system.

On the other hand, the analysis of the initial versions of such diagrams provides new roles and tasks. After this initial roles and task identification, an iterative refinement process will provide with a higher quality model, which will conclude with a complete specification of the system.

Traceability between the requirements gathering stage and the analysis stage provides a comprehensive and coherent specification, and similarly traceability intra-stage between its steps. Such traceability will be detailed later.

17.4   Case Study

In order to illustrate the proposals we present in this chapter, a simple case study will be described in this section. It is a groupware application which allows several authors to create the same document through the Internet. When the authors of the document have done a draft, one of them is responsible for sending, through the same application, the document which is candidate to be published to some reviewers. Then, the reviewers discuss about the document and they give their own opinion on whether it should be published or not. A published document can be read by all the users of the system, even if they are not authors or reviewers.

Throughout this chapter, the examples presented concern this simple case study. Reasonably, it is not a complete specification for lack of space. It is only to clarify some points.

17.5   Roles and Tasks Identification

In the first stage of requirements gathering, the *actors* of the system and information concerning *requirements* among other things should have been identified, what will lead to the identification of the *roles* the users will able to play and the *tasks* they will have to perform in the system [11, 12]. The relationship between roles and tasks is so close that their identification and description will be done in parallel and closely linked.

Once the requirements of the system and the actors involved in it are known, it is possible to establish some roles that determine who makes what. This is a key aspect when designing a collaborative system.

Some *templates*, which are similar to and based on the ones used by [2] in the requirements gathering stage, are used to describe the roles and the tasks identified. They are simpler templates in terms of the number of metadata describing a concept, but necessary to describe quickly all the roles and tasks.

In addition, some *traceability matrices* [2] will be used. They put into relation *actors* with *roles* and *requirements* with *tasks*. Traceability matrices explicitly show information that is in the specification in an implicit manner. This way of showing the traceability relationships eases the developers the access to such information. It is also easier to carry out the subsequent activities of maintenance and evolution. A final matrix puts into relation tasks and roles.

The identification of the roles and the tasks, their description and the use of templates and traceability matrices are described in the following sections.

17.5.1 Identification and Description of Roles

The concept of *role* has been defined as a set of tasks an actor performs. An *actor* is what it is due to the *role* it plays in the system [12]. A role model is a list of roles described in terms of behaviours, responsibilities and so forth. Every role has an associated name that captures its nature. Constantine proposes a series of questions to ease the identification of roles [1].

It is common to start thinking about real users (agents or groups) to identify the roles. Then some features are generalized and abstracted in order to identify the different ones. Brainstorming technique is proposed in [1] for reaching the final model of roles from a list of candidates roles.

The different roles to be performed by the end users (actors in general) that will use the application, can be extracted from the study of the information collected at the requirements gathering stage.

In a refinement step, the candidate roles which were identified previously are then grouped by similarities. The objectives are to avoid having too similar roles that really could be one, to avoid duplicated roles, to simplify and to generalize the model, etc. [1].

Roles will be described using a template such as the one shown in Table 17.1. Since the roles are described on the basis of tasks, there is a matrix that links explicitly these concepts (see Sect. 17.7). Such metadata provides the necessary information about the roles in order to establish the organizational model:

- The first three fields (*Version*, *Authors*, *Sources*) are also in the requirements gathering templates and their meaning is the same [2].
- Roles can be performed by actors if they fulfil certain restrictions. A Capacity is an ability or a responsibility associated to an actor, which allows him to play certain roles and to perform tasks [3]. Therefore, an actor could play a role

Table 17.1 Description of the Writer Role from the template to describe the roles of the system

Role-1	Writer
Version	v1.0 (March 22, 2007)
Authors	Víctor M. R. Penichet (LoUISE)
Sources	Internal study (LoUISE)
Description	A user of the system playing this role could write documents
Responsibilities	Actor's required responsibilities to play this role are the following ones:
	R1: He is responsible of the content
	R2: The content should be original
	R3: He should elaborate contents
Abilities	Actor's required abilities to play this role are the following ones:
	H1: Researcher capacity
	H2: Expressiveness capacity
Permissions	He will be able to write, create, modify and delete documents
Comments	No additional comments

according to his Abilities and roles could require an actor to have some
Responsibilities in order to play such a role.
- Actors which play a role will have a series of *Permissions* or privileges to per-
form certain actions in the system. *Description* outlines how this role is, while
Comments give some kind of additional information.

If we take a look at the case study presented in Sect. 17.4, according to the aforementioned steps, it is possible to identify some roles that would play the actors of
the system. The identification of the roles has been carried out at the requirements
gathering stage, so it will not be shown in detail. Roles identified are as follows:

- A *Writer* is a role played by a user who writes a document collaboratively. Table
17.1 shows the description of this role. A *Chair_writer* is a role played by a user
who decides if a candidate document could be sent to a review process.
- A *Reviewer* is a role played by a user who gives opinions about if a candidate
document could be published or not. A *Chair_reviewer* is a role played by a user
who decides if a candidate document could be published.
- A *Notifier* is a role played by an actor. It is an agent that informs automatically
about the result of the revision process to the authors. It also informs readers if
there is a new document published.
- A *Reader* is a role played by an actor who can read published documents.

17.5.2   Identification and Description of Tasks

In this chapter, the idea of task is inspired in ConcurTaskTrees [10], a notation for
task modelling. A common definition can be stated as follows: 'a *task* is a piece of
work required to achieve an objective'. This definition of task simplifies the idea
about what every user has to perform.

The number of tasks identified will be increased during the study and analysis of the tasks, mainly for two reasons: by decomposition of complex tasks into other simpler ones; and by the identification of new tasks. It is a matter of describing the work performed in the system.

As mentioned before, the notation CTT has been used extensively for task modelling. This diagram is also used in this methodology to represent the tasks the actors should accomplish. CTT is used to model the human–computer interaction; however, the human–computer–human interaction, that is, the interaction between people through the machines, is not modelled so intuitively. To solve this lack, we propose a new diagram to model the collaboration between users.

The model we propose for the analysis of user interfaces in collaborative systems also describes the tasks by means of templates similarly to the ones used to describe roles. The metadata used in the template for the description of tasks are as follows:

- The first three fields (*Version*, *Authors*, *Sources*) are common to the requirements gathering template ones and its meaning is the same [2].
- *Objective* represents the sub-problem linked to the task. The set of tasks linked to such an objective solve this objective of the system, that is, this sub-problem.
- *Requirement* shows the relationship between this task and any of the requirements identified in the previous stage.
- *Description* allows describing what the task does.
- *Sub-Task-of* shows the parent one.
- *Objects*. Tasks are related to or affect some domain objects of the system. This is something the designer should be aware of. System objects and their relationships are represented through the classic UML class diagrams.
- *Task Allocation* indicates how the performance of the tasks is allocated according to several possibilities [10]: *User, Interaction, Application* or *Abstract*. We consider this classification open, so you also can match some other possibilities, for example, composite tasks.
- *Composite* indicates whether the task is composite or atomic.

If it is a composite task, there are two additional metadata:

- *Dependent Tasks* lists the decomposition of tasks (only one level). *Composite Task Description* would provide additional information regarding composition, if necessary.

Finally, if it is a *group task*, it also provides the following metadata:

- *CSCW* characterizes the task according to the CSCW characteristics: *coordination, communication, collaboration* and/or *cooperation. Time* characterizes the task as *synchronous* or *asynchronous*, that is, in real time. *Space.* A group task can be performed in the *same place* or in *different places. Group Task Description* provides additional information about its group task condition.

For the example depicted in Sect. 17.4, some tasks are identified: *writing in the document, sending documents, responding comments*, etc.; as well as several group tasks such as *sharing a document* and *sending/receiving the document.*

In the following sections, we show some diagrams that model the interaction and these and other tasks can be seen. In the analysis process such tasks have been previously identified and described by the use of templates, which are similar to the ones used to describe the roles shown in Table 17.1.

17.6   Structure and Behaviour

The division between structure and behaviour has been traditionally used in Software Engineering for modelling the system throughout the software life cycle.

The analysis stage of the model process proposed provides a set of structural and behavioural diagrams to support a complete and coherent analysis of collaborative systems. The diagrams we present have been developed to increase the expressiveness of the specifications and to make them more complete, especially from the point of view of the user as part of a group and the interactions among them. Table 17.2 shows the organizational items used in the diagrams and their notation. Similarly, Table 17.3 summarizes their possible relations.

17.6.1   Structure Analysis

Two structural diagrams are used to represent the structure of the system, which model its static part. First, we assume the *class diagram* from the *class package* in UML 2.0 [9], which shows the domain objects used in the system as well as the

Table 17.2 Organizational items of the diagrams

Description	Notation
An *actor* is one or several persons or another external system that interacts with the system. Actors directly interact within the collaborative system to accomplish individual tasks, but they can also interact with each other, through the system, to perform group tasks.	ACTOR_1
A *group* is a set of individual or collective actors which play roles. Such a set of actors needs to interact together and to collaborate in order to achieve a common objective.	GROUP_1
An *individual* item is a unique actor which plays a role.	Individual_1
A *user* is a human individual item who interacts with the system.	User_1
An *agent* is a non human individual item who interacts with the system.	Agent_1
A *role* is defined by means of the set of tasks which an actor performs. An actor is what it is due to the roles it plays.	ROLE_1

Table 17.3 Relationship between items

Description	Notation
A *play* relationship is a structural organizational relationship among a role and the actor playing such a role.	
An *aggregation* relationship is a structural organizational relationship that identifies an association between the whole and its parts.	
A *hierarchy* relationship is a structural organizational relationship that identifies a grade dependency among two actors.	
A co-interaction is a group organizational relationship between two actors which means an interaction between them to achieve a common objective thatwould be unreachable without such an interaction.	

relationships among them. Then, another diagram is used to describe the organizational structure of the actors involved in a CSCW system: OSD, Organizational Structure Diagram. It specifies the participants of the system, their organization and the roles they play.

17.6.1.1 Organizational Structure Diagram

The *Organizational Structure Diagram*, OSD, describes how the different organizational items are related to constitute the structure of groups, roles and actors which are going to use the system under consideration, that is, how actors are organized and interrelated to constitute groups and hierarchies and so forth.

An OSD provides designers with a view of the system in which the different actors appear organized according to their belonging and hierarchical relationships. Furthermore, the role the actors can play in the system is also depicted, thus this diagram gives a structural view without taking into account what the users do.

It is possible to model the organizational structure of the future system's participants by means of *actors*, *groups*, *individuals*, *users*, *agents* and *roles*, connected between them by means of *play*, *aggregation* and *hierarchy relationships*. Such elements and relationships have been briefly described in Tables 17.2 and 17.3. Figure 17.1 shows an example of OSD for the case study described in Sect. 17.4, where most of the organizational items and relationships are shown.

17.6.2 Behaviour Analysis

We use the Co-interaction Diagram (CD) and the Task Diagram (TD) to analyze and model the behaviour of the system. The first one models the collaborations

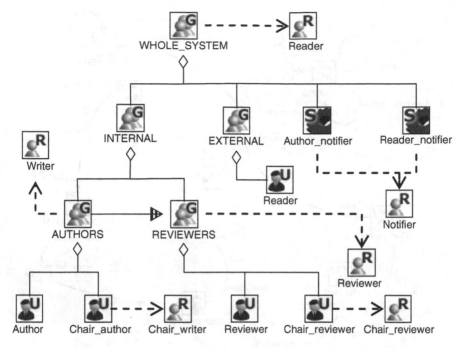

Fig. 17.1 Organizational structure diagram for the case study

among the actors. As a task diagram we have adopted CTT [10]. A TD models what an actor does in the system, that is, its interactions with the system.

17.6.2.1   Co-interaction Diagram

The CD models the interactions established among the organizational items in the system. The idea is not to model users' interactions, which is modelled through the TDs, but to model the interaction among the users through computers and networks, that is, human–computer–human interaction.

When structuring the whole system with different primary objectives, a CD is developed for each one. Each CD will explain the existing interaction among the organizational items (groups, roles, actors) needed to achieve such objectives. The whole set of CDs describes all the collaboration in the system.

To model this particular kind of interactions, *actors*, *groups*, *individuals*, *users agents*, and *roles* are used to represent the different participants which are connected by means of *play relationships*, if it is necessary to show the roles, and *co-interaction relationships* to depict human–computer–human interactions. Such elements and relationships have been briefly described in Tables 17.2 and 17.3.

Figure 17.2 shows an example of CD for the case study described in Sect. 17.4, where several co-interaction relationships among actors (groups, agents or users) are shown.

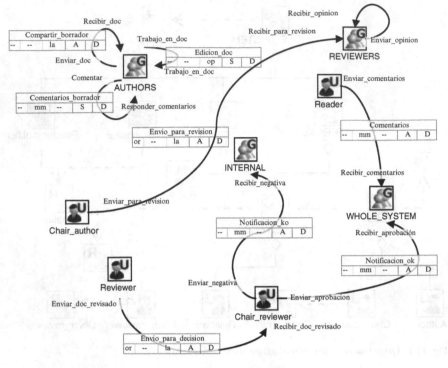

Fig. 17.2 Organizational structure diagram for the case study

17.7   Traceability Inter- and Intra-Stage

Coherence and consistency among the elements that appear between the different development stages, as well as in every stage, are two aspects which have been taken into account. Since this chapter regards analysis in CSCW systems, we will describe the traceability intra-stage, the one that happens within the analysis stage, not the traceability that take place between this stage and requirements gathering and design stages.

The traceability to be considered in this stage regards roles and tasks as they are concepts closely related, but identified separately. Once both the roles and the tasks of the system have been identified and described, the aforementioned diagrams model the organizational structure of the actors in the system, the collaborations between them and the interactions of the users with the system. Modifications of elements in a model deserve a special attention because many of the elements used in a diagram are also used in the others. Therefore, the use of elements unambiguously identified should maintain the coherence and consistency of the model.

Roles have been defined regarding a set of tasks, so that roles and tasks are inextricably linked. The number of roles and tasks (especially tasks) of a system can be very high. We use a task–role two-dimensional matrix to express this association in an explicit way.

17.8 Conclusions

In this chapter we present a methodology to tackle the analysis stage when developing collaborative systems. Traditional software engineering methods defined to tackle the analysis stage takes into account static and behavioural issues but regarding collaborative systems, where interactions among users are specially important, these methods are not enough to give account of the specific features of these systems. To tackle this lack, we propose new diagrams for analysis purposes. In this sense, some issues have been specially considered such as collaborations among the participants of the system or human–computer–human interactions, participant's organization and the roles they play. Some diagrams have been proposed to perform these models. The methodology supports the modelling of user interactions as well as the modelling of the objects manipulated in the problem domain and their relationships. To prove the method proposed, we have applied it successfully to different case studies, and a part of one of them is shown in this chapter to help the understanding of the proposal.

Acknowledgements This work has been partially supported by the Spanish CICYT TIN2004-08000-C03-01 and the JCCM PAI06-0093-8836 grants.

References

1. Constantine LL, Lockwood LAD (1999) Software for use: a practical guide to the models and methods of usage-centered design. Addison Wesley, Reading, MA
2. Durán A (2000) Un Entorno Metodológico de Ingeniería de Requisitos para Sistemas de Información. PhD. University of Sevilla
3. Garrido Bullejos JL (2003) AMENITIES: Una metodología para el desarrollo de sistemas cooperativos basada en modelos de comportamiento y tareas. PhD. University of Granada
4. Greif I (1988) Computer-Supported Cooperative Work: A Book of Readings. Morgan Kaufmann. San Mateo CA
5. Grudin J (1994) Computer-Supported Cooperative Work: History and Focus. Computer 27, 5
6. Jacobson I, Booch G, Rumbaugh J (1999) The Unified Software Development Process. Addison-Wesley Longman Publishing Co. Inc.
7. Johansen R(1988) Groupware: Computer support for business teams. New York. The Free Press
8. Molina AI (2006) Una Propuesta Metodológica para el Desarrollo de la Interfaz de Usuario en Sistemas Groupware. Tesis Doctoral. Universidad de Castilla-La Mancha
9. OMG (2005) Object Management Group. UML Superstructure Specification, v2.0
10. Paterno' F (1999) Model-based Design and Evaluation of Interactive Applications. Springer Verlag, Berlin. ISBN 1-85233-155-0
11. Penichet VMR, Lozano MD, Gallud \JA, Tesoriero R (2007) Task Modelling for Collaborative Systems. 6th International workshop on TAsk MOdels and DIAgrams: TAMODIA 2007.

Lecture Notes in Computer Science, Springer Verlag; I.S.B.N.: 978-3-540-77221-7 vol 4849. Toulouse, France

12. Penichet VMR, Lozano MD, Gallud JA (2008) An Ontology to Model Collaborative Organizational Structures in CSCW Systems. Springer, Berlin. Vol. Engineering the User Interface: From Research to Practice. ISBN: 978-1-84800-135-0

13. Pinelle D, Gutwin C, Greenberg S (2003) Task analysis for groupware usability evaluation: Modeling shared-workspace tasks with the mechanics of collaboration. ACM (TOCHI) Volume 10, Issue 4, Pages: 281–311. ISSN:1073-0516

14. Poltrock S, Grudin J (1994) Computer Supported Cooperative Work and Groupware. Companion on Human Factors in Computing Systems. Boston, Massachusetts, United States. C. Plaisant, Ed. CHI'94. ACM, 355–356

15. Poltrock S, Grudin J (1999) CSCW, groupware and workflow: experiences, state of art, and future trends. CHI'99 Human Factors in Computing Systems. Pittsburgh, Pennsylvania. ACM Press, New York, NY, 120–121

16. Van der Veer GC, Van Welie M (2000) Task based groupware design: Putting theory into practice. Symposium on Designing Interactive Systems. ACM, 326–337

Chapter 18
CIAT, A Model-Based Tool for Designing Groupware User Interfaces Using CIAM

William J. Giraldo, Ana I. Molina, Cesar A. Collazos,
Manuel Ortega and Miguel A. Redondo

Abstract In this chapter, we introduce CIAT (Collaborative Interactive Applications Tool), a software tool based on models supporting designers and engineers to create models based on CIAN notation. This software tool supports the interface design of groupware applications that enable integration with software processes through UML notation. We introduce our methodological approach for dealing with the conceptual design of applications that support work in groups, called CIAM. A study case using the Congress Management System is presented in order to describe our Model.

18.1   Introduction

The interactive groupware system design integrates disciplines such as Software Engineering (SE), CSCW, and Usability Engineering (UE). Therefore, it requires interaction between multiple stakeholders using their own specific workspaces [1, 2]. This process is, in itself, a collaborative process in which each stakeholder needs support to design artifacts on multiple abstraction levels and perspectives. Therefore, the specified information on each workspace must serve as a complement for the modeling on other workspaces, both in the same perspective and in others at the same abstraction level. In addition, although there is a growing number of proposals in the development of collaborative systems, there are deficiencies in trying to model the collaborative aspects [3, 4], particularly for proposals that combine group work application aspects and interactive aspects. In the same way, those that are especially dedicated to the modeling of the interactive aspects of the applications do not usually give support for modeling collaborative aspects. Within the CSCW field and the representation of application workflow, the proposals do not allow concepts relating to the design of groupware systems and their more interactive parts to be combined. In addition,

W.J. Giraldo (✉), A.I. Molina, C.A. Collazos, M. Ortega and M.A. Redondo
Systems and Computer Engineering, University of Quindío, Quindío, Colombia
e-mail: wjgiraldo@uniquindio.edu.co

V. López-Jaquero et al. (eds.), *Computer-Aided Design of User Interfaces VI*,
DOI: 10.1007/978-1-84882-206-1_18, © Springer-Verlag London Limited 2009

these proposals are not easily integrated with software methodologies. The disciplines of software engineering and human–computer interaction (HCI) consider user interfaces from different points of view. Therefore, linking the activities that take place in these two disciplines has been complex [5]. For all these reasons, we have defined *CIAM*. *CIAM* (*Collaborative Interactive Applications Methodology*) is a methodological approach that implies adopting different viewpoints in order to create models of interactive groupware systems.

In this chapter, we introduce our methodological approach for developing the presentation layer of a collaborative system and the integration with the software engineering process. This chapter is organized in the following way: Section 18.2 introduces our methodological approach for designing interactive groupware applications, presenting a brief explanation of its stages and the aspects that can be specified in each one. Also, some aspects of the CIAN notation are described in this section. Section 18.3 introduces the eclipse framework, especially the GMF framework. Section 18.4 presents the CIAT tool, which is used as an example. Finally, the conclusions are presented.

18.2   CIAM: A Methodological Approach for User Interface Development of Collaborative Applications

In this section, we present the stages in our methodological approach. CIAM considers interactive groupware modeling in two ways: group-centered modeling and process-centered modeling. To start with, the social relations are studied and an organizational scheme is specified. Next, the group work is modeled. The modeling becomes more user-centered when we go deeper into the abstraction level in which interactive tasks are modeled [6]. In other words, a dialog arises between an individual user and the application. In this way, collaborative aspects (groups, processes) and interactive (individual) modeling problems are tackled jointly. CIAM guides designers in creating conceptual specifications of the main aspects that define the presentation layer in CSCW systems. The stages of this proposal and their objectives are enumerated as follows:

Sociogram Development. In this phase, the organization structure is modeled, as well as the relationships between its members. Organization Members belong to these categories: *roles, actors, and software agents*, or in the aforementioned associations, forming *groups* or *work teams* consisting of several roles. The elements in these diagrams can be interconnected by means of three kinds of basic relationships (*inheritance, performance,* and *association*).

Inter-Action Modeling. In this phase, the main tasks (or processes) that define the group work in the previously defined organization are described. For each process, the roles involved, the data manipulated, and the products generated are specified. Each task must be classified in one of the following categories: *group* or *individual tasks*. Processes will be interconnected by means of several kinds of relationships that, in many cases, can be interpreted as dependence.

Responsibilities Modeling. In this phase, the individual and shared responsibilities are modeled. We can see that the specified information in this phase is supplemented by that of the previous one. Both models must be consistent with each other.

Group Tasks Modeling. In this stage, the group tasks identified in the previous stage are described in a more detailed way. There are two different kinds of tasks, which must be modeled in differentiated ways: (a) *Cooperative Tasks* are specified by means of the so-called *responsibilities decomposition graph*, in which subtasks make up the group task, so that, at a lower abstraction level, only an *individual task* must appear. (b) *Collaborative Task* modeling includes specification of the roles involved, as well as the data model objects manipulated by the work team (i.e., the *shared context* specification). Shared context is defined as the set of *objects* that are visible to the user set, as well as the *actions* that can be executed on them. Once the objects that make up the *shared context* have been decided, it is necessary to fragment this information into three different parts: the objects and/or attributes manipulated in the *collaborative visualization area*, the ones which appear in the *individual visualization area,* and the ones that make up the *exclusive edition segment* (a subset in the data model that is accessed in an exclusive way by only one application user at a time).

Interaction Modeling. In the last phase, interactive aspects of the application are modeled. An interaction model for each individual task detected in the diverse phases of the gradual refinement process is created. An interactive task decomposition tree in CTT [3] is developed. The interactive model is directly derived from the shared context definition. Our methodological approach includes the way of obtaining this model from the shared context modeling [7].

CIAM is supported by a notation called CIAN (Collaborative Interactive Applications Notation). This notation is a simplification of another notation for workflow modeling, called APM (Action Port Model), proposed by Carlsen [9]. This notation has been enriched to support differentiated modeling of cooperative and collaborative tasks, although it has been simplified in some aspects (to characterize a task, only the task identification, the roles involved, and the objects manipulated are included).

18.3   Eclipse Framework

The Eclipse Framework provides tools for guiding the software modeling by using metamodel concepts [10]. By using EMF (Eclipse Modeling Framework) and GMF (Graphical Editing Framework), we can design the CIAT tool as an Eclipse Plug-in. Eclipse has established itself in the area of application development. Its main success factor is the ability to extend its functionality through the use of plug-ins [11, 12]. Eclipse is not a monolithic program, but rather consists of a small kernel called "Plug-In Loader" surrounded by hundreds of plug-ins [11]. Each plug-in provides services for the other ones, and in turn, it can be used for other services.

Eclipse provides support for MDD by means of the Eclipse Modeling Framework (EMF) for developing models from a specification. It supports key MDA concepts such as the development and integration of software guided by models. EMF is the modeling framework within Eclipse and provides mechanisms to persist the model data to an XML file. EMF is designed to facilitate the design and implementation of structured models, because the modeling concepts and their implementations are directly related [10, 13].

The Graphical Editing Framework (GEF) facilitates the development of graphical representations of models. These displays are made through the Draw2D Framework, which is based on SWT and is the standard drawing of Eclipse.

By combining GEF and EMF, we can implement an Eclipse plug-in in the java Eclipse framework. To enable the definition of a graphical modeling tool in multiple domains is the aim of GMF [14].

A block diagram of the structure of the CIAT GMF project is shown in Fig. 18.2, which was implemented through the following steps:

(1) *Specification of graphical model of the CIAN notation.* This model defines the graphical component structure used to represent the CIAN concepts. Figure 18.1 illustrates the graphical design of the Inter_Action individual task of CIAN (middle), and the graphical results (right) are quite similar to the initial graphical specification (left). Each graphical component of the CIAN notation should be specified by using the GMF model elements, for example, Rectangle, Label, Node, and Link. It is necessary to understand this GMF graphical model because all the graphical elements for which information should be stored should then be added to the domain model of the notation.

(2) *Domain model specification of the CIAN modeling concepts (using EMF).* The domain model defines the persistence model of information from the models generated by CIAT. This information includes data about graphical aspects of the CIAN notation. See Fig. 18.2(a).

(3) *Implementing the CIAT graphical model.* Figure 18.2(b) shows the implementation of the graphical specifications on GMF.

(4) *Generating the CIAT toolbar model.* Figure 18.2(c) shows the implementation of the CIAT toolbar by using GMF.

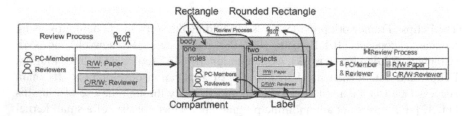

Fig. 18.1 Graphical specification of the Inter-Action task on CIAT

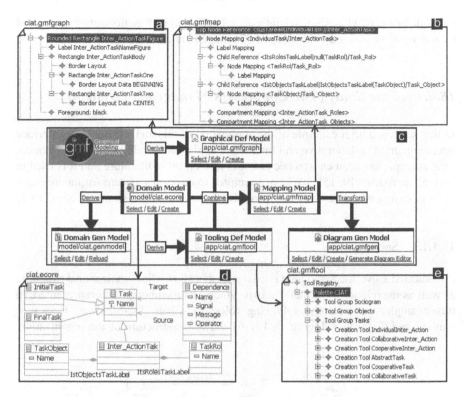

Fig. 18.2   GMF Project structure. CIAT tool example

(5) *Generating the CIAT mapping model.* The relationship between the graphical
    elements, the domain model, and the toolbar is established for the mapping
    model. Figure 18.2(d) shows the implementation of the mapping model by
    using GMF.

Thus, a functional plug-in is created for the CIAT tool. CIAT is built by combining
all the modeling capabilities of Eclipse.

18.4   CIAT: The Collaborative Interactive Applications Tool

CIAT (Collaborative Interactive Applications Tool) is a software tool based on
models supporting designers and engineers to create models based on CIAN notation. This software tool supports the interface design of groupware applications,
enabling integration with software processes through UML notation. The ECLIPSE
Modeling Framework (EMF) and Graphic Modeling Framework (GMF) provide

support for the CIAT design. We introduce CIAT, and its functionality is presented by means of a case study, the Congress Management System.

18.4.1 Case Study (The Congresses Management System)

In this section, a brief example of the application of this method for User Interface development of collaborative and interactive applications using CIAT is presented. This example has been chosen because it is referenced in literature and it is used in several approaches [9, 15]. We have attempted to develop a system for the management of congresses. The modeling process follows the stages shown in Sect. 18.2.

18.4.1.1 Sociogram

As indicated above, the Sociogram is a diagram that allows the organizational structure, as well as the relationships that can exist among its members, to be represented. In this example, we have the following roles: PC-Chair, PC-Member, Reviewer, Author, and Co-Author. Figure 18.4 (left) shows the structure of the organization.

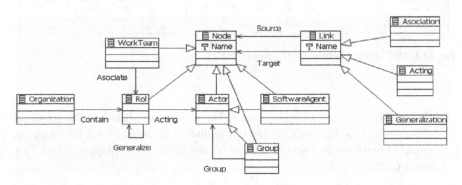

Fig. 18.3 Sociogram metamodel

Fig. 18.4 Sociogram model of case of study (*left*), XMI code generated by CIAT (*right*)

A PC-Member can be considered a specialization of a Reviewer, since he or she carries out the same work (revising), but is specialized in carrying out another, wider, group of tasks or responsibilities. In addition, we can see that the PC-Chair and PC-Members' roles are associated. This indicates that there are tasks in which both, with their respective responsibilities, take part.

CIAT provides designers with models in XMI files, as shown in Fig. 18.4(b). The XML Metadata Interchange (XMI) is an OMG standard that facilitates the interchange of models via XML Documents [16]. CIAT uses XMI files to maintain the system domain models and also because it is the format used by the ATL plug-in on model transformations.

18.4.1.2 Work In-Group Tasks Modeling Stage

In this phase, the level of detail, with which the previously identified group tasks (collaborative or cooperative) are specified, increases. CIAM defines the cooperative tasks and the collaborative tasks in a differentiated way. This distinction is translated into two important aspects (the division of tasks and the manipulated objects) which are considered in the definition by Dillenbourg [17].

As an example, we will show the specification of a task of each type in detail. In particular, we will show the modeling of the cooperative task, Reviews Distribution Task, and the collaborative task that allows the Final List of Papers to be created.

In Fig. 18.5 (left), the model of the task that allows papers to be distributed for subsequent revision is shown in detail. On the left, we can see the roles involved and the objects manipulated. On the right is the *responsibilities decomposition graph*. Figure 18.5 (right) shows the appearance of the collaborative task specification making the final list of papers. As in the cooperative tasks specification, the area on the left shows the roles involved, the objects manipulated, and the access mode to these objects (reading and/or writing).

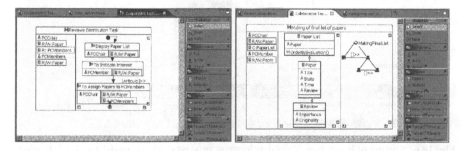

Fig. 18.5 Modeling of the cooperative and collaborative tasks on CIAT

18.4.2 Integration of CIAM into the Software Development Process

The integration of model-based design approaches and development with UML notation makes it conceptually possible to relate the main concepts of HCI to the classic ones in SE [18]. The approach used in the fields of HCI (Human–Computer Interaction) and SE (Software Engineering) has gained importance and attention in recent years [5]. On the one hand, SE begins to consider *usability* as a quality attribute that must be measured and promoted [19]. On the other hand, if the techniques proposed in HCI want to gain solidity within the SE field they should clearly indicate how to integrate their techniques and activities within the process of software development.

The scheme of integration between the development process, the model-based UI development process (UI), and the CIAM proposal is presented in Fig. 18.6. The CIAM requirements analysis is based on an ethnographic analysis [20]. This is the most extended requirement-gathering technique for the development of CSCW systems. The data obtained in this stage is linked to the analysis information of the other two methods considered, so that the system requirements are complete and can be used as the starting point for the three development methods.

The taxonomy for classifying and separating information is defined in CIAM. A conceptual modeling approach based on taxonomies has great advantages in

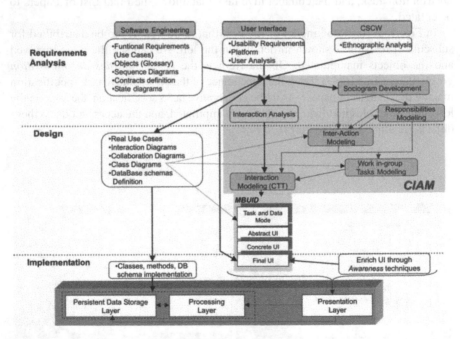

Fig. 18.6 Scheme of integration of the development process (ES), the model-based UI development process (UI), and the CIAM proposal (CSCW)

broad domains [21]. The proposed taxonomy is based on the Zachman Framework [22], which is defined in two dimensions, called perspectives (owner, designer, builder) and views (Data, Function, Network, People). The integration of models in UML and CIAN is done through transformations.

MDD proposes model transformations to reduce the complexity of software design [8, 23]. The integration of models in UML and CIAN is done through an integration layer; see Fig. 18.7. The integration layer is populated by using transformations applied to CIAN models; see Fig. 18.7(a). Each transformation uses only information that is useful in generating UML diagrams. Both the CIAN notation and the notation used by the taxonomy are MOF-compliant.

The ATLAS Transformation Language (ATL) is used to implement transformations between models. The ATL plug-in is used to transform CIAM diagrams into a set of model elements in the integration layer.

Figure 18.8 illustrates the integration between the CIAN models and UML models by using the CIAT tool. The information about roles and relationships in the Sociogram is extracted through the transformation, which is used in the "Business Model" and "System Model" perspectives and the "People" view, mainly; see Fig. 18.8(c). There is no direct translation of the acting and association relationships of CIAN into UML. However, this information should be stored in order to generate other artifacts.

The Inter_Action diagram [see Fig. 18.8(a)] illustrates the system's macro-activities and their interdependencies. This model is essential, because certain temporary information (precedence and coordination information) is represented. This information can be enriched by using information related to the domain (which is extracted from the models of the ES process). This diagram provides information about the pre-conditions, post-conditions, messages, and data that are required or generated by the activities. UML lacks a diagram of this type.

It is necessary to point out that the use cases provide information of interest for the development of the task models. The Business use cases identify the tasks, at the upper abstraction level, that must be performed by the users and the system, and

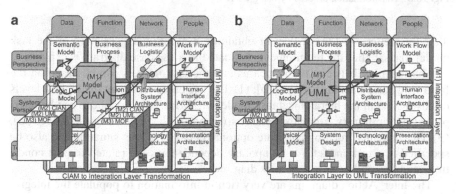

Fig. 18.7 CIAT transformation process

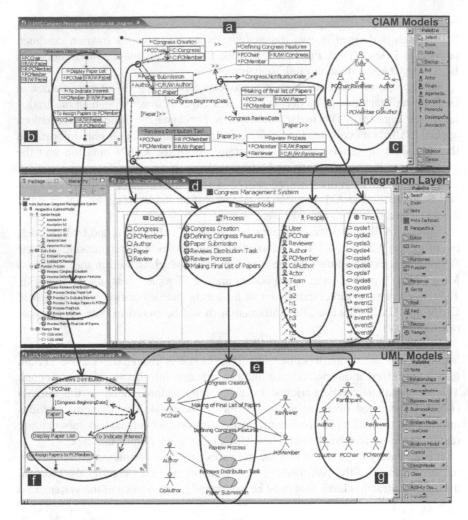

Fig. 18.8 Transformation process by using CIAT

their interaction. In [24], a way of obtaining a preliminary structure of the task
model that satisfies the requirements indicated in a use case diagram is explained.

The mapping between the use cases and the task models can be based on the
following basic transformations [25]: (1) The use cases represent the highest levels
of abstraction in the hierarchical task models. (2) The "uses" relations can be interpreted as temporary order expressions (in particular a sequence connection).
(3) The "extends" relations indicate optional behaviors. This situation can also be
specified in a task model. (4) Temporary dependencies are related to post conditions and preconditions in activities diagram.

The Inter_Action diagrams are very rich in information to populate the integration layer. Figure 18.8 illustrates the information extracted from this diagram.

The transformations separate information as follows: (1) The Inter-Action activities are associated with business use cases. The cooperative activities are transformed into activity diagrams. (2) The interdependencies are associated with preconditions, post-conditions, and events between various activity diagrams. (3) The domain objects are associated with business entities. A business object diagram is derived from the information in each activity, which is related to roles and objects.

The process of transformation and integration is controlled through the integration layer metamodel. The first transformation uses the CIAN metamodel as the input metamodel and the taxonomy metamodel as the output metamodel. The second transformation uses the taxonomy metamodel as the input metamodel and the UML metamodel as the output metamodel. CIAT recognizes these three metamodels and it is possible to edit models using editors for each one.

18.5 Conclusions

In this chapter, we have presented a brief picture of our methodological proposal and our proposal for the integration of the interaction design into the Unified Development Process. In particular, we have presented CIAT, a model-based software tool that enables a user-centered approach for Model Based User Interface Development of Collaborative Applications. We have introduced our methodological approach for dealing with the conceptual design of applications for supporting work in groups, called CIAM. This approach is organized into several stages in which conceptual models are created, using the CIAN notation.

CIAT is intended for supporting the early design cycle of a user interface or integration with the software engineering process. It allows stakeholders to construct models without losing touch with other stakeholders, because each one has support for designing artifacts in their specific domain.

We have used a study case to present the appearance and configuration of the CIAT tool. The taxonomy has been useful for integrating model elements from CIAN into UML. The use of an integration layer based on the taxonomy has facilitated the integration between CIAN and UML. Finally, thanks to the use of GMF, CIAT can integrate with other tools and services available in the Eclipse project.

Acknowledgments This work has been supported by Universidad del Quindío, the Castilla – La Mancha University and the Junta de Comunidades de Castilla – La Mancha in the projects AULA-T (PBI08-0069), M-CUIDE (TC20080552), and mGUIDE (PBC08-0006-512).

References

1. A. I. Molina, M. A. Redondo, and M. Ortega, "A conceptual and methodological framework for modeling interactive groupware applications," CRIWG 2006, Valladolid. Spain.
2. C. Gutwin and S. Greenberg, "Design for Individuals, Design for Groups: Tradeoffs between power and workspace awareness," presented at ACM CSCW'98, Seattle, 1998.

3. F. Paternò, "ConcurTaskTrees: An Engineered Notation for Task Models," presented at The Handbook Of Task Analysis For HCI, 2004.
4. M. v. Welie and G. v. d. Veer, "Groupware Task Analysis," presented at Handbook of Cognitive Task Design, 2003.
5. T. Granollers, J. Lorés, M. Sendin, and F. Perdrix, "Integración de la IPO y la ingeniería del software: MPIu + a," presented at III Taller en Sistemas Hipermedia Colaborativos y Adaptativos, Granada España, 2005.
6. H. Beyer and K. Holtzblatt, Contextual Design: Defining Customer-Centered Systems. Morgan Kaufmann, CA, 1998.
7. A. I. Molina, M. A. Redondo, M. Ortega, and U. Hope, "CIAM: A methodology for the development of groupware user interfaces," *JUCS*, 2007.
8. D. S. Frankel, "An MDA Manifesto," MDA Journal: Business Process trends, 2004.
9. S. Carlsen, "Action Port Model: A Mixed Paradigm Conceptual Workflow Modeling Language," *3rd IFCI*, 1998.
10. B. Moore, D. Dean, A. Gerber, G. Wagenknecht, and P. Vanderheyden, *Eclipse Development using the Graphical Editing Framework and the Eclipse Modeling Framework*: ibm.com/redbooks, 2004.
11. E. Clayberg and D. Rubel, *Eclipse: Building Commercial-Quality Plug-ins, Second Edition*, second ed: Addison Wesley Professional, 2006.
12. B. Burd, *Eclipse For Dummies*. Wiley, River Street, 2005.
13. F. Budinsky, D. Steinberg, E. Merks, R. Ellersick, and T. J. Grose, *Eclipse Modeling Framework: A Developer's Guide*: Addison-Wesley, Reading, 2003.
14. R. gronback and D. roy, "Tutorial GMF," vol. 2007: Eclipse Wiki, 2006.
15. H. Trætteberg, "Model-based User Interface Design," in doctorade thesis: Norwegian University of Science and Technology, 2002.
16. J. Miller and J. Mukerji., "MDA Guide Version 1.0.1," vol. 08-07-2007: http://www.omg.org/docs/omg/03-06-01.pdf, 2003.
17. P. Dillenbourg, M. Baker, A. Blaye, and C. O'Malley, "The Evolution of Research on Collaborative Learning," presented at Towards an interdisciplinary learning science, 1995.
18. J. Artim, M. Harmelen, K. Butler, and J. Guliksen, et al., "Incorporating work, process and task analysis into industrial object-oriented systems development," *SIGCHI Bulletin*, vol. 30, 1998.
19. X. Ferré, "Integration of Usability Techniques into the Software Development Process," ICSE-2003, Portland (OR), USA, 2003.
20. H. Schwartzman, "Ethnography in Organizations," *Qualitative Research Methods Series 27, Sage*, Newbury Park CA., 1993.
21. Y. Tzitzikas, N. Spyratos, and P. Constantopoulos, "Mediators over taxonomy-based information sources," *The VLDB Journal*, vol. 14, pp. 112–136, 2005.
22. J. F. Sowa and J. A. Zachman, "Extending and formalizing the framework for information systems architecture," *IBM Systems Journal*, vol.31, pp. 590–616, 1992.
23. F. Jouault and I. Kurtev, "On the architectural alignment of ATL and QVT," In the 2006 ACM symposium on Applied computing, France, 2006.
24. F. Paternò, "Towards a UML for Interactive Systems," In the 8th International Conference on Engineering for Human-Computer Interaction, 2001.
25. S. Lu, C. Paris, and K. Vander Linden, Towards the automatic generation of task models from object oriented diagrams. In Engineering for Human-Computer Interaction. Kluwer, Boston, 1999.

Chapter 19
Towards a Methodological Framework to Implement Model-Based Tools for Collaborative Environments

Montserrat Sendín and Ana I. Molina

Abstract Collaborative systems for mobile environments require being adaptable to various physical and computing scenarios with varying conditions due to mobility restrictions. Assuming that, it is recommendable to reuse as far as possible the work already realized to deal with problems inherent to mobility, device heterogeneity and adaptation in the groupware work. Our conceptual framework, the so-called *Collaborative EPF*, has been defined in this line. It is conceived as a reference instrument that offers a set of directives and heuristics for supporting the design of plastic and groupware User Interfaces. In addition, CIAM is a methodology for obtaining the conceptual modelling of CSCW applications, providing thus a complement for the *Collaborative EPF*. In this chapter, we show the integration of both works providing a comprehensive and original methodological framework to be instantiated in operative Model-Based tools for work in-group.

19.1 Introduction

It is widely recognized the increasing utilization of mobile devices in collaborative environments. Current groupware approaches focus on the restrictions and affordances that mobility provides, but they do not address in a satisfactory way the huge heterogeneity and the adaptation to varying constraints at the same time. An ideal infrastructure should provide the capacity to adapt interactive systems to the context of use, considering aspects related to user, platform or environment, but without neglecting the group conditions, integrating *awareness* issues.

The approach par excellence for the systematic development of multi-contextual User Interfaces (UIs henceforth) is the Model-Based (MB henceforth) approach. We have developed a conceptual framework for supporting this type of tools, which offers some directives for the collaborative work: the so-called *Collaborative*

M. Sendín (✉) and A.I. Molina
GRIHO Research Lab, University of Lleida, 69, Jaume II St., 25001 Lleida Spain
e-mail: msendin@diei.udl.cat

V. López-Jaquero et al. (eds.), *Computer-Aided Design of User Interfaces VI*,
DOI: 10.1007/978-1-84882-206-1_19, © Springer-Verlag London Limited 2009

Explicit Plasticity Engine (C-EPF henceforth). It is conceived as a reference instrument to construct flexible MB tools able to develop adaptable and group-aware UIs for multi-environment collaborative and interactive systems.

The main difficulty of this kind of tools underlies in the complexity in the specification of the system's conceptual modelling, in whose definition the group considerations have also to be incorporated. In particular, certain issues such as the support to cooperative procedures and spaces for sharing information become requirements to be considered during the development of this kind of systems, affecting specially the design of the UI. There are several proposals that have tackled the problematic of the conceptual modelling of work in-group systems. Some representative examples are CTT [7], GTA [10], APM [2] and COMO-UML [3]. The study of these proposals has allowed us to detect the need for *theoretical and computational models* that allow specifying the activities in group in a suitable way and the scarce variety of *notations* that support in a joint way interactive and groupware aspects. CIAM (*Collaborative Interactive Applications Methodology*) [6] offers a solution to these lacks. It obtains the conceptual modelling of groupware applications, considering jointly the work in-group and the interaction.

This chapter shows the integration of the CIAM methodology in the development process defined in the C-EPF. The inclusion of a methodology as CIAM provides an appropriate formalism that complements C-EPF. The result is a comprehensive methodological framework to support the construction of this kind of tools as instantiations of the conceptual framework.

This chapter is structured as follows. Section 19.2 presents the C-EPF. Section 19.3 presents the CIAM methodological approach, some of the notations and specification issues, which are applied in a case study. Finally, the conclusions and further work conclude the chapter.

19.2 C-EPF: A Conceptual Framework for Designing Plastic Group-Aware UIs

According to the approach known as *dichotomic view of plasticity* [8], a MB tool, located in a certain *plasticity server*, tackles those contextual changes that cannot be solved locally in the target device, due to the complexity of the adaptation to be performed. In these cases, it is emitted an explicit request from the device to the corresponding server, triggering so the process to produce a UI accommodated to the new situation. As a consequence, a MB tool is being iteratively reactivated by receiving a request with the current contextual restrictions.

Our conceptual framework fosters the separation of concerns usually found in *model-based approaches* with a progressive multi-layer design of the UI. Hence, it is structured in the four levels of abstraction that were proposed in the CAMELEON project [1]. The goal is to progressively shape the suitable UI for each case, taking into account all the contextual circumstances.

The models included in the highest level of abstraction are the following ones: the task model (TaskM in Fig. 19.1), which has to be specially accommodated to a group scenario considering the distinction between the individual or collaborative features of each task, including little actions aimed at promoting collaboration; the domain model (DomainM in Fig. 19.1), which must include specific collaborative concepts such as actors, roles, places, and events; and the dialogue model (DialogueM in Fig. 19.1), which has to specify the relationship among the different states of the UI and the possible situations related to the group.

Apart from these models, there are those that collect different aspects from the context: the contextual models. One of the contextual models considered in C-EPF is the *group model*, specially included for collaborative systems. It is aimed to gather a shared understanding of the common problem in order to be assimilated by the group members. We are referring to a certain kind of working group memory that represents all those aspects of the collaborative work that can help in the development of the common activity in a collaborative manner. A wide explanation about the models and the conceptual framework can be consulted in [9].

The C-EPF contemplates three types of operations: *reification* or descendant derivation (transformation from more abstract to more concrete models), *abstraction* or ascendant inference, following a reverse engineering process and *adaptation* or horizontal transformation (accommodation of a particular UI design to a different contextual situation). According to this *multi-path UI development* [4] and following the multi-layer structure presented above, the C-EPF defines six stages in all, being one of them common in the two vertical paths: the so-called *Preparation of Initial Models* (PIM in Fig. 19.1). Figure 19.1 shows this stage.

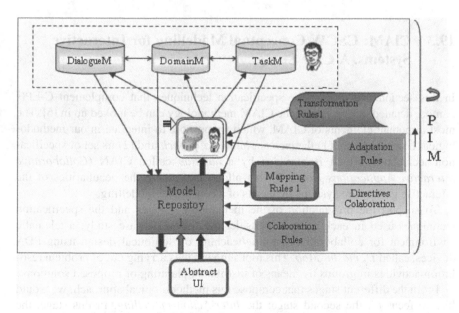

Fig. 19.1 *Preparation of Initial Models*, the first stage in a pure derivation process

Details about the sequencing of the stages, their objectives, as well as other additional components that also intervene in each stage can be consulted in [9].

Regarding the components specific for Groupware, a part from the shared-knowledge the conceptual framework also integrates these two:

- *Collaboration rules*. Specific rules that govern the collaborative behaviour of the system at hand from a global perspective. These are the rules applied when the server receives a request by a group member, containing collaborative issues. They provide mechanisms to infer global properties and the group social dynamic from the *shared-knowledge* in order to support decision-making upon specific situations. These rules are particular to each system.
- *Collaboration directives*. Define some guidelines and directives that gather the experience accumulated by the groupware researchers, trying to promote participation between group members and to contribute to a real collaboration. One of the most important directives is the integration of diverse *global awareness mechanisms*. By *global awareness mechanism* we are referring to any mechanism destined to capture, maintain, update and increment the *shared-knowledge*, as well as its distribution to the entire group members, aiming at contributing and promoting a real collaboration and a major effectiveness in the development of the group activity. These guidelines intervene along the whole process.

Next section presents CIAN, the formalism that complements C-EPF providing a conceptual modelling methodology. The explanation is focused on those specification techniques that provide an input to the groupware components in the C-EPF; in particular, the *collaboration rules* and the *task model*.

19.3 CIAM: CSCW Conceptual Modelling for Interactive Systems. A Case Study

In this section, we present the specification techniques that complement C-EPF. A more detailed description of the CIAM methodology can be looked up in [6]. The most important elements of CIAM, which we propose to integrate in our methodological framework, are (1) the *methodological approach* and (2) its set of specification techniques, which is provided by a *notation* called CIAN (*Collaborative Interactive Applications Notation*) that allows expressing the peculiarities of the interactive groupware systems by means of a conceptual modelling.

To support the presentation of the methodology stages and the specification techniques used in each one, we consider the following case study: a telematic environment for collaborative learning/teaching of domotical design using PDA devices, called *Domosim-Mob*. This tool supports the carrying out of problem resolution activities in groups by means of distributed planning of proposed solutions.

From the different stages that compose this methodological approach, we would like to focus on the second stage: the *Inter-Action modelling*. In this stage, the

Responsibility	Task Type	Object in Domain Model	Pre-requirement	
			Task	Data
Configure Experiences		C: Activities	INI	
Argumentative Discussion		L/E: Individual Plan C/L/E: Discussion Tree C/L/E: Group Plan	Individual Planning	Individual Plan
Design		L/E: Group Plan C/L/E: Detailed Design	Argumentative Discussion	Group Plan
Parameterization		L/E: Detailed Design	Design	Detailed Design
Cases and Simultacion Hypothesis Definition		L: Detailed Design C: Cases C: Hypothesis	Design	Detailed Design
Simulation		L/E: Detailed Design L: Cases L: Hypothesis	Cases and Simulation Hypothesis Definition	Papers

Fig. 19.2 *Responsibilities Model of Teacher role*

abstract tasks (or processes) that define the work in-group developed in the organization, as well as the temporal and data dependencies that exist among them are described, generating the so-called *participation table*. It provides an initial idea about the division of the work at the highest level of abstraction. Then, the *Responsibilities Model* can be defined, which specifies in more detail and in an individual perspective the responsibilities associated to each one of the roles in the organization. Figure 19.2 shows the Responsibilities Model of the Teacher role.

Finally, we want to pay attention to the last stage: the *Interaction Modelling*. For each task of individual nature detected in the previous stages, an *interaction model* is created, in order to model the interactive aspects of the application. These models facilitate the obtaining of the final UI. The notation used for the interactive models is the *interactive tasks decomposition tree* from CTT [7]. Figure 19.3 shows the *interaction model* associated to the collaborative task *Collaborative Design*.

19.4 Conclusions and Further Work

Our work intends to offer a methodological framework that integrates (a) the C-EPF conceptual framework; and (b) CIAM, a methodology that guides the modelling of collaborative systems. According with the MB approach, CIAM starts with abstract specifications, which are diminishing when advancing in the process. CIAM provides a formalism that enriches C-EPF because C-EPF proposes some collaborative work directives, but it does not include issues related with work in-group modelling. In this sense, CIAM provides a coherent set of notations for modelling

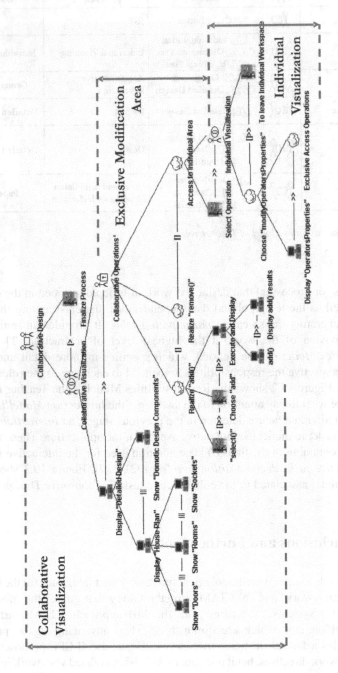

Fig. 19.3 Interaction model associated to the collaborative task *Collaborative Design*

this kind of systems. To be more precise, the *interaction models* in CTT obtained from the application of CIAM become the models to be used in the highest level of abstraction in C-EPF. Moreover, certain diagrams included in the CIAM approach can be used to model the *collaborative rules* component defined in C-EPF. We are referring to the participation table and the responsibilities model. As a result, both frameworks seem to be supplementary. In short, the output from CIAM serves as input to the C-EPF, providing so an adequate work in-group approach from the scratch. As far as we are concerned, the integration of all these considerations can improve groupware design in a significant way. As further work, we are preparing integrating the groupware components presented in a concrete MB tool: the AB-UIDE [5].

Acknowledgements   Supported by Castilla–La Mancha University. M-CUIDE (TC20080552).

References

1. Calvary, G., et al. (2003) A Review of XML-Compliant User Interface Description Languages. Interacting with Computers. *Vol. 15, No.* 3, 289–308.
2. Carlsen, S. (1998) Action Port Model: A Mixed Paradigm Conceptual Workflow Modeling Language. *3rd IFCIS International Conference on Cooperative Information Systems.*
3. Garrido, J. L. (2003). AMENITIES: Una metodología para el desarrollo de sistemas cooperativos basada en modelos de comportamiento y tareas. Phd. Thesis, University of Granada.
4. Limbourg, Q., et al. (2004). UsiXML: a Language Supporting Multi-Path Development of User Interfaces. *Proc. of 9th IFIP Conf. on Engin. for Human-Computer Interaction*, LNCS 3425, 200–220.
5. López-Jaquero, V. (2005). Interfaces de Usuario Adaptativas Basadas en Modelos y Agentes Software. PhD Thesis. University of Castilla-La Mancha.
6. Molina, A.I., M.A. Redondo, and M. Ortega (2008). CIAM: A methodology for the development of groupware user interfaces. Journal of Universal Computer Science. Vol. 14, No. 9, 1435–1446.
7. Paternò, F (2004). ConcurTaskTrees: An Engineered Notation for Task Models. *The Handbook of Task Analysis for HCI.* Diaper and Stanton (Ed.). LEA, Mahwah, NJ., 483–501.
8. Sendín, M. (2007). Infraestructura Software de Soporte al Desarrollo de Interfaces de Usuario Plásticas bajo una Visión Dicotómica. PhD Thesis. University of Lleida.
9. Sendín, M., López-Jaquero, V.M., Collazos, C.A. (2007). Explicit Plasticity Framework: Towards a Conceptual Framework for the Generation of Plastic User Interfaces for Collaborative Environments. Journal of Universal Computer Science. Vol. 14, No. 9, 1447–1462.
10. Welie, M, Veer, G. (2003). Groupware Task Analysis, Handbook of Congnitive Task Design.

Chapter 20
Toward a Formal Task-Based Specification Framework for Collaborative Environments

Maik Wurdel, Daniel Sinnig and Peter Forbrig

Abstract A precise model of the behavioral dynamics involved in collaborative environments is a necessary precondition for the development of smart, proactive user interfaces (UIs). In this chapter, we present a formal task-based specification framework for collaborative environments. The framework consists of two components: A formal specification languages (called CTML) and a tool for editing and animating CTML specifications. The former has a formally defined syntax and semantics and is designed to model actors, roles, and their collaborative tasks. The latter is an Eclipse IDE for the interactive creation and simulation of CTML specifications.

20.1 Introduction

A necessary precondition for the design of proactive UIs and smart environments is a thorough understanding of the user's objectives and their tasks. In a collaborative environment, tasks are barely carried out in isolation, but have to synchronize with other users' tasks. Cooperation among actors is needed to accomplish personal as well as team goals. Some tasks cannot be started while others are still in progress. Imagine the following scenario of a conference session:

> The session chair, Dr. Smith, introduces herself and defines the topic of the session. Afterward she gives the floor to the first speaker who sets up her equipment, the laptop switches to presentation mode and the speaker starts with the talk. During the presentation the audience accesses additional information related to the talk using their personal devices. After finishing the talk the chairman asks for questions from the plenum which are answered by the speaker. Eventually the chairman closes the talk and announces the next one. Subsequent talks are given in the same manner until the chairman encourages an open discussion, wraps up the session and finally closes it.

By analyzing the scenario one can detect several important aspects to consider. The scenario includes multiple actors (Dr. Smith, each presenter, and the listeners),

M. Wurdel (✉), D. Sinnig and P. Forbrig
Department of Computer Science, University of Rostock, Rostock, Germany
e-mail: maik.wurdel@uni-rostock.de

whose behavior is characterized by the role they are fulfilling (chairman, listener, presenter). Personal devices are employed to support the tasks the actors are currently performing. Task performance of users is usually embedded in a social context consisting of team and individual goals [1]. Team goals, such as "performing the conference session," are decomposed into individual goals like "giving my talk" and "manage the session"; however, these goals cannot be accomplished autonomously but require cooperation.

In this chapter, we present a formal specification framework for collaborative environments. The framework consists of two main components: (1) A formal task-based specification language and (2) an interactive editor and simulator. The formal specification language is able to model dependencies between users, devices, and the infrastructure needed to accomplish team and individual goals. The editor and simulator tool provides software engineers with a tool environment to create and test the specification.

The specification language with its tool support is useful to gather requirements for the development of predictive applications in collaborative scenarios, such as smart environments, by helping to identify potential tasks for implicit human–computer interaction (HCI) [2].

In the next section we distill a set of requirements that should be addressed by any behavioral specification framework for smart environments. In Sect. 20.3, we reiterate through relevant background information and review related work. Section 20.4 introduces the collaborative task modeling language (CTML). The tool CTML Editor and Simulator is presented in Sect. 20.5. Finally we conclude and provide an outlook to future avenues.

20.2 Requirements of a Formal Specification Framework

In this section, we compile a set of requirements that are particular to a formal specification framework for collaborative applications. We have summarized the requirements into five distinct categories:

Task-Based Specification: The concept of a "Task" is central to collaborative environments. Typically various actors collaborate and interact with each other by sharing, synchronizing on, and triggering common and related tasks, respectively. Therefore, we believe that a specification framework for collaborative environments should be built around the concept of a task. It should furthermore intrinsically support well-known task-related concepts such as decomposition into subtasks and temporal constraints.

Modeling Cooperation: In order to model collaborative work, synchronization constructs to coordinate task performance are needed. Examples of such constructs are preconditions and effects. The former denote additional constraints defined over the state of the collaborative environment whereas the latter define state modifications as a result of task execution.

Formal Syntax and Semantics: In order to make effective use of the task-specification language formally defined syntax and semantics are needed. The underlying formal model will not only rule out ambiguities but also serve as a reference point for the definition of a refinement relation between two specifications. It is also an obvious precondition for sophisticated tool support.

Support for Refinement: In general, software development consists of a series of transformations in which models are iteratively refined. Modeling collaborative environments is no exception to this rule. Often a coarse grained, even incomplete, specification is successively transformed into more complete fine-grained specifications. With each transformation step, it is important to ensure that the resulting model is a valid refinement of the based specification.

Tool Support: Another key requirement for a formal specification framework is tool support that assists developers in handling collaborative task-model specifications. In particular, tools can facilitate the creation of the actual specification of the collaborative model, perform automated refinement checks, and simulate/animate the specification.

The chapter covers the items (1), (2), (3), and (5). Even though (4) is an interesting issue to investigate, it is out of scope here and needs further investigation. Thus, the focus of this chapter is the introduction of a task-based specification language for collaborative systems together with its formal syntax and semantics. In addition, we present the tool CTML Editor and Simulator which is used to create and animate collaborative task specifications.

20.3   Background and Related Work

In this section, the reader is reminded of the core concepts involved in classical task modeling. We then examine existing collaborative task-model notations and review additional formalisms and relevant-related work in this area.

Task modeling and analysis is a well-established research field in HCI. Various notations for task modeling exist. Among the most popular ones are GOMS [3], HTA [4], CTT [5], and WTM [6]. Even though all notations differ in terms of presentation, level of formality, and expressiveness, they assume the following common tenet: tasks are performed to achieve a certain goal. Moreover, complex tasks are decomposed into more basic tasks until an atomic level has been reached. Within the domain of HCI, CTT is the most popular notation, as it contains the richest set of temporal operators and it is supported by a tool, CTTE [7], which facilitates the creation, visualization, and sharing of task models. A comprehensive overview on CTT can be found in [5].

In order to support the specification of collaborative (multi-user) interactive systems, CTT has been extended to CCTT (Collaborative ConcurTaskTrees) [7]. Similar to the corporative task modeling language presented in this chapter, CCTT uses a role-based approach. A CCTT specification consists of multiple task trees.

One task tree for each involved user role and one task tree that acts as a "coordinator" and specifies the collaboration and global interaction between involved user roles. This approach is not sufficient in our case since CCTT does not provide means for modeling several actors fulfilling the same role simultaneously involved in the collaboration.

In [6, 8], Klug et al. and Bomsdorf introduced an extension to task models where a task is not regarded as an atomic entity (like in CTT) but has a complex life cycle, modeled by a so-called task-state machine. The approach by Klug et al. does not consider a temporal operator as state chart whereas the approach by Bomsdorf does not consider abortion or skipping of tasks. In this chapter, we adopt the same idea for the definition of CTML but try to overcome the limitations mentioned above. Additionally, we integrate instruments to model collaboration.

20.4 The Collaborative Task Modeling Language

In this section, we present the first component of our formal specification framework for collaborative systems, namely, the *collaborative task modeling language* (CTML). We first define the syntax of CTML, explain its design rational, and provide an example. Then we present the semantics of collaborative task expressions and collaborative task models.

20.4.1 Syntax and Design Rationale

The design of CTML is based on two fundamental assumptions: (1) In limited and well-defined domains the behavior of an actor can be approximated through its role and (2) the behavior of each role can be adequately expressed by an associated collaborative task expression. Based on these assumptions, we define a collaborative task model as a tuple consisting of a *set of actors,* a *set of roles,* and a *set of collaborative task expressions* (one for each role) where each actor belongs to one or more role(s).

Definition 1: (Collaborative Task Model)

A collaborative task model G is a tuple G = (A, R, T, a, r) where:
A, R, T are non-empty sets of actors, roles, and collaborative task expressions, respectively,
a: A $\rightarrow 2^R$ is a function that associates an actor with a set of roles, and
r: R $\rightarrow$ T is a bijective function that associates a role with a task model.
Each collaborative task expression has the form of a task tree, where nodes are either tasks or temporal operators. Each task is attributed with a (unique) identifier, a precondition, and an effect. Intuitively, the precondition defines a required state of the collaborative environment for executing the task, whereas an effect denotes the resulting state after having executed the task. Both, preconditions and effects are needed to model collaboration and synchronization across collaborative task expressions.

Definition 2: (Collaborative Task Expression)

A collaborative task expression CTE is a tuple CTE = (T, h) where:
T is a non-empty set of tasks of the form <id, precondition, effect>
h:T → List(T) × Op, with Op = {[],| = |, |||, >>,|>,[>,*,#,opt} is a function that maps a task t to an ordered list of tasks and a temporal operator. The former represents the children of task t, whereas the latter denotes the execution order of the children.

An *effect* denotes a state change of the system or environment as a result of task execution. A *precondition* adds an additional execution constraint to a task. In particular, a task may only be performed if its precondition is satisfied. Conditions can be either defined over the system state or the state of other tasks, which potentially may be part of another task definition. Examples of preconditions are given in Table 20.2. The semantics of the quantifiers *oneInstance* and *allInstances* are discussed in the next section.

We say a collaborative task expression is *well formed* if the corresponding task tree is connected and free of cycles such that each task (except for the root task) has exactly one parent. Moreover, we demand that if a task has more than two children it is associated with an n-ary operator ([],| = |, |||, >>). If a task has exactly two or one child(ren) it is associated with a binary (|>,[>) or unary operator (*, #, opt), respectively. Leaf tasks (tasks with no children) are not related to any temporal operator by the function h.

Figure 20.1 depicts a subset of the collaborative task model for the introductory example of Sect. 20.1. The task model was interactively created using the tool CTML Editor (will be presented in Sect. 20.5). For the sake of readability, for each task, only the hierarchical breakdown and temporal relations are shown, using concrete syntax. Preconditions and effects have been omitted. Additionally, an overview of the entire specification is given in the lower left corner.

20.4.2 *Formal Semantics*

We start with defining the execution semantics of a single collaborative task expression. The execution order of the tasks contained in a well-formed collaborative task expression is determined by the following three criteria: (1) The defined temporal operators, (2) the task–subtasks decomposition, and (3) the preconditions defined for each task.

In order to illustrate the interplay of all three criteria, let us consider the life cycle of a generic task. As depicted in Fig. 20.2, each task starts in the state *disabled*. Upon receiving the message "enable" a task moves from state *disabled* to *enabled*. If, and when, an "enable" message is sent depends on the super-ordinate temporal operator as well as the task state of the sibling tasks. Table 20.1 gives an intuitive definition of the semantics of all temporal operators defined in CTML. Note that most of the operators (except for instance iteration) have similar counterparts in CTT [5]. Upon receive of message "start" an enabled task starts executing by tran-

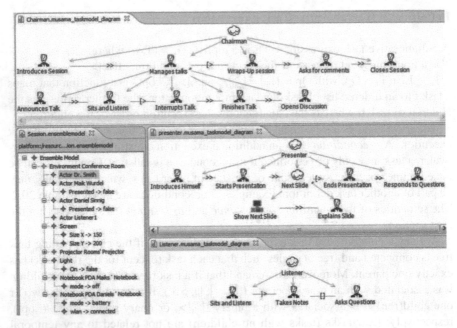

Fig. 20.1 Specification of the example using the CTML editor

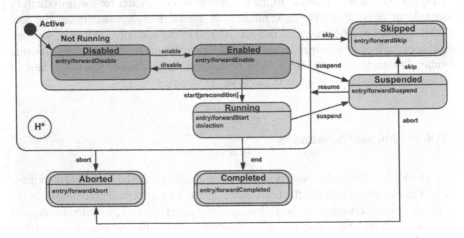

Fig. 20.2 Generic task state chart

siting into state running, given that its precondition is satisfied. In state running the task executes its predefined action (denoted by "do/action") and its effect to the environment becomes externally visible. A successful run of the task is denoted by the "end" transition to state *completed*. At any time, a task may be prematurely aborted, as a result of the disabling operator (see Table 20.1 for details). A task that is enabled, or already running can be suspended upon receive of the "suspend"

Table 20.1 Semantic of CTT operators

N-Ary Operators		
Choice	[] $(t1,t2,...,tn)$	Only one operand task is executed
Order independence	$\|=\|(t1,t2,...,tn)$	Operand tasks are executed in any order with no interleaving of subtasks
Concurrent	$\|\|\|(t1,t2,...,tn)$	Interleaved execution of operand tasks and their subtasks
Enabling	$>>(t1,t2,...,tn)$	Operand tasks are executed sequentially
Binary operators		
		Execution of $t1$ is aborted as soon as $t2$ becomes
Disabling	$t1[>t2$	enabled
		At any time the execution of $t1$ may be interrupted by $t2$. After $t2$ has finished its execution $t2$ resumes
Suspend/Resume	$t1\|>t2$	tion $t2$ resumes
Unary operators		
Iteration	t^*	Repetitive execution of t
Instance iteration	$t^\#$	Interleaved repetitive execution of t. Please consult [9] for more details
Optional	t^{opt}	Execution of t is optional

message. Once a task is suspended it returns back to its previous state when it receives "resume." As long as a task is not started, it can be skipped, which is either due to an optional, iterative, or choice operator.

Note that each state of the task-state chart is equipped with so-called entry actions whose purpose is to notify the state charts of sub- and super-ordinate tasks of state changes. This implements an update mechanism to assure synchronization between all state charts.

In CTML, not only each task but also each temporal operator is represented by a state chart which formally implements the semantics given in Table 20.1. By mapping each task and operator to a state chart a network of communicating state charts is created, where operator-state charts mediate messages between task-state charts of adjacent levels of abstraction.

This far, we have defined the execution semantics of individual collaborative task expressions. We now continue with the definition of semantics of a collaborative task model. The main principle is as follows: (1) For each role, based on the associated task expression, we create a network of communication state machines (as shown previously). (2) For each actor, an individual copy (instance) of the corresponding role state machine network is created. (3) The resulting state machine networks are composed and run concurrently at simulation time. In essence, a collaborative task model is transformed into a set of concurrently running networks consisting of task-state machines and operator-state machines.

Synchronization across networks is achieved by means of preconditions and effects. As shown in the previous section, preconditions are logical statements which may contain *allInstances* and *oneInstance* quantifiers. Using the quantifiers it is possible to "refer" either to all task models (state machine networks, respectively)

Table 20.2 Subset of preconditions used in "Session" scenario

Number	Role	Task	Precondition
(1)	*Presenter*	*StartsPresentation*	*Chairman.oneInstance.AnnoucesTalk.completed*
(2)	*Listener*	*AsksQuestion*	*Chairman.oneInstance.OpensDiscussion.completed*
(3)	*Chairman*	*Wraps-UpSession*	*Presenter.allInstances.EndsPresentation.completed*

Table 20.3 Subset of effects used in "Session" scenario

Number	Role	Task	Effect
(1)	*Presenter*	*EndsPresentation*	*this.presented = true*
(2)	*Presenter*	*StartsPresentation*	*Projector.inputSource = this.notebook*

that belong to a given role *or* one particular task model of a given role. The preconditions given in Table 20.2 represent a subset of the preconditions used to model our scenario and express the synchronization points between the task executions of different actors. The meaning of the presented statements is as follows:

A presenter is allowed to start her presentation after the chairman has announced the talk.

The listeners are allowed to ask questions after the chairman has opened the discussion session.

The chairman can wrap-up the session after all presenters have finished their talk.

Table 20.3 depicts the subset of the effects used for the "Session" scenario. In general, effects can affect either a set of tasks (e.g., enabling/disabling/trigger tasks) or the environment by changing the state of objects or actors. For our example (Fig. 20.1), we found the following effects of task execution expedient:

After ending her presentation the Presenters' state is set to *presented*.

When the Presenter starts her talk the projector connects with the Presenters' notebook.

Please note that "this" denotes the actor currently performing the task in the style of common object-oriented languages. "Point-notation" is used to refer to attributes or associated objects similar to OCL.

20.5   Tool Support: CTML Editor and Simulator

Having defined the syntax and semantics of CTML in the previous section we now introduce the second component of our formal framework; the CTML Editor and Simulator. As hinted by the name, the tool was designed to assist software engineers with (1) the creation of CTML models and (2) the animation and interactive simulation of CTML models. In what follows, both key purposes are described in detail followed by a proposal of an iterative development life cycle for collaborative task models. As an illustrative example we will use the "Session" scenario of Sect. 20.1.

The CTML Editor provides software engineers with an Eclipse-based IDE to create and manipulate all parts of the CTML model. In particular, the tool assists with the specification of roles, actors, and collaborative task expressions (Fig. 20.1, in Sect. 20.4). In case of the latter, the user conveniently defines the task–subtask hierarchy by "dragging" tasks into a task tree. Only tasks at the same hierarchy level can be related with temporal operators. The tool ensures that the resulting task expression is well-formed according to the criteria presented in the previous section.

Additionally, the editor provides assistance in creating a preliminary device specification. Devices are defined by a set of properties; more precisely name-value pairs. The device specification can then be used in preconditions to check whether a device property has a certain value. Figure 20.3 portrays the CTML Editor in specification mode.

Once a CTML model has been defined it is compiled into a network of communicating state machines. At this point, the CTML Simulator can be used to interactively walk through the CTML model (Fig. 20.4). At startup the simulator shows the various involved tasks in form of task trees. The icons defined for each task symbolize the current state of the respective task-state machine. Hereby each state of the state machine is mapped to a different symbol. Upon mouse-click the tool attempts to execute the respective task. This is however only possible if the corresponding task-state machine is in state *enabled* and the assigned preconditions (in brackets after the task name) are fulfilled. Every task execution triggers the execution of associated effects.

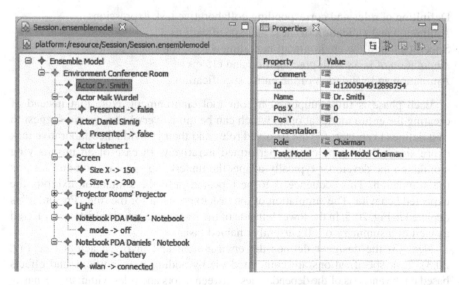

Fig. 20.3 Specification of the environment using the CTML editor

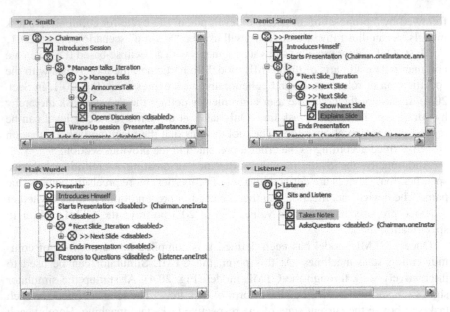

Fig. 20.4 Interactive simulation of the collaborative task model for "Session" scenario

We conclude this section by proposing a life cycle for the iterative and incremental creation of CTML models. We believe that a CTML model is best developed in five steps:

Definition of roles and corresponding collaborative task expressions
Animation and validation of these sub-specifications
Specification of the environment including actors, roles, and devices
Annotation of tasks with precondition and effects
Animation and validation of the entire specification

Each phase is fully supported by our tool environment. Note that instead of creating the entire model at once, which can be quite overwhelming, we suggest to first define (1) and test (2) the involved roles and their individual collaborative task expressions. Both steps can be performed iteratively. In case of an unsatisfying simulation the developer typically adapts the underlying specification and restarts the simulation. This sequence is to be repeated until the simulation exhibits the expected behavior. The simulation of the task expression for the role "Presenter" is depicted in Fig. 20.5. In the lower left side of the figure an execution history is offered as well as a summary of all currently enabled tasks.

Next (3) the designer defines the environment and involved actors (see Fig. 20.3). Task specifications are completed (4) by adding preconditions and effects based on the analysis of the dependencies between actors and roles within the scenario. Finally (5) the entire specification consisting of several concurrently executing task expressions is tested and simulated (see Fig. 20.4).

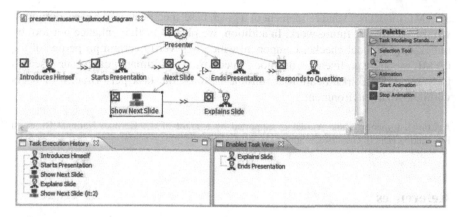

Fig. 20.5 CTML simulation of the "Session" example

20.6   Conclusion and Future Research

In this chapter, we presented a formal specification framework for collaborative environments. First, we distilled a set of key requirements that should be fulfilled by a specification framework for smart environments. That is, the framework should include a (1) task-based specification language which (2) models cooperation among actors and (3) has a formal syntax and semantics. Furthermore the framework should (4) include a notion of refinement and be (5) supported by tools. Based on these requirements, we presented our specification framework consisting of two components: the collaborative task modeling language (CTML) and the tool CTML Editor and Simulator.

The design of CTML is based on the assumption that the behavior of an actor can be approximated through its role. CTML incorporates concepts for the specification of interrelation between different actors based on roles, where the behavior of a role is defined by collaborative task expressions. Collaborations of actors are specified by means of an OCL-like notation used to specify preconditions and effects defined over the state of the tasks and the environment. In order to make CTML amendable for tool support and formal analysis a formal syntax and semantics has been defined as well.

To effectively make use of CTML we presented the tool CTML Editor and Simulator. It provides software engineers with a convenient way to handle formal CTML specifications. In particular the tool can be used to create, validate, and simulate collaborative task models. Based on our experience, we determined that simulation is a very helpful validation device especially during early stages of development as it helps to gain understanding about the behavioral dynamics involved in the collaboration.

In its current state, our framework fulfills four of the five originally elicited requirements. The only remaining requirement that is yet to be satisfied is the definition of a formal refinement relation. It will address the question "under which circumstances a CTML model is a valid refinement of a given base specification?" Such a definition will be part of our future work. In addition, we plan to further enhance our tool by integrating a model checker component which will verify certain properties of the CTML model (e.g., liveness, deadlock freedom). The ultimate goal of our research is to use CTML specification at runtime to track the task performance of users within a smart environment.

Acknowledgments Maik Wurdel is supported by a grant of the German National Research Foundation (DFG), Graduate School 1424, MuSAMA

References

1. Schmidt, A., M. Beigl, and H.W. Gellersen, There is more to Context than Location. 1998, University of Karlsruhe: Karlsruhe.
2. Schmidt, A., Implicit Human Computer Interaction Through Context. Personal and Ubiquitous Computing, 2000. 4(2/3): p. 191–199.
3. John, B.E. and D.E. Kieras, The GOMS Family of User Interface Analysis Techniques: Comparison and Contrast. ACM Transactions on Computer-Human Interaction, 1996. 3(4): p. 320–351.
4. Annett, J. and K.D. Duncan, Task Analysis and Training Design. Journal of Occupational Psychology, 1967. 41: p. 211–221.
5. Paterno, F., Model-Based Design and Evaluation of Interactive Applications. 1999, London, UK: Springer-Verlag.
6. Bomsdorf, B., The WebTaskModel Approach to Web Process Modelling. TaMoDia, 2007. 4849: p. 240–253.
7. Mori, G., F. Paternò, and C. Santoro, CTTE: Support for Developing and Analyzing Task Models for Interactive System Design. IEEE Transactions on Software Engineering, 2002. 28(8): p. 797–813.
8. Klug, T. and J. Kangasharju, Executable Task Models, in TaMoDia. 2005: Gdansk, Poland.
9. Sinnig, D., M. Wurdel, P. Forbrig, P. Chalin, and F. Khendek, Practical Extensions for Task Models, in TaMoDia. 2007, Springer, Berlin. p. 42–55.

Chapter 21
Task-Driven Composition of Web User Interfaces

Stefan Betermieux and Birgit Bomsdorf

Abstract This chapter proposes an approach to flexible user interface generation. The basic idea is to extend a task model with fragments of the abstract user interface and to pass over this information to the runtime system. The system is based on an architecture that separates a task controller and a page composer. The controller enables the user to interact with the web application according to the specification. The composer is responsible for creating the concrete description of web pages.

21.1 Introduction

Web sites have been developing toward highly interactive web applications, by which web pages evolve more and more into user interfaces – besides providing content they have to support user-system interaction in the style of conventional user interfaces (UIs). In the field of model-based UI design it is well established to develop a UI based on the models of user tasks and conceptual entities. Task modeling has also entered the development process of web applications, strengthening the usage-centered view within the early design steps. In current approaches, however, this view is not kept up during subsequent activities to the same degree as this is the case in the field of Human–Computer Interaction (HCI). In WSDM [7], for example, task models are used as a high-level dialog description to guide navigation design. In OOHDM [13], task descriptions are analyzed to identify data items which are to be exchanged between the user and the web application.

All in all, in both the field of web modeling and the field of UI modeling as applied in the HCI field task models are used to guide UI and navigation design,

S. Betermieux (✉)
Faculty of Mathematics and Computer Science, Information Systems and Databases,
University of Hagen, Hagen, Germany
e-mail: stefan.betermieux@fernuni-hagen.de

B. Bomsdorf (✉)
Applied Computer Science, University Fulda, Germany
e-mail: Birgit.Bomsdorf@informatik.fh-fulda.de

V. López-Jaquero et al. (eds.), *Computer-Aided Design of User Interfaces VI*,
DOI: 10.1007/978-1-84882-206-1_21, © Springer-Verlag London Limited 2009

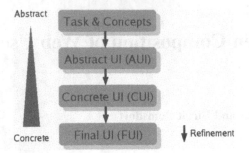

Fig. 21.1 Design time overview

respectively. In such approaches, the hierarchical task structure is transformed into an initial dialog model [11, 12] or navigation model [7] at design time. These models are taken as input to subsequent development steps, to create an abstract user interface (AUI), a concrete UI (CUI), and a final UI (FUI), see Fig. 21.1. In the case the task model is modified, all these steps have to be re-performed. The transitions from the task model to the CUI model require the most human effort. Developers, for instance, have to take care of already assigned elements of the CUI or have to link new elements once the task model and/or AUI is altered.

This chapter presents an approach by which the CUI or parts of it are composed at runtime shortly before a web page is delivered to the user. The composition is based on CUI elements by which the task model is extended. The main distinction to the above-mentioned approaches is that in our work the hierarchical task model is not only a build-time model but also used at runtime. Task model descriptions are passed over to a *task controller*, whereas the assigned CUI elements provide main input to a *page composer*. The remaining transition (from CUI to FUI) is performed by making use of an existing web UI framework (Java-ServerFaces [9]).

The main motivation of our work is the support of multi-platform user interfaces, particularly cases in which the user switches the end device while working with the application. In contrast to other approaches, we do not transform the task model into dialog models, but determine a current dialog state based on which the web page is dynamically composed. The focus of this chapter is on the task-related concrete user interface description, which is part of the whole approach. First of all, in the next section, we introduce our task modeling approach. Afterwards we present how a task model is extended by CUI fragments (Sect. 21.3). This will be followed by an explanation of the page composition technique (Sect. 21.4). In Sect. 21.5, the impact of task model modifications is discussed, which is followed by a conclusion in Sect. 21.6.

21.2 The WebTaskModel Approach

The WebTaskModel (WTM) [5, 6] is a further development of our previous work [4] providing conventional task modeling concepts, such as hierarchical decomposition of task into subtasks, temporal relations, and pre- and post-conditions. WTM

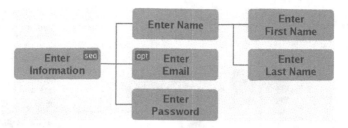

Fig. 21.2 Task model example

incorporates additional concepts to account more appropriately for characteristics of interactive web applications, for example, session timeouts and functional transactions. The main difference to existing task models is the introduction of a task state machine as a modeling concept. The state machine defines a generic task life cycle and is automatically assigned to each task of a model. At build time the developer can extend each task state machine with application specific rules, for example, to define the behavior in the case a task fails. In addition, the task state information is used at runtime to control task execution. Since the focus in this chapter is on the runtime concepts, we introduce our approach by means of a simplified WTM example.

The example used throughout the chapter describes a web-based registration process. Figure 21.2 shows a part of the example task model.[1] The root task Enter Information is decomposed into the subtasks Enter Name, Enter E-mail, and Enter Password. The order of task execution is given by temporal relations, which are assigned in WTM to the respective parent task so that the same temporal relation is valid for all of the subtasks. In the example, the user has to perform the three subtasks of Enter Information strictly one after the other, which is defined by the temporal relation seq (used as an abbreviation for sequential). Please note that in the diagram used in Fig. 21.2 the exact execution order is given by the top–down placement of the task symbols. Enter Name is further refined into Enter First Name and Enter Last Name. Since in this case no temporal relation is given, these subtasks can be performed in an arbitrary order. The Enter E-mail task is optional and may be omitted by the user.

Tasks undergo different state changes while the user is working on them. The states are also significant to users since in their planning of follow-up activities they take into account current task situations. It is important to a user, whether he can start to work on a task (initiated) or not because of unfulfilled conditions, or if he is already performing a task and thus its subtasks (running). Further task states and the possible transitions between them are given in Fig. 21.3. All in all, the behavior of each task is represented by its state machine aiming at task control at runtime. The static task model is transformed into a hierarchy of task state machines for this purpose. Conditions and temporal relations are translated into specifications of the transitions, that is, preconditions of a task are linked to the transition from initiated

---

[1]The example of this chapter is deployed at our runtime engine. It is online available at http://sirius.fernuni-hagen.de.

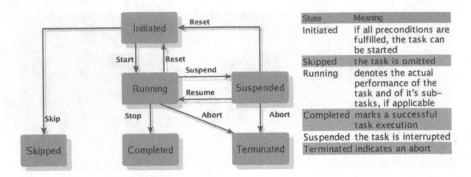

Fig. 21.3 Task state machine

to running, so that the task can only be started if the conditions are fulfilled.
Performance of subtasks, that is, invocation of their state machines, is coordinated
by the superior task state machine.

21.3 Concrete UI Information

In most approaches, for example, in [12], the task model is transformed into an
initial dialog model based on which the UI is developed. In contrast to this, in the
work proposed here, the task model is extended with CUI information which is
used at runtime to dynamically generate the final CUI. The generation is performed
by a so-called page composer taking into account the current task states information
and the UI information assigned to the task states during modeling. Figure 21.4
shows on the left-hand side a draft of a possible final UI, which result in our example
from the semi-automatic page composition according to the task model shown in
Fig. 21.2.

21.3.1 Abstract User Interface Components

The corresponding XML description of the concrete UI is depicted on the right-hand
side of Fig. 21.4. In our approach, we make use of existing JavaServerFaces (JSF)
components [9], which are similar to CUI elements of UsiXML [12] and Interactors
of Teresa [10]. The JSF components used in the example are as follows:

Output is a concrete component for textual output.
Input is a concrete component for textual input.
Command is a concrete component to create a navigation element.
Panel is a component to create a concrete layout for subcomponents.

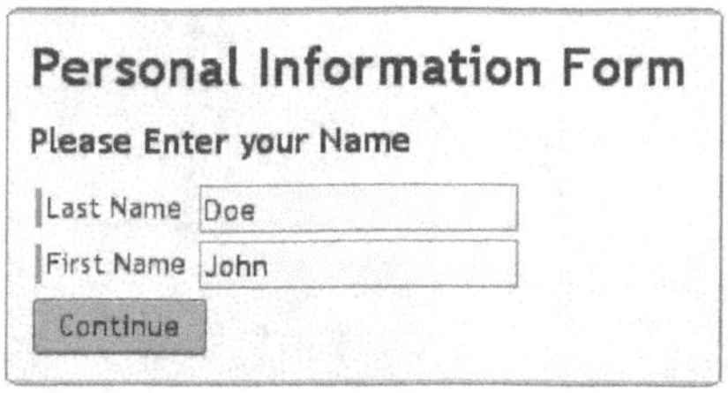

Personal Information Form

Please Enter your Name

| Last Name | Doe |
| First Name | John |

Continue

```
1 <Output value="Personal Information Form"/>
2 <Output value="Please Enter your Name"/>
2 <Panel columns="2">
3   <Output value="Last Name"/>
3   <Input .../>
4   <Output value="First Name"/>
4   <Input .../>
2 </Panel>
2 <Command value="Continue" .../>
```

Fig. 21.4 Example of a final UI (HTML page) and a corresponding abstract UI (XML description)

For the purpose of simplification of the example the components are not linked to the domain model, that is, the XML specification does not show to which domain entities the input fields are mapped and which events a command button generates. Also, the output is statically coded into the components. In the XML descriptions, the omitted information is replaced by an ellipsis. A description of the domain mapping can be found in [2].

The structure of a user interface is created by organizing the components hierarchically. Leaf components are to be presented in the UI whereas a panel component acts as a "grouping" operator specifying subcomponents of the next hierarchical level. The concrete UI in Fig. 21.4, for example, contains a two level hierarchy by which the first name/last name fields are presented by means of a two column layout.

21.3.2 UI Fragments

CUIs are composed of task-related elements. However, to explain our composition approach, the example CUI is split into such elements: The first Output–Input pair (marked with 3) is related to the task Enter First Name, the second pair (marked with 4) to Enter Last Name. The Output-Panel-Command (marked with 2) elements are related to the task Enter Name. The first Output (marked with 1) is related to the task Enter Information.

We call a subset of concrete UI components that is related to a single task a *UI fragment*. Later on the page composer takes different fragments into account depending on the current state. Figure 21.5 shows how our example task model is extended by UI Fragments: The above-mentioned concrete UI components become UI fragments (white boxes) by relating them to the running states of the respective tasks. Furthermore, UI fragments are defined for the tasks Enter E-mail and Enter Password.

In our example, UI fragments mainly exist for the running states of the tasks. The optional Enter E-mail task possesses an additional UI fragment assigned to the state-initiated defining CUI elements that enable users to skip the task, whereas the running-fragment specifies the CUI element by which the user can enter an e-mail address.

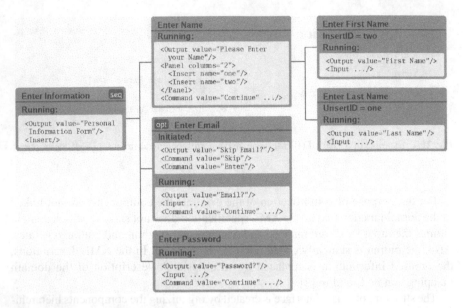

Fig. 21.5 Enhanced task model with dialog templates

As shown in Fig. 21.5, UI fragments are not only assigned to leaf tasks but also to superior tasks. They define CUI information to be presented independently of the subtasks and their current states. This reduces redundancy by not repeating the same elements in different leaf task's UI fragments but concentrating them on UI fragments of more abstract tasks (more close to the root task). The UI fragment of the root tasks will always be rendered in the final UI.

The generated layout depicted in Fig. 21.4 is based on this rule. If the user wants to perform the task Enter Name he has to provide the first and last name. Since no temporal relation is explicitly given (see the task model in Fig. 21.2), the subtasks can be executed in arbitrary order. Thus, the related fragments are part of the same page. In addition the fragments of the superior task are taken into account, that is, the UI elements attached to Enter Name and the root task. Hereby the information is given what has to be put on the web page; however, we cannot just concatenate the four fragments to generate the final CUI. All in all, the task states define which UI fragments are to be considered by the page composer. Additional information is needed defining how the CUI components should be arranged within a page.

21.3.2.1 Layout Information

We have been introducing the Panel component to describe an abstract spatial layout (e.g., a two column layout). Additional information is needed to define which fragment should be arranged before another one. For example, the title output from the UI fragment of the Enter Name task should appear before the subtask's UI fragments, but the continue button should appear afterwards. For the purpose of specifying such spatial relations we introduce the element Insert:

Insert defines a placeholder inside a UI fragment that may be filled later at runtime by UI fragments of subtasks.

Insert elements mark within fragments of non-leaf tasks the spaces where the page composer has to insert so-called subfragments (UI fragments of the subtasks).

If no abstract layout specification is given, the final UI structure results from an automatic layout algorithm (see below), which takes into account the task model structure and the current task states. A problem when dynamically generating UIs based on this information is the lack of direct control over the final result. The "same" page may look differently according to the states all tasks adopted at a subsequent point in time because UI elements that ought to be static tend to "jump" when the follow-up page is generated. It is difficult to maintain a consistent UI layout through different dialog steps since the states of the leaf tasks tend to change frequently from one dialog step to the next. In our approach, UI fragments assigned to higher level tasks stabilize the layout since states change less frequently the closer they are positioned to the root task. The root task itself will be in the running state most of the time. After a dialog step the resulting user interface will remain the same for all those parts the task state has not changed and will differ only in cases of state changes of lower level tasks. Our experience gained so far shows that this does not have a big impact on page layout.

Several *insert* elements can be used within a fragment at different places denoting the insertion of subfragments. In such cases, the page composer requires the exact connection between an insert and the corresponding fragment. This is established, as the example has been showing, by means of unique names for the place holding insert elements, for example <Insert name = "main content"/> or <Insert name = "page footer"/>. The subtasks need to define to which insert position they belong, that is, if the subfragment is to be included at runtime, the page composer will insert it at the corresponding placeholder.

There are two use cases for such multiple placeholders. The first one is to create an abstract layout and define several placeholders at different positions within the concrete UI, for example, to insert the main content, a page header, and a page footer. This concept is similar to the templating techniques of Web site creation tools, where a single template (with a common page structure) is used for all pages of the site to create a consistent look and feel. In our example, the root task contains a UI fragment to display a common header for all generated pages (<Output value = "Personal Information Form"/>). This can be easily enhanced by the definition of a more complex page layout.

The second use case (which is applied in Fig. 21.5) is to specify the order of subfragments, for example, the first name/last name input fields in the UI fragment of task Enter Name. The subtasks are inserted by default according to the order of appearance in the task model. Using the inserts one and two, we are able to change the order of presentation without "touching" the subtasks.

21.4   Runtime Generation of the Final AUI

While the last section described the design time actions to model the user interface
based on a task model, this section takes a detailed look at the runtime processing
as summarized in the processing pipeline (see Fig. 21.6). A request from the user,
which contains the *user events*, starts the processing system and leads to a HTML
page which is returned to the user.

The task controller maps the user events (Buttons clicked, etc...) to task events
(Start, End, Skip, etc...), based on which the follow-up task states are evaluated.
The WTM task model is transformed into an executable task model for this purpose.
An executable task model represents the runtime version of a task model holding,
for example, information concerning current task states and transitions that can be
performed. The task controller uses it to ensure that all task states adhere to the task
model definition. For example, in the case of a sequential relationship it guarantees
that no more than one subtask adopts simultaneously the state running. Furthermore,
the task controller determines at each point in time all active tasks that are used to
create the concrete UI in response to a user request. A task is denoted as active task
if its state machine is either in the state running or if at least one transition will fire
once the assigned event is received.

The set of all active tasks is conceptually the tree of the task model with some
inactive branches being "cut out" (comparable to enabled task sets from CTTs, see
our previous work [3] and [2]). Figure 21.7 shows an example of an active task tree
providing the information for the generation of the concrete UI in Fig. 21.4. In
general, the page composer creates the CUI by scanning recursively the active task
tree, starting with the root task, performing the following steps (where T denotes
the currently visited task):

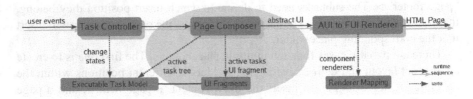

Fig. 21.6 Processing pipeline

Fig. 21.7 Active task tree

- Determine the UI fragment which is defined for the current task state of T
- Determine for each active subtask of *T* the UI fragment which is defined for the current subtask state
  - Replace each *Insert* element of *T*'s UI fragment by its corresponding subfragment

  If there is no corresponding subfragment, then the *Insert* element is left empty.
  If more than one subfragments are determined and thus to be inserted, all of them replace the Insert element, ordered by the appearance of the subtasks in the task model.
  - If there are subfragments to be inserted but the *Insert* element is missing in *T*'s UI fragment, then the UI fragments of the subtasks will be inserted at the end of *T*'s UI fragment (i.e., there is always an implicit *Insert* element at the end of a UI fragment).

This section so far described the conceptional algorithm the page composer is based on. Inserting UI fragments into each other on every request reduces system performance.

Thus in the implementation we make use of the *composite view* pattern [1] to delegate the creation of the final abstract UI to the Facelet framework ([8]). Through this, the UI fragments are not modified but only read by the page composer that creates for each request a *composite document*. It is transformed by the framework into an abstract UI. The composite document is described in XML and makes use of two predefined elements:

- For each UI fragment a *Composition* element is inserted into the composite document. It possesses an attribute named *fragment*, by which the UI fragment is referenced (which consists of, as shown in Fig. 21.8, the task name and the task state). The composition elements contain further composition elements according to the "Insert/subfragment" cases described above.
- If the name attribute of an insert element is defined, a *Define* element is inserted. It possesses the attribute *name*, the value of which is identical to the value of the *Insert*'s name attribute. The subelements of this *Define* element will be placed at the corresponding *Insert* element.

```
<Composition fragment="Enter Information (Running)">
  <Composition fragment="Enter Name (Running)">
    <Define name="one">
      <Composition fragment="Enter Last Name (Running)"/>
    </Define>
    <Define name="two">
      <Composition fragment="Enter First Name (Running)"/>
    </Define>
  </Composition>
</Composition>
```

Fig. 21.8 Generated intermediate composite document

Figure 21.8 shows the composite document which the page composer generates from the active task tree (Fig. 21.7). The hierarchy of the composite document corresponds to the hierarchy of the active task tree. It includes the UI fragments based on task state and uses the *define* element to define groups of UI fragments.

The Facelet framework creates a concrete UI (see right-hand side of Fig. 21.4) from the dynamically created composite document in combination with the UI fragments defined at design time. The last step, the transformation of the concrete UI to a final UI is delegated to existing generators (e.g., [9]), which use a standard one-to-one mapping to render the HTML page.

21.5 Modifications of the Task Model

Our approach starts with a task model, which is extended by UI fragments. Hereby, the CUI is partitioned into the UI elements that are composed at runtime to create the "final" CUI, or more precisely, parts of it. But how do we cope with modifications of the task model later on?

If we add a new task to an existing task model and want to assign UI elements to this task, then we have to create new UI fragments for this task. It is advisable to have extensibility of the task model in mind, that is, to define placeholders inside the UI fragments, where (future) subtask's UI fragments can extend this new task. If we remove a task, then the UI fragment will not be represented in the abstract UI any longer, since the page composer uses the task model structure as a starting point to create the abstract UI. The removal of a task removes also all subtasks from the task model, since they are not any longer accessible.

If we re-sort the subtasks in relation to their superior task then we change the order of appearance of the UI fragments. The result will be a temporally changed order based on the relation (e.g., in a sequential relation). The re-sorting can also have a spatial effect if there are more than one subfragments displayed at the same time (e.g., in the decomposition without a relation), because the page composer will insert the subfragments consecutively based on the order of appearance in the task model at the *Insert* element of the superior task's UI fragment.

If we move a task to another parent task, then we move also its subtask hierarchy (and all assigned UI fragments) to another destination. The concrete UI generated by this task will be accessible in another context based on the new position in the task model.

If we copy a task hierarchy to another parent task, then we can effectively reuse task hierarchies in the task model. We can create small task hierarchies for commonly used interactions and insert them multiple times in the same task model. If we modify our task model, we have to take a look at the consistency of our multiple insert elements from Sect. 21.3.2.1. There are two possible conflicts:

- There are uniquely named inserts in the superior task's UI fragments, but there are no subtasks which provide UI fragments for this insert ID. This does not pose a serious problem, since the page composer can cope with empty insert elements. But since the designer of the superior task's UI fragment had a concept

of multiple insert positions which would now be permanently unfilled, at least a
warning should be presented at design time.

- There are subtasks which provide UI fragments for an insert ID, which is not
available as an insert element in the superior task's UI fragment. The page composer
will insert UI fragments of subtasks, for which it cannot find a suitable insert
position, at the end of the superior task's UI fragment. But since the UI fragment
which belongs to an insert ID, is probably made to fulfill a specific group-related
task, a warning should be presented at design time.

21.6   Conclusion

In our approach

- We use a task model that is extended by so-called UI fragments to create the
final dialog at runtime.
- A UI Fragment defines the concrete UI for a certain task. UI fragments are independent from each other (i.e., no links exist between them) and are only associated
with tasks.
- Non-leaf tasks do not only act as containers for leaf tasks, but provide UI fragments
common to all subtasks.
- Our approach supports easy modification of the abstract UI. Since it is finalized
by the page composer, effects of task model modifications are postponed to
runtime in a lot of cases.
- Temporal and spatial relations are explicitly specified, either in the task model
or in the UI fragments. Both are input to the page composition.

Still there are some limitations and design decisions, which the user of our
approach should be aware of. We are focusing on web applications, we do not support
multi-modal applications or non-HTML output at the moment (thus we make
currently no use of an AUI). We have reduced redundancy by using UI fragments
but we have also introduced complexity, since the content of a web page is divided
on multiple UI fragments and the change of a single UI fragment can affect many
generated pages. However, by means of appropriate development tools complexity
can be reduced. We use the hierarchy and the temporal relationships of the task
model to create the dialog/navigation model implicitly at runtime. There are no
means to create an explicit dialog model at design time.

References

1. Deepak Alur, John Crupi, and Dan Malks. Core J2EE Patterns: Best Practices and
DesignStrategies. Prentice Hall, NY, 1st edition, 2001.
2. Stefan Betermieux and Birgit Bomsdorf. Finalizing dialog models at runtime. In Luciano
Baresi, Piero Fraternali, and Geert-Jan Houben, editors, Proceedings of the 7th International
Conference on Web Engineering, volume 4607 of LNCS, p 137–151. Springer, Berlin, 2007.

3. Stefan Betermieux, Birgit Bomsdorf, and Patrick Langer. Towards a generic model for specifying different views on the dialog of web applications. In Proceedings of HCI International.
   Lawrence Erlbaum Associates, NJ 2005.
4. Matthias Biere, Birgit Bomsdorf, and Gerd Szwillus. The visual task model builder. In
   Proceedings of CADUI 1999, Louvain-la-Neuve, 21–23 October 1999.
5. Birgit Bomsdorf. Modelling interactive web applications: From usage modelling towards
   navigation models. In Proceedings of the 6th International Workshop on Web-Oriented
   Software Technologies, pages 194–208, 2007.
6. Birgit Bomsdorf. The webtaskmodel approach to web process modelling. In Proceedings of
   the 6th International Workshop on Task Models and Diagrams for User Interface Design,
   pages 240–253, 2007.
7. Olga de Troyer. Audience-driven web design. In Information modelling in the new millennium.
   IDEA Group Publishing, Canada, 2001.
8. Jacob Hookom. Facelets – JavaServer Faces view definition framework. Technical report, Sun
   Microsystems, 4150 Network Circle, Santa Clara, CA 95054 USA, 2005.
9. Craig McClanahan, Ed Burns, and Roger Kitain. JavaServer faces specification, v1.1, rev. 01.
   Technical report, Sun Microsystems, 4150 Network Circle, Santa Clara, CA 95054 USA, 2004.
10. Giulio Mori, Fabio Patern`o, and Carmen Santoro. Tool support for designing nomadic appli-
    cations. In Proceedings of IUI 2003, Miami, Florida, January 2003.
11. Fabio Patern'o, Cristiano Mancini, and Silvia Meniconi. Concurtasktrees: A diagrammatic
    notation for specifying task models. In INTERACT'97: Proceedings of the IFIP TC13
    Interantional Conference on Human-Computer Interaction, pages 362–369, London, UK,
    1997. Chapman & Hall, Ltd, London.
12. Jean Vanderdonckt and Quentin Limbourg. Usixml: A user interface description language
    supporting multiple levels of independence. In M. Matera and S. Comai, editors, Engineering
    Advanced Web Applications, pages 325–338. Rinton Press, USA, 2004.
13. Patrícia Vilain and Daniel Schwabe. Improving the web application design process with UIDs.
    In Proceedings of 2nd International Workshop on Web-Oriented Software Technology,
    Málaga, Spain, 2002.

Chapter 22
Collaborative Modelling of Tasks with CTT: Tools and a Study

Jesús Gallardo, Ana Isabel Molina, Crescencio Bravo
and Miguel Ángel Redondo

Abstract The design and systematic development of usable user interfaces (UI) is becoming increasingly important. The use of task models is considered to be the main approach for the specification of the presentation tier in interactive applications. The task modelling for specification of the interaction in a complex application may require the participation of several designers/engineers. In this paper, the use of a generic modelling groupware tool, SPACE-DESIGN, is proposed for task modelling using CTT notation. To evaluate the benefit of the approach, a comparative study has been conducted with two groups of experienced users: the first group carried out a task modelling activity with SPACE-DESIGN and the other one with the CTTE tool shared by means of Microsoft NetMeeting. Results and conclusions of the study are discussed.

22.1 Introduction and Motivation

The user interface (UI) is a fundamental part in the development of any application. Over recent years, researchers in the field of human computer interaction (HCI) have created several tools for supporting the development of IUs. Thus, there are model-based approaches that propose the use of several models and notations for the specification of the presentation tier in interactive applications. The CTT (*ConcurTaskTrees*) notation [7] is one of the most widespread ones in the HCI community. CTT is a notation for interaction modelling based on the specification of task trees made up of tasks and temporal relationships among them. The CTT approach includes a CASE tool, called CTTE (*ConcurTaskTrees Environment*) [6], which allows editing, verifying and simulating the models.

J. Gallardo (✉), A.I. Molina, C. Bravo and M.Á. Redondo
Computer Science and Engineering Faculty, Department of Information Technologies and Systems, University of Castilla-La Mancha, Paseo de la Universidad, 4, 13071, Ciudad Real, Spain
e-mail: jesus.gallardo@uclm.es

V. López-Jaquero et al. (eds.), *Computer-Aided Design of User Interfaces VI*,
DOI: 10.1007/978-1-84882-206-1_22, © Springer-Verlag London Limited 2009

Task modelling for the specification of the users' interaction in a complex application may require the participation of several designers/engineers. For example, it might be interesting for the UI engineer to carry out the modelling work together with the customer/user at the same time but from different locations. And it would also be interesting for several members of the same team (e.g., UI designers) to be able to carry out the modelling in a collaborative way. Taking into account this setting, the need to use a collaborative application or *groupware* tool [4] becomes evident.

For this situation, we propose the use of a groupware tool called SPACE-DESIGN [2], which is a collaborative modelling tool able to adapt itself to several application domains by means of a procedure of domain specification. This tool is framed in the context of a *model-driven architecture* for groupware system generation [5]. Another way to work collaboratively for creating task models in CTT is by sharing the aforementioned tool (CTTE) by means of a shared window system. This paper is based on the hypothesis that the use of a groupware tool such as SPACE-DESIGN provides advantages over this latter possibility.

The next section explains in more detail the two ways of making a CTT model collaboratively that have been considered. In the third section, the study carried out for validating the initial hypothesis is described. Finally, we present the conclusions drawn as a result of this study and the future lines of work arising from it.

22.2   Tools for Task Modelling with CTT

The validation of our hypothesis has two aims: the analysis and comparison of the modelling process in each of the systems studied and the study of the users' opinion as far as the facility of modelling and other aspects are concerned. To compare the modelling processes, a study in which users with experience in modelling with CTT work together will be made.

Two different ways of carrying out a modelling task working with CTT notation in groups are considered. On the one hand, the use of the single-user CTTE application (Fig. 22.1, left), which allows the flexible edition of the hierarchy of interactive tasks, together with a shared window application is studied. For it, version 1.5.9 of CTTE was used. Regarding the shared window environment used, Microsoft NetMeeting, one of the most commercially known systems, was the one chosen. This way, CTTE is used simultaneously by several users who carry out a single modelling task in a collaborative way.

On the other hand, the SPACE-DESIGN tool has been used as an infrastructure to create the necessary support for collaborative task modelling with CTT. The SPACE-DESIGN tool (Fig. 22.1, right) is a tool that is included within a methodological approach for the model-driven development of synchronous collaborative modelling systems [5]. In particular, SPACE-DESIGN is a tool with support for

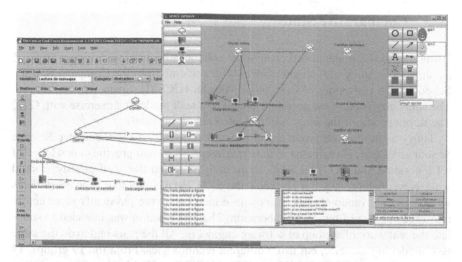

Fig. 22.1 Examples of use of CTTE (*left*) and SPACE-DESIGN (*right*)

distributed synchronous work that allows users to carry out modelling tasks. It is domain-independent since the tool processes the specification of the application domain expressed by means of an XML-based language and spawns the user interface and the necessary functionality to support that specific modelling. In particular, SPACE-DESIGN has already been tested with application domains such as digital circuits, use case diagrams, conceptual maps, Bayesian networks, etc.

As shown in Fig. 22.1 (right), SPACE-DESIGN has a shared whiteboard on which the users can work with the different elements that make up the application domain (objects and relationships). Both types of elements are instantiated from the toolbars located on the left side of the user interface. These toolbars will vary according to the application domain on which the tool is working, and the objects and relationships contained will be those appearing in the domain specification.

An important characteristic of SPACE-DESIGN is the awareness techniques [3] and collaboration support that it includes by default. These elements are a session panel, the identification of the elements that the users select by means of colours, telepointers, a structured chat and a list of interactions. The presence of these elements is one of the features that differentiate SPACE-DESIGN from other similar tools, such as Synergo [1] or CoolModes [8].

To adapt SPACE-DESIGN to the characteristics of CTT notation and thus to evaluate the initial hypothesis, a specification of CTT that can be processed by SPACE-DESIGN has been obtained. Starting off from this specification, SPACE-DESIGN adapts its UI to give support to modelling with this notation. This, consequently, provides a collaborative tool that enables task modelling with the CTT notation, which will serve to validate the research hypothesis by means of the comparative study that will be explained in detail later.

22.3 Comparative Study

Using the two aforementioned choices for collaborative task modelling with CTT, a comparative study of both alternatives with students from the Computer Science School of the University of Castilla-La Mancha (UCLM), Spain was carried out. The study consisted of the accomplishment of a task modelling exercise with CTT. The development of the study is commented below in detail.

Thirty-eight students, who attend a course on HCI in the Computer Science School at UCLM, participated in the experiment. They had previous knowledge of CTT notation and of CTTE application, both of which they had already worked with. Nevertheless, they did not know the SPACE-DESIGN tool. The 38 students were organized randomly into pairs whose members were physically separated to reinforce the idea of remote collaboration. That distribution was intended to simulate the real work of a group of software engineers. All the pairs had to do the same task modelling exercise, but using different technologies. From the 19 groups, 11 had to work with SPACE-DESIGN and 8 with CTTE + NetMeeting. The study was recorded to identify later possible usability problems.

Once the modelling was completed, the students filled in a survey with a series of questions whose answers would be used to compare different aspects of both systems. As far as the general aspects of the functioning of both systems are concerned, the students working with SPACE-DESIGN rated much more highly its facility of configuration and execution than those using the CTTE + NetMeeting combination. In the other two questions, referring to the ease of use and to the capability for solving any task activity, the difference between values is also favourable to SPACE-DESIGN, although not so significant.

Regarding the questions referring to the awareness mechanisms, the advantage of SPACE-DESIGN with respect to CTTE + NetMeeting is noticeable, as almost all the indicators give a greater value to SPACE-DESIGN. The difference in the values given to the aspects referring to the perception of the other users and their work in the shared workspace is especially important. Finally, the global evaluation given by the users to the awareness mechanisms is also quite significant.

Later, the users were asked about their personal impressions regarding other aspects of the collaborative modelling tasks. In this case the questions were yes–no questions. When the users were asked whether they had felt comfortable when carrying out the collaborative CTT modelling, the difference was remarkable. Although 77% of the users who worked with SPACE-DESIGN answered affirmatively, only 38% of those who worked with CTTE + NetMeeting gave a positive answer. The answers to the question about the existence of conflict situations during the modelling process are also important. Ninety-four percent of the users who worked with CTTE + NetMeeting confirmed having encountered conflict situations whilst in the case of those who used SPACE-DESIGN it was only 68%.

Finally, the users could freely answer two questions about the main problems arising in the interaction with the system and about their final impressions about the experiment. Among SPACE-DESIGN users, the main problems that arose were the conflicts when trying to work on the same objects and the difficulty in reaching an agreement between the participants in the session. As far as possible improvements of the system are concerned, users suggested that the use of an audio tool or of a video conference system would improve communication between the members of the design session. In relation to the users who had worked with CTTE + NetMeeting, more than 50% criticized the way in which turn taking is implemented in NetMeeting.

Taking these results into account, a first conclusion that can be obtained is that the benefit of the approach of using a modelling groupware tool for task modelling with CTT has been validated. Most users have evaluated very positively the useful-ness of SPACE-DESIGN, its facility of configuration and its awareness mecha-nisms in contrast with the same characteristics in the combination of CTTE and NetMeeting. Similarly, SPACE-DESIGN has caused fewer situations of conflict, mainly due to the relatively inflexible way in which turn taking is implemented in NetMeeting.

One point, however, that received a low evaluation by the users is the question asking whether any task of CTT modelling can really be carried out with SPACE-DESIGN. The reason for this may be the evident limitations of a generic model-ling tool with respect to a tool that has been developed specifically for a certain notation. However, the difference in the evaluation with respect to CTTE is very small.

Apart from this, a possible improvement in the tool that would facilitate com-munication would be, as previously mentioned, the inclusion of an audio tool or of a desktop video conference system. Regarding awareness mechanisms, although they have been generally well valued by users, those referring to the identification of the place in which the users carry out the different actions could be improved. It would also be useful to provide some information about the following actions to take and about how they are framed within greater goals. To provide the tool with these mechanisms, a job allocation tool could be developed and integrated with SPACE-DESIGN.

Finally, as regards turn taking, the comments of the users indicate that the use of a tool for turn taking is useful. Thus, it would be possible to implement a simple tool that by means of a given low-level protocol of actions would regulate the use of the collaborative whiteboard.

22.4   Conclusions and Future Work

In this study the benefit of an approach based on a generic collaborative modelling tool for the design of task models with CTT has been presented and analyzed. It has been demonstrated by means of a study that this approach has numerous advantages in comparison to the use of a single user tool combined with a shared window sys-tem. On the other hand, some features of the proposed approach that could be improved have also been identified. Thus, we can state that SPACE-DESIGN can contribute to the support of the collaborative design of task models with CTT and, therefore, to the design of fundamental models for the development of UI. In addition, it provides a more suitable support than other choices such as, for instance, the sharing of the CTTE application by means of NetMeeting.

In the future, the usefulness for more application domains of the approach described will be validated by carrying out further studies similar to the one described. In so doing it will be possible to verify whether the tool is really valid for a wide set of collaborative modelling tasks. In these future experiments, professionals of each specific field will participate, to obtain a more powerful evaluation than the one extracted from the experiment with students. In addition, the comparative analysis of the products obtained will be done.

Acknowledgments This work has been partially supported by the Ministerio de Educación y Ciencia (Spain) in the TIN2005-08945-C06-04 project and by the Junta de Comunidades de Castilla-La Mancha in the PBC08-0006-5212 project.

References

1. Avouris N, Margaritis M, Komis V (2004) Modelling interaction during small-groups synchronous problem-solving activities: The Synergo approach. In: Proceedings of the Second International Workshop on Designing Computational Models of Collaborative Learning Interaction, Maceio, Brazil.
2. Bravo C, Gallardo J, García-Minguillan B, Redondo MA (2004) Using specifications to build domain-independent collaborative design environments. In: Luo Y (ed.), Cooperative Design, Visualization and Engineering. LNCS 3190. Springer, Berlin, pp. 104–114.
3. Dourish P, Bellotti V (1992). Awareness and coordination in shared workspaces. In: Proceedings of the Conference on Computer Supported Cooperative Work CSCW'92, Toronto, Canada. ACM Press, New York.
4. Ellis CA, Gibbs SJ, Rein GL (1991) Groupware: Some issues and experiences. *Communications of the ACM*, vol. 34, no. 1, pp. 38–58.
5. Gallardo J, Bravo C, Redondo MA (2007) An ontological approach for developing domain-independent groupware. In: Proceedings of the 16th IEEE International Workshops on Enabling Technologies: Infrastructures for Collaborative Enterprises (WETICE 2007), IEEE Computer Society, Paris, pp. 206–207.
6. Paternò F (2002) CTTE: Support for developing and analyzing task models for interactive system design. In: IEEE Transanctions on Software Engineering, vol. 28, no. 9, pp. 1–17.
7. Paternò F (2004) ConcurTaskTrees: An engineered notation for task models. In: Diaper D and Stanton NA (eds.), The Handbook of Task Analysis for HCI. LEA, Mahwah, NJ, pp. 483–501.
8. Pinkwart N, Hoppe U, Bollen L, Fuhlrott E (2002) Group-oriented modelling tools with heterogeneous semantics. In: Cerri S, Gouardères G, Paraguaçu F (eds.), Intelligent Tutoring Systems. LNCS 2363. Springer, Berlin.

Chapter 23
A Generic and Configurable Electronic Informer to Assist the Evaluation of Agent-Based Interactive Systems

Chi Dung Tran, Houcine Ezzedine and Christophe Kolski

Abstract The evaluation of user interactive systems has been an active subject of research for many years. Many methods have been proposed but most existing evaluation methods do not take the specific architecture of an agent-based interactive system into account, nor do they focus on the coupling between the architecture and evaluation phase. In this article, we propose an agent-based architecture of interactive systems that is considered as being mixed (it is both functional and structural). On the basis of this architecture, we propose a generic and configurable model of an evaluation tool, called "electronic informer," designed to assist evaluators in analyzing and evaluating interactive systems with such architecture.

23.1 Introduction

Nowadays, in spite of the existence of several methodologies for the development of interactive systems, designing, developing, and assessing, in terms of utility and usability [2, 9, 14], an agent-based interactive system is still a difficult task. It is, therefore, necessary to provide methods, models, and evaluation tools to make it easier.

Subheading 23.2 of this paper presents a brief state of the art concerning the architectures for traditional interactive systems as well as for agent-based interactive systems. Subheading 23.3 proposes an architecture that is both functional and structural. By using this architecture as a basis, in Subheading 23.4, we propose a generic and configurable model of an evaluation tool called "electronic informer"; it aims at assisting the evaluation of interactive applications of this architecture. The last section is used for our experiment and the conclusion.

C.D. Tran, H. Ezzedine and C. Kolski (✉)
LAMIH–UMR CNRS 8530, University of Valenciennes and Hainaut-Cambrésis,
Le mont Houy, F-59313 Valenciennes Cedex 9, France
e-mail: christophe.kolski@univ-valenciennes.fr

V. López-Jaquero et al. (eds.), *Computer-Aided Design of User Interfaces VI*,
DOI: 10.1007/978-1-84882-206-1_23, © Springer-Verlag London Limited 2009

23.2   Interactive System Architectures

Architecture of an interactive system supplies the designer with a generic structure from which he/she can build an interactive application. It is a set of structures that include components, the outside visible properties of these components, and the relations between them [4]. Researchers have proposed several architecture models over the past 20 years. These architecture models recommend the same principles, based on the separation between the functional core of system (application) and the human–machine interface. This separation makes modifications easier; it allows modifying the interfaces without affecting the application. Two main types of architecture can be singled out: (1) functional models, such as Seeheim [12], Arch [1] and (2) structural models, such as PAC proposed by Coutaz [3], and its variations, AMF [15] or MVC [7] and its variations.

The functional model splits an interactive system into several functional components. For example, the Seeheim model is made up of three logical components (presentation, dialogue controller, application interface); the Arch model defines a functional breakdown of an interactive system into five components in which both the presentation and interaction components are a decomposition of the presentation of the Seeheim model, the functional kernel component, the domain adapter component, and the dialogue controller component. The functional models enable to separate system analysis-design difficulties by decomposing into different modules. Nevertheless, the functional models show some disadvantages. First, they do not define the internal structure of modules and the communication between them. Second, Arch and Seeheim provide canonical functional structures with big grain; the functionalities are mixed in the too macroscopic components [15]; they are useful as a structural framework for a design or a rough analysis of the functional decomposition of an interactive system [16]. These decompositions are generally not enough for complex applications. These inconveniences make functional systems inadaptable to complex applications in general and to industrial supervision systems in particular.

The structural models aim at a finer breakdown by using structural components, and in particular those said to be distributed or agent approaches suggest grouping the functions together into one entity, the agent. The agents of this type of architecture are then organized in a hierarchical manner according to principles of composition or communication. For example, a MVC agent is made up of three facets: Model, View, and the Controller. The PAC model defines an agent using three facets: the Presentation, the Abstraction, and the Control. The decomposition into many autonomous and cooperative entities enables to accelerate the feedback of system to the user. This advantage is very useful to the supervision applications that can be highly interactive; in consequence, the intensive dialogue between the user and the application can slow the system down. In spite of this advantage, the structural models have also the following disadvantages: the number and the role of agents are not made clear. Moreover, the designer of a supervision application can have difficulty in following the global interface because the interface is distributed in many facets such as "Presentation" of agents. The functional models can solve this problem because they provide only one *Presentation* component to represent the interface. Our approach is intended to be mixed as its principles borrow from both types of model; it is both functional and structural.

23.3 Agent-Based Architecture Proposed as a Mixed Model

The mixed model is a combination of these two aforementioned models to exploit advantages of each of them. The proposed agent-based architecture [6] has to be considered as a such mixed model. We suggest using a division into three functional components recommended in the Seeheim model, which we have called, respectively, *interface with the application* (connected to the application), *dialogue controller*, and *interface* or *presentation* (this component is directly linked to the user). Each of these components can be broken down further in a structural approach in the form of agents. These components are built like three multiagent systems and they are considered as working in parallel, at least, at a theoretical point of view (Fig. 23.1).

The application agents, manipulating the field concepts of the application, cannot be directly accessed by the user. One of their roles is to ensure the real-time transmission of the information necessary for the other agents to perform their task. The interface agents are in direct contact with the user (they can be seen by the user) through the associated user interface events. These agents coordinate between them to intercept the user commands and to form a presentation that allows the user to gain an overall understanding of the current state of the application. The control agents in the Dialogue Controller component provide services for both the application and the interface agents to guarantee coherency in the exchanges emanating from the application toward the user, and vice versa. Their role, in particular, is to link the two other components together by distributing the user commands to the application agents concerned, and by distributing the application feedback toward the interface agents concerned. All these agents communicate amongst themselves to answer the

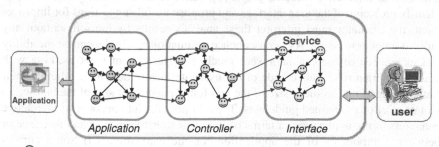

☺ *Application* Agents
☺ *Controller* Agents
☺ *Interface* Agents

Fig. 23.1 Our agent-based architecture

user actions. Each agent of this architecture associates with a set of services that are the actions that this agent can execute. The communication between agents is realized by the invocation between services of agents. This architecture as well as its events (user interface events, services) has been formally described before proposing a generic and configurable electronic informer, designed to assist evaluators in analyzing and evaluating interactive systems of this architecture.

23.4 Proposition of an Electronic Informer Adapted to Agent-Based Interactive Systems

An electronic informer is a software tool that ensures the automatic collection, in a real situation, of users' actions and their repercussions on the system. The collection of information is done in a discreet and transparent way for the user, who must not at any time feel hampered by the presence of the informer. This is an advantage of such a tool. Objective data collected through interactions can be treated, analyzed, and shown in a synthetic shape to the evaluator. This facilitates the analysis of the results. At this moment, many evaluation tools have been proposed but they have some disadvantages and limitations: (a) The current evaluation tools do not take into account the specific architecture of an agent-based interactive system [16], and there are rarely propositions concerning the coupling between the architecture and evaluation phase. (b) The current electronic informers often contain some stages such as collecting interaction data, and then retrieving these data to realize some analysis such as counts, summary statistics, detecting patterns, etc., and finally visualizing analysis results in a synthetic shape to the evaluator. For example, the tool WET [5] collects only interaction data between user and the interface without any later analysis; the tools RemUSINE [11] and WebRemUSINE [10] realize some analysis such as calculations, summary statistics concerning tasks executed, and Web pages visited by the user, and then visualize analysis results to the evaluator in terms of diagrams and WebQuilt that represent sequences of visited Web pages in terms of an interactive directed graph [8]. After tools show analysis results, to identify problems of the user interface and propose useful suggestions for improvement, the evaluator must interpret these analysis results by himself without any indications or assistances. As a consequence, evaluation results depend on the ability and experience of the evaluator very much. (c) The current tools working with guidelines often read source code of the user interface to determine whether their static presentations (color or size of the text fonts, position or size of the button,...) violate a set of predefined guidelines. They do not take into account of interactive behaviors of the application in terms of interactions between user and interface or between components of the application for the evaluation. (d) Some current "feedback quality agents" are only softwares used to gather data about what was happening in the application whenever it crashes. The feedback quality agents only gather technical information about the context and state of the application when it had problems such as OS version, processor type, display type, register, functions that were called just before the failure, etc. And then, these data are sent to the development team to help them identify problems, the cause of the crash more readily, and then improve the future version of the application. Feedback quality agents can permit the user to report what he/she was doing when the failure appears to the development team. These tools only take into account of the context and state of the application when it had problems; as a consequence, assistances in evaluating interactive applications are limited compared with other tools such as electronic informers or tools working with guidelines.

We propose a generic and configurable model of an electronic informer to remedy these limitations. The first version of an electronic informer has ever been studied and developed [16]. However, it is not a generic tool but only a specific one. This first specific tool aims at evaluating a specific agent-oriented applicative application that is intended to manage the passenger information on a public transport system in a project called SART [13]. It cannot be used to evaluate other agent-oriented applications because it depends on the number of agents, the structure and the content of such systems. Furthermore, it also shows some inconveniences and shortcomings. We solve such problems by proposing and developing a generic and configurable model of an electronic informer made up of seven main modules (Fig. 23.2). Our tool takes into account of the architectural specificities of interactive applications of the proposed architecture. In particular, our tool collects interactions between the user and the interface agents in terms of occurred user interface events and interactions between agents themselves in terms of executed services to evaluate interactive applications. After analyzing collected data, this tool provides the evaluator with an open list of determined criteria, which can be ergonomic criteria or quality attributes. These criteria are associated to analysis results to give to the evaluator clear indications and assistances in interpreting analysis results to identify problems of the application based on these criteria, and then he/she can propose useful suggestions to the designer for necessary modifications to improve the application. These associations should be automated as much as possible in the future version of this tool.

Module 1 (M1): This module can run in background to collect events that appear (occurred user interface events and executed services) from all agents of the concerned interactive system and save them into a database, which will be exploited by other modules. This module 1 and evaluated application can be in the same or other place. That means the evaluation can be done remotely. The module 1 and the other modules do not communicate directly with each other. The data collection and its treatment are separated. As a result, the module 1 can be modified without affecting the other modules and vice versa.

M2: This module enables the evaluator to associate events in intermediate level (user interface events and services) with each task. Several events in intermediate level can be realized to obtain a certain task. For example, the user interface events *Image_Vehicule_Click*, *TabDriver_click*, *TextBoxMessage_OnChange*, and *buttonOK_Click* can be associated with the task "Send a message to the driver/voyagers" of the system intended to supervise the passenger information on a public transport system in the SART project.

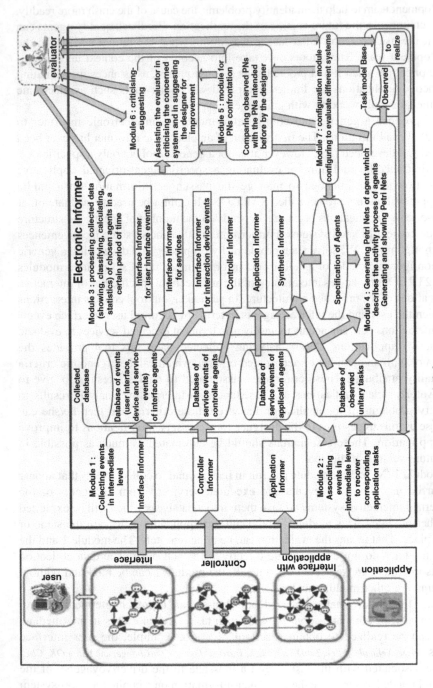

Fig. 23.2 Generic and configurable model of the proposed electronic informer

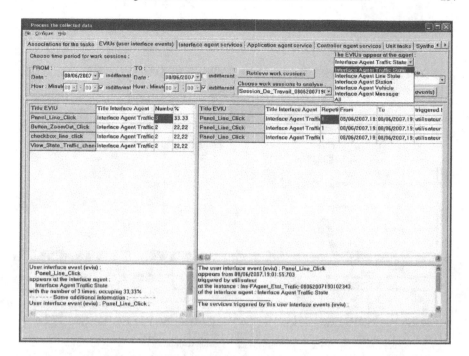

Fig. 23.3 One of screen pages of M3: UI events occurred in the interface agents in table form

M3: Processing collected data of a chosen agent (interface, control and application agents) or all the agents in a certain period of time and showing results in forms understandable for the evaluator. Here are examples of calculations and statistics: response time for interactions between services; time for a certain user interface event (time for typing a text box...); time for completing a service and a task; the percentage of services accomplished and, furthermore, of tasks accomplished, the error percentage, the percentage of services and, furthermore, of tasks achieved per unit of time, the ratio of failure or success for interactions between services, the ration of failure or success for each or all the tasks, the ration of appearance of each user interface event of a certain interface agent, the percentage of execution for each service of a certain agent, and so on. The results are showed in table or graph form (Figs. 23.3 and 23.4).

M4: Generating Petri Nets (PNs) to describe activity process of agents and users in the system from collected data. Indeed, it describes process of interactions between services of different agents and process of activity of user (in terms of user interface events) to realize a certain task. We call them "observed" PNs. Generated PNs bring evaluators visual views of all real activities of the user and the concerned system and can be used for comparison purposes later. The left part of Figs. 23.5 and 23.6 illustrates generated PNs describing the activity process to realize the task "Send a message to stations" of the application that supervises the vehicles of urban common transport in the SART project. The generated PNs are described by PNML

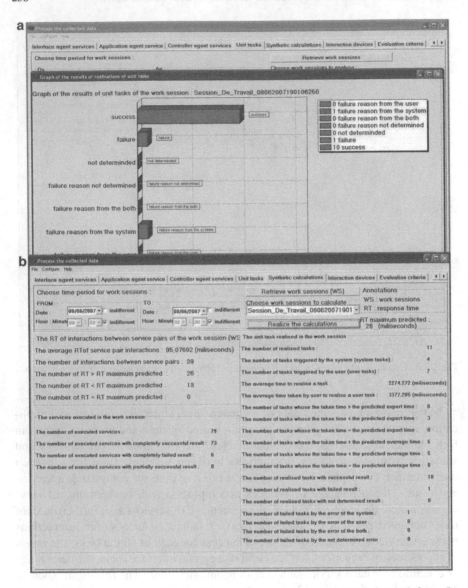

Fig. 23.4 Two screen pages of M3. (**a**) The results of the realizations of tasks in graph form. (**b**) Some calculations (the ratio of successful tasks, average response time, confrontation between real and predicted time to realize tasks, and so on)

(Petri Net Markup Language) and are opened by the tool Renew version 2.1. In the Figs. 23.5 and 23.6, eviuM,N-I stands for user interface event M of the interface agent N and sM,N-I(A) stands for service M of the interface (application) agent N.

M5 (Figs. 23.5 and 23.6): Comparing PNs generated earlier with theoretical PNs that system designer has intended. This comparison assists the evaluators in detecting

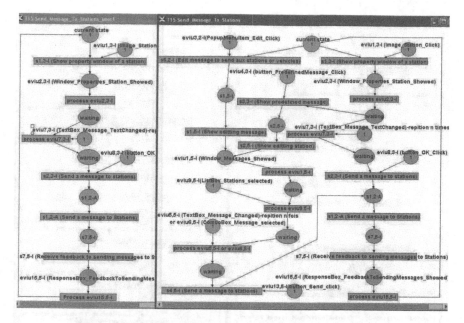

Fig. 23.5 Comparing generated PNs of user 1 (*left side*) with PNs intended by designer (*right side*) to realize the task "Send a message to stations"

use errors; for example, one can perceive that the user has done useless manipulations or chosen a nonoptimal way to realize a task. These comparisons can also be used to assist the evaluator in learning habits of users or in evaluating and comparing the ability of different users to use a system.

For example, Fig. 23.5 tells the evaluator about the way chosen by the user to realize the task among three ways predicted by the system designer. Figure 23.6a let the evaluator know that the way chosen by the user 1 is optimal but the one chosen by the user 2 is not. Figure 23.6b let the evaluator perceive two problems: (1) The user 3 realized the task unsuccessfully because of an error of the service *s2,3-I*. This service must invoke the service *s1,2-A* but in fact, the service *s1,2-A* is not executed. One can also perceive this problem by comparing generated PNs of user 2 with theoretical PNs that the system designer has intended. (2) The user 4 executed an useless manipulation through the UI event button_*Cancel_Click* (red arrow on the figure). As a result, the UI event *Window_Properties_Station_Hidden* was triggered and the user 4 had to execute the manipulation through the event *Image_Station_Click* again.

M6: The evaluator must interpret analysis results to evaluate agent-based user interactive systems as mentioned earlier. M6 is responsible to assist the evaluator in doing that. As a result, the evaluator can criticize the concerned system and give useful suggestions to the designer for necessary modifications to improve it. M6 is not an expert system but a tool to assist the evaluator in evaluating the concerned system by providing him/her with an open list of criteria, which can be ergonomic

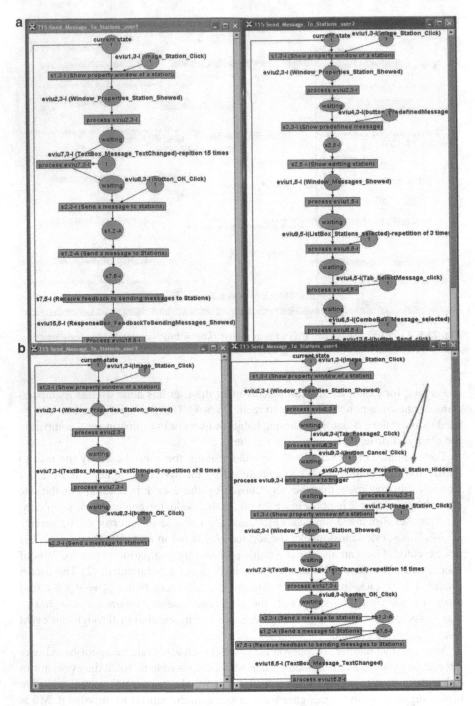

Fig. 23.6 Confrontation between PNs to realize the task "Send a message to stations." (**a**) Comparing generated PNs of user 1 (*left side*) with PNs of user 2 (*right side*). (**b**) Comparing generated PNs of user 3 (*left side*) with PNs of user 4 (*right side*)

criteria or quality attributes. These criteria must respect some principles: (1) they aim at evaluating three different aspects of agent-based interactive systems: user interface, user ability to manipulate systems, some nonfunctional properties such as response time, reliability, so on. (2) These criteria must be evaluated completely or partially using the data collected and processed by the other modules. In other words, the evaluator has to be able to interpret the data collected and processed by the other modules to evaluate the systems based on these criteria. In the future, the electronic informer can be combined with other methods to evaluate more enough and exactly such criteria. (3) The list of criteria is open and modifiable. The evaluator has to be able to add new criteria or modify the old criteria. He/she can use the criteria from available sources or determine the criteria by himself/herself. (4) The criteria can be generic or specific for the evaluated application. For example, the criteria such as *response time, complexity,* and *immediate feedback* are generic and can be used to evaluate all the agent-based interactive systems but the criteria such as *"Does the regulator find easily the necessary vehicle?,"* and *"Does the regulator find easily the necessary station?"* are specific for the agent-based interactive system in the SART project. These specific criteria influence much the satisfaction of user of this system. Figure 23.7 illustrates this module. Each criterion is composed of four parts: *title, definition, interpretation* (explain to the evaluator how to use the collected data as well as its analysis results to evaluate this criterion), and *evaluation of this criterion* (according to this criterion, the evaluator enters his/her critiques for

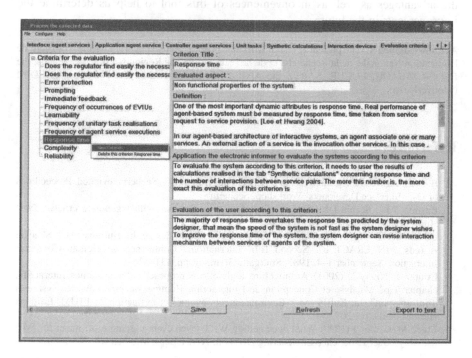

Fig. 23.7 Screen page of the module 6

the system and suggestions to fix it). Because of lack of place, it is not possible to describe in detail this module in the paper.

M7: This module enables the evaluator to configure electronic informer to evaluate different agent-oriented systems by entering the specific data of the evaluated system, for example, the *Specification of Agents* that describes agents, associated services, and so on, and the tasks that the user can realize to reach his/her goal and some other configuration parameters.

23.5 Conclusions

We have presented a brief state of the art concerning interactive system architectures and proposed a mixed architecture as well as a generic and configurable model for assisting the evaluation for agent-oriented interactive systems. An electronic informer has been proposed and its constitutive modules have been described. We intend to combine this electronic informer method with other methods (questionnaire, interview,...). That needs to combine data collected from the electronic informer and data collected from the other methods to evaluate such systems more efficiently. An experiment is planned during the first semester of 2008 at the laboratory LAMIH, University of Valenciennes and Hainaut-Cambrésis, France with about five to ten participants. This experiment is the final stage of the SART project and it will show the advantages as well as inconveniences of this tool to help us determine the improvements in the future.

Acknowledgments The present research work has been partially supported by the Ministère de l'Education Nationale, de la Recherche et de la Technologie, the Région Nord Pas-de-Calais, the FEDER (MIAOU, EUCUE, SART), the ANR ADEME (Viatic.Mobilité), and the PREDIM (MouverPerso).

References

1. Bass L, Little R, Pellegrino R, Reed S (1991) The Arch model: Seeheim revisited. Proceedings of User Interface Developers' Workshop, Seeheim.
2. Bastien JMC, Scapin DL (1995) Evaluating a user interface with ergonomic criteria. *Int J Hum–Comput Interact*, 7, 105–121.
3. Coutaz J (1987) PAC, an object-oriented model for dialog design. In: Bullinger H-J, Shackel B (eds.), INTERACT 87, Second IFIP International Conference on Human–Computer Interaction, September 1–4, 1987, Stuttgart, Germany, pp. 431–436.
4. Coutaz J, Nigay L (2001) Architecture logicielle conceptuelle des systèmes interactifs, chapter 7 of "Analyse et Conception de l'Interaction Homme-Machine dans les systèmes d'information". In: Kolski (ed.), Environnements évolués et évaluation de l'IHM, Éditions Hermes, Paris, pp. 207–246.
5. Etgen M, Cantor J (1999) What does getting WET (Web event-logging tool) mean for Web usability? User Experience Engineering Division, AT&T Labs, Middletown, NJ, 1999.

6. Grislin-Le Strugeon E, Adam E, Kolski C (2001) Agents intelligents en interaction homme-machine dans les systèmes d'information. In: Kolski C (ed.), Environnements évolués et évaluation de l'IHM, Éditions Hermes, Paris, pp. 207–248.
7. Goldberg A (1983) Smaltalk-80, the interactive programming environnement. Addison-Wesley, Reading, MA.
8. Hong IJ, Heer J, Waterson S (2001) WebQuilt: A proxy-based approach to remote Web usability testing. In: *ACM Transactions on Information Systems*, 19(3), 263–385.
9. Nielsen J (1993) Usability Engineering, Academic, Boston, MA.
10. Paganelli L, Paterno F (2002) Intelligent analysis of user interactions with Web applications. In: Proceedings of ACM IUI 2002, January 2002, San Francisco, CA.
11. Paterno F, Ballardin G (2000) RemUSINE: a bridge between empirical and model-based evaluation when evaluators and users are distant. *Interact Comput*, 13(2), 229–251.
12. Pfaff GE (1985) User Interface Management System. Springer,Berlin.
13. SART (2007) Système d'Aide à la Régulation de Trafic du réseau de transport valenciennois et de ses pôles d'échanges. Final report, co-operative project SART, INRETS, France.
14. Shneiderman B (1998) Designing the User Interface: Strategies for Effective Human–Computer Interaction. Addison-Wesley, Reading, MA.
15. Tarpin-Bernard F, David B (1999) AMF: un modèle d'architecture multi-agents multi-facettes. *TSI*, 18, 555–586.
16. Trabelsi A, Ezzedine H, Kolski C (2004) Architecture modelling and evaluation of agent-based interactive systems. In: Proc. IEEE SMC 2004, October, The Hague, pp. 5159–5164.

Chapter 24
Quality of Adaptation: User Cognitive Models in Adaptation Quality Assessment

Víctor López-Jaquero, Francisco Montero and Pascual González

Abstract Adaptation capabilities are becoming more and more popular in applications due to several facts, including heterogeneity of users, devices, and physical contexts of use where applications are currently used. Adaptation is not per se good, and poor adaptations usually lead to disappointed users who reject or disable adaptation mechanisms. Therefore, for adaptation to reach the mainstream mechanisms guaranteeing the *quality of adaptation* (QoA) is required. In this paper one of those mechanisms is proposed, which is based on results coming from cognitive models developed in the literature as a means to asses quality of adaptation.

24.1 Introduction

In the global village where we are immersed, a growing interest for interaction with computers can be observed in our societies. Nevertheless, as more and more people get attracted to interaction with computers new needs arise. The range of user typologies is widening; expert users are no longer the critical mass of software applications, and people from many different social and cultural backgrounds need to use the same applications. Besides, the number of available platforms to interact with is drastically increasing, providing many different platforms with a great range of variability in their capabilities for graphics, networking, computing power, or interaction techniques. Furthermore, the uses that users give to software applications and the ubiquitousness of computing are introducing new exciting possibilities regarding the physical contexts where interaction can take place; users can use their applications at home, in a bar, in the streets, or even in the countryside.

V. López-Jaquero (✉), F. Montero and P. González
Laboratory on User Interaction & Software Engineering (LoUISE), Instituto de Investigación en Informática (I3A), University of Castilla-La Mancha, 02071, Albacete, Spain
e-mail: victor@dsi.uclm.es

V. López-Jaquero et al. (eds.), *Computer-Aided Design of User Interfaces VI*,
DOI: 10.1007/978-1-84882-206-1_24, © Springer-Verlag London Limited 2009

This situation has introduced an awesome challenge to software engineers: creating software applications able to work under all those situations illustrated earlier. Obviously, it is impossible to create a version of each application for each situation; therefore, applications need to be able to be adapted or to adapt themselves to the situations described earlier (or at least to a set of those situations). When the user is the actor in charge of adapting the application to the new situation, the application is called adaptable. On the other hand, when the application itself is the actor that makes the adaptation automatically, the application is said to be adaptive [1]. Nevertheless, adaptation per se is not necessary good. There are numerous examples of adaptive systems that failed and were rejected by users. Thus, not every adaptation is valid, but just those adaptations that are good enough for the user interacting with the application being adapted, for the given context of use. Therefore, it is necessary to devise approaches supporting the assessment of the quality of an adaptation with respect to the user to select the right adaptation for a given context of use.

In this paper, an assessment method for the evaluation of the *quality of adaptation* (QoA) is presented that takes into consideration the cognitive model of users.

24.2   The Adaptation Process

To achieve the goal of adapting a user interface (UI) a series of steps are required. The most accepted sequence of steps for adaptation is the one proposed by Dieterich et al. in [5]. The four steps proposed in this adaptation framework are (1) Initiative: one of the entities involved in the interaction suggests its intention to perform an adaptation. The main entities are usually the user and the system. (2) Proposal: if a need for adaptation arises, it is necessary to make proposals of adaptations that could be applied successfully in the current context of use for that need for adaptation detected. (3) Decision: as we may have different proposals from the previous stage, which adaptation proposal best fits the need for adaptation detected should be decided, and whether it is worth applying for each proposal. (4) Execution: finally, the adaptation proposal chosen will be executed. One important factor when making any changes in the UI is how the transition from the original UI to the adapted one is performed. Before the execution stage, a prologue can be executed to prepare the UI for the adaptation. For instance, if the adaptation includes switching from one code to another code, the prologue function should store the current state of the application, so it can be resumed after the adaptation takes place. On the other hand, an epilogue function can be provided to restore the system after adaptation takes place. This epilogue will take care of restoring application state and resuming the execution of the application.

However, these four steps suffer from several shortcomings, being the most relevant to this paper the inability of this adaptation process to consider the evaluation of the adaptation. This drawback, among some others, led us to propose a new framework for adaptation called ISATINE [7], which specializes Norman's mental model [9] for adaptation.

24.3   ISATINE: A Framework for Adaptation

The specialization of Norman's model for adaptation results into the ISATINE framework, whose seventh stage, evaluation of adaptation, includes the assessment of the quality of the adaptation produced. The work described in this paper can be framed into this seventh stage of ISATINE framework. Next, a description of all seven stages of adaptation according to ISATINE framework is presented: (1) *Goals for user interface adaptation*: any entity (U, S, or T) may be responsible for establishing and maintaining up-to-date a series of goals to ensure user interface adaptation. Although this adaptation is always for the final benefit of the user, it could be achieved with respect to any aspect of the context of use (with respect to the user herself, the computing platform used by the user, or the complete physical and organizational environment in which the user is carrying out her task). The goals are said to be *self-expressed, machine-expressed, locally* or *remotely*, depending on their location: in the user's head (U), in the local system (S), or in a remote system (T). (2) *Initiative for adaptation*: this stage is further refined into formulation for an adaptation request, detection of an adaptation need, and notification for an adaptation request, depending on their location, U, S, or T, respectively. For example, T could be responsible for initiating an adaptation when an update of the UI is made available or there is a change of context that cannot be detected by the system itself (e.g., an external event). (3) *Specification of adaptation*: this stage is further refined in specification by demonstration, by computation, or by definition, depending on their origin: U, S, or T, respectively. When the user wants to adapt the UI, she should be able to specify the actions required to make this adaptation, such as by programming by demonstration or by designating the adaptation operations required. When the system is responsible for this stage, it should be able to compute one or several adaptation proposals depending on the context information available. When the third party specifies the adaptation, a simple definition of these operations could be sent to the interactive system so as to execute them. (4) *Application of adaptation*: this stage specifies which entity will apply the adaptation specified in the previous stage. Since this adaptation is always applied on the UI, this UI should always provide some mechanism to support it. If U applies the adaptation (e.g., through UI options, customization, personalization), it should be still possible to do it through some UI mechanisms. (5) *Transition with adaptation*: this stage specifies which entity will ensure a smooth transition between the UI before and after adaptation. For instance, if S is responsible for this stage, it could provide some visualization techniques, which will visualize the steps executed for the transition, e.g., through animation, morphing, progressive rendering [15]. (6) *Interpretation of adaptation*: this stage specifies which entity will produce meaningful information to facilitate the understanding of the adaptation by other entities. Typically, when S performs some adaptation without explanation, U does not necessarily understand why this type of adaptation has been performed. Conversely, when U performs some adaptation, she should tell the system how to interpret this evaluation. (7) *Evaluation of adaptation*: this stage specifies the entity responsible for evaluating the quality of the adaptation performed so that it will be possible to check whether or not the goals initially specified are met. For instance, if S maintained some internal plan of goals, it should be able to update this plan according to the adaptations applied so far. If the goals are in the users' mind, they could be also evaluated with respect to what has been conducted in the previous stages. In this case, the explanation of the adaptation conducted also contributes to the goals update. Collaboration between S and U could be also imagined for this purpose.

24.4 Adaptation Quality Assessment

We define *quality of adaptation* (QoA) as the extent to which a set of adaptations produce a user interface to achieve specified goals with usability (ISO 9241-11; ISO 9126-1) in a specified context of use. The term *quality of adaptation* has been used also to describe services to provide adaptation facilities in [12], but focusing on networking environments.

In this work the context of use is conformed by the characteristics of the user, the platform (both hardware and software), the physical environment where interaction takes place, and the current task the user is doing.

The adaptation engine should guarantee a certain degree of QoA, similar to the way QoS[1] (quality of service) does for network data flows. No adaptation should be applied that would produce a QoA value below the guaranteed threshold.

To address the assessment of the quality of each adaptation applied, a description of which parameters characterize the quality of adaptation is required. In this work the quality of adaptation is parameterized in terms of two concepts: migration cost and adaptation benefit. Migration cost [3] represents the physical, cognitive, and conative effort the user requires to migrate from one context to another. Adaptation benefit represents how good an adaptation will be for the user in the new context. In this work, the assessment of the adaptation cost is based on migration cost, but other approaches are possible, such as the constraint-solving solution found in [11]. For the evaluation of the migration cost an association of the components in the definition with the criteria used in their assessment has been made (Fig. 24.1). In the current version physical effort has been left out, because it is relevant just in some interaction environments, such as virtual environments where the effort required to manipulate the equipment (head-mounted displays, data gloves, etc) is really relevant in the evaluation of the interaction.

The cognitive effort is assessed by means of two criteria: discontinuity and cognitive load, while conative effort is assessed according to user preferences. Discontinuity appears when the user is forced to divide his attention between two entities. For instance, continuity would be preserved if an adaptation would replace a *widget* with another one that occupies the same screen area as the original,

---

[1]http://www.cisco.com/univercd/cc/td/doc/cisintwk/ito_doc/qos.htm.

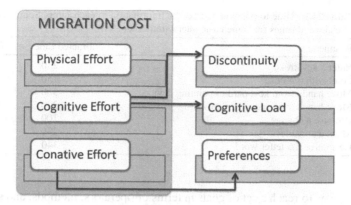

Fig. 24.1 Migration cost components and their relationship with the assessment criteria

because the user does not need to draw his attention from the same screen area. However, if a small widget, for instance a *comboBox*, is replaced with a group of radio buttons with a medium amount of items, the user will need to regain the focus on the right place before continuing using normally the UI, to be able to cope with the noticeable change in the size of the screen area where the user focus needs to be. Cognitive load in a UI adaptation is represented as the increase/decrease of the amount of information the user is asked to process to perform his current tasks. Therefore, those adaptations directly affecting the amount of information shown (i.e., when applying techniques such as *stretch text* or *accordion* [2]) have an impact in the cognitive load.

Finally, user preferences will be applied as a corrective measure to the metrics for migration cost previously discussed. Thus, for example, if the user has some kind of visual impairment and prefers a textual representation of information, despite it implying a higher cognitive load, the migration cost will be weighted to reflect the aforementioned user preference.

Discontinuity is assessed according to the mental effort required to resume the activity interrupted by the adaptation process. To support the evaluation of this mental effort an estimation based on interaction cognitive modeling, especially in the empirical and theoretical results obtained from HCI is used. More exactly, the evaluation is based on results obtained by means of GOMS-inspired techniques [4].

24.4.1 GOMS-Based Interaction Time Estimation

Cognitive models are mainly used to make predictions about how a person will behave given a specific situation. In human–computer interaction the most extended one is GOMS (goals, operators, methods, and selection rules) [4]. GOMS is based on the Human Processor model [4]. This model provides a hierarchical specification

Table 24.1 Time to position and get the information in each jump. Summary of estimated times for some basic interaction tasks

Parameter	Estimated time (ms)
Enter a keystroke	230
Point with a mouse	150
Move hands from keyboard to pointing device	360
Move hands from mouse to keyboard	360
Perceive a change	100
Make a saccade[2]	230
Recognize a 6-letter word	340

describing how to reach a set of goals in terms of operators, methods, and selection rules. The operators can be perceptual, motorial, or cognitive acts. Methods are sequences of subgoals and operators used to structure the specification of how to reach a goal. Finally, the selection rules provide a means to decide which method should be used in a given situation to reach a goal (if several methods are available to reach that goal). GOMS supports [8], among other things, estimating the time required to perform a task and finding out what interaction steps take longer or are more error-prone. By using some GOMS specifications and the final applications for them, an estimation of each basic interaction task was achieved.

The values empirically estimated by Card et al., Dieterich et al., Newell and Card [4, 8, 10] used within the assessment of adaptation quality in this work are summarized in Table 24.1.

24.4.2 Discontinuity Evaluation

Evaluating the discontinuity produced due to a UI adaptation includes the evaluation of the different influences that an adaptation can produce on the UI resulting in some kind of discontinuity. It is also necessary to consider that as a result of an action different collateral effects can arise. In Table 24.2 the adaptation effects considered in the context of this work are listed. Notice that several effects can appear at the same time. For instance, the size of a widget could change at the same time it is moved. Collateral effects can also appear. For instance, when a widget is removed, the rest of the widgets can move to occupy the screen space freed.

Next, how the discontinuity in an adaptation is computed will be illustrated for one the items listed in Table 24.2.

24.4.3 Discontinuity When Enlarging/Reducing a Widget

When an adaptation enlarges/reduces a widget discontinuity can appear because of changes in the widget size. Besides, discontinuity can also appear as a collateral

Table 24.2 Adaptation effects considered for discontinuity

Adaptation effect
Enlarge/reduce a widget
Move a widget
Delete a widget
Add a new widget
Replace a widget
Add a new container
Change the layout of the widgets/containers of a container
Enlarge/reduce a container
Delete a container

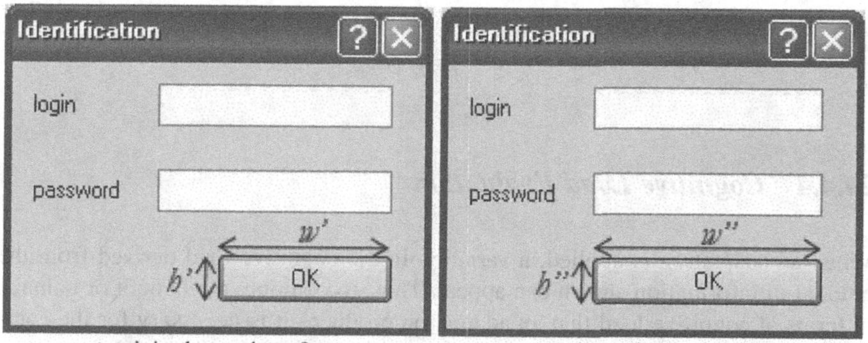

a) original user interface   b) adapted user interface

Fig. 24.2 Example of a simple adaptation where the size of a widget is changed

effect produced by the elements included in the same container than the enlarged/reduced widget. These elements can be pushed by the enlarging/shrinking widget to accommodate themselves to the new available screen space.

In Figure 24.2 a simple example for an adaptation where a widget size changes is shown. In the left part of the figure the original presentation for the UI is illustrated. In the right part the adapted presentation is shown.

In (24.1) a formula to compute the discontinuity when the widget e_i changes its size is shown, where h' is the height of e_i in the original UI and w' is the width of e_i in the original UI. Similarly, h'' and w'' are the height and width of e_i in the adapted user interface, respectively. Finally, h and w are the current horizontal and vertical screen resolution of the device, respectively. The denominator in the formula ($h \times w$) weights the discontinuity according to the screen resolution. This is important, since a widget size change of 25 pixels for a desktop PC can be nearly noticeable, while in a PDA with a much more reduced screen resolution it can be really important. Discontinuity is expressed in percentage. The rightmost part of the formula represents the discontinuity produced as a collateral effect by the rest of the widgets on the same screen.

Table 24.3 Adaptation effects considered for cognitive load evaluation

Adaptation effect
Add widgets
Delete widgets
Add text
Delete text
Replace some widgets with other widgets

$$Discontinuity(e_i) = \left(\frac{h'' \times w'' - h' \times w'}{h \times w} \right) \times 100 \qquad (24.1)$$
$$+ \sum_{j=1, j \neq i}^{n} Discontinuity(e_j)$$

24.4.4 Cognitive Load Evaluation

When an adaptation is applied, a variation in the cognitive load derived from the amount of information shown can appear. Thus, to compute the benefit or damage in terms of cognitive load that an adaptation produces it is necessary for the computation of cognitive load differential between the original user interface and the adapted one.

This differential is computed in terms of the increment, or decrement, of the information the user is asked to process to perform his tasks. Table 24.3 summarizes the adaptation effects considered when computing cognitive load differential in an adaptation.

Next, to illustrate how this computation is made, how cognitive load is computed for one of the effects shown in Table 24.3 will be described.

24.4.5 Cognitive Load Variation When Adding Widgets

When some widgets are added to the UI as a result of applying an adaptation, cognitive load increases, because the user needs to understand these new widgets that were added (see Fig. 24.3).

In (24.2) a formula to calculate the cognitive load differential when adding some widgets in the adapted user interface is shown. In this formula *perceive* is the time required to perceive an information unit (see Table 24.1), *Visibility* [6] is a function that computes the visibility ratio of a widget (computed in terms of the screen space it requires to be shown), and *UnderstandWidget* is the time required to understand how a widget works. Therefore, to compute the cognitive load of a widget we take

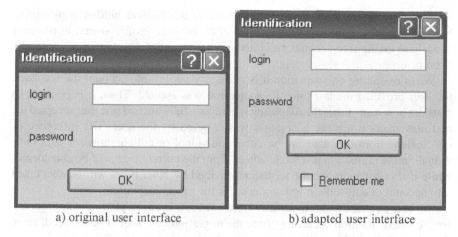

a) original user interface   b) adapted user interface

Fig. 24.3 Example of an adaptation where a widget is added

into account the time to perceive the widget elements, as long as the time to understand how the widget works. Thus, CC_k computes the cognitive load resulting from the inclusion of the widget CC_k in the adapted user interface. To compute the increment of cognitive load in the adapted user interface we need to calculate first the cognitive load for each new widget added (where m is the number of widgets added), because an adaptation can result in the addition of several widgets. When the computation of the cognitive load for m widgets is done, it is divided by the total cognitive load of widgets in the original user interface (n), to actually compute the increment of cognitive load.

$$CC_K = \frac{perceive \times visibility(w_k) + undersandWidget}{2},$$

$$\Delta CC = \frac{\sum_{i=1}^{m} CC_I}{\sum_{j=1}^{n} CC_J}. \tag{24.2}$$

24.4.6 Adaptation Benefit Evaluation

Discontinuity and cognitive load increments represent the negative part of applying an adaptation for the user. Nevertheless, adaptation has also a positive facet that needs to be assessed. This positive facet comprises preferences, context frequency, and user feedback.

Preferences represent the extent to which the adaptation meets the user preferences. Thus, this criterion is mostly assessed in terms of the data collected by data mining the feedback provided by the user to discover hidden preferences, because the preferences in the description of the user profile stored in the user model are taking into account previously to determine if an adaptation should be fired or not.

When executing an adaptation it is necessary taking into account the feedback the user provided the last time the adaptation was applied. Thus, it is possible to consider how many times the adaptation was successfully applied (the user accepted it), and how many times the adaptation was rejected by the user. The inference of conclusions from this data can be either individual or collaborative. If it is individual, in the evaluation just the feedback from the current user will be considered, while if it is collaborative the feedback provided by other users will be also taken into account to adjust the migration cost for the given adaptation.

Context frequency also modifies migration cost. If an adaptation is appropriate for a context situation occurring often, the migration cost should be reduced, since the adaptation will be applied once but used many times.

Finally, some adaptations are mandatory and they will be applied regardless of their migration cost. For instance, this is the case when the switching from a platform where there is audio playback support to a platform where there is not. Regardless of the migration cost all the audio elements of the user interface must be removed and replaced with equivalent elements for a nonauditory modality.

24.5 Conclusions and Future Work

In the path to provide meaningful adaptations to the user that actually improve the usability of the applications it is necessary to provide mechanisms to assess how good or bad an adaptation is and to guarantee a certain *quality of adaptation* (QoA) to the user.

In this paper a mechanism is proposed that allows the evaluation of QoA in terms of migration cost and adaptation benefit concepts. The migration cost is computed by some expressions that take advantage of the basic interaction task times obtained empirically in GOMS-based studies.

Adaptation can be a powerful tool to improve user experience, but unless it is properly applied it can produce undesired effects that might lead users to reject or disable adaptation mechanisms. Therefore, adaptation quality mechanisms as the one proposed in this paper are required by adaptive applications to guarantee the quality of the adaptations applied. In our future work we plan to extend the concepts proposed for virtual environments where additional parameters in the migration cost should be considered. Further testing with real-world applications is also one of our immediate goals.

Acknowledgments This work is partly supported by the PAI06-0093-8836 grant from the Junta de Comunidades de Castilla-La Mancha, Spain.

References

1. Benyon, D., Murray D. Developing adaptive systems to fit individual aptitudes. In: Proceedings of the First Int. Conf. on Intelligent User Interfaces, Orlando, USA. ACM Press, New York, 1993, pp. 115–121.
2. Brusilovsky, P. Adaptive Web-based systems: technologies and examples. In: The Twelfth International World Wide Web Conference, 20–24 May 2003, Budapest, Hungary.
3. Calvary, G., Coutaz, J., Thevenin, D. A unifying reference framework for the development of plastic user interfaces. In: Proceedings of IFIP WG2.7 (13.2) Working Conference EHCI'2001 (Toronto, May 2001). Springer, Berlin, LNCS 2254, pp. 173–192.
4. Card, S., Moran, T., Newell, A. The Psychology of Human Computer Interaction, Lawrence Erlbaum, Hillsdale, 1983.
5. Dieterich, H., Malinowski, U., Kühme, T., Schneider-Hufschmidt, M. State of the Art in Adaptive User Interfaces. Adaptive User Interfaces: Principle and Practice. Elsevier Science, Amsterdam, 1993.
6. López-Jaquero, V. Adaptive User Interfaces Based on Models and Software Agents, Ph.D. Thesis. University of Castilla-La Mancha, Albacete, Spain, 2005 (in Spanish).
7. López-Jaquero, V., Vanderdonckt, J., Montero, F., González, P. Towards an extended model of user interface adaptation: the Isatine framework. In: Proc. of Engineering Interactive Systems 2007, EHCI/DSVIS (Salamanca, 22–24 March 2007). Springer, Berlin, 2007.
8. Newell, A., Card, S.K. The prospects for psychological science in human–computer interaction. Hum–Comput Interact 1985, 1, 209–242.
9. Norman, D.A. Cognitive engineering. In: Norman, D.A., Draper, S.W. (eds.): User Centered System Design. Lawrence Erlbaum, Hillsdale, 1986, pp. 31–61.
10. Olson, J.R., Olson, G. The growth of cognitive modelling in HCI since GOMS. Human–Computer Interaction, Vol. 5. Lawrence Erlbaum, Hillsdale, 1990, pp. 221–265.
11. Gajos, K., Weld, D.S. SUPPLE: automatically generating user interfaces. In: Proc. of the Ninth Int. Conf. on intelligent User interfaces, IUI'04 (Funchal, Portugal, 13–16 January 2004). ACM, New York, 2004, pp. 93–100.
12. Gjorven, E., Eliassen, F., Aagedal, J.O. Quality of adaptation. In: Proc. of Int. Conf. on Autonomic and Autonomous Systems (19–21 July 2006). ICAS. IEEE Computer Society, Washington, DC, 9, 2006.

Chapter 25
Design by Example of Graphical User Interfaces Adapting to Available Screen Size

Alexandre Demeure, Jan Meskens, Kris Luyten and Karin Coninx

Abstract Currently, it is difficult for a designer to create user interfaces that are of high aesthetic quality for a continuously growing range of devices with varied screen sizes. Most existing approaches use abstractions that only support form-based user interfaces. These user interfaces may be usable but are of low aesthetic quality. In this paper, we present a technique to design adaptive graphical user interfaces by example (i.e., user interfaces that can adapt to the target platform, the user, etc.), which can produce user interfaces of high aesthetic quality while reducing the development cost inherent to manual approaches. Designing adaptive user interfaces by example could lead to a new generation of design tools that put adaptive user interface development within the reach of designers as well as developers.

25.1 Introduction

More and more computing devices have been appearing on the market, each having very different characteristics in terms of CPU power, display size, memory, etc. This situation has led to a renewal in HCI research about user interface (UI) adaptation, which is nowadays often referred to as plasticity. Plasticity is defined by Calvary et al. [1] as the capacity of a UI to withstand variations of contexts of use while preserving predefined usability properties. The context of use is defined in terms of user (e.g., expert, novice…), platform (e.g., memory, screen size…), and environment (e.g., noise, luminosity…). Instead of trying to cover all, we target the creation of UIs adapted to different screen sizes. Most of the research that has been done up to now tried to achieve plasticity by relying on automatic approaches [6]. This reduces the cost to create and maintain a user interface for each platform significantly. In addition, creating different user interfaces for different screen sizes manually may lead to inconsistencies between the designs. Unfortunately, most of

A. Demeure (✉), J. Meskens, K. Luyten and K. Coninx
Hasselt University – tUL – IBBT Expertise Centre for Digital Media, Wetenschapspark,
2, B-3590, Diepenbeek, Belgium
e-mail: alexandre.demeure@uhasselt.be

V. López-Jaquero et al. (eds.), *Computer-Aided Design of User Interfaces VI*,   277
DOI: 10.1007/978-1-84882-206-1_25, © Springer-Verlag London Limited 2009

the automatic UI generation approaches use abstractions that lead to the "greatest common divisor" interfaces that work for all targeted platforms [9]. In practice, the greatest common divisor lead to form-based UIs.

In this paper, we introduce the possibility to adopt a manual approach to create aesthetic graphical user interfaces (GUIs) at low cost. This is achieved with design by example that gives the designer full control over the adaptation process. In this paper, we do not focus on preserving consistency between GUIs, neither on how to provide guidance to the designer.

There are two main advantages of design by example, as pointed out by Frank [5]. First, the designer manipulates a concrete object rather than its abstractions. Second, providing examples is less complex than programming the corresponding algorithm, which puts the control back in the hand of the designer instead of the developer.

In addition, we blur the distinction between runtime and design time by letting the designer specify examples on the running UI. Thus, the effect of an example is immediately perceivable, which highly facilitates a trial and error approach. In the remainder of this paper, we first discuss the philosophy of our approach.

Next, we introduce the algorithms that we use. Afterward, we discuss how our approach addresses some issues that are often perceived in example-based UI design tools. Finally, we discuss relevant related works, draw the conclusions, and provide ideas for future work.

25.2   Design by Example

We define a design space as a set of user interfaces that have similar behavior and goals and support the same set of interaction tasks. Each UI in this design space is appropriate for a certain range of screen sizes.

Figure 25.1 illustrates the design space of a UI that supports the user task of selecting a slide number from a running presentation (e.g., PowerPoint). Different UIs can be defined to support this task and populate the design space; the UIs of examples *a* and *b* are adapted according to the available screen width, while they are not influenced according to the height. Example *c* is adapted according to the increase in screen height primarily, while example *d* is adapted to both an increase in width and height. This example design space shows that the presentation for the same task can differ significantly: the structure, style, and layout of the user interface are tailored according to the screen size when the functionality that is offered remains unchanged.

In our approach, the designer can create these example UI designs for different screen sizes. These UI designs are interpolated and extrapolated to generate user interfaces for all other sizes the designer did not take into account explicitly. Interpolation and extrapolation mean that, given some examples for certain screen sizes, the system will propose UIs for all intermediate window sizes (*interpolation*) and even smaller or bigger ones (*extrapolation*). In this sense, interpolation can be considered as a specialization of the design space, while extrapolation extends the coverage of the design space.

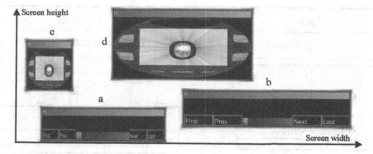

Fig. 25.1 Illustration of a design space of UIs that supports the user task of selecting a slide

The cornerstone of the approach presented here is that the design space can be changed at design time as well as at runtime. The designer can specify examples and view the results of interpolation or extrapolation directly on the final running UI [1], and manipulate the design space this way. The designer can use the UI the same way the end user will use it and edit the design space if the behavior is not what is expected. To be really effective and usable by designers, this approach requires the underlying mechanism of interpolation and extrapolation to be easily understandable but yet remain powerful enough to also allow the end users to change the UI according to their preferences. Artistic resizing [4] demonstrates this for the graphical aspect of a user interface.

We aim at maintaining a semantic equivalence during the adaptation process. Therefore, each modification of the UI needs to preserve the semantics (i.e., the user task). That is, tools should ensure that the substitution of an interactor is only possible with one that is compatible with respect to the original semantics.

25.3 Example Inter- and Extrapolation

The algorithm we use to interpolate examples is based on the orthogonal interpolation technique used in Artistic resizing [4]. This algorithm is simple and easily understandable even by nonprogramers but yet allows for interesting results. However, the algorithm focuses on the graphical representation only and does not deal with semantical equivalence when resizing. We generalize Artistic resizing by providing a common infrastructure to express dependencies between any combinations of UI variables.

Figure 25.2 shows a UML schema of the data structure we use to compute interpolation and extrapolation on the base of the given examples. A zone defines a subspace in the screen size space, i.e., a set of points <window width, window height> for which a set of examples is defined. These examples will be used to compute other required user interfaces through the interpolation and extrapolation mechanism whenever the window is resized within the zone boundaries, e.g., the window stays larger than (100,100) and is smaller than (200,200).

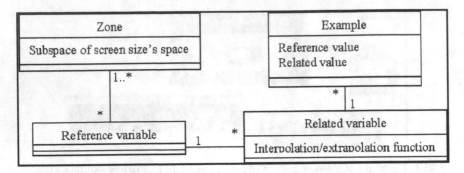

Fig. 25.2 UML class diagram representing the interpolation data mechanism

Each example is composed of two values: a reference value (e.g., the width of the window when the example was defined) and a related value (e.g., the button position within the window when the example was defined). Every example is linked to one related variable (e.g., the related variable corresponding to the *x*-coordinate of the button position). A related variable contains a function for computing interpolation and extrapolation from a set of examples (e.g., linear interpolation). Each related variable is linked to one reference variable (e.g., the reference variable corresponding to the window width). Each reference variable is linked to one or more zones.

The designer can define zones in which examples are taken or are not taken into account to compute the inter- and extrapolation. As mentioned before, zones are subspaces in the space of reference variables (usually width and height). To correct the behavior of the UI, the designer may define two zones as shown in Fig. 25.3. A subset of the examples can be associated with each zone (Fig. 25.3): a and b for the lower zone and c and d for the upper one.

Using this technique, the designer has the possibility to construct fine-grained UI behavior. This behavior is not only restricted to interactors' position, size, or rotation, but also to its type. The key point for success is how to give the designer the right tools to edit these zones and examples. We currently explore ways to realize such tools (http://iihm.imag.fr/demeure).

25.4 Related Work

Artistic resizing [4] was a source of inspiration for this work. It allows designers to build visual variants of graphical objects by using their traditional tools (e.g., Adobe Illustrator). These variants are used as examples, which are interpolated and extrapolated afterward. Given our objectives, the two main restrictions of this work are as follows: (1) it is not possible to substitute a graphical object by another, and (2) the designer has to switch between tools such as Adobe Illustrator and the Artistic resizing runtime environment to verify the effects.

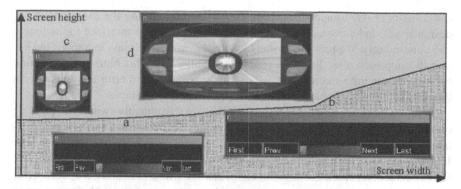

Fig. 25.3 Designer can define zones where only a subset of examples applies

Collignon et al. [2] propose an intelligent editor for multipresentation UIs. This editor allows specifying several versions of the UI, each adapted to a certain screen size. To build each UI version, another editor is used (GraphiXML in this case). The selection of the right version is done at runtime, depending on the available screen size. However, the designer cannot edit the behavior of the UI when it is already in operation. Therefore, with respect to our objectives, [2] only applies at design time. Moreover, the different versions of the UI are built separately, which makes it difficult to keep them consistent. On the contrary, in our approach, all examples are related to the others since they are just a different view of the same UI. Therefore, every example is semantically equivalent to the others by construction.

Most of the works done in programming by example focus on inferring the mappings between application data and its visual representation [8]. However, Li and Landay [7] propose a system to create UI prototypes by graphical demonstration. This system does not aim to design plastic user interfaces but instead provides interesting insights on algorithms that could be used to construct examples. In particular, the authors demonstrate how to detect pivot points and make use of movement paths. This confirms that it is possible to specify more complex behaviors using design by example. We will explore this in the future.

Finally, Stuerzlinger et al. [10] demonstrate the possibility to dynamically substitute interactors of legacy UIs. The philosophy is clearly close to the one that underlies our work: giving the designer (or even end user) the ability to fully control the adaptation process by directly manipulating the UI. However, "Façades" are quite static; it is currently not possible to resize them. Moreover, it is not possible to build different versions of the UI that will be dynamically chosen while resizing.

25.5   Conclusion

In this paper, we presented a design by example approach to create adaptive GUIs. Using this approach, the designer can achieve plastic user interfaces of high aesthetic quality while keeping full control over the design process. This design process consists of three main steps: providing examples, editing the examples in the design space, and viewing the behavior of the adaptive user interface immediately and continuously. We provided some tools based on the toolglass metaphor to support this approach directly on the running user interface. This blurs the distinction between design time and runtime, which encourages trial and error and thus lowers the threshold for developing adaptive user interfaces by example.

In future work, we will explore the possibility to dynamically switch – depending on the available screen space – between complex layout algorithms, such as tree-maps, flow layout, etc. This would only require small modifications to the toolglass. In addition, we will explore ways to give the designer the possibility to generalize the behavior of an element to a set of elements. We will also explore ways to trigger graphical transitions when changing zone. Those transitions should help the user to understand how the UI was reconfigured (e.g., by using morphing). Finally, we will conduct evaluations in cooperation with designers. Videos of the system can be found at http://iihm.imag.fr/demeure.

Acknowledgments Part of the research at EDM is funded by ERDF (European Regional Development Fund). The AMASS++ (Advanced Multimedia Alignment and Structured Summarization) project IWT 060051 is directly funded by the IWT (Flemish subsidy organization).

References

1. Calvary G., Coutaz J., Thevenin D., Limbourg Q., Souchon N., Bouillon L., Vanderdonckt J.: Plasticity of user interfaces: a revised reference framework, In *TAMODIA 2002*, Bucharest, Romania, 2002.
2. Collignon B., Vanderdonkt J., Calvary G.: An intelligent editor for multi-presentation user interfaces, In *23ème ACM Symposium on Applied Computing. SAC'2008*, Ceará, Brazil, 2008.
3. Demeure A., Calvary G., Coutaz J., Vanderdonckt J.: The COMETs inspector: towards run time plasticity control based on a semantic network, In *TAMODIA'2006*, Hasselt, Belgium, 2006.
4. Dragicevic P., Chatty S., Thevenin D., Vinot J.: Artistic resizing: a technique for rich scale-sensitive vector graphics, In *Proceedings of the 18th Annual ACM Symposium on User Interface Software and Technology*, Seattle, WA, USA, October 23–26, 2005.
5. Frank M.: Model-Based User Interface Design by Demonstration and by Interview. PhD Thesis, Georgia Institute of Technology, College of Computing, Atlanta, GA, December 1995, 275 pp.
6. Gajos K., Weld D. S.: SUPPLE: automatically generating user interfaces, In *Proceedings of the Ninth International Conference on Intelligent User Interfaces*, IUI'04, Funchal, Madeira, Portugal, January 13–16, 2004.
7. Li Y., Landay J.A.: Informal prototyping of continuous graphical interactions by demonstration, In *ACM SIGGRAPH 2006 Sketches*, Boston, MA, 2006.
8. Lieberman H.: Your Wish Is My Command, Morgan Kaufmann, San Francisco, 2001, ISBN 0262140535.
9. Nilsson E.: Combining Compound Conceptual User Interface Components with Modelling Patterns – A Promising Direction for Model-Based Cross-Platform User Interface Development, Springer, London, DSVIS 2002.
10. Stuerzlinger W., Chapuis O., Phillips D., Roussel N.: User interface façades: towards fully adaptable user interfaces. In *Proceedings of the 19th Annual ACM Symposium on UIST*, Montreux, Switzerland, 2006.

Chapter 26
A Method to Design Information Security Feedback Using Patterns and HCI-Security Criteria

Jaime Muñoz-Arteaga, Ricardo Mendoza González, Miguel Vargas Martin, Jean Vanderdonckt, Francisco Álvarez-Rodriguez and Juan González Calleros

Abstract To design a user interface of a secure interactive application, a method is provided to designers with guidance in designing an adequate security information feedback using a library of user-interface design patterns integrating security and usability. The resulting feedback is then evaluated against a set of design/evaluation criteria called human–computer interaction for security (HCI-S). In this way, notifications combining visual and auditive channels required to achieve an effective feedback in case of a security issue are explicitly incorporated in the development life cycle.

26.1 Introduction

The term "user feedback" is often referred to as to any form of communication directed from a system toward the user. Similarly, information security feedback is any information related to the system's security conveyed to the end user. This information must to be shown in an adequate manner to the final user. A good alternative to generating a well-designed information security feedback consists of applying design patterns, because it is well known that a pattern represents a proven solution for a recurrent problem within a certain environment. From a computer science perspective, human–computer interaction (HCI) deals with the interaction between one or more users and one or more computers using the user interface (UI) of a program [13]. The concepts of traditional HCI can be used to design the interface or improve some interface currently available, considering aspects such as usability. Usability determines the ease of use of a specific technology, the level of effectiveness of the technology according to the user's needs, and the satisfaction of the user with the results obtained by using a specific technology to perform specific tasks.

J. Muñoz-Arteaga (✉), R. Mendoza González (✉), M. Vargas Martin, J. Vanderdonckt, F. Álvarez-Rodriguez and J.G. Calleros
Universidad Autónoma de Aguascalientes, Centro de Ciencias Básicas, Av. Universidad, 940, 20100 Ciudad Universitaria Aguascalientes, Mexico
e-mails: jmunozar@correo.uaa.mx, mendozagric@yahoo.com.mx

V. López-Jaquero et al. (eds.), *Computer-Aided Design of User Interfaces VI*,
DOI: 10.1007/978-1-84882-206-1_26, © Springer-Verlag London Limited 2009

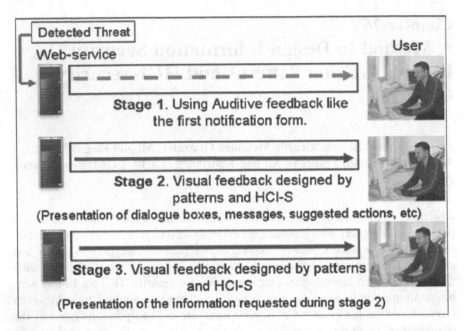

Fig. 26.1 Our model is divided into three stages: first, an additional notification form is triggered to notify end user about some security threat, possibly augmented with auditive notifications or any other kind of feedback; then, the visual feedback is effectively designed based on the design patterns that are explicitly based on HCI-S criteria; finally, the feedback is constructed

Security HCI (HCI-S) has recently being introduced [15] to reflect the need to explicitly support security in the UI development life cycle. The concept of HCI-S modifies and adapts the concepts of the traditional HCI to focus in aspects of security and to find how to improve security through the elements of the interface.

Our contribution consists of a set of design patterns to design usable information security feedback combining the concept of user interface patterns and HCI-S criteria. We create a basic model to exemplify the presentation of information security feedback to the end user when a threat is detected (see Fig. 26.1).

Combining visual and auditive channels in an alert benefits from the following advantages [12]: A sound may be more interruptive than other types of alerts; this combined with some specific colors and images may represent a very good way to notify users about some threat or error detected, and permits an efficient sensorial correlation. Auditive feedback, in theory, should permit to assign a specific sound to a specific threat. A particular sound may be identified by the users in a set of auditive alarms.

To address this shortcoming, this paper introduces a method for designing visual and auditive user feedback based on design patterns. The remaining of this paper is organized as follows. Subheading 26.2 explains the HCI-S design/evaluation criteria. Subheading 26.3 describes the general problem within the framework of our research work. Subheading 26.4 defines the steps of the method for designing information security feedback that is then applied in a case study in Subheading 26.5. Subheading 26.6 compares this work with respect to other relevant and related works. Finally, Subheading 26.7 summarizes our concluding remarks and provides some potential avenues for future work.

26.2   HCI-S Design Criteria

To achieve a successful application of the HCI-S's concepts, it is necessary to consider the design criteria proposed by Johnston et al. [15]. These criteria facilitate developing usable interfaces that are used in a security environment, based on Nielsen's heuristics traditionally used for heuristic evaluation [18]:

- Visibility of system status: The UI must inform the user about the internal state of the system (e.g., using messages to indicate that a security feature is active, etc.).
- Aesthetic and minimalist design: Only relevant security information should be displayed. The user must not be saturated with information and options, and the UI must avoid the use of technical terms as much as possible.
- Satisfaction: The security activities must be easy to realize and understand. Without the use of technical terms in the information showed to the user, in some cases, it is convenient to use humor situations or pictures to present important security concepts to the user in an entertaining manner.
- Convey features: The UI needs to convey the available security features to the user clearly and appropriately; a good way to do it is by using pictures or draws.
- Learnability: The UI needs to be as nonthreatening and easy to learn as possible; it may be accomplished using real-world metaphors, or pictures of keys and padlocks.
- Trust: It is essential for the user to trust the system. This is particularly important in a security environment. The successful application of the previous criteria should typically result in a trusted environment. The concept of trust can be adapted for the HCI-S criteria of trust [15] to "the belief, or willingness to believe, of a user in the security of a computer system."

Similarly, D'Hertefelt [10] identified six primary factors (i.e., fulfillment, technology, seals of approval, presentation, navigation, and brand) that convey trust [1] in an e-commerce environment. Four of these factors are related directly to HCI-S as illustrated in Table 26.1. Applying these concepts in a security environment using the HCI-S criteria, it is possible to achieve the user trust in the specific system's security.

26.3   Problem Outline

We believe that the security information of a specific Web service must be shown in an easy-to-understand manner. According to Dhamija [9], and Johnson and Zurko [14], a usable security information feedback could reduce possible errors caused by final users when important notifications are ignored, nevertheless most of the designers or/and programmers do not consider the available design criteria because their application is frequently complex and the criteria are not specified

Table 26.1 HCI-S and the primary factors that convey trust in an e-commerce environment

HCI-S criteria	Primary e-commerce factors	Relation
Convey features, visibility system	Fulfillment, seals of approval	Appropriate notification of available security features using a minimalist Web site design. This leads to a more satisfying experience for the users
Aesthetic and minimalist design	Presentation, navigation	The users must be appropriately informed about which security features are available, and when these are being used
Learnability	Navigation	A Web site with a minimalist design is easier to use and navigate
Satisfaction	Fulfillment, Presentation	A Web site that is easy to navigate is also easy to learn by the users

enough [9, 14, 19, 20]. Another problem may be the insufficient consideration of the end users by the current design specifications. Braz et al. [3] demonstrated the importance of finding equilibrium between security and usability. Nevertheless, most of the security researches do not consider usability topics during its development; for this reason, it is necessary to provide a support for security, by means of design criteria and guides based on usability and ergonomic principles. In accordance with Atoyan et al. [1], such design rules must be considered during the design of trust systems to increase its proper use and interpretation. An adequate feedback is necessary to reduce the possibility that the final users misunderstand security notifications or other information related with the internal state of the system [2, 5, 14, 22]. Our classification is oriented toward the design of a usable security information feedback, easy to understand and interpret by users with different experience and backgrounds (experts, advanced, and beginners).

26.4 Designing Security Feedback Using Patterns and HCI-S Criteria

It is well known that secure Web services must keep informed their end user about the internal state of the system and the technologies used by the system to protect confidential information during a transaction. We propose a classification of interactive patterns based on HCI-S criteria intended to design a usable security information feedback (Fig. 26.2).

The classification proposed is divided in the following levels, which are oriented to represent the basic aspects to handle a UI:

- Informative feedback: This level includes the interactive patterns useful to present information about available security features, the correct way to use these features, detection of threats, and internal status of the system.
- Interaction feedback: This level brings together the interaction forms useful to establish the feedback's navigation and operation.
- Interactive feedback: This level includes the interactive patterns to specify the security feedback needed to convey information to the end user when the

elements of the interface are handled by means of the mouse or the keyboard. We incorporate auditive feedback in the first level to enhance the visual notifications considering the sonification prototype [12]. We complement such relationship with visual notifications, assigning a specific color to each threat under consideration (Table 26.2). It is important to mention that the five potential threats considered in [12] are specified in a network log; this log file is available publicly and was generated by DARPA [7]. We also bear in mind the explanation of these threats presented by Dass [8].

To present a general view of our classification, we define some of the interactive patterns presented in Fig. 26.2, considering a possible recurrent problem

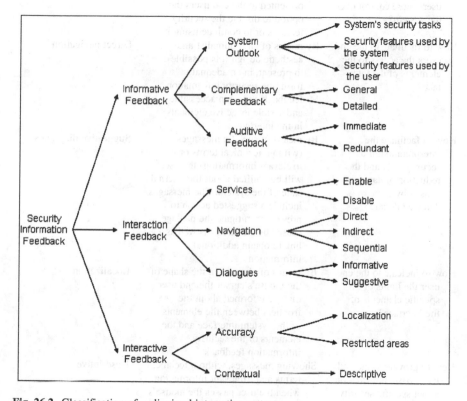

Fig. 26.2 Classification of audiovisual interactive patterns

Table 26.2 Enhanced sonification prototype with visual feedback

Color	Sound effect	Detected threat
Yellow	Frog	Guess
Orange	Cat	rcp
Red	Horse	rsh
Purple	Cock	rlogin
Violet	Bird	port-scan

Table 26.3 Description of some interactive patterns included in the classification proposed

Problem	Solution	Interactive pattern
How to permit the user to get specific information about the security of the system?	By giving in the notifications presented to the end users links to obtain, by e-mail, specific information about the security features, the detected threats, among other security topics	Detailed complementary feedback
How to inform to the end user about a detected threat?	Using an additional feedback form to enhance the visual notifications established to inform about detected threats	Immediate auditive notification
How to give to the end users more control over the system?	By giving in specific notifications presented to the end users the option to disable the security features or to continue using it	Disabling of services
How to facilitate to the end users the access to the elements of the inter-face?	By means of an minimalist and aesthetic design it is possible to present, in an adequate form, the security information feedback and keep accessible and visible its active elements in the interface.	Direct navigation
How to facilitate the interpretation of a security alert and the reduction of damages caused by some detected threat?	By means of specific messages (without technical terms or irrelevant information) the users will be notified about the internal state of the system. The messages include a suggested action to prevent or mitigate the damage caused by the threat, as well as a link to obtain additional information	Suggestive dialogues
How to indicate to the end user the limits of specific elements of the interface?	By means of changes in the shape of the mouse's cursor the end user may be informed about the frontiers between the elements of the system interface and the elements of the security information feedback	Localization
How to provide to the end users basic information about specific security information feedback elements?	Showing messages, without technical terms and irrelevant information, when the user passes the mouse's cursor over a specific element of the security information feedback	Descriptive

based on the HCI-S criteria, and a suggested solution offered by the patterns (Table 26.3; Fig. 26.3).

We consider that our proposal could facilitate, to designers and programmers, the planning and construction of a usable security information feedback, which could make easier for end users the comprehension and use of the security features

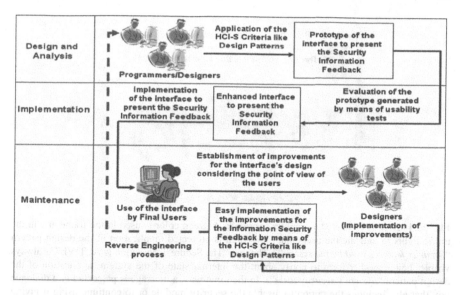

Fig. 26.3 This figure graphically depicts a general view of the application of our method. The graphical model is divided in three basic stages to represent an alternative collaboration between three types of users (end users, programmers, and designers) to improve security information feedback of a secure Web service

available in a specific secure Web service. Other advantages of the application of our proposal are that the implementation of the improvements could be easy and quick, for designers and programmers, because the feedback was originally generated by means of design patterns and considering the HCI-S criteria.

26.5   Case Study

As a case study we considered the next scenario: "It is required an UI that informs users, in a clear manner, about detected threats, and the security features available in a specific application. Furthermore, the security information feedback must include suggested actions to avoid or mitigate the damage caused by some detected threat, as well as provide options to obtain additional information about the detected threat, and the security features of the system." The design of the security feedback required by this specific example was generated applying the most appropriate design patterns of the classification proposed (Fig. 26.2). The example is illustrated in Figs. 26.4 and 26.5. We complement this example with the specification of the patterns used.

1. *Patterns*: Security features used by the system, System's security tasks, and Enable/Disable all the security features. *Problem*: How to convey the security features of the Web service clearly? *Solution*: Using an image of traffic lights

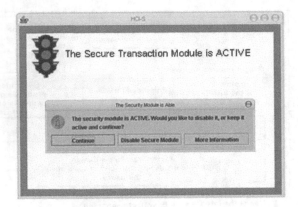

Fig. 26.4 Here is presented a graphical example. A green color is used in the frame and in the traffic lights to indicate the users that the system is protected (application of the design pattern *"Security features used by the system"*). The text "The Secure Transaction is ACTIVE" is always visible, being another form to notify about the internal state of the system (application of the design pattern *"System's security tasks"*). In the same way, a message is presented in a dialogue box that also includes the option to disable the security module or to continue using it giving the user more control over the system (application of the design pattern *"Enable/Disable all the security features"*)

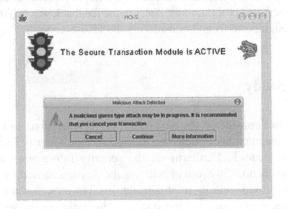

Fig. 26.5 This graphic shows the appearance of the UI when a "guess" potential threat is detected; in this case, a frog sound is generated (a frog sound is mapped to this threat, Table 26.2); yellow color is used in the frame and in the traffic lights (application of the design pattern *"Immediate notification of threats"*). Immediately, the interface presents a message in a dialogue box that includes the options "Cancel" and "More Information" (application of the design pattern *"Dialogue with suggested actions to follow"*). At the same time, the dialogue shows a frog picture at the top right corner of the screen. In this dialogue was considered a specific threat–color–sound–picture relation (see Table 26.2)

and the message "The Security Module is ACTIVE," the users will be alerted about the protection of the system.

2. *Patterns*: Dialogues with suggested actions to follow, and immediate notification of threats. *Problem*: How to present a clear visibility of the system status? *Solution*: By means of a sound alarm, changing the color of the interface's frame and the traffic lights, and a specific message (without technical terms or irrelevant information) the users will be notified about the internal state of the system. The messages include a suggested action to prevent or mitigate the damage caused by the threat, as well as a link to obtain additional information.

The security feedback designed for this case study also was considered and it covered the following HCI-S design criteria:

1. *Learnability*: The UI is easy to learn and friendly because the use of colors in the frame that notify about some threat detected and the use of real-world metaphors such as traffic lights.
2. *Aesthetic and minimalist design*: The UI informs about the security features available and when they are being used, showing only relevant information in the messages and notifications of the security features, maintaining a simple design.
3. *Trust*: The interface may help to achieve that the user trusts in a system, through adequate notifications, and clear suggested actions to prevent or mitigate the damage caused by the threat.

It is important to mention that the size of the messages, dialog boxes, and other notifications, presented in Figs. 26.4 and Fig. 26.5, was increased to show more clearly the texts of the notification's examples.

26.6   Related Work

In this section we present some of the most significant related work. We use the following criteria to identify advantages and disadvantages of our research: Proposal of a usable security information feedback, presentation of security aspects to the users, consideration of HCI-S design's criteria, and consideration of more than a sensory channel. We have considered the research works of Rode et al. [20], Yurcik et al. [22], Cranor et al. [5, 6], Ka-Ping [16], and McCrickard et al. [17] (Table 26.4). Table 26.4 illustrates the criteria performed by each research work. The focus of Rode's proposal [20] has been on providing final users with information they can use to understand the implications of their interactions with a system, as well as assessing the security of a system. The authors have been exploring two design principles for secure interaction: visualizing system activity and integrating configuration and action. The research shows a very good design strategy, but they have not considered the HCI-S design criteria, or the incorporation of sonification, which may complement this research. Similarly the work of Yurcik et al. [22] tries to facilitate the realization of specific activities related to security by means of

Table 26.4 Comparison of research works

Criteria Researches	Proposal of usable security information feedback	Presentation of security aspects to the users	Consideration of HCI-S design's criteria	Consideration of more than a sensory channel
Rode et al. [20]	X	X	–	–
Yurcik et al. [22]	X	X	–	–
Cranor et al. [5, 6]	X	X	–	–
Ka-Ping [16]	X	X	–	–
McCrickard et al. [17]	X	X	–	–
Current work	X	X	X	X

simple instructions and suggestions offered to the users through the interface elements. The research work presented by Cranor et al. [5, 6] proposes a very interesting strategy to facilitate the creation of simple interfaces, easy to understand and use by users, emphasizing some challenges that face the designers during the development process of security and privacy software configuration options. The objective of the research presented by Cranor in [6] is very similar to the goal of our work; nevertheless, in [6] are not considered auditive notifications or an additional feedback form. In the same way, the incorporation of the HCI-S criteria is not included. The research of Ka-Ping [16] consists of the proposal of a model of ten points to represent the interaction of the users with secure systems. The model is based on actors and their abilities, and it provides the actors some authority to assist users in determining whether a particular action is secure or not. In a similar way, McCrickard et al. [17] propose a very interesting strategy to design and evaluate usable feedback but do not consider the application of the HCI-S design criteria and the incorporation of sonification. In general terms, we believe that the application of the new HCI-S criteria, and the incorporation of sonification, may increase the usability of the works mentioned earlier. With the research work presented in this paper we try to perform the four comparison criteria (Table 26.4), and thus provide a complement for other research works.

26.7 Concluding Remarks and Future Work

Bearing in mind previous works, such as those described in [9, 14, 16, 20, 22], we present a first version of a nonexhaustive classification of information security feedback based in patterns. Our proposal is intended to facilitate the way some security aspects are conveyed to the end user. With the proposed classification, it is possible to achieve an appropriate feedback through the elements of the interface by means of visual and auditive notifications about information related to the security and the internal state of a particular on-line system. Similarly, the interactive patterns are oriented to designing and generating information security feedback easy to understand and interpret by users with different levels of experience and backgrounds (experts, advanced, and beginners) avoiding, as much as possible, the use of technical terms. We consider that specific visual notifications using intuitive elements designed by means of our guidelines application may represent a very good way to notify users about the security and the internal state of a specific Web service. There are several aspects to explore as future work, such as increasing the number of elements of the classification, and improving the classification, to be a component of a formal specification for the feedback of security information design. Also, it is necessary to perform a number of usability studies that consider aspects analyzed in research works such as those presented in [4, 21] to formally evaluate our proposal. In the near future, we also would like to investigate how other interaction modalities (e.g., speech, or haptic feedback) could complement or supplement the existing ways to provide feedback to the end users.

References

1. Atoyan, H., Duquet, J., Robert, J.: Trust in New Decision Aid Systems. In: Proc. of the 18th Int. Conf. of the Association Francophone d'Interaction Homme-Machine IHM'2006 (Montreal, April 18–21, 2006). ACM Press, New York (2006) 115–122.
2. Berry, B., Hobby, L. D., McCrickard, S., North, C., Pérez-Quiñones, M. A.: Making a Case for HCI: Exploring Benefits of Visualization for Case Studies. In: Proc. of World Conf. on Educ. Multimedia, Hypermedia & Telecom. EDMEDIA'2006 (Orlando, June 26–30, 2006).
3. Braz, C., Seffah, A., M'Raihi, D.: Designing a Trade-off Between Usability and Security: A Metrics Based-Model. In: Proc. of 11th IFIP TC 13 Conf. on Human–Computer Interaction INTERACT'2007 (Rio de Janeiro, September 10–14, 2007). Lecture Notes in Computer Science, Vol. 4663. Springer, Berlin (2007) 114–126
4. Lee, J.C., McCrickard, S.: Towards Extreme(ly) Usable Software: Exploring Tensions Between Usability and Agile Software Development. In: Proc. of Agile Conference AGILE'2007 (Washington, DC, August 13–17, 2007). IEEE Comp. Soc. Press (2007) 59–71.
5. Cranor, L.F.: Designing a Privacy Preference Specification Interface: A Case Study. In: Proc. of ACM CHI'2003 Workshop on Human–Computer Interaction and Security Systems (Fort Lauderdale, April 5–10, 2003). ACM Press, New York (2003).
6. Cranor, L.F., Garfinkel, S.: Security and Usability: Designing Secure Systems that People Can Use. O'Reilly, Sebastopol (2005).
7. DARPA Intrusion Detection Evaluation: Data Sets, Massachusetts Institute of Technology, Lincoln Laboratory, Boston (1999). Accessible at http://www.ll.mit.edu/IST/ideval/data/1998/1998_data_index.html.
8. Dass, M.: LIDS: A Learning Intrusion Detection System. B.E. Thesis. Nagpur University, Nagpur (2000).
9. Dhamija, R.: Security Usability Studies: Risk, Roles and Ethics. In: Proc. of ACM CHI'2007 Workshop on Security User Studies (San Jose, April 28 – May 3, 2007). ACM Press, New York (2007).
10. D'Hertefelt, S.: Trust and the Perception of Security, 2000. Accessible at http://www.interactionarchitect.com/research /report20000103shd.htm.
11. Dustin, E., Rasca, J., McDiarmid, D.: Quality Web Systems: Performance, Security, and Usability. Addison-Wesley, New York (2001).
12. García-Ruiz, M., Vargas Martin, M., Kapralos, B.: Towards Multimodal Interfaces for Intrusion Detection. In: Audio Eng. Society: Pro Audio Expo and Convention (Vienna, 2007).

13. Hewett, T., Baecker, R., Card, S., Carey, T., Gasen, J., Mantei, M., Perlman, G., Strong, G., Verplank, W.: ACM SIGCHI Curricula for Human–Computer Interaction. ACM, New York (2004). Accessible at http://www.acm.org/sigchi/cdg/cdg2.html.
14. Johnson, M.L., Zurko, M.E.: Security User Studies and Standards: Creating Best Practices. In: Proc. of ACM CHI'2007 Workshop on Security User Studies (San Jose, April 28 – May 3, 2007). ACM Press, New York (2007).
15. Johnston, J., Eloff, J., Labuschagne, L.: Security and Human Computer Interfaces. *Comput Security* 22, 8 (2003) 675–684.
16. Ka-Ping, Y.: Secure Interaction Design and the Principle of Least Authority. In: Proc. of ACM CHI'2003 Workshop on Human-Computer Interaction and Security Systems (Fort Lauderdale, April 5–10, 2003). ACM Press, New York (2003).
17. McCrickard, S., Czerwinski, M., Bartramc, L.: Introduction: Design and Evaluation of Notification User Interfaces. *Int J Hum Comput Stud* 58 (2003) 509–514.
18. Nielsen, J.: Ten Usability Heuristics. Nielsen & Norman Group, Mountain View (2005). Accessible at http://www.useit.com/papers/heuristic/heuristic_list.html.
19. Reeder, R.W., Karat, C.-M., Karat, J., Brodie, C.: Usability Challenges in Security and Privacy Policy-Authoring Interfaces. In: Proc. of 11th IFIP TC 13 Conf. on Human–Computer Interaction INTERACT'2007. LNCS, Vol. 4663. Springer, Berlin (2007) 141–155.
20. Rode, J., Johansson, C., DiGioia, P., Silva Filho, R., Nies, K., Nguyen, D. H., Ren, J., Dourish, P., Redmiles, D.: Seeing Further: Extending Visualization as a Basis for Usable Security. In: Proc. of Second ACM Symposium on Usable Privacy and Security SOUPS'2006 (Pittsburgh, July 12–14, 2006). ACM Press, New York (2006) 145–155.
21. Roth, V., Turner, T.: User Studies on Security: Good vs. Perfect. In: Proc. of ACM CHI'2007 Workshop on Security User Studies (San Jose, April 28 – May 3, 2007). ACM Press, New York (2007).
22. Yurcik, W., Barlow, J., Lakkaraju, K., Haberman, M.: Two Visual Computer Network Security Monitoring Tools Incorporating Operator Interface Requirements. In: Proc. of ACM CHI'2003 Workshop on Human–Computer Interaction and Security Systems (Fort Lauderdale, April 5–10, 2003). ACM Press, New York (2003).

Chapter 27
Domain-Specific Model for Designing Rich Internet Application User Interfaces

Marino Linaje, Juan C. Preciado and Fernando Sanchez-Figueroa

Abstract The development of Rich Internet Applications User Interfaces is attracting researches from different communities such as Web Engineering and Human Computer Interaction. Proposals coming from both fields have their own benefits and disadvantages. The real fact is that, to our knowledge, there is no proposal covering all the new issues regarding User Interfaces that appear in Rich Internet Applications. In this paper we present a domain-specific model for the systematic development of User Interfaces for Rich Internet Applications. This model is defined in the context of RUX-Method, which includes several languages and techniques coming from the HCI, Web, and Multimedia Engineering fields.

27.1 Introduction

Currently, HTML is showing its limits when considering high levels of interaction and multimedia support in Web applications. From a technological point of view, one solution to this limitation resides in the use of Rich Internet Applications (RIAs), which combine the benefits of the Web distribution model with the User Interface (UI) interactivity of desktop applications.

RIAs are characterized by adding new capabilities to the conventional hypertext-based Web. Some of the novel features of RIAs affect the human–computer interaction (HCI) (such as the UI presentation and the interaction paradigm) while others influence architectural issues (such as client–server communication and the distribution of the data/business logic). Regarding architectural issues, they support online and offline usage, data storage and processing capabilities directly at the client side, lower bandwidth consumption, and deeper separation between presentation and content, among others. Regarding HCI, they provide sophisticated UIs and powerful interaction tools leading to better usability and personalization.

M. Linaje (✉), J.C. Preciado and F. Sanchez-Figueroa
Quercus Software Engineering Group, Universidad de Extremadura, 10071 – Cáceres, Spain
e-mail: mlinaje@unex.es

V. López-Jaquero et al. (eds.), *Computer-Aided Design of User Interfaces VI*,
DOI: 10.1007/978-1-84882-206-1_27, © Springer-Verlag London Limited 2009

From a technological point of view, and according to [1], RIA approaches have four key characteristics: *runtime environment, graphic UI, business logic*, and the *back-end services*. In [2] we find another group of key capabilities of RIA: new *user interface* (rich and multimedia), new *data management* (user creates and consumes), *richer platforms* (the whole Web), *richer applications* (richer Web services, mashups...) and new *strategies* (self-service, self-organized...). The real fact is that, from the end-user perspective, RIA's most appreciated key characteristics are their capabilities in graphics, animation, and multimedia to enrich UIs.

Over the past few years, Web applications have been designed using Web models and methodologies. However, as a result of RIA's technological characteristics and requirements, current models and methodologies cannot be directly applied for modeling and generating RIA UIs [3].

Designing RIAs with Web engineering methodologies requires adapting the Web development flow of traditional Web applications to consider the new client-side capacities, the different communication flows between the client and the server, and the new presentation features coming from the HCI field.

Recent works [4, 5] have extended some Web models to deal with the design of RIAs. However, in these proposals UI models are either missing or they do not fully cover many concepts regarding UIs, which have been well established in the HCI field to increase productivity, decrease maintenance costs, etc., facilitating, for example, multidevice, multimodal, or multiplatform support. This is the reason why the development of a RIA requires a long development period. The new HCI issues arising in RIA have to be added in an ad hoc manner. However, proposals coming from the HCI field do not provide the richness of data modeling and navigation that Web models provide. Existing presentation models/description languages cannot be directly applied to model RIA UIs [3] and this is the point where the work shown in this paper comes into the scene. It serves as a bridge between HCI and Web engineering when considering the development of RIAs.

Recently, the authors proposed RUX-Method [6], a Model Driven Development (MDD) method for the definition of multidevice, multimodal, multiplatform UIs with high levels of interaction and multimedia temporal relationships. RUX-Method is intended to be used over an existing Web model to provide it with the necessary features to model the presentation issues appearing in RIAs. In previous works e.g., [6], we focused on aspects more relevant for the Web Engineering community than for the HCI community (e.g., how to extract and connect with the underlying Web model). However, different parts of RUX-Method regarding UI specifications were briefly described or just avoided. The main contribution of this work is showing the specification of a Domain-Specific UI Model common to different RIA rendering technologies (e.g., Flex or DHTML Ajax). To show how to use this specification over an existing UI modeling language, we apply it to RUX-Method, but many concepts can be applied to other UI models (e.g., UsiXML [7] or UiML [8]).

The rest of the paper is as follows. In Subheading 27.2 an introduction to RUX-Method is provided. Subheading 27.3 explains the Domain Specific Language (DSL) in detail while Subheading 27.4 shows how to use the method in practice. Finally, Subheadings 27.5 and 27.6 show related works and conclusions, respectively.

27.2   RUX-Method Introduction

RUX-Method is based on the Cameleon reference framework [9] where an UI can be decomposed into four levels: Concepts and Tasks, Abstract Interface, Concrete Interface, and Final Interface. For the last three levels, RUX-Method uses standards or well-known techniques when a standard is not available (more details about languages and models used to create the RUX-Method specification can be found at [6]). In RUX-Method each Interface level is mainly composed by Interface Components.

At design time, RUX-Method uses existing data, business logic, and presentation models offered by the underlying Web model being enriched. RUX-Method maps this information into a UI abstraction, which is then transformed until the desired RIA UI is reached. At run time, while a new UI is generated using RUX-Method, the data and business logic remain the same.

The development process in RUX-Method has the next stages (Fig. 27.1): connection with the previously defined Web model (marked CR in Fig. 27.1), definition of the Abstract Interface, definition of the Concrete Interface, and specification of the Final Interface, which ends in code generation. In RUX-Method each stage is fed by the previous one, as well as the mapping possibilities specified in the RUX-Method Component Library (also in Fig. 27.1).

So, the first stage in RUX-Method deals with the process of connecting with the previous Web model. Web models can be seen as task-specific models with the aim of providing an abstract specification of the data and hypertext of Web applications. That is the reason why RUX-Method does not introduce a task model, just extracting the required information already modeled using existing Web models (underlying Web model). At this first stage, the presentation elements and the relationships among them are extracted, as well as the defined operations on the Web model. The Connection Rules ensure RUX-Method to adapt to the system requirements shaped in the previous Web model including data, business logic and navigational features.

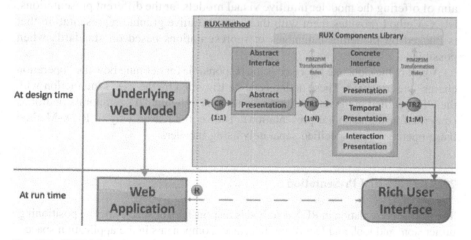

Fig. 27.1 RUX-Method overview

In the second stage, from the Abstract Interface (device and platform independent) a draft version of the Concrete Interface is obtained through the application of the first transformation rules set (Transformation Rules 1, marked TR1 in Fig. 27.1). In the third stage, from the Concrete Interface (platform independent) and through a second transformation rules set, the Final Interface is obtained (Transformation Rules 2, marked TR2 in Fig. 27.1).

The relationship among the stages in the method follows an MDD approach where: for each hypertext model you get an Abstract Interface (Platform Independent Model: PIM); for each Abstract Interface (PIM) you get n Concrete Interfaces (PIM); for each Concrete Interface (PIM) you get m Final Interfaces (Platform Specific Model: PSM).

27.3 The RIA Domain-Specific Model of RUX-Method

The concepts related with the description of a domain-specific model for the specification of fine-grained RIA UIs can be achieved in many different ways attending to the UI model/language that we want to use. In RUX-Method these concepts are described in two separated but interrelated parts: the Component Library and the Concrete Interface specification.

27.3.1 Concrete Interface

The Concrete Interface is in charge of specifying the presentation and behavior of the UI that has to be modeled, depending on how we want the application to be.

The Concrete Interface is formed by three additional "presentations layers" to minimize cross-cutting: spatial, temporal, and interaction presentations. With the aim of offering the modeler intuitive visual models for the different presentations, RUX-Method provides them with their own intuitive graphic representation that is backed by modeling languages or representations based on standards when possible.

A part of the Concrete Interface is the responsible for defining how the "operation chains" are triggered. These actions can be triggered by the user's interaction with the UI (specified in the interaction presentation) or by the UI's temporal conditions (specified in the temporal presentation). That is the reason why in RUX-Method these operations are specified separately using handlers.

27.3.1.1 Spatial Presentation

The spatial presentation in RUX-Method is responsible for specifying the positioning, dimension, and look and feel of the Interface Components in the application space.

RUX-Method gives the modeler a set of native RIA Components, which have been defined on the basis of a component set, which is currently present in nearly all current RIA rendering platforms. The choice of these Components is the fusion among the groups of available components in Adobe Flex, Flash [10], and Open Laszlo [11] as platforms that have been largely used. RUX-Method Concrete Interface Components can be classified in three categories: (1) Controls: components used to gather the user entries or to provide the user with output information, (2) Layouts: components able to distribute and/or gather the elements in the Concrete Interface, and (3) Navigators: components able to provide navigation among the stack layout and other typical navigation Components.

27.3.1.2   Temporal Presentation

The temporal presentation is defined on the spatial presentation for specifying how time-based changes affecting the RIA UI will take place. The temporal presentation is formed by the temporal presentation elements, which are Concrete Interface Components or groups of Concrete Interface Components, whose spatial presentation is already defined.

It is possible to establish the temporal relationships logic between the elements (E) of the temporal presentation and also group temporal presentation elements (G), which can contain one or more temporal elements to share the same temporal logic among all of them. SMIL [12], the W3C standard, is currently used for expressing temporal logic relations. In RUX-Method, the graphical representation of the temporal presentation is lightly inspired by sequence diagrams defined in OMMMA. The set of possible temporal relations in RUX-Method has been validated by correspondences of the set of temporal relations defined in HMT [13].

Because of the length of this paper and the fact that temporal presentation is usually treated by the Multimedia community, we recommend [6] for further information.

27.3.1.3   Interaction Presentation

The objective of the interaction presentation in RUX-Method is to capture and represent those behaviors triggered by the user interaction.

In RIAs, capturing the user interaction with the UI is generally carried out by the application components that are able to capture certain event types.

In RUX-Method, an event is the representation of some asynchronous occurrence (such as a mouse click on the presentation of the element) that is associated with a Concrete Interface Component. An action is some way of responding to an event; a handler is some specification for such action; a listener is a binding of such handler to an event targeting some Component.

As the event capture definition language, RUX-Method uses XML Events [14], the W3C Standard language for the event capture specification. The XML Events module provides RUX-Method with the ability to uniformly integrate event listeners and event handlers.

27.3.1.4 Handlers

Interaction in RUX-Method follows an Event-Condition-Action (ECA) model. Each ECA is defined by the Event (in RUX-Method defined in the interaction presentation) and a Condition-Action-Tree (CAT) defined in the handler. ECA makes RUX-Method able to define rules with actions that are triggered when some conditions are met. This behavior model is more than enough to express both, changes in the UI and calls to the business logic expressed in the defined hypertext model.

The proposed ECA model represents in a declarative way the system of conditions and actions of RUX-Method, and helps solving a great part of the problems with handlers regarding the triggering of operation chains and spatial presentation changes. Additionally, RUX-Method provides an OCL Syntax to those models requiring an extra expressiveness out of the CAT usage domain provided by ECA.

27.3.2 The Component Library

Each Interface level is mainly composed by Interface Components whose specifications are stored in the Component Library (Fig. 27.2), which is responsible for (1) storing the Components specification (name, properties, methods, and events), (2) specifying the transformation capabilities for each Component from an Interface level in other Components in the following Interface level, and (3) keeping the hierarchy among Components at each Interface level independently to every other level.

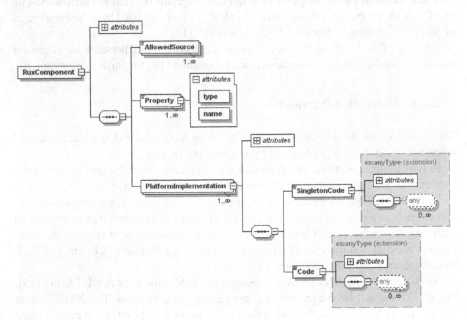

Fig. 27.2 Part of the RUX-Method Component Library scheme

In this document and due to the RUX-Method nature, when we talk about Components, we refer to User Interface Components where they can have different complexity levels and intrinsic functionality (also called widgets).

A Component can only belong to an Interface level. The Component Library has a dynamic nature, which means that the set of Components can be increased or adapted by the modeler according to its needs and the specifications of the project. Properties, methods and events of each Component can be extended at any time. The Component Library stores the interface level structure by means of skeletons and it also stores how the transformations among Components of different levels are carried out.

For the transformations specification contained in the Component Library we have extended the XICL [15] specification (Fig. 27.2) to declaratively specify which are the transformation options available to be carried out on each Interface Component.

In the Abstract Interface the different kinds of media and views define the grouping and the type of elements that the user is going to perceive. In the Concrete Interface level, *Control* Components are used for data I/O (e.g., *Textcontrol*), *Layout* Components are used to organize the content (e.g., *Dividedlayout*) and *Navigational* Components are used for navigating the content (e.g., *Tabnav*).

Each Component can be composed of different parts and not all of them are required (according to the Interface level of the Component): *Caption, Capability, Properties, Methods, and Events.* Caption specifies the Component name and the list of Components from the previous Interface level that can be transformed into this Component. *Capability* expresses the functionality needed to express the Component behavior. It is composed of a Header and a Body. While the Header is used and shared by all the instances of this Component in the application, the Body is specific for each instance. To clarify this abstract specification, let us explain an example for an AJAX-specific Component: the Header can be a snippet CSS or JavaScript function placed once in the application. On the other hand, the Body is placed once for each instance defining different values in each case as necessary (e.g., example values for size, font color, etc), sharing all the instances of a Component in the same header. A *Property* indicates a Component characteristic that contains a value according to its Interface level. For example, in the Abstract Interface a common property is *connectorid* that contains a reference (value) to the connector of the underlying Web model. In the Concrete Interface the *size* property, for example, is available in the *Tabnav* Component. *Methods* express a way to communicate the whole interface with the Component (e.g., invoking Component functionality). *Events* state for the list of events listened by the Component (e.g., ondrag or onmouseover).

A skeleton describes abstractly the basic structure of an application in a specific Interface level (i.e., that we call metadescriptor). There is a close relationship between skeletons and Components, since Components are placed in the Interface level according to the skeleton specified. A skeleton may include a set of common resources needed by Components.

Regarding the transformation among Components, both transformation rules (TR1 and TR2) follow the same steps: (1) use the skeleton defined (in the Component Library) for the target interface level, (2) transform each Component in the source interface level into its corresponding default Component in the target interface level, (3) enrich this skeleton including the Components obtained from step 2. This process distributes the Component Headers and Bodies across the skeleton preserving the Component hierarchy.

27.4 The Method in Use

RUX-Tool has been developed based on RUX-Method, and real-life applications are being developed by the *Homeria Open Solutions* Company. At the moment, RUX-Tool works with WebRatio 5.0 in commercial and academic terms allowing the design of rich UIs over Web applications designed and generated with WebRatio (the WebML CASE tool). RUX-Tool is a full cloud platform, i.e., to model the UI it provides a browser-based RIA editor that works online and it is to communicate with the server-side to apply the Transformation Rules. The Final UIs generated are automatically deployed at server side. This RIA cloud platform avoids any kind of installation at client-side. Nowadays, the available UI code generators are FLEX, Laszlo, and AJAX (using the jquery framework). All of these RIA frameworks are free and open source.

RUX-Tool has been validated using several projects where high interactivity, multimedia synchronization, and device independency are mandatory. The results obtained are satisfactory in terms of design time, effort, and final appearance. RUX-Tool is ready to be used online and additional information (video demo, screenshots, architecture, etc.) is available at http://ruxproject.org/. Next, we show several screenshots describing some steps for the RIA UI definition using RUX-Tool.

In Fig. 27.3 the spatial presentation is depicted, automatically obtained from the Abstract Interface by means of the TR1 defined by RUX-Method.

In Fig. 27.4a a chunk of a temporal presentation is depicted. Figure 27.4b represents the listener properties where the event *onclick* triggers the handler described in Fig. 27.4c. This handler invokes the method *closeWindow* defined in the Component Library over a *windowlayout* Component. Figure 27.4d depicts the generated RIA Final Interface (the full example is available online at *ruxproject* Website).

To complain with the extensibility and flexibility of RUX-Method, RUX-Tool Component Library and code generators have a plug-in architecture for allowing the inclusion of new Components and target platforms. Each Component is a template based on the Declarative Velocity Style Language (DVSL).

In practical terms, the skeleton indicates physically the set of files and folders to place the application and Component resources and designates where and how to put the Component Header and each Component Body for a RUX-Method Component. This is carried out using skeletons written in XSL language for generating a XML file that describes the folders/files hierarchy for the whole application.

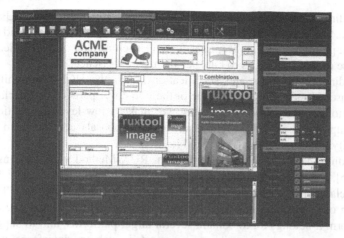

Fig. 27.3 Spatial presentation using RUX-Tool

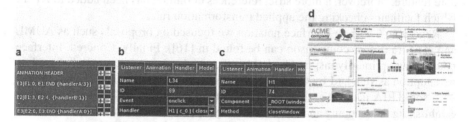

Fig. 27.4 (**a**) Temporal presentation definition. (**b**) Listener properties. (**c**) Handler properties. (**d**) Generated RIA Final Interface

27.5   Related Work

Different proposals related with RIAs are coming from both, Web Engineering community and the HCI community. The main problem of those proposals coming from the Web Engineering community is that not all of them consider the presentation issues as first-class citizens (e.g., [4]), being their focus on other aspects such as business logic distribution. Only a few cover presentation issues and this is the case of [5], a work close to ours, which incorporates RIA-specific presentation features in a model-driven Web development process. However, it only copes with the Abstract Interface level design while RUX-Method goes further including the Concrete and Final Interface design stages achieving a full RIA Model-based UI.

On the other hand, the HCI community is also taking into account RIA presentation specific features. We can differentiate between those proposals only providing specifications for the description of the UIs (i.e., just describing a DSL) and those providing a MDD where mapping and transformations play a pivotal role. Although RUX-Method follows MDD, it also takes ideas from the formers.

Regarding model-based proposals, [7] is an interesting one. It uses UsiXML to describe a first draft of RIA UIs incorporating the MDD. However, and due to it being in a preliminary stage, it misses features such as temporal specification that is the base of many RIA UIs to enhance the user experience.

Regarding those DSLs and specifications from the HCI community, RUX-Method uses ideas coming from some of them to cover parts of its Interface levels specification. In the rest of this section we make a low-level description of the relationships between RUX-Method and those proposals coming from the HCI community used to inspire and/or build it.

Regarding the Components specification, RUX-Method is mainly inspired by XICL [15], which was originally designed to create HTML components. The properties declaration has been modified to adapt them to RUX-Method. The XICL definition of Component has been largely extended, mainly to make reference to the platform it belongs to, to contain several target platforms, and to support skeletons. Some elements and attributes are avoided, such as <interface> where UIs could be specified mixing spatial arrangement and interaction, which is not a desirable feature. Moreover, a more strict references definition has been added to XICL, which facilitates checking the applied transformation rules.

Regarding Concrete Interface notation we focused on proposals such as AUML and XUL (a deeper comparison can be found in [16]). Finally, Concrete Interface notation was primarily inspired by UIML [8], which selection was mainly based on its adoption as standard by OASIS. Notwithstanding, UIML is not enough to deal with some RIA necessities [3], so RUX-Method extends it with many features to establishing the mapping and relations among RUX-Method Components, interface levels, and presentation types.

The textual specification of the spatial presentation is also based on a subset of the specification proposed by UIML, which is formed by part of the children defined in UIML inside the node <interface>. This includes the nodes <structure> and <style>, avoiding the use of <content> and <behavior> nodes.

For the interaction presentation notation, RUX-Method uses XML Events, which is based on the definition of listeners that are used to declare event listeners and register them with specific nodes in the DOM. It is important to note that XML Events does not specify available event types or actions. This feature is really important in RUX-Method where event-type availability is declared independently for each Component in the dynamic Component Library.

In RUX-Method, handlers are textually represented in a declarative way. The specification is based on a subset of UIML behavior module that is composed by the next basic elements: (1) behavior: the behavior root element; (2) rule: this element defines a binding between conditions and actions (that RUX-Method uses for the binding between temporal/interaction presentations and actions to be evaluated and performed); (3) condition: element that contains a logical expression based on the <op> element. <op> may also contain hierarchical op elements to composite more complex conditions. UIML <op> available logical conditions are ==, !=, >, <, &&, and ||. <op> available operators are constant, property, reference, call, op, and event; (4) action: element that contains one or more elements that are executed in the order they appear in the UIML document. Actions in UIML may do procedure calls (<call> element), changes on properties (<property> element), and other actions such as UI restructuration, or event activations (<restructuration> and <event>). Additional action subelements are <whentrue>, <when-false>, and <by-default> conditions.

To define actions in RUX-Method, we use a subset of UIML <action> element. In RUX-Method there are two kinds of actions: those which modify the UI and those that affect the underlying Web business logic. For those actions that affect the UI, we avoid using <restructuration> element to change the UI. RUX-Method at this point is richer than UIML proposal, since RUX-Method facilitates not only property changes available in UiML but also the definition of transitions calling the temporal presentation specified by RUX-Method. For those actions that affect the underlying business logic, we use UIML <call> element. The name of the procedure and a set of arguments configure the typical syntax to call a function in procedural languages and that is the way in which UIML does it using <param> elements. However, RUX-Method extends it to specify both synchronous and asynchronous communications, using GET or POST request methods.

27.6   Conclusions

The RIA UI design can be seen from two different, but complementary, perspectives: Web engineering and HCI. While proposals belonging to the former do not cover fully many concepts that have been well established in the HCI field, proposals coming from the latter do not provide the richness of data modeling and navigation that Web models provide, which are necessary to cope with the requirements of the Web application and to increase the user experience in many cases (e.g., storing data at client-side for data filtering operation). In this sense, RUX-Method can be seen as a bridge between HCI and Web engineering fields when considering the development of RIAs.

In RUX-Method we have tried to systematize the RIA UI design by lessons learned from HCI, Web, and Multimedia engineering fields. The proposal has been validated, in practical terms, by the implementation of a CASE tool (RUX-Tool) and several case studies have been carried out during the last 2 years. Readers can find the tool and many video demos online at http://ruxproject.org.

Acknowledgments The work is partially supported by the Spanish projects: TIN2008-02985 and TSI020501-2008-47.

References

1. Stearn B (2007) XULRunner: a new approach for developing rich internet applications. Internet Computing, *IEEE*, Vol. 11, No.3, 67–73.
2. Butler Group, http://www.butlergroup.com/research/research.asp Accessed on 30 January 2009.

3. Preciado JC, Linaje M, Sanchez F, et al. (2005) Necessity of methodologies to model rich Internet applications. Proceedings of International Symposium on Web Site Evolution, Budapest, Hungary, IEEE Computer Society 7–13.
4. Bozzon A, Comai S, Fraternali P, et al. (2006) Conceptual modeling and code generation for rich internet applications. Proceedings of the International Conference on Web Engineering, ACM Vol. 263, Palo Alto, CA, 353–360.
5. Urbieta M, Rossi G, Ginzburg J (2007) Designing the interface of rich internet applications. Proceedings of Latin American Web Conference, IEEE Computer Society, Santiago, Chile, 144–153.
6. Linaje M, Preciado JC, Sanchez-Figueroa F (2007) A method for model based design of rich internet application interactive user interfaces. Proceedings of the International Conference on Web Engineering, LNCS Vol. 4607, Como, Italy, 226–241.
7. Martínez-Ruiz FJ, Muñoz Arteaga J, Vanderdonckt J, et al. (2006) A first draft of a model-driven method for designing graphical user interfaces of rich internet applications. Proceedings of Latin American Web Conference, IEEE Computer Society, Cholula, Mexico, 32–38.
8. Abrams M, Phanouriou C, Batongbacal AL, et al. (1999) UiML: an appliance-independent XML language. Computer Networks: The International Journal of Computer and Telecommunications Networking, Elsevier, Vol. 31, 1695–1708.
9. Calvary G, Coutaz J, Thevenin D, et al. (2003) A unifying reference framework for multi-target user interfaces. Interacting with Computers, Vol. 15, No. 3, 289–308.
10. Adobe RIA, http://www.adobe.com/devnet/ria. Accessed on 14 May 2008.
11. Open Laszlo, http://www.openlaszlo.org/. Accessed on 14 May 2008.
12. SMIL W3C, http://www.w3.org/TR/2005/REC-SMIL2-20051213/. Accessed on 14 May 2008.
13. Specht G, Zoller P (2000) HMT: modeling temporal aspects in hypermedia applications. International Conference on Web-Age Information Management, Shanghai, China, 256–270.
14. XML Events W3C, http://www.w3.org/TR/2003/REC-xml-events-20031014/. Accessed on 14 May 2008.
15. Sousa G, Leite JC (2004) XICL – An extensible markup language for developing user interface and components. Proceedings of Computer-Aided Design of User Interfaces, Kluwer Academic Publishers, Portugal, Vol. 1, 1–10.
16. Pohja M, Honkala, M, Penttinen M, et al. (2006) Web user interaction – comparison of declarative approaches. Proceedings of WEBIST, Setúbal, Portugal, 295–302.

Chapter 28
Design Patterns for User Interface for Mobile Applications

Erik G. Nilsson

Abstract In this paper we present a collection of user-interface design patterns for mobile applications. The patterns in the collection are grouped into a set of problem areas that are further grouped into three main problem areas. After presenting this problem structure we present one of the patterns in some detail. Then, we present some relevant findings from a validation of the patterns collection. This validation shows that both the patterns collection and the individual patterns are relevant and useful for usability professionals with a mixed background. Finally, we discuss pros and cons of using a patterns format for documenting design knowledge, related work, and future research.

28.1 Introduction

In the UMBRA and FLAMINCO projects, we have developed a set of design guidelines to aid developing more user-friendly applications on mobile devices (PDAs/SmartPhones), giving practical advices for how to solve various problems that arise when designing user interfaces on mobile devices. The main part of these design guidelines is a collection of user-interface design patterns for mobile applications [5] (the patterns collection is available at http://www.sintef.no/flaminco). Each problem is presented on a design pattern format [3]. The "sources" for the problems addressed in the patterns collection are problems identified in the requirements elicitation phase of the UMBRA and FLAMINCO projects, and practical experience in developing and using mobile applications among the project partners.

E.G. Nilsson
SINTEF ICT, Postboks 124, Blindern, N-0314, Oslo, Norway
e-mail: egn@sintef.no

V. López-Jaquero et al. (eds.), *Computer-Aided Design of user Interfaces VI*,
DOI: 10.1007/978-1-84882-206-1_28, © Springer-Verlag London Limited 2009

Table 28.1 UI design patterns and their connection to problem areas

Main problem area	Problem area	Individual problems/UI design patterns
Utilizing screen space	Screen space in general	Presenting elements in lists
		Principles and mechanisms for grouping information
		Mechanisms for packing information
	Flexible user interfaces	**Handling dialogs when SW keyboard is shown/hidden**
		Supporting switching between portrait and landscape mode
		UIs that should run on equipment with different screen size
Interaction mechanisms	Handling input	Mechanisms for entering text
		Mechanisms for entering numerical data
		Multimodal input
	Not using the stylus	Interacting with applications without using stylus
		Retrieving data from a database without using keyboard
Design at large	Guidelines	Standard features in an automatically generated prototype
		Combining branding, aesthetics, and screen space
	Difficult to understand	User interaction during synchronization
		User interaction during long-lasting operations

28.2 Main Problem Areas

The design guidelines presented in the patterns collection follow a given structure. On the top level, they are grouped into *three main problem areas*. Within each of these three main problem areas, a small number of *problem areas* are defined. Within each of these problem areas, a number of problems are identified. In Table 28.1 some of the 26 identified problems (UI design patterns) with their connection to problem areas are listed. A brief version of the problem in bold font is presented in the next section.

28.3 Handling Dialogs When Software Keyboard Is Shown and Hidden

Background: On PDAs without keyboard, a common solution for entering text is to show a software keyboard on the bottom of the screen where the user can enter text using the stylus. This area may already be used by the application, thus leaving less room for its "normal" interaction.

Problem: The main problem is how to resize the dialogs to avoid some parts of the dialogs becoming invisible. The severity of this problem depends on the type/style of the user interface. It is most challenging for forms-based UIs, while for UIs containing arbitrary text or visual presentations adding or adjusting a scroll bar is usually sufficient. Handling tab folders and buttons that are placed on the bottom of the screen is also a challenge.

Solutions: The most obvious and most simple solution to this problem is to *add or adjust scroll bars* when the keyboard appears. The other solutions presented later are solutions where the need for adding scroll bars is removed or reduced.

In some cases it is OK *letting the keyboard cover part of the UI*. How "bad" this solution is depends on what is placed on the part of the screen that will be covered by the keyboard. If this part is occupied by output fields, the solution may work fine as long as the keyboard is removed when not needed. If this part of the screen contains important input fields or tab folders the solution is useless.

Another simple, but seldom very practical solution is to *just use the part of the screen that will not be covered by the keyboard*. In practice, what this solution does is reducing the size of the screen. This solution may be OK for dialog boxes, but is seldom practical for normal windows.

A more advanced, but still fairly easily implemented solution is to *use one large UI control as a buffer*. By this we mean that when the keyboard is added, one of the controls is reduced vertically to be just as much smaller as the size of the keyboard. Controls that may be used for this are primarily list boxes and multi line text boxes.

Yet another fairly simple solution is *having two variants* of the UI, one that uses all the screen space and one that makes room for the keyboard. The main disadvantage with the solution is – in addition to added development work – that the user may be confused when the UI changes.

The buffer solution may also be used with two or more large UI controls sharing the amount of size reduction to be applied. Generalized, this solution ends up as *dynamic resizing* of the controls in the UI. This may be done using two different approaches. The first is to decide a resizing rule for each window and apply that as tailored code for each window. The second is to have a general layout adjustment algorithm doing it for all windows.

28.4 Validation

The patterns collection was presented at a half-day tutorial at the HCI International conference in 2007 [6]. At the tutorial, the structure of the patterns collection was presented, and all patterns were presented at a very brief level. Then, 12 of the 26 patterns were presented in more detail. During the presentation, the participants filled in a questionnaire. They scored the relevance of the main problem areas, the relevance and usefulness of each of the presented patterns, and finally the relevance and usefulness of the patterns collection as well as their expectations for future use of the patterns collection. Relevance, usefulness, and future use were scored on a scale from 1 (lowest) to 6 (highest).

Twenty nine of the participants at the tutorial handed in the questionnaire. There was a small majority of males (age varied from 25 to 50), most being around 30 years old. A majority had their origin in Asia, the rest coming from Europe and America. The majority has an education on master's level, the rest split among undergraduates and PhD holders. The educational background was equally split between technical and nontechnical. UI development experience varied from 0 to 12 years, the majority having 5 years or less experience. Experience in developing mobile solutions varied from 0 to 6 years, the majority having 2 years or less experience.

28.4.1 Results

Scores on the main problem areas show an average score on relevance of 5.3 for Utilizing screen space, on 5.4 for Interaction mechanisms, and 4.9 for Design at large. Scores on the patterns collection as such show an average score on relevance of 5.0, and on both usefulness and future use of the patterns collection of 4.5. All these scores verify that the patterns collection both addresses relevant problems and gives useful and practical advices on how to solve these problems.

Looking at the scores for the individual patterns that were presented in more detail, the scores vary a bit but are still fairly high. Figure 28.1 shows the average scores for relevance and usefulness for the 12 patterns, sorted descending on scores for relevance.

As for the patterns collection as such, the average scores for relevance are higher than the corresponding scores for usefulness. This is not surprising, as it is usually

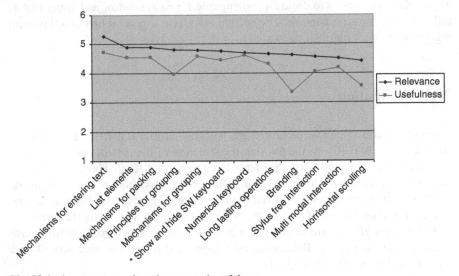

Fig. 28.1 Average scores for relevance and usefulness

easier to agree with a problem description than a proposed solution. Although all but one of the average usefulness scores are on the top half of the scale, the patterns where the usefulness scores are lowest, and the patterns where the difference between relevance score and usefulness scores is highest are candidates for further work. It may also be noted that correlation analyses show that the scores for relevance and usefulness correlate on the 0.01 level for 7 of the 12 problems, and on the 0.05 level for 2 of the other 5. Also, the scores for relevance and usefulness for the patterns collection as such correlate on the 0.01 level.

28.5   Using Patterns Format to Document Design Knowledge

The chosen patterns format is in many ways well suited to document user-interface design knowledge, as it captures the essential aspects of a problem. Also, as design patterns may be on different abstraction levels they can be used to describe problems of different "sizes." Furthermore, dividing a problem field into a limited number of well-defined problems makes it possible to handle a set of manageable problems separately. Finally, having a patterns collection makes it possible to combine the just mentioned "divide and rule" principle with having an overall structure.

The biggest challenge we had using the patterns format is the connection between problems and solutions. Very often, this is a many to many connection. Presenting the same or very similar solutions to a number of problems, either causes a lot of cross-references or large amounts of repetition. We chose to use cross-references, as is being done in other patterns collections [2]. Currently we are considering restructuring the patterns collection so that each pattern represents either one solution or a unique combination of one problem and one solution. Both these approaches will reduce the need for cross-referencing, but both will increase the number of patterns, thus making it more difficult to get an overview of the patterns collection.

28.6   Related Work

There are a number of patterns collections and even collections of patterns collections on the Web; see also [1] for an assessment of such collections. There are also a few collections of patterns for mobile user interfaces, such as The Design Pattern Wiki[1] and Little Springs mobile UI design patterns.[2] The latter overlaps with two of our main problem areas, but while our collection is organized by problems, this collection is organized by solutions. The patterns presented in [8], although focus-

---

[1] http://www.gibbert.net/DPWiki (in German).
[2] http://patterns.littlespringsdesign.com/~newlsdpatterns/index.php/Main_Page.

ing on mobile interaction, are much wider in its scope than our collection, with only two user interface patterns. The works [2, 4] present a design patterns collection for ubiquitous computing that is fairly large but has a broader scope with patterns that are on a higher abstraction level and/or are less comprehensive in the suggested set of solutions than our patterns.

28.7 Conclusions and Future Work

In this paper we have presented a structured collection of user-interface design patterns for mobile applications. The structure is valuable as an index and it gives a comprehensive overview of design problems for mobile UIs.

The patterns collection has been validated using a questionnaire at a tutorial. This validation shows that both the individual patterns assessed and the whole collection were perceived as relevant and useful by the participants, and that it is likely that they will use the collection in future work. It also identifies patterns that need more work.

Finally, we have discussed pros and cons of using a patterns collection for documenting design knowledge: the main pro being the ability to divide a large problem area into a structured set of manageable problems and the main con being that the same solution may apply to a number of problems, causing a lot of cross-references between the patterns. The collection is continuously being improved and enhanced, e.g., in the areas of multimodal interaction and exploiting context [7].

Acknowledgments The work on which this paper is based is supported by the UMBRA and FLAMINCO projects funded by the Norwegian Research Council and the industry partners in these projects. I would also like to thank my colleagues Asbjørn Følstad and Jan Heim for contributions to designing the questionnaire used for the validation and in analyzing the results.

References

1. Deng J, et al. (2005) Managing UI pattern collections. In Proceedings of the Sixth ACM SIGCHI New Zealand Chapter's International Conference on Computer–Human interaction, Hamilton, New Zealand.
2. Duyne D K & Landay J A (2004) Design Patterns, Course documentation.
3. Gamma E, Helm R, Johnson R, Lissides J (1995) Design Patterns – Elements of Reusable Object-Oriented Software. Addison-Wesley, Reading, MA.
4. Landay JA & Borriello G (2003) Design patterns for ubiquitous computing. IEEE Comput 36(8), 93–95.
5. Nilsson E G (2005) Design guidelines for mobile applications. SINTEF Report STF90 A06003, ISBN 82-14-03820-0.
6. Nilsson E G (2007) Design patterns for user interfaces on mobile equipment. Tutorial documentation, HCI International, Beijing.
7. Nilsson EG, Floch J, et al. (2006) Model-based user interface adaptation. Comput Graph 30(5), 692–701
8. Roth J (2002) Patterns of mobile interaction. Personal Ubiquitous Comput 6(4), 282–289.

Chapter 29
On the Reusability of User Interface Declarative Models

Antonio Delgado, Antonio Estepa, José A. Troyano and Rafael Estepa

Abstract The automatic generation of user interfaces based on declarative models achieves a significant reduction of the development effort. In this paper, we analyze the feasibility of using two well-known techniques such as XInclude and Packaging in the new context of reusing user-interface model specifications. After analyzing the suitability of each technique for UI reutilization and implementing both techniques in a real system, we show that both techniques are suited to be used within the context of today's existing model-based user interfaces.

29.1 Introduction

The automatic generation of user interfaces (UIs) through model-based user interface development environments (MB-UIDEs) [1] is likely to become a candidate technology for reducing the development effort in software industry. MB-UIDEs use abstract models (named user interface models or UIMs), which can be used for developing and automating the generation of user interfaces. Although these models could potentially be expressed through graphical or textual languages, they are commonly coded through XML-based user interface description languages (UIDLs) [2]. In fact, XML has became a de facto standard to specify UIMs potentially suited for MB-UIDEs.

In addition to automation, another way to reduce the development effort is through reuse. Software reuse is a well-known area of study in software engineering, which aims to reduce redundant work. There is a wide range of reusable assets: requirements, test cases, etc. The reuse of UIMs is not a new idea. Some techniques such as UI patterns, multi-device user interface development, etc. have been proposed [3]. However, few efforts have been made to inquire about the reusability of UIs through the reuse of UIMs specifications.

A. Delgado (✉), A. Estepa, J.A. Troyano and R. Estepa
Escuela Superior de Ingenieros, C/ Camino de los descubrimientos s/n, 41092, Sevilla, Spain
e-mail: aldelgado@trajano.us.es

V. López-Jaquero et al. (eds.), *Computer-Aided Design of User Interfaces VI*,
DOI: 10.1007/978-1-84882-206-1_29, © Springer-Verlag London Limited 2009

Only a few of current UIDLs provide mechanisms for reusing fragments of the UI models: UIML templates [4], XICL components [5], and XUL overlays [6]. However, the methods used are specific of the UIDL used [4, 5] (i.e., define their own tags) and consequently, incompatible between them, or use special XML processing instructions [6].

The objective of this work is to propose and analyze the pros and cons of two techniques for UIMs reuse: *XInclude* [7] and *Packaging*. Both methods are commonly applied in contexts different from UI reuse but we believe that both are potentially valid in the reuse of UIMs specifications, being UIDL-independent and having a minimum impact in the actual UIDLs syntax. To validate our proposal, we have implemented both techniques in a real MB-UIDE [8] using this experience as a feedback for our analysis.

29.2 User Interface Models: Reuse

MB-UIDEs attempt to formally describe the users, tasks, and presentation for a UI, and then use this set of formal UIMs to guide the full process of developing the UI. To identify what portions of the UIMs are eligible for reuse, we should first describe the models commonly included in MB-UIDEs as well as the objects included in each model. This will let us have a view of the reusability degree of each model. There seems to be a common agreement in defining the following UIMs [1]:

- The Domain Model (DOM): Defines the data objects that a user can view, access, and manipulate through a UI. The elements included in this model are typically classes, entities, attributes, operations, and relationships. Developers are familiar with these objects and the reusability degree depends typically on the model's subject and developer's expertise.
- The User Model (UM): Specifies a hierarchical decomposition of the user population into stereotypes. Each stereotype brings together people sharing the same value for a given set of parameters. Components of this model are users, groups, relationships between them, and their properties. Initially, we do not think that reusing users or groups can be very interesting because they are usually centralized in shared directories (e.g., LDAP repository). However, some parameters from the UM specifications such as user preferences or profiles are potentially interesting for reusing (e.g., accessibility issues).
- The Task-Dialogue model (TDM): Describes the tasks that the users are able to perform as well as its interrelation. The elements commonly used to define the TDM are tasks, goals, actions, preconditions, and postconditions. The definition of tasks is likely to become a reusable asset since some tasks can be repeated in different projects. Tasks are usually defined in a hierarchical way (e.g., Concurrent Task Trees), so full trees of task definitions or portions of them can be defined as reusable components.
- The presentation model (PM): Two different submodels can be distinguished:

- The abstract presentation model (APM) provides a conceptual description of the structure and behavior of the visual parts of the UI. Commonly the APM is composed by views and abstract input objects. Reusing abstract interface specifications is an interesting feature since the abstract definition of a UI can be repeated in other projects (e.g., login dialog).
- The concrete presentation model (CPM) details the visual parts of the UI. The components of this model are windows, concrete interaction objects, and layouts. Reusing CPM specifications is particularly interesting in projects where several applications are interrelated since it provides a consistent presentation across project-wide UIs.

Depending on the target, we might be interested in reusing parts of some UIMs as a whole reusable parameterized asset or subsystem (e.g., an instant message system) or just single model elements such as a user profile, a form, or a widget.

29.3   Approaches for Reuse

Since most MB-UIDEs use text-based languages for UIMs specification, one natural temptation is to just copy–paste reusable pieces of code. This is identified as a bad practice for code development (*cut&paste programming* [9]) leading to an unmaintainable and oversized code. A better solution is to encapsulate the reusable component properly as presented in following subsections.

29.3.1   Model Specification Reuse Using XInclude

XInclude [7] introduces a generic mechanism for merging XML documents in applications that need an inclusion mechanism to facilitate modularity. An obvious requirement to apply XInclude in a UIDL is that it must be XML-based. The use of XInclude provides some immediate advantages. First, large specifications can be modularized in fragments easier to handle. Second, any model component in a specification of the UI can be coded in a XML file and included in any other specification, which requires using the functionalities offered by that component.

XInclude also has some drawbacks that should be noticed. It defines no relationship with the document validation or transformation. XInclude describes an infoset-to-infoset transformation but it does not specify the XML parsing behavior. Therefore, a document can be validated before or after inclusion, or both, or neither. Consequently, one needs to take into account the following:

- If we decide to perform document validation before the inclusion of the components, the validation method (DTD o XML Schema) should support the validation of XInclude tag elements. Consequently, we should add the definition of these elements in the UIDL validation method. Additionally, the included components should have been previously validated to avoid errors. Also, the validation mechanism can not be used to validate the included components because they are just fragments from other specification and consequently are not well-formed documents.

- If we validate the declarative specification after inserting the included components we need a method to be aware of the correctness of the included code, which is not always possible. In addition, the line numbers that we would obtain in case of error messages would be wrong. Therefore, whatever option we choose would require specific tools for component validation.

XInclude can be a good solution for those UIDLs that specify all the UIMs in one XML-based document (e.g., UsiXML or XIML). However, a number of current UIDLs only support two or three UIMs [2] (e.g., UIML, XUL, or XICL) leaving the rest models out of the XML document.

29.3.2 Models Specification Reuse Using Package Management

Packages are widely used today in computing: from operating systems (e.g., MSI, RPM, DEB) or file management (e.g., TAR, ZIP, CAB) to programming languages (e.g., JAR, WAR). However, to the best of our knowledge, its use for reuse UIM components has never been proposed. To be able to use packaging for reusing MB-UIDE components, it would be necessary to meet the following requirements:

1. The UIMs need to be in a format allowing the extraction of model objects, which are parts of the reusable component (e.g., textual language).
2. A file format must be set for package building.
3. It is necessary to define the metainfo that will be included in the package for each component (e.g., package version, dependencies, etc.).
4. The use of packages in MB-UIDEs creates the need of implementing a package management system to automate the process of installing, upgrading, configuring, and removing component packages.

Packages allow reusing either a complete subsystem or part of its components by including the corresponding fragments in the package content. In addition, the use of packages would allow to include different UI specifications written in different languages (even those which are not XML-based) in the same package.

However, the use of packaging also has some problems to be addressed – first, the problem of dependencies [10]. This problem is not new and it can cause situations such as the commonly known "DLL hell" experienced by Microsoft Windows developers and users. Common problems in software packaging are also conflicts or security issues [11]. Finally, the solutions adopted are typically platform dependent, and errors in package definitions can only be fixed by the package developer.

29.3.3 Testing the Approaches

The previous approaches have been tested in a MB-UIDE (WAINE) [8] oriented to the development of Web-based management applications. The MB-UIDE uses a XML-based language named ASL to specify the UM, TDM, and APM. WAINE uses other languages such as class diagrams or ERDs for DOM specification, and configuration text files, HTML templates, and CSS for CPM issues. Thus, WAINE represents a high-complexity case since it uses both XML and non-XML specification languages in the UI development.

The XML-based UIDL has been upgraded from its original version to allocate the use of XInclude. Currently we are validating the ASL specification before the inclusion of the components. This led us to modify the original DTDs for validation to add the XInclude element. In addition, we have developed new utilities to validate not well-formed documents (UIM components).

We also developed a package management system specifically for this MB-UIDE, which let us reuse components of any complexity. Their main components are the *wpk* files and the *wpkg* tool. The wpk files are tar gzipped files that can, among others, contain an ASL file in addition to other files that can be necessary to describe a complete component (fragments of the DOM, CPM, files, etc). Wpk files also contain a directory with metainformation about the package and two scripts *preins.sh* y *postins.sh*, which are executed before and after the component installation, respectively. The *wpkg* tool allows to list, add, or remove packages to a user interface.

Since our system does not specify all UIMs in XML, the use of XInclude can be useful to modularize a large project or to reutilize single fragments of models, but it lacks the completeness needed to reutilize complete subsystems since they typically need pieces of every UIM. So, in practice we often use WAINE packages instead of XInclude as our main reusing technique. However, the development effort to implement a package management system is bigger than modifying the document validation system (for XInclude use).

To summarize the analysis done in this paper, Table 29.1 shows a brief comparison between the proposed reutilization approaches.

Table 29.1 Comparison between reuse approaches

Feature	XInclude	Packages
Based on standards	Y	N
Allows to reuse isolated components	Y	Y
Allows to reuse complete subsystem	[a]	Y
Needs to modify validation System	Y	N
Needs package management system	N	Y
Independent of UIDL	Y	Y
Independent of MB-UIDE	Y	N
Implementation effort	Very low	High

[a]Valid only for those UIDLs supporting all UIMs

29.4 Conclusions

The reuse of MB-UIDE's specification models can achieve a reduction of the UI development time. We have analyzed two mature standard UIDL-independent techniques for UIM reuse: XInclude and Packaging. Both are typically applied in diverse fields but never been proposed for UIM reuse in the software development process. We conclude that both techniques are well suited for UIM reuse.

References

1. Pinhero, P. (2001): User interface declarative models and development environments: A survey. Interactive Systems – Design, Specification, and Verification: 7th IWS, pp. 207–226
2. Souchon, N., Vanderdonckt, J. (2003): A review of XML-compliant user interface description languages. LNCS. Interactive Systems. Design, Specification, and Verification, 7th International Workshop, DSV-IS 2000, Limerick, Ireland.
3. Feng, S., Wan, J. (2007): User interface knowledge reuse and multi-device user interface development. IEEE International Conference on Automation and Logistics, Shandong, China.
4. OASIS UIML TC (2004): User Interface Markup Language Specification.
5. Gomes de Sousa, L., Leite, J.C. (2005): XICL: An Extensible Mark-Up Language for Developing User Interface and Components. Springer, Netherlands.
6. Mozilla Developer Center: XUL overlay. http://developer.mozilla.org/en/docs/XUL_Overlays.
7. W3C: Xml inclusions, http://www.w3.org/tr/xinclude.
8. Delgado, A., Estepa, A., Estepa, R. (2007): Waine: Automatic generator of Web based applications. Third International Conference on Web Information Systems and Technologies, Barcelona, Spain.
9. Cheng, Y.P., Liao, J.R. (2007): An ontology-based taxonomy of bad code smells. Proceedings of the third conference on IASTED International Conference: Advances in Computer Science and Technology, Phuket, Thailand.
10. Hart, J., D'Amelia, J. (2002): An analysis of rpm validation drift. Proceedings of the 16th USENIX Conference on System Administration, Philadelphia, PA.
11. Mancinelli, F. (2006): Managing the complexity of large free and open source package-based software distributions. ASE 2006, Tokyo, Japan.

Index